My Time in Hell

My Time in Hell

*Memoir of an American Soldier
Imprisoned by the Japanese
in World War II*

by

Andrew D. Carson

McFarland & Company, Inc., Publishers
Jefferson, North Carolina, and London

Front Cover: Torture of American war prisoners, Cabanatuan Prison Camp, 1942. Drawing by unknown artist. (Courtesy of American Ex-Prisoners of War, Arlington, Texas.)

British Library Cataloguing-in-Publication data are available

Library of Congress Cataloguing-in-Publication Data

Carson, Andrew D.
    My time in hell : memoir of an American soldier imprisoned by the Japanese in World War II / by Andrew D. Carson
        p.   cm.
    ISBN 0-7864-0403-5 (sewn softcover : 50# alkaline paper) ∞
    1. Carson, Andrew D.   2. World War, 1939–1945 — Prisoners and prisons, Japanese.   3. World War, 1939–1945 — Personal narratives, American.   4. World War, 1939–1945 — Concentration camps — Philippines — Cabanatuan.   5. Cabanatuan (Philippines)
6. Prisoners of war — United States — Biography.   7. Prisoners of war — Philippines — Biography.   I. Title.
    D805.P6C27   1997
    940.54'7252'095991— dc21   97-23520
                                                                CIP

Manufactured in the United States of America

McFarland & Company, Inc., Publishers
    Box 611, Jefferson, North Carolina 28640

To Lainie Maloy,
the only angel I ever met
in the City of Angels

Acknowledgments

I would like to acknowledge each and every member of the brave American and Filipino forces that fought so gallantly in defense of the Philippines.

Surrounded by the enemy, outmanned and outgunned, unaware that they were being sacrificed on the altar of expediency, they held back the might of the Japanese Empire for five incredible months.

After the surrender of Bataan and Corregidor, 36,000 American troops disappeared into the oblivion of the Japanese prisoner-of-war camps, there to suffer starvation, brutality, and inhuman treatment while working as slaves. When they emerged from the darkness at the end of the war, some three-and-a-half years later, there were only 15,000 survivors. Dead and buried along the way were 21,000 others.

I salute the memory of each of them, both the living and the dead, and I am proud to have been one of them.

I would also like to acknowledge the editorial assistance of my wife, Elaine Carson, for the countless hours she devoted to reading the manuscript, correcting my mistakes, and always offering encouragement and constructive criticism.

Contents

Preface

Like most GIs of World War II, I was raised during the years of the Great Depression. I dropped out of high school in the tenth grade to look for work, but jobs of any kind were virtually nonexistent, and preference was usually given to heads of families rather than to unskilled teenagers. The Army, on the other hand, offered good food, all of my clothing, a place to sleep, an opportunity to travel, and thirty dollars a month. At the time, it seemed like an attractive option.

I enlisted at Fort MacArthur, near Los Angeles, on March 20, 1941, and was shipped immediately to Angel Island, the Army embarkation station in San Francisco Bay. Within a couple of weeks I found myself on a ship bound for the Philippines. This wasn't a regular troop ship but a luxurious transatlantic passenger liner, complete with civilian crew and all the amenities, hastily chartered by the Army for the express purpose of getting a few hundred raw recruits to the Philippines in a hurry.

We arrived in Manila on May 8, 1941, just seven weeks after I enlisted. No boot camp, no basic training, not one minute of close-order drill. My only preparation for active duty was a single ten-minute lecture on who, how, and when to salute. I was ferried to Corregidor and two weeks later saw the ship that brought me over, the S.S. *Washington*, leaving for the States fully loaded with dependents, with officers' wives and children.

I trained on the big guns as a buck private, was promoted to private first class just before the start of the war, and remained at that rank throughout our five months of combat and three-and-a-half years as a prisoner of the Japanese. After the war, after our release from the Japanese prison camps, all surviving ex–POWs were given an automatic one-rank promotion, so I was discharged from the Army as a corporal. In terms of the military hierarchy, mine is a story written by a guy at the bottom of the rank ladder.

I arrived back in the States on November 1, 1945, and was discharged at Fort MacArthur on February 4, 1946. Shortly thereafter I married Lainie Maloy, my childhood sweetheart, a lovely young woman whom I had met when she was just fifteen and I was seventeen. We moved to San Francisco, where I found a job as a longshoreman on the San Francisco waterfront.

As far as education I was still a high school dropout, but in 1948, at my wife's

The author today

urging, I managed to pass a G.E.D. test and was admitted to a small college in Los Angeles. I was uneducated but eager, and they were kind. My first college assignment was scrawled in pencil on a torn-out sheet of paper from a spiral notebook.

In my first semester both a VA physician and a wise old psychology professor advised me to bring my POW experience out into the open by writing it out as a form of therapy. I wrote and wrote, and the recurrent nightmares seemed to lessen, but at that time most of us who survived the Japanese prison camps were either reluctant to speak openly about our experience or unable to put our thoughts into written words. Admittedly, my first completed manuscript was awful, and it remained hidden on a closet shelf for many, many years.

Only now, some fifty years later, do I feel that I can adequately express the feelings and emotions that have lain buried these many years — though I sometimes still tremble as I write.

This is my own story, a true account of what happened to me as a prisoner of war. In a sense, however, with variations as to time and place, it is also the story of every American who surrendered to the Japanese. It is my fervent wish that those who read this account will learn to know and understand what really happened to a bunch of American kids who fought and lost and who for the next three-and-a-half years paid a terrible price for delaying the Japanese conquest of the Philippines for five months.

Note to the Reader

Shortly after the end of World War II, at a meeting of former prisoners of war, the author was approached by a woman seeking information about her son who had died while a prisoner. During the conversation she told the author that when the Army informed her that her son was dead, they also told her *how* he died. He was doused with gasoline and burned alive. This horrible information caused the premature death of her husband and left her with lifelong emotional trauma.

Even at this late date, after fifty years, every monthly issue of the *American Ex-Prisoner of War Bulletin* publishes requests from persons still seeking information about loved ones — a father, husband, son, or brother who died in the camps.

In view of the above, the author has changed the names of actual persons mentioned in the book. Those still alive will find themselves easily; other readers may be spared unnecessary heartache.

May 6, 1942:
Fort Drum Surrenders
to the Japanese

Cease fire! Cease fire! Stand by. The command came through the loudspeaker loud and clear. I'd heard it a thousand times. Routine. It came again, sharp, crisp, military as hell. Cease fire! Cease fire! Then a pause and a distinct sob. I could sense the pain in the first sergeant's voice. He was crying. Voice breaking, he told us that we had been ordered to surrender.

I was tired, so damned tired the words didn't really sink in. We had been fighting for five months, for the last month, since the fall of Bataan, almost continuously. The Japanese artillery, now largely unanswered, pounded Corregidor and the three smaller fortified islands around the clock. Their bombers, unopposed by a single American plane, hit us thirty, forty, sometimes fifty times a day. The fury of our little battle, perhaps insignificant when compared to the greater battles yet to come, was reaching a crescendo. And now, without warning, this unbelievable order to surrender.

Looking back, I am still amazed at how calmly soldiers can accept the inevitable. Bataan had fallen, seventy-eight thousand American and Filipino troops overrun, simply overwhelmed by superior numbers. There were still ten thousand men on Corregidor and the three smaller forts, but after five months of combat, with the sick and wounded, only about four thousand able to fight. And though only a portion of them were directly confronting us, there were nearly a quarter of a million Japanese troops in the Philippines. We knew we were isolated, cut off, surrounded by the enemy, but we didn't yet know we had already been written off as expendable, abandoned by our country. Abandoned? Not really. We didn't believe it, wouldn't accept it. Until the last day, until the last damned hour, in the occasional lull in the fighting, we strained our eyes watching the China Sea, waiting, hoping, praying for the relief convoy General MacArthur had promised, the relief convoy that never came.

On the other side of the coin, more realistically, we had talked among ourselves and decided we would probably die in battle. In preparation for this ultimate event we made one final "thumb your nose gesture of defiance" at the enemy. From colonel to private, we took all of the little treasures that an American kid usually carries into battle, family photos, letters from Mom and Dad, perhaps a watch that had been a gift at graduation, and threw them into the water on an outgoing tide. Now we were ready. The victorious Japanese would pick no souvenirs from our dead bodies.

The final assault began shortly after dark on the night of May 5, the Japanese attacking with overwhelming force, the American and Filipino troops defending with fury and courage born of sheer desperation. Corregidor was a shambles. Japanese artillery, amassed on Bataan, had pounded her defenses into rubble, and the never-ending stream of bombers, completely unopposed, only added to the devastation. The battle raged all through the night and into the following morning. The men on Corregidor met the Japanese on the beaches, tried to hold them off with rifle and machine-gun fire. My outfit on tiny Fort Drum had the only big guns not yet put out of action, two naval turrets taken from a remodeled battleship, each turret mounting a pair of fourteen-inch naval rifles. Our mission was to fire across Corregidor and hit the Japanese jumping-off sites on Bataan. Meanwhile, Japanese artillery on the shore behind us tried to blast us out of existence.

Morning came. Corregidor was nearly hidden from sight under a dense cloud of smoke. Our big guns were so hot that just to touch them would sear the flesh. Our job now was to destroy the Japanese landing craft crossing the narrow strait between Bataan and Corregidor. Our last order from Corregidor — just fire into the smoke, they're so damned many you can't miss. The smoke was so heavy our spotters could no longer see their targets. We were still firing when we learned the Japanese had managed to put tanks on the island and Corregidor had nothing to oppose them. Then, between our salvos, the order to surrender.

In those days firing our four turret guns was a complex procedure involving almost all of the two hundred men in the fort, each man's every movement carefully timed, coordinated, choreographed like a modern ballet. In the magazines deep in the bowels of the fort, crews moved projectiles, each weighing more than twenty-one hundred pounds, to the hoisting mechanism, which took it up three decks and positioned it directly behind the gun. An electric rammer shoved the projectile far up into the barrel. Then came the powder, hundreds of pounds, neatly packaged in round silk bags that the rammer shoved into the breech behind the projectile. The huge breechblock was slammed shut, rotated electrically until it was securely locked, and the gun was ready to fire. Meanwhile, forward observers had been phoning data to fire control, the crew in the plotting room that factored in corrections for distance, target elevation above sea level, wind speed and direction, temperature and humidity, temperature of the gun (a hot gun fires farther than a cold one), even time of flight and rotation of the earth during that time. Final data were transmitted to the turret crew, who fired the guns on a timing bell that rang every twenty seconds. Alternating the sequence like the old "Row Row Row Your Boat" medley, we could fire one gun every twenty seconds or a four-gun salvo every minute and twenty seconds.

Top: Looking toward Manila, a prewar view of the Topside parade ground at Corregidor. Topside Barracks is unseen to the left. The small building, top left, is the post theater. The buildings on the right and top center are officers' quarters. Bottom: Taken before the war, this photo shows one of Corregidor's 12-inch disappearing guns being fired out to sea. These guns, designed before World War I and obsolete before World War II, were defenseless against bombs dropped from bombers flying overhead or against Japanese artillery, which fired from behind them from both the Bataan and Cavite sides of the bay. (United States Army photos.)

Usually when the command to cease fire came over the intercom, it meant a lull in the fighting, a change of target, a break in the action. The standby meant a chance to relax. Don't go away, don't go back to your bunk, don't wander off; just stop where you are, sit down, lie down, close your eyes and rest, but be ready to resume firing any minute, any second.

I was functioning on instinct, unthinkingly going through a series of motions programmed into my brain by hours of repetitive dry runs in the months of training before the war. I was operating like a man who finds himself parked in his driveway yet who cannot remember the last few turns on the familiar road home. When I heard the words, we've been ordered to surrender, I simply stopped in my tracks, tired, dazed, unable to think. I felt nothing, no relief, no despair, no fear, nothing. I just stood there, not understanding, not comprehending. I didn't know what, if anything, I was supposed to do. The only thought I can remember is, what now? What comes next? I was in the plotting room, the nerve center of our fire-control system. I looked around the room. Officers, noncoms, enlisted men, we just stared at one another. No one moved, no one spoke. We were like an audience in a movie theater when the film breaks, staring stupidly at a blank screen, waiting for someone, somewhere, to fix things, to resume the continuity. We had been trained to act instinctively, immediately, to commands like "Attention," "At ease," "About face," "Man your battle stations," and "Fire when ready," but the word "Surrender" was foreign. It had not been programmed into our minds and therefore brought no response. Like pressing a new doorbell not yet hooked up to the buzzer, there is no connection, the bell does not ring on the other side of the door.

This mental logjam was broken by the intercom. Colonel Kirkpatrick was speaking. Slowly, quietly, in a voice pitched much lower than usual, he told us that the surrender would go into effect at twelve o'clock. We had twenty minutes to get ready, to destroy our equipment. The colonel wished us good luck and God bless. I could sense his reluctance as he gave this final, hateful order. The intercom snapped off and was silent, leaving us with one last final order that had to be obeyed.

Twenty minutes to destroy our equipment. We didn't talk, didn't think, didn't question, just went to it. Sergeant Timothy Murray, "Spud" Murray to the crew, grabbed me by the arm. Murray was an "old-timer," a likable, lovable Irishman with a brogue who had already been in the Army longer than I had been alive, and he knew exactly what had to be done. Together we went up through the casemates and out onto the open deck. It was a bright day with a cloudless sky and a hot sun, and it was eerily quiet. Corregidor was hidden under a pall of smoke, but no shells were bursting. There were no bombers in the sky, and on the ground neither side was firing. No bombs, no artillery shells, not even the sharp crack of a rifle, just an unnatural silence. For the moment, the world was holding its breath.

Out on the deck I knew damn well the Japanese observers could see us, and their artillery was already zeroed in, but they didn't fire. There was a Japanese artillery shell, a big one from an eight-inch howitzer, unexploded on deck. Some of the shell craters in the cement were still smoking, and hundreds of jagged pieces of shrapnel littered the deck. Except for these visual reminders of the fury of battle, it was uncanny, peaceful, almost idyllic. Our big guns were at rest, swiveled to face the China Sea, muzzles lowered to horizontal. Even in this position I could still stand upright under the huge barrels. Working at arm's length above our heads, Murray and I managed to shove two or three large sandbags down the barrel of each gun in the lower turret. Someone else was taking care of the upper turret. Out of sight, inside the turrets, crews drained the oil from the recoil cylinders and smashed control mechanisms with sledges. Murray and I ran for cover. We had to get off the deck before we went to hell with the guns. Down three decks and back to the plotting room. One final check to make sure everyone was in the clear, and at precisely twelve o'clock our guns fired their final salvo. The shells exploded in the tubes, muzzles burst, one gun tore free from its carriage, and in a fraction of a second they were scrap.

With the thunder of our own guns still ringing in our ears, we hauled down the Stars and Stripes and fastened a white bedsheet to the flagpole at the afterend of the fort. We had surrendered. We waited. Nothing happened.

I think it was Sergeant Murray, but it could have been someone else, who carried the flag down to the sally port, where Colonel Kirkpatrick, Captain Wing, and my battery commander, Lieutenant Folley, together with a few enlisted men burned it. It's a point of pride in military tradition. You don't let your flag fall into enemy hands, so we burned our flag. We burned another one too, the fancy parade-ground flag that stayed in the colonel's office, the one with the battle streamers naming all the battles in all the wars the regiment had fought since its formation during the Civil War. The fancy flag, the one with the gold braid and the battle streamers, it didn't seem to matter. It was the loss of our plain old everyday battle flag that brought the tears. Somehow, to us, that flag symbolized the entire defense of the Philippines. Our battle flag, it was more rag than flag, had big holes and little holes, rips and tears and pieces missing, but it had flown defiantly through five months of bombing and shelling and strafing, and incredibly, the Japanese had never been able to knock it down. Smoke-blackened, seared by flame, so tattered as to be almost unrecognizable, it must have been a pain in the ass for the Japs to see, every morning, like the words of our National Anthem, "that our flag was still there."

No bombers, no artillery fire, no Japs, nothing. We were running around the fort like a nest of ants that had just been disturbed, every man to his own thing. Destroy your equipment. We didn't recognize the finality of what we were doing. Destroy your equipment. Like puppets moving to the strings of the puppeteer, we obeyed.

My partner and I went on deck and dismantled our thirty-caliber machine gun. (We all had different jobs to do, depending on whether we were responding to attack by dive-bombers, heavy bombers, artillery, or landing craft. On "beach defense" I was a machine gunner.) We threw the machine-gun parts as far as we could into the deep water. Rifles and bayonets followed, then the spare ammo and grenades. I remember thinking, foolishly, "God Almighty! If this is a mistake the Army will be taking it out of my pay for the rest of my life." Army pay in those days was thirty bucks a month, a rumored six dollars extra for combat pay. Everybody threw everything he had into the water. The ocean bed must have been covered with guns and pieces of guns. In the engine room, the power source for the entire fort as well as the big guns, the black gang revved the monstrous diesel engines up to maximum speed and then cut off the lubricating oil. When the diesels ground to a screeching halt the fort was dead. We had some lighting from a small emergency generator, nothing else.

Joe was crying, but silently, of course. I could see the furrows the tears had cut in the grime on his face. Me too. I think we were all crying, but mostly inside, not outside. It just wasn't manly to cry. John Wayne wouldn't have cried. And Joe was swearing softly, half under his breath. "Sonsabitches, Goddam sonsabitches." I heard the words repeated over and over again.

In my thoughts I might have worded it differently, but my feelings were the same as his. I sensed what he was feeling, knew what he was thinking. Without a word or a look or a gesture we shared this common moment between the two of us. Joe wasn't swearing at the Japanese, just swearing in general at a situation that had gone out of control. Swearing, not at any individual, not the people as a whole, just swearing in general at that vague entity that we called our country, our home, and that we felt had somehow let us down. To us it was still inconceivable that America, that great and powerful country we belonged to, would abandon its soldiers and leave them to die. Suddenly we felt very much alone.

Personally I felt bewildered, betrayed. I knew nothing of military expediency, nothing of the possible need to sacrifice a smaller force to protect a larger one, nothing of our country's need to arm itself, to train, to prepare itself for the greater battles yet to come. I only knew that we had done our very best. Through blood and tears and sacrifice we had held back the tide for five incredible months. We had bought, for our country, some desperately needed time. Five months, hell, a convoy could have reached us in rowboats in five months.

Late afternoon and still no sign from the Japs. Night came. Everything possible had either been destroyed or thrown over the side. We had time on our hands. With the ventilation system gone the fort was too hot below decks, way above a hundred degrees. Cautiously, in groups of two or three or four, we crept out on the open deck to breathe the cooler air. It was strange. Soldiers were sitting, standing, lying down, smoking cigarettes, talking quietly in a place where no life could have survived only a few hours ago. In the tropics the stars sometimes seem close enough to touch. With the unnatural silence of the cease fire, the touch of a tropical breeze as it brushed my cheek, the soft gurgle of the outgoing tide, this could have been peacetime, a typical night before the war.

No shots were being fired from either side, but my survival instinct kept me in the shadow of the turrets. I was uneasy, I just didn't feel right. I knew we were still targeted. The Japanese had a number of artillery batteries zeroed in on our fort. A pull of the lanyard and shells would be bursting on deck before we could clear, before we even heard the sound of the guns firing. And there was always "the little bastard." The little bastard was a Japanese machine gunner who had become as irritating as a sore tooth. He had rigged a fifty-caliber machine gun, probably one of our own they had captured, rigged it on a fixed mount so it was always zeroed in on us. He wasn't accurate at that distance, but a single shot whistling across the deck or a short burst of fifty-caliber slugs ricocheting off a turret could send you running like hell for cover. In my machine-gun nest on night watch I spent a lot of hours searching through binoculars for "the little bastard." Never found him. I figured he must have hung a piece of burlap in front of his gun, firing through it, using it as a screen to hide the muzzle flash.

I asked Joe what he thought our chances were. We were hunkered down in our machine-gun nest, now without its gun. He felt, because we couldn't hurt them anymore, that the Japanese might decide to just leave us sit where we were, starve us out. It was a good possibility that deserved some consideration.

The gun emplacement was a snug little place, just large enough for the two of us, one on either side with the gun in the middle. After many nights sitting there guarding against a possible landing attempt, we felt safer there than out on the open deck. We had been safe there, safe except for the one time the Japanese had literally scared the living hell out of us. A stray four-inch artillery shell had apparently passed between us, ripped the top row of sandbags from the back of our nest, and embedded itself in the sandbag wall of an ammunition bunker some twenty feet behind us. No, it didn't explode. Thank God, it was a dud.

It was a very strange time, those hours immediately after the surrender. From the hell of intense conflict we had suddenly moved into the eye of the hurricane, a quiet eddy in time, after the battle but before the enemy took us over. We could stroll freely about the open deck, a killing zone only nine or ten hours earlier. We talked, laughed, relaxed, sat on our backsides and looked at the sky. The night was beautiful, and our war, like the stars, was a million miles away. We were like passengers on a transatlantic flight whose plane had passed the point of no return with only an hour's fuel left in the tanks and with the nearest land six hours away. Yet we were completely unconcerned because we didn't know. There was no more need to keep a tight ass because our part in the battle was over, yet unknowingly we were hurtling through the night toward a head-on collision with a world we could not even imagine.

The illusion was shattered when the sound of exploding artillery shells came from Corregidor. The island had surrendered at noon and was, by now, naked and defenseless, yet the Japanese laid down a saturation barrage that lasted nearly three hours. I watched in horror. I had a front-row seat in an arena where helpless men were being slaughtered. Meanwhile, not a shot was fired at our fort. Maybe the Japanese looked at us as a ripe plum that could either be plucked at will or left to fall under its own weight.

There would be no more rest, no sleep for me this night. What the hell, maybe the Japs wouldn't accept our surrender. Maybe they were going to kill us all. I put my thoughts into words. No need. Every man on the fort was thinking the same damn thing. Wish to hell we hadn't destroyed our guns. Better to die in battle than to sit here, caged like stray dogs in a pound waiting to be executed at the whim of the keeper.

There were three of us huddled together. What a disparate trio. I was from California. Stearman was a country boy from Texas, and Joe was fresh from the back streets of Brooklyn. Stearman was a likable fellow, slow of speech and easy going. When there was a lull in the fighting we would sit around in one of the casemates and talk or just listen while he sang softly and strummed on an old guitar. Joe was different. Cocky, aggressive, outgoing, Italian. New York City exuded from his pores. Joe was proud of the fact that he had over three hundred books in his library at home and that he had read every damn one of them. Joe also had a flaming red scar above his right eyebrow that bothered the hell out of him. Peacetime, he kept it meticulously covered with a fresh strip of white adhesive tape every day. Army doctors had him scheduled for an operation to remove the scar, but the Japs attacked and blew that dream all to hell. Bet the first thing he did when he got home after the war was have that scar removed.

At any rate, the three of us put our heads together and came up with a plan. We would escape to Australia. We recruited a fourth member of our escape party, a civilian ordnance man who had prospected all over the islands, spoke Tagalog, and knew the islands like a book. First we went into the plotting room and on a sheet of transparent silk traced all the islands between us and Australia. Now we needed to get off the fort and across nearly a mile of water to land. We went into the powder magazine and carried four empty powder cans up to the sally port. The powder cans were round metal cylinders, eight feet long, and large enough in diameter to hold the big bags of powder that propelled the projectiles from our fourteen-inch guns. Sealed airtight, four of them lashed together made a fine raft. In the small-arms firing range we found a twenty-two-caliber target rifle that had been overlooked in the flurry of throwing things overboard. This would be our only weapon. We figured we would have to escape by stealth, not by force. The twenty-two was light and would not make a lot of noise, and we could carry hundreds of rounds of ammunition. Used carefully, it might provide us with birds and small game to eat along the way. A barracks bag full of canned goods from the kitchen, some basic medical supplies from the infirmary, and we were ready to shove off. After the noontime surrender and the rush to destroy our equipment there were no more orders, no military formations. Every man was on his own and nobody paid a damn bit of attention to what the four of us were doing. We were stowing our gear on the raft when Colonel Kirkpatrick walked into the sally port. He didn't pull rank, didn't give us any orders, simply pointed out that the Japanese had said they would accept only total, unconditional surrender, and that if we were caught it could make it tough on the guys we left behind. What the hell, it was probably a stupid idea anyway. We gave the raft to some Filipinos who worked in our laundry and with tearful good-byes they disappeared into the night.

Night was gone. First light was showing on the horizon beyond the China Sea. I went into the storeroom and put on a new pair of khaki trousers and a new khaki shirt. I rolled my blanket and a couple of pairs of socks into a tight bundle, slipped two pocket books, one of Shakespeare, the other of short stories, into my backpack, picked up some iodine and bandages from the infirmary, took a can of peaches from the kitchen, went on deck and waited. I sat with my back against the turret and stared at the peaches. I had no way of knowing it would be three-and-a-half years before I tasted another peach.

It's a trite saying, but ignorance is bliss. I wasn't scared, wasn't too worried. For me, nothing had changed except that the fighting had stopped.

About nine o'clock in the morning a string of small boats came from behind Limbones Point and headed straight for our fort. This was it. Whatever their intentions, the Japs weren't going to starve us out. They were coming after us. When the boats drew near to the fort, we formed in four ranks across the width of the deck. Though I couldn't see them, I heard the putty-put-put of the motors, the thumping as they came alongside, the excited rattle of voices — speaking Japanese. Colonel Kirkpatrick gave his final command, and we snapped to attention. In the lingo of the Mexican bullfighter, this was the moment of truth.

A scuffling sound from the casemate, then a bayoneted rifle followed by a helmeted Japanese in full battle gear came up the ladder. He saw us, crouched with bayonet at the ready, and waited for reinforcements. He seemed nervous, scared, ready instantly to pull the trigger. Obviously, this was a new situation to him, and he didn't know what to do next. Twenty or thirty soldiers followed, then a Japanese lieutenant in a dirty field uniform, with a pistol strapped to his hip. Colonel Kirkpatrick walked to him, saluted, and formally surrendered the fort. Lots of Japanese soldiers on deck now. They surrounded us, walked back and forth between the ranks, rifles, bayonets, pistols ready for instant use. A gun crew set up a machine gun directly in front, loaded it, pulled the bolt back, slipping the first shell into the chamber. It made an ominous sound. A Japanese radio operator sent a message to someone on shore, and we waited.

I stood stiffly at attention, suspended in time, suspended in space. The rest of the world became indistinct, faded away. There was nothing, nothing except me and a Japanese soldier with his bayonet touching my throat. Each passing second seemed an eternity. Hell, each second was an eternity. I knew, instinctively, the Japanese lieutenant was waiting for a message from his superior on shore, and that message would determine whether I lived or died. I was afraid, damn right I was afraid, but I hoped I didn't show it. My Japanese soldier was smaller than I, and I stared beyond him. I didn't look directly at him, didn't make eye contact, didn't want him to see the mixture of hate and fear that surely must have shown. We stood there, two hundred unarmed, defenseless men, standing at attention, dangling momentarily between life and death. The Japanese may have thought we were well disciplined soldiers. We were. But for me, I know I was using stiff military posture as a crutch. I was rigid. I didn't move, I didn't breathe, I'm not sure that I even blinked my eyes. I was rigid because I was bracing, with every muscle in my body, for the thrust of a bayonet or the smashing impact of a bullet. Seconds passed, mere ticks, unnoticed in the eternal scheme of the universe, but each second filled with incredibly concentrated feeling, sensation, experience, the very stuff of life itself. I was acutely aware of the blueness of the sky, the warmth of the sun, the tangy smell of the salt sea air. Suddenly it was as if I could gather all the sights and sounds and feelings, from horizon to horizon, and funnel them into one tiny spot in my brain. I wasn't dead. I was alive, and I didn't want to die. I wanted to live. God, how I wanted to live. I stood frozen, my body motionless, my mind racing. I wondered if death would be slow, painful, or would it be quick, like turning out a light? I wanted the tension to end before my mind burst from the intensity of the moment, but somewhere, in a little corner of that same mind, I was aware that each second passing was an added bit of life, a postponement of my death.

The radio crackled. I didn't understand the words, but I knew they meant life or death. They meant life. Obviously disappointed, the lieutenant motioned to his soldiers to start moving us off the deck.

A blow from a rifle butt gave guidance and the first man in line stumbled down through the fort, out from the sally port, and onto a waiting boat. I was in the first rank, somewhere among the first fifty men. A feeling of relief surged through my body, touched my very soul. I sucked it in through my pores like the first breath of air to a man who has been under water for too long. I didn't try to reason, didn't try to think ahead. The moment was enough. I was alive!

I had to run a gauntlet of Japanese soldiers stationed at intervals throughout the fort, and the change from the brightness outside to the darkness below decks left me temporarily blinded. Most of the Japanese were quiet, impassive, but a few seemed to enjoy their work. I knew the way, but when I hesitated in the dark a rifle butt to the shoulder or across the buttocks got me started again. I hardly felt the blows. Along the way a guard motioned for me to drop my backpack. He let me keep my mess kit, which was hanging from my belt.

The boat was a very small, very old fishing craft, at the most maybe twenty-five or thirty feet long. Only God knows how they managed to bring it down from Japan. Maybe instead it was one confiscated in the Philippines. I was shoved through a small square opening into what had been the cargo hold. I could tell from the strong smell and the fish scales sticking to the wood it had been used to store the catch. The space was small. We could barely sit and couldn't stand up. When it was full the hatch was closed and we were in the dark. I heard the speed of the engine increase, felt the motion of the water, and we were on our way. During those few minutes, at most a half hour, since we had snapped to attention on deck, there had been no time for conversation. I had spoken to no one; no one had spoken to me. Strange how in the midst of a crowd a man can be absolutely alone.

Now we began to speak, cautiously, as if afraid the Japanese would overhear. Someone asked if I was all right, if I had been hurt. I had to think a minute to be sure. I knew I had been hit on the head with a rifle and my head was bloody, but I wasn't seriously hurt. I wondered about where we were going, where they were taking us, what they were going to do to us. (Not what are they going to do *with* us, but what are they going to do *to* us?)

Questions, concern about one another. Unanswerable questions, probing into the future. We had no idea that we were entering into a lifestyle far beyond our wildest imaginings The hatch cover opened and light, daylight, came into the hold. Someone tossed down a box of prunes. Funny, yesterday we had been killing each other, today, a box of prunes. The Japanese soldier sitting on a box beside the hatch opening spoke in very broken but understandable English. I think he wanted to show off his English in front of the other Japanese.

He told us that all the soldiers on his boat were Marines, the elite, Japan's best. They had taken part in the assault on Corregidor. He wasn't angry, he was philosophical about it. Some die, some don't.

I had no idea where we were going, what was going to happen to us. We chugged along, the strong stink of dead fish in my nostrils, a two-foot square of blue sky visible overhead. I think I was on the fishing boat for two or three hours. I don't know, time is meaningless, not really measurable at a time like that. Physically, I was okay. A few bruises from being banged around running the gauntlet coming out of the fort, but basically unhurt. And at the moment there was no brutality, no mistreatment of any kind. For the moment I was content with my lot, not accepting, but damn glad to be alive. Under extreme stress, I believe the mind assumes a defensive posture, blanks out certain realities, dulls the impact of the situation. I think this happened to me. In a matter of minutes life had done a flip flop, had taken a reverse turn. My brain seemed ready to explode. My mind spun like the wheels of a slot machine, and continued spinning, endlessly. I was a bundle of contradictions. I felt relaxed, but my body was trembling, every muscle taut to the hurting point. I was calm, apprehensive, fearful, complacent, full of rage, all of these, all at once. I felt as though I had jumped off a cliff in absolute blackness and I didn't know how far I had to fall or what lay at the bottom. My mind continued to probe into the future but returned empty. As yet, there simply was no answer. Obviously I knew I was a prisoner of war, but what the hell did that mean? Prisoner of war was a concept utterly beyond my scope of experience, meaningless. Vaguely, I sensed that I had somehow lost control of my life, that I was a ship without a rudder.

I couldn't see the Japanese Marine who sat on deck above the hatch opening, but I could hear him as he struggled with his little-used English. It wasn't a conversation. He just rattled on and we listened, tried to extract meaning from his garbled words. He told us it had been a great battle and the Japanese had won.

Our Japanese Marine liked to talk, but we couldn't always understand him. Little by little, a word here, a phrase there, we began to realize what he was trying to convey. It wasn't the least bit reassuring. It came in bits and pieces.

Our guns had created havoc among the Japanese soldiers who had attacked Corregidor. By their own account the Japanese lost more than three thousand men in the attack, most of whom never reached shore. He himself was not mad at us, but his superiors were very angry.

For this we were being separated from the other Americans and taken away for "special severe punishment."

The Japanese lieutenant who had accepted the surrender of our fort had an older brother, a colonel, who commanded an assault regiment. We had killed the lieutenant's older brother, killed him with our gunfire.

I'll admit I was slow, but when the words came together it was like the clap of doom. Special severe punishment. We had killed the lieutenant's older brother. Jesus Christ!

The clatter of the motor dropped off to a whisper, then ceased altogether. Our boat drifted silently, bumped hard against something solid and stopped. We had reached our destination.

Japanese soldiers scream "Banzai" as they attack. American paratroopers yell "Geronimo" as they hurtle into space. We managed nothing more than a feeble "this is it," or, "here we go again." No heroics, no bravado. Contrary to the way the movies portray it, there were no wisecracks, no witty remarks. We were still disciplined, still composed, still soldierly, but I cannot honestly say we were defiant. There were no John Waynes among us. We were just a bunch of scared kids, caught up in a raging torrent being swept toward a waterfall. I, myself, said nothing. All of my faculties were focused on myself and on the enemy. As a soldier I had been conditioned to accept the possibility of injury or death in battle, conditioned to face bombs and bullets and artillery fire. But conditioned to be a prisoner of war? No way. There is no parallel, no equivalent in the American experience to prepare a man to be a prisoner of war.

In my turn I climbed out of the cramped smelly hold and took my place in line on the pier. As my eyes adjusted to the bright sunlight, I could see we were near a village at the end of a small bay. On one side a long pier jutted into the water, on the other a building covered with corrugated tin, evidently a warehouse, and beyond that the nipa huts of a Filipino village. The point of land where we stood, where the pier started, was bare, but a hundred yards farther back and all around was the usual scatter of coconut palms and dense jungle underbrush. Between us and the village, blocking any possible escape from the pier area, were Japanese soldiers, rifles, bayonets, and machine guns. This was my first sight of Nasugbu, an insignificant little sugar port and fishing village, thirty miles south of Manila Bay.

The Japanese lost no time in getting right down to the business of teaching us how to be prisoners. Our talkative Imperial Marine had disappeared with the docking of our boat and no one in my little group understood the Japanese language, but we were quick to understand their meaning. A bayonet in the ass or a rifle butt to the back is understandable in any language. I got the idea. The guards wanted us to place everything we carried on the ground in front of us. Damn, I was in the front row again, always in the front row. I was six foot two and two hundred twenty pounds, and the smaller Japanese seemed to take a personal interest in cutting me down to size. Most of the prisoners were permitted to keep canteens and mess kits, but not me, I had to place mine on the ground. Never saw it again. I had been prisoner less than six hours and was already down to hat, shirt, pants, shoes, and underwear.

We were divided into two groups of about a hundred men each and herded toward the pier at gunpoint. No particular order, officers, noncoms, enlisted men mixed together. And we went to work, hard work. There was a huge hole in the pier a hundred feet from shore. It could have been from a bomb, but more likely our own troops had blasted it when they retreated to Bataan. Our job was to fill this hole with rock from a pile on shore. By hand. The water was thirty feet deep and the gap twenty feet wide. It would have taken a small mountain to fill the damn thing to pier level.

I was one of a line of prisoners passing chunks of rock and coral from hand to hand, the last man dropping the rock into the hole. Night came. I was taking a rock from the man on one side and handing it to the man on the other. I couldn't see much of what was going on, only those men close to me. Don't remember who they were. My mind was blurred with the enormity of the transition from American soldier to Japanese prisoner. We talked, tried to comfort, to support one another, but our guards slapped the hell out of us for talking, and we were reduced to short whispers when our guards were at another part of the line. From the darkness a soft voice advised us not to antagonize the guards, reminded us that things could be a hell of a lot worse. Good advice. I wondered when the little bastards were going to knock this crap off. Little bastards soon became our favorite expression when referring to the Japanese.

An angry shout and our guards came running. No more whispers. Language barrier or not, I learned that "hyaku," "hyaku" meant hurry, hurry. And we hurried. There's no reasoning with a sharp bayonet. I was dripping, my clothes literally soaked with sweat, sticking to my body. My hands were sore, nearly raw, sharp edges of the coral chunks grinding away at bare flesh. I was tired. At eleven o'clock we changed shifts. My bunch filed off the pier and the other half came on. Great! Now I would get a drink of water, something to eat, sit down, maybe even stretch out on the ground and catch a few minutes sleep. Bullshit! So much for wishful thinking. Our guards marched us off the pier and up on the rock pile. No water, no food. Sit down on the rock pile but sit at attention. Knees under my chin, arms locked around my knees. Don't talk, don't sleep, don't even rest your head on your arms. Sit at attention. The Japs were mean, rough as hell, but they didn't try to kill us, just wear us down, hurt us, make us suffer. I did doze off, and a rifle butt left a hell of a lump on my head behind my ear. I got the message.

I lost track of time, but I got one more long shift passing rocks during the night. Again, as we moved onto the pier we passed the other bunch coming off. I could see in their faces that they were tired, dirty, and dead beat. Old Ben Wing was in the second group. Captain Wing really, but we called him "Old Ben" because he was at least forty. Captain Wing passed by with his hands clasped together above his head like a victorious fighter in the ring. He smiled and kept repeating, "Hang on men. Don't let them see you're hurting." It was corny as hell, but he was an inspiration. By God, if that old man could make it, so could I.

Next to the colonel, Captain Wing was the oldest officer on the fort. He was wiry and he was tough. He'd been a Texas Ranger before he came into the Army, and when war came he refused to wear the regulation forty-five automatic pistol. Said he was more comfortable with the two six shooters he had carried as a Ranger. He made it too. He was the senior surviving officer from Fort Drum.

Daylight came and I was sitting on the rockpile again. It was my second day as a prisoner. Still no water, no food, no rest. I was hungry but more thirsty than hungry. I had not been smart enough to think to take a big drink of water just before the Japs took us over, not smart enough to fill my belly with food. None of us had thought ahead. We were too concerned with just staying alive through the first few minutes of the Jap takeover to plan ahead, and now we were paying the price.

Days heat up quickly in the Philippines. By nine o'clock I was uncomfortable. By ten I was sweating profusely. I was hurting. I was young, big, and in relatively good physical condition, but I was hurting. I had not slept for at least forty-eight hours. Maybe it was seventy-two, I couldn't remember. The last day and night of fighting, the day of surrender, of tearing up the fort, the day the Japs took us from the fort and put us to work on the rockpile. Anxiety, fear, tension had carried me this far, but I was beginning to run down. Up off the rockpile and back in line. It was my turn to work again, to endlessly pass rocks from man to man and toss them into the hole. The chunks of coral had sharp edges and some of them were quite heavy. We were handling them barehanded. Scrapes became abrasions, became little cuts. I tried to protect my hands by cradling the rocks in my forearms and tore holes in my shirt. The muscles in the small of my back ached. I didn't have to move my feet, just swing to the left to take a rock from the man on that side, swing to the right to hand it off to the next guy. I developed some sort of rhythm: swing, pick, swing, let go, swing, pick, swing, let go. Who were the guys next to me? Don't know. Americans, of course, friends, certainly, but they were just bodies with faces, and I don't remember the faces. There were no units, no squads, no platoons. When the Japs hollered, we got off the rockpile amid a shower of kicks and blows, formed a single line on the pier and started passing rocks. One shift I might be standing next to an officer, the next shift beside a private. What mattered was that I was still alive, tired, miserable, hurting, but alive, and I damn well wanted to stay that way.

The day was hot and the coral was dusty. I had coral dust in my eyes, in my nostrils, in my mouth. The dust stuck to my sweaty skin where skin was exposed, stuck to my clothes where the sweat soaked through. I was hungry and thirsty, but the thirst was the worst. My mouth was so dry I couldn't even spit out the dust. Japanese soldiers walked along the line. Hyaku, hurry, hurry. They weren't vicious, but they were damn methodical. A rifle butt across the buttocks, a blow from a clenched fist, the stinging slap of an open hand. They didn't want to kill us. They could have done that easily. They only wanted to hurt us, to humiliate us, to make us look bad. One of the guards took my hat. Oh, I know they took everybody's hat, but this guard took *my* hat. It became personal. Out of all the Japanese soldiers surrounding us, I hated this little son of a bitch the most.

The heat, the work, the lack of sleep, the thirst began to take their toll. We didn't talk. The Japanese slapped the hell out of anybody they caught talking. Here and there along the line men pooped out, couldn't handle the rocks anymore, simply stood with arms hanging. We skipped them, passed the rocks around them. As long as a man was on his feet the Japanese ignored him. If he fell they beat him, tried to get him up. If he didn't get up we passed rocks across the unconscious body.

Midafternoon. Still working the rockpile, passing rocks from man to man and dropping them into the water. This was the second day of our incarceration. The sun was at its hottest. There were no trees, no bushes, no buildings near the pier. Working or resting, there was no way to get out of the sun. Today was May 8, 1942. Happy anniversary! Exactly one year ago today I had landed on Corregidor. Then, because of the heat, it had been a court-martial offense for a recruit to be caught without a hat or without a shirt between sunup and sundown.

There were fewer guards now. Still the machine guns cut off any chance of escape, but fewer guards watched us work. We began to talk, only in whispers when the guard was farthest away, but we began to talk and get away with it.

The sun was too damned hot, and I was thirsty as hell. I remember wishing that I had a drink of water. I would have given anything for just one big drink of cold water. A fellow prisoner asked me if I was makin' it all right, asked how I was getting along. I answered that I was still OK but didn't know how long I could keep it up. We stopped whispering. The guard was coming.

The guard passed. Walked slowly farther along the line. Probably getting tired of this damn monkey business and thinking his own thoughts.

I could whisper again. Best time to talk was when a rock was being handed from one man to another. We were face-to-face then, didn't have to turn our heads, to draw attention. I had two men I could whisper to, the man on my left who handed his rock to me and the man on my right who took it out of my hand. The three of us, we were the exact center of our little universe. I don't know who the other two men were, but we were whispering, struggling, suffering together. Other prisoners were there, but farther away, and kinda faded into the background. How strange, how tiny one's world becomes. I was at the center of my three-man group, but the man next to me was the center of his own trio, and I was on the edge of that one. To the third man down the line I probably didn't exist, didn't matter at all.

Wish I was back on the fort takin' a shower. I'd just stand there with my mouth open and let the goddamn water run down my throat. Just thinking about it brought a smile to my face. Once when I was a kid a bunch of us went swimmin' in the creek. I wouldn't get in. Scared. Water was too cold. Boy! I'd jump in, turn somersaults in that creek right now.

I was caught off guard. A Japanese soldier appeared out of nowhere, bayonetted rifle slung over his shoulder. He stopped directly in front of me. He was a big fellow, and his eyes were level with mine, an arm's length away. I knew I had been caught, waited for the rain of blows. None came. We stood for an instant face-to-face, the victor and the vanquished. I could see him making up his mind.

Then he reached out with thumb and middle finger and flicked me hard on the end of my nose, motioned for me to get back to work. Highly amused, chuckling to himself and shaking his head, he walked on down the line. Son of a bitch!

The ice was thawing a little bit. We talked more freely now. Still working our asses off, still under the hot sun with no water, no food, no rest, but we talked and the talking helped. There is no way a man can share the pain in his gut, the icy wrenching fear in his heart, the hurting of his body. But through words, communication, his soul can reach out and make contact with another soul, can exchange thoughts, ideas, anxieties, fears, feelings, can be not alone. Talking helps.

The work went on, the hurting went on, the suffering went on. No letup. Men were dropping regularly now, intense heat and exhaustion getting the better of willpower. Sometimes a few kicks could get them up again; sometimes they just lay there and the Japs walked away in disgust.

A water truck drove up to the end of the pier, a tanker that held perhaps a thousand gallons. Thank God! Water at last, lots of it.

I could see the water sloshing out the top. The Japanese soldiers gathered round, filled their buckets, drank their fill, spilled water on the ground, but no water for us. They circled the truck with a ring of bayonets. We were dying for lack of water and water was there aplenty, but none for us, not a drop. It was savage.

After dark. Another shift, passing rocks from hand to hand, was over. We straggled from the pier, no longer as a military unit, just a ragged bunch of dirty, utterly exhausted men dragging their asses. This time the Japanese let us sit on a spot of level ground, still uncomfortable, but much better than sitting on the rocks. I was tired, so tired that I had more than once fallen asleep on my feet. "He was out on his feet." I had heard the term applied to fighters in the ring but never knew what it meant. Now I knew. During these last hours there had been intervals when my body functioned, taking a rock from one man and handing it to another, but when my mind was blanked out.

I was dying of thirst. I knew damn well I was dying, and it didn't seem to matter. I could have managed the hunger, the fatigue, even the pain, the hurting, but I had to have water. I just couldn't get along without water. But there was yet another factor, indescribable, more difficult to put into words. I had youth and strength on my side. Physically I was able to withstand damn near anything the Japs could give, but I was totally unprepared for the psychological change. Changing from a combat soldier to a prisoner of war is not like putting on a clean shirt. Consciously I was totally preoccupied with the minute-to-minute reality of just staying alive. This was my conscious thought. But somewhere way back in the unconscious part of my mind I had become a prisoner of war, and I didn't even know what a prisoner of war was. It was a term without meaning. I sensed I had stepped across an invisible line, and there was no stepping back. I was horrified at the finality of what had happened. Psychologically it was as though a feeling of dread had enveloped my body and penetrated to the depths of my soul. Life was dragging me down an unknown path toward an unknown destination, and I didn't want to go. Years later my wife told me that when she was in the delivery room with her first child she became frightened, told the nurse she had changed her mind about having the baby. I already knew a little something of the fear that she felt.

This was the third night since the surrender. No water to drink, but the Japs gave us food. Were they toying with us, trying to break us? They gave us one flat six-ounce tin of sardines to divide among four men. Hardly a sumptuous feast. I wolfed mine down, both bites. Had great difficulty swallowing.

Hunger and thirst I could put aside, the pain and bodily fatigue was bearable, but there was no denying the need to sleep. My eyelids were heavier than the rocks I had been carrying. We were crowded together, and the Japs still wanted us to sit at attention. Maybe the Japs were growing tired of their little game. There weren't so many of them around to watch us. Without moving we formed little self-help groups. Five, six, eight, eight men close enough to touch.

There were three men in my little group. One suggested that we take turns, two men trying to sleep while the third stayed awake and kept an eye on the guards. Good idea if we could get away with it. I watched for a while; then it was my turn.

Sleep, blessed sleep. I rested my head on my drawn-up knees. A minute, two minutes, I don't know. An elbow jammed hard into my ribs, jammed again. It hurt.

Ssssst! The fellow on watch told me to get my damn head up and try to open my eyes. One of the guards was coming our way.

I struggled mightily to sit straight, to resume the pose of sitting at attention. There were little stirrings around me as other prisoners straightened their bodies. The guard passed without incident. I dropped my head, went to sleep like turning off a light switch. Pretty soon it would be my turn to stand watch. A minute, two minutes, five minutes, don't know. This time I woke to the sound of a shower of blows. Startled grunts, gasps of pain from the prisoners, an angry harangue from the guard. No rifle butts this time, just a lot of hard whacks with a bamboo stick. A bamboo stick is better than a rifle, doesn't break bones, hurts like hell. Poor bastard, our lookout had fallen asleep.

I made it through the night. Most of the time I got away with it, but sometimes I got the bamboo stick. I had reached the irrational point where my mind and body no longer gave a damn. It hurt more to stay awake than to take a couple of licks from the bamboo stick. Morning came, the fourth day, and the same hot sun popped up again. Still no water for us, but I must have rested a little during the night because I think I felt better. I read somewhere that the human body gets more rest from the first two hours sleep than it does from all the rest of the night, no matter how long you stay in bed. Wonder if this holds true for the first one, two, or five minutes?

The heat was tremendously intense, and the hours passed in a monotonous blur. I took rocks from one man, handed them to another, and farther down the line someone dropped them into the water. Prisoners began hitting the ground regularly, dropping to the ground exhausted, getting up, dropping again. The only shade was underneath the water truck still sitting near the end of the pier. Whenever a prisoner dropped from the heat, absolutely couldn't get up again, the Japanese let us drag him to the water truck and lay him in the shade. Soon there was room for only heads to lie in the shade. By midafternoon there were too many even for that. Most of these men got up and returned to work. Some, a few, never revived at all.

Colonel Kirkpatrick had a lot of guts. He went to the boat the Japanese commander used as an office and raised hell. I could hear the shouting, both in English and Japanese, but I couldn't make out the words. The Japanese respected courage. They beat hell out of the colonel, but he came back bloody and triumphant. They gave us water. They brought it to us in canvas buckets. Not enough, not nearly enough, but sufficient to keep us going. My God! It was good. I could feel my strength returning. My body had forgotten how to urinate, but it sucked up water like a sponge. I could feel it. When my bunch was not handling rock, when it was our turn to rest, the Japanese fed us again. This time it was a small can of pork and beans split among each four men. It is difficult to divide one little can of beans evenly among four hungry men, but we tried. I think the last man got the best of it. He got to wipe the inside of the can with his finger and then lick his finger.

This night passed like the previous one — work a while, rest a while. Sit at attention. Sleep a minute if you can. But this night was different. I'd had a drink of water, I'd been given a bit of food, and I'd managed a few minutes sleep. I wasn't aware of it, but I was already learning the most basic law of survival as a prisoner. Adapt. Bend with the pressures. Bend but don't break. Give up what you absolutely have to, but hold on to what you can. Learn to beat the "little bastards" at their own game.

Morning again, the fifth day. Something was in the wind, something different. We formed up about ten or eleven o'clock and marched away under heavy guard. We must have walked two or three miles. Another village, nipa huts, coconut palms, and a large open field near a schoolhouse. We stopped briefly on the dirt road that bordered one end of the field. We were ringed with guards and bayonets. Filipino women, old women, so old and wrinkled and bent with age they could barely walk, tried to give us food. The guards shoved them back. The old women tossed the food over the heads of the guards. Bits of fish, little packages of cooked rice wrapped in large green leaves, twists of crude tobacco. God bless them. Some of them were beaten for their efforts. Little kids too. Boys and girls maybe six or seven years old ran up and threw little bits of food. It's still a warm memory, the love and generosity of these Filipino people.

These Japanese quickly moved us into the field, kept the Filipinos away. Eight or ten Japanese officers, big shots probably, sat on chairs at one side of the field, a makeshift reviewing stand. Our guards formed us into ranks and marched us past this bunch of Japanese officers. They watched in impassive silence. Wasn't good enough. We tried it again. We looked like hell. Very unmilitary. We were filthy dirty, our clothes were torn, our hair was matted, and we were unshaven. They weren't satisfied. Hour after hour we formed ranks, marched around the field and passed in review. They were taking pictures with an old newsreel camera. Maybe a newsreel to send back to Japan to demonstrate their glorious victory. I don't know if we looked too good or too bad but they made us do it over and over. How in the hell could we look military in our condition? We'd march, a man would drop, two men would pick him up and all three would drop. The bastards weren't satisfied. Every man had to be on his feet. It was late afternoon before the officers finally nodded their heads and our guards marched us back to the pier. I never found out what that afternoon was all about.

We got back to the pier and God Almighty, there was hot food waiting for us. Plain unsalted cooked rice and more water to drink. I was in heaven. In our condition a bowl of rice and a drink of water was indeed heavenly, a gift from the gods. I had been stripped of all my eating gear except a spoon and the rice was too hot for my hands, so I held out my shirttail. I ate out of that shirttail for the next two weeks.

After eating we were lined up again and told that fifteen volunteers were going on detail to work in a sugar mill. We were in a bit of hell on earth, and we wanted out, so there were two hundred immediate, eager volunteers. Everyone wanted to go. Walter Allen, "Cy" to us, stood on one side of me, Corporal Sunderland on the other. We all wanted to go, to get anywhere else, away from where we were. When the Japs came down the line, two privates and an officer, I stepped forward. The guard shoved me back with his rifle and took Cy Allen instead. I was bitterly disappointed. I wanted out. I wanted to go. Fifteen happy men waved their good-byes, climbed into the back of a truck, and set off down the road to the sugar mill. The Japanese worked them for a few days, put them into a pit in the ground, doused them with gasoline, and set them afire, burned them alive.

The rest of us were moved into the empty tin warehouse. No more moving rock on the pier. Once in the warehouse, the Japs left us pretty much alone. There was barely room to lie down on the cement floor, but I stretched out and fell asleep immediately. The warehouse was closed all round except for one door that was left open, secured by a single waist-high two-by-four and guards with rifles and bayonets. Inside there was no water and no toilets.

Until now, since leaving the fort, I had not felt the need for either a bowel movement or to urinate. Under the stress, normal bodily functions had been suspended. Now that we were eating again and drinking water, things would be different. A guard took one of our officers outside to the back of the warehouse and showed him a rude plank walkway, two feet wide and without handrails, that stretched out a hundred feet over the water. This was our toilet. The guard indicated that during daylight hours, one man at a time could walk to the end of the walkway, drop his pants, hang over the water, and do his do.

When my turn came I dutifully walked to the end of the runway. My God! There were two nipa huts not fifty feet away with porches built over the water and families living in them. I had to drop my pants and bare my ass, as the old saying goes, "in front of God and everybody." It was a humiliating, degrading experience, one of the many humiliations I endured as a prisoner of war. The Filipino women ignored us, never looked at us, went about their household duties as if we didn't exist. It was a kindness I was thankful for.

We stayed in the warehouse, gradually recovering strength. Compared to the first few days our situation was now much better but things were still bad. For instance, though we were given rice every day, we were still filthy dirty. None of us had been able even to wash our hands or faces. I was developing ulcers under my arms and in my groin, from the heat and the sweat and the dirt. Before the war, in barracks, I took two or three showers a day just to keep fungus infections away. Here we smelled, and we were dirty and getting dirtier. There was no toilet paper, one of the taken-for-granted peacetime luxuries I was learning to do without. No toilet paper meant raw irritation between the cheeks of my buttocks and an added stink to the already stinking smell of my body.

A head count told us that the Japs had kept Spud Murray, who spoke some Japanese, and nine men from the engine-room gang to show them how to run the machinery on the fort. When the Japanese took us from the fort, they had no way of knowing how completely we had destroyed everything. Murray and his nine men didn't have a chance in hell of getting the machinery running again. The Japs must have been furious once they realized the full extent of our destruction. At any rate, we never saw Murray or his men again. Unlucky bastards. Figure the Japanese must have executed them on the fort and tossed the bodies into the bay.

We spent a week in the warehouse, cooped up, doing nothing. Our guards seemed to come to us on a rotating basis, a certain bunch today, a different bunch tomorrow. Probably detached from some larger unit stationed nearby. The contrast in the way the Japs treated us was unbelievable, dark to daylight, hell to heaven. This was a good week for me. It gave me time to think, to regroup. For the first five days I knew I was going to die, knew the Japanese intended to kill us and wondered why they didn't just shoot us and get it over with. Now, I began to think in terms of being allowed to live. The physical part was the easiest. I was young, healthy, and still well over two hundred pounds. My bruises were fading and the general soreness was leaving my body. I had ulcers under my arms, in my groin, and on one leg, and literally hundreds of small cuts and scratches on my hands and arms. Every damn one of these was oozing and infected, but with a little medicine and some clean gauze bandages I would be all right. I had no idea that my next medication was three-and-a-half years down the road. Psychologically, my mental regrouping was much more difficult than my physical adaptation. I was still thinking in American terms. In the United States even a man on death row had rights, privileges, things he was entitled to. He was clothed, fed, permitted, even encouraged to wash up, to shave and shower on a daily basis. He was given books, a radio, medical and dental attention. He was permitted to write and receive letters, to communicate with people outside the prison. And he was spared physical brutality. These things were considered his rights, human rights. It took me a while to realize that I was entitled to nothing, that I had no rights, that I lived or died at the whim of my captors, and that I could do absolutely nothing to change this.

This week in the warehouse was our first real chance to talk among ourselves, and talk we did. But we were young and foolish and full of optimistic hope, not yet old enough or wise enough to see the realities of our situation.

We deceived ourselves by thinking that the relief convoy was only delayed but that it was still on its way. When it got here our troops would lick these little bastards and get us out. We knew the United States would win the war quickly and then we would all go home. At the worst we felt there would be a prisoner exchange and we would be among the first traded. Any day now we would get the good word.

We were filled with youthful optimism. To youth reality comes slowly, and hope dies hard.

One afternoon I stood at the warehouse door behind the wooden barrier trying to get some fresh air, trying to see what was going on outside. I could see a few other prisoners, Philippine Scouts, but the Japs kept them separated from us. I lingered in the doorway, breathing air not yet contaminated by the stench of unwashed bodies. The warehouse was dark, gloomy, filled with misery and suffering, but outside the day was warm, bright, full of life. Two completely different worlds, separated by a piece of two-by-four across a doorway. On my side the prisoners, a tiny island of despair and suffering, on the other side the whole rest of the world. The difference, a two-by-four, a couple of armed guards, and that magical, sometimes indefinable thing called freedom. I kept a wary eye on the guards, hoping to stay near the doorway but not wanting to attract the guards' attention. Luckily, they were absorbed in their own affairs, talking among themselves. I smelled a mixture of odors, all pleasant. There was the tang of salty sea air, of seaweed washed up on the beach, of dry grass, strange flowers, freshly turned earth from a nearby farm.

A small soldier, small even for a Japanese, came to the door. I backed away but he beckoned unmistakably to me. He was unarmed, not one of the regular guards.

He placed his hands on his hips and stared at me sternly. Then in very poor but understandable English he told me that I had a very big nose, a very much big nose.

Big nose? Didn't seem all that big to me. Continuing in his schoolbook English he asked me if I knew Shakespeare. I didn't. Then he told me that he knew more Shakespeare than me, that he knew more Shakespeare than all of us. He waved his hand contemptuously at the roomful of prisoners, snorted and turned on his heel. Never saw him again.

I had been a prisoner almost two weeks. It seemed a lot longer. We learned that our Japanese lieutenant, the one whose brother we had killed, had been reassigned. We had a new Japanese commander, a lucky twist of fate. I think the first commander fully intended to kill every one of us. Had he remained in charge, the fifteen men he burned to death would have been just the beginning.

Guards took us out on the pier, motioned for us to take off our clothes and get into the water. First chance I had to wash since the surrender. Believe me, a man can accumulate a lot of stink in two weeks. The salt water stung. Seemed like I had a million little cuts and scratches. When I was a kid in Tampa, Florida, I heard that salt water had a healing effect on cuts. Hoped it was true. After washing the worst of the dirt from my body I swam under water for a ways. I came up behind one of the Japanese fishing boats and a Jap guard sitting on deck sighted his rifle directly at my head. He wasn't more than ten feet away, and it was scary as hell. I could see his finger on the trigger, knew he wanted to kill me. Panicky, I ducked under and swam as far as I could without coming to the top. When I ran out of breath I came up in the middle of a crowd and stayed there. With my eyes I measured the distance across the small bay. Not more than half a mile. The other side was covered with dense underbrush and small trees. I could make that, could swim it easily. Maybe there was a way out after all. After dark, if I could convince the guards that I had to take a crap, maybe I could slip into the water, swim across the bay and be hidden in the underbrush before they knew I was gone. Maybe. It was a hard decision to make, a chancy one, and I kept turning it over in my mind all night.

Next morning Harold Gardener and one other man were missing. They must have taken the water route because they went without their shoes. The Japs killed them both.

Something was in the wind. We were moving. Back on the boats and the smelly little fish holds. Nobody knew where, why, what for. And our guards told us nothing, just shoved us below decks, closed the hatch, and off we went.

I was relieved, glad to go. Always, whenever the Japs moved me from one place to another, I had the feeling, the hope that the next place would be better than the last. I was leaving Nasugbu, a place that a week ago had seemed to offer only certain death. What else could I think? Get the hell away from here, anywhere, any way you can. The next place had to be better. Snatches of conversation, overheard. The usual question was, "How ya doin'?" or "What's up?" For me the answer was "lousy." I was hurting from top to bottom. Nothing serious, just lots of little cuts and bruises and sore all over. Sitting in the darkness we didn't talk much, nothing much to talk about. We all had the same gripes, the same cuts and bruises, the same aches and pains. We all had the same hopes and unvoiced fears, and not one of us could see a single minute into our future. Crammed below decks in the blackness of that little fishing boat, we were all afraid of what might happen to us when the Japanese opened the hatch and let us out. Were they taking us to a place with food and a place to sleep, maybe even a shower? And if so, where was all the gear they had taken away from us? Personally, I was glad to get away from the pier with a whole ass and no busted bones. Although my head still ached from a blow from a rifle butt when I had fallen asleep on the rockpile, basically I was still in pretty good shape.

An hour or so in the hold and the motor stopped. The hatched opened. We were a long way from shore, next to a rusty old freighter. Up the gangway and down into an empty cargo hold. No words, no explanations, not a minute on deck, just off the little boat and onto the big one. The Japs closed the hatch and left us in the dark again. I didn't know what to think. I was relieved, glad to be getting away from the brutality of Nasugbu, but scared of what might be ahead because ahead was still unknown. I'm sure all of us were the same, tight guts, tight asses, but we tried not to show it in front of each other. Were we really out of the woods? Were we really going to get better treatment? What about the "special severe punishment"? Were they going to kill more of us? Maybe their hatred, their thirst for revenge had been satisfied with the fifteen men they had already burned to death. Maybe?

The big ship was moving. Wish I knew where it was taking us. Wish I knew when we were going to eat again. Wish I knew for sure if we were going to eat again.

We were stopped. I heard the rumble of the anchor chain as the ship dropped its anchor. The hatch covers opened and daylight streamed in. In any other circumstance it might have been laughable. Without noticing it we had been loaded into an empty coal bunker. I was covered with coal dust. Every time I sat down, lay on the steel deck, brushed against a bulkhead, wiped my hands across my face, I had smeared myself with black. We were a mess.

Off the big ship and onto small boats again. Different boats but small, like landing craft. Looked like the Japs had brought us up the coast and into Manila Bay. I could see Manila a few miles away. Maybe we were going to Manila. At least there'd be food, buildings, beds, a place to sleep. We stepped in neck deep water, and the Japs made us wade ashore. It wasn't just my outfit, not just the men from Fort Drum. I could see other freighters, other landing craft. This must be everybody, all the guys from Corregidor.

By the time I reached shore my shoes were full of sand. I wanted to take my shoes off, to shake the sand out, to brush off my feet, but the Japs started raising hell and using clubs. We started walking toward the city. The guys from Corregidor had evidently been treated differently from the guys from Fort Drum. They still carried their backpacks, still wore their hats. Some of them carried blanket rolls, and many had barracks bags filled with food and clothing. We had nothing.

We marched toward Manila along Dewey Boulevard, a wide, beautiful street that follows the edge of the bay. As we neared Manila the street was lined with throngs of Filipinos, ordered into the street by the Japanese for the occasion. Then came the cavalry, the goddamn Japanese cavalry. They were sharp. The horses were beautifully groomed and every buckle, every piece of metal, had been polished to perfection. And their riders, the Japanese cavalrymen were mirror perfect. Their helmets were polished, their carbines glistened, not a wrinkle in their clothing, not a hair out of place. We were on parade, a victory parade to impress the Filipino people. The Japanese cavalry looked good and we looked bad, unbelievably bad. The Filipinos watched dutifully as our beaten remnant of an army trudged past, but I could see many of them were crying, tears streaming down their faces.

It was a long march. The pace was fast and the sun was hot. Exhausted men were dropping their gear. I saw backpacks, blanket rolls, full barracks bags left on the street. I thought about grabbing a full barracks bag off the street. Probably full of clothes and food, but I wasn't sure I had the strength to carry it. Anyway, the cavalry would have none of it. I saw an American prisoner get the hell beat out of him for picking up a bag.

This march through Manila was an experience I shall always remember. I knew it was a show for the Filipino people, this parade of victorious Japanese and defeated Americans, and I was filled with mixed emotions. My feet hurt. The sand in my shoes was grinding away between my toes, but the pain faded into the background. I was on an emotional high, tense, keyed up. Every faculty was totally absorbed in the business of learning to be a prisoner of war. It wasn't quick and it wasn't easy. The physical part was simple. One minute I was an American soldier fighting a battle. The next minute I was a prisoner of the Japanese. Psychologically, emotionally, the transition is more difficult. Being a prisoner of war was not just something I did; it was something I became over a period of time.

On this afternoon's march through Manila my emotions were jumbled, confused. Of course the fear, the anxiety, not knowing what to expect next, these feelings were paramount. I felt humiliated, degraded, but I was not ashamed. Instead, I felt proud that we had fought so well for so long. True, the Japanese Army had whipped our asses, but I knew in my heart that with help from home, even a little help, we would have won.

I was learning fast. A man had to learn quickly just to survive. I had seen one prisoner beaten for it and already knew that on this march, picking up abandoned gear was a no no. Later on the same day I saw a Japanese soldier strike an American prisoner repeatedly across the face. The American struck back, hit the Japanese, and a second later the American was dead. Hard lessons, bitter lessons, but I learned.

The day's march ended, still in the city, at the Bilibid Prison. Old Bilibid, as it was called, had been built during the Spanish occupation of the Philippines in the late eighteen hundreds. It was very old, crude, but surrounded by a massive brick wall and quite secure. My contingent, the men from Fort Drum, was the last to pass through the gates. Once we were inside Bilibid the Japanese left us alone. Apparently they were satisfied with the showing they had made by parading our ragtag army through the streets. Bilibid Prison was chaos. All the survivors from Corregidor were there before us, and the place was overflowing. We had absolutely no organization, no chain of command. The march through the city had mixed us so thoroughly that even though our officers were somewhere among us, there was no one to tell us where to go, what to do. We were on our own.

There were a few crude buildings within the walls, barracks probably, with dirt floors and planks for beds. These rough shelters had been taken by earlier arrivals and were more than full. Even sleeping space on the ground was limited.

I wandered from barracks to barracks looking for a plank to sleep on, even a place to lie on the ground. No luck. I was too late. It was dark, very dark, and I was stumbling over people in the blackness. I saw a light in the open area, firelight, and I gravitated toward it. Four prisoners, probably among the first arrivals, had found a five-gallon tin and were cooking fritters over a small wood fire. The fritters were just flour and water, bits of dough dropped into hot grease. Don't know how they made it through the march with flour and oil. My mouth watered at the smell. I was hungry. No use asking for any though. I could see there wasn't enough to go around. They had food, I didn't. They ate, I didn't. We were already in the dog-eat-dog stage, every man for himself. I was alone, one man among several thousand prisoners of war, each man doing his damndest to look out for himself.

On the ground near the fire I found the top of the five-gallon tin. It had been cut out of the can with an old-fashioned can opener or a crude knife. It was square but the edges were rough, sharp, jagged. I bent the edges with a rock to form a crude plate. This would be my mess kit. Rough, but better than eating off my shirttail. I ate from that piece of tin for more than a year.

Nosing around some more I found an unlocked door, a small room with no furniture and a dirt floor. Grateful for the space, I stretched out and fell asleep in the dirt. I awoke with daylight streaming in through small windows high up in the walls. I could see and I didn't like what I saw. One wall was pockmarked, full of bullet holes and spattered with dried blood. I had spent the night in the execution chamber. I got the hell out of there.

In the prison yard word was that a detail of five hundred men was leaving Bilibid. Where, nobody knew. When, right now. I got in line. I knew that the first fifteen-man detail from my outfit had been executed, burned alive, but five hundred, the Japs could more easily shoot us right here. I decided to take the chance. Bilibid was going to be a hellhole. No place for me if I could get out.

Because our circumstance was identical, we had found the buildings full and no place to sleep, most of the prisoners from Fort Drum managed to be in this first five hundred. At a checkpoint the Japanese were passing out baseball-sized balls of cooked rice mixed with a few soybeans. I put mine inside my shirt. I ate mine quickly, hustled about, got back into line and got a second. Thank God, to the Japanese all Americans looked alike.

Out the gate, out of Bilibid. I was elated, my first little victory, my own choice. The Japanese didn't know who was going on that detail, didn't give a damn. They counted five hundred bodies as they passed through the gates and that was it. The gates slammed shut. Bilibid was behind me, and I was on my way.

Heavily guarded, we walked two or three miles to a railroad yard. No brutality, no mistreatment, just an occasional "hyaku, hyaku" as we slouched along. It was full daylight when we reached the rail yard, but there were no civilians about. The Japanese had cleared the area. The boxcars were tiny, almost toylike, and the Japanese filled them to capacity. They crammed us in like sardines in a can, like animals, just room to stand, no room to move, hardly room to breathe. Paul Brisco, a Marine who had fought beside us on Fort Drum, was near me in

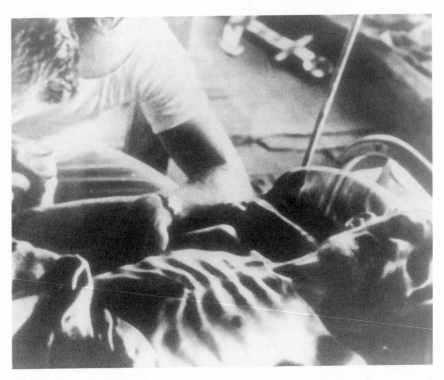

Prisoner dying from beri-beri in the prison hospital at Bilibid. There was no actual medical treatment. All the American doctors could do was try to make the dying a little easier. Yet this type of suffering and painful death could easily have been averted with sufficient food and a little medicine. (Photo courtesy of American Ex-Prisoners of War, Arlington, Texas.)

the crowd. We knew each other because we had fought together on the fort. Paul joined me and we formed an instant temporary alliance.

We decided to be careful and held back, jockeyed for position in the crowd so as not to be the first prisoners loaded into the boxcar.

We thought the guards would stand in the doorway and that the first prisoners into the car would be away from them, out of their immediate reach but we weren't sure.

In these first two weeks I had learned that it was wise to stay as far away from the guards as possible and not to attract their attention. Nevertheless, I stayed with Paul and we were among the last four or five men shoved into the rail car. My God! Only two weeks and already we were looking for that little edge, that little advantage that might make the difference between living or dying.

Paul and I were in the doorway, standing against the waist high barrier that had been put across the door. Two Japanese guards stood shoulder-to-shoulder, body-to-body beside us. It was tight for them too. They had barely room to stand, and it would have been difficult for them to use their rifle butts or bayonets. Still, there was no thought of escape. I knew there were more guards with machine guns sitting on the roof.

The trip began easily. The cars swayed and lurched along the track and we were moving. Soon I was dripping sweat, and I was in the doorway. By midafternoon it was unbelievable, pure torture. Americans were dying in the back corners of the car. Dead but still standing because there was no room to fall down.

Most people don't know, but when a man dies his muscles relax, his sphincters relax. Sometimes after death he urinates or defecates. The stench was horrible. I could smell death in the air, and there was nothing I could do about it.

The train stopped. For a minute or a half hour, no one knew why or for how long. Paul had to urinate, badly. His face was contorted; it was killing him. Paul made motions to the guards with his hands, made hissing noises between his teeth. The guard nodded and motioned for Paul to get off the train. With his hands raised above his head Paul walked about thirty feet, then very slowly lowered his hands and unbuttoned his pants. Nothing happened. He tried so hard his face grew red with the effort. Nothing. He had struggled, held it in for so long his sphincter was locked. He couldn't release. The guard shouted angrily in Japanese. Paul made helpless gestures with his hands. After all that trouble he didn't dare come back without urinating and if the train started without him the guards would simply shoot him where he stood. The guard shouted again, raised his rifle and sighted it directly at Paul. I was sure Paul was going to be shot. Perhaps the threat of imminent execution made the difference. Paul urinated, long and hard. He was so relieved he giggled a little hysterically. The guards laughed too, even put down their hands and helped him back into the car. A triviality, perhaps, but a prisoner of war often lived or died by just such trivialities.

The train stopped at dusk, and most of us, those of us who were still alive, were herded like cattle into a fenced open field behind a one-room schoolhouse. No food, no water, but at least we were out of the rail cars with a chance to rest, to breathe freely again, maybe even to sleep. It began to rain, hard. In the Philippines, during the rainy season, most rains are real downpours. The earth becomes saturated, and water runs in sheets across the ground. I crawled beneath it to get out of the rain. There was a slight slope to the ground and rivulets of water began coming under the building. The earth under the schoolhouse was inches deep in dust. With my hands I scraped a ridge of loose dust around me and curled up in a little ball. I slept sound and dry throughout the night. The poor bastards in the field lay in the rain all night.

In the morning, without a head count, the Japanese herded us down the road. Four men from my outfit, Turman, Burlon, Garland, and Law, had formed a self-help group, and decided to stick together. One of them was too weak to walk, so they hid in some tall weeds, lay quietly while the rest of us marched off. I was strongly tempted to stay with them but at the last minute decided against it.

We walked all day, maybe ten or twelve miles. No breaks, no food, no water, no hurry, just a slow plodding walk. Our guards trudged beside us. Once a Japanese staff car came roaring down the road. It came from behind and passed so close, the fender actually brushed my clothing. I was startled. Better stay awake, better watch, these bastards won't swerve an inch to keep from running over an American prisoner.

I was tired, hungry, and just plodding along when we reached the camp, our first real camp. I hadn't eaten since I ate my rice ball the day before, but I had managed a drink of water from a puddle alongside the road. The puddle was covered with green scum and the water was full of wiggly things, but I scooped it up in my hands and drank it anyway. Glad to get it.

The camp had been built to help train the Philippine Army. It was rough, nothing like an Army camp back home. The barracks were about fifty feet long, twenty feet wide, and raised a little off the ground. There were no doors; they were wide open at both ends. The roofs were thatched and the sides were one thickness of woven palm leaves. There were long, horizontal windows with no glass, no screens. The windows opened out and up and could be propped open with a stick. The buildings were all alike, dirt floor, a six-foot aisle down the middle, and sleeping shelves along each side and over the aisle. The shelves were seven feet wide and ran the length of the building, one a foot above the ground, one four feet above that, and one high up over the center aisle. The sleeping shelves were covered with bamboo strips nailed to two-by-fours, a strip, a space, another strip. This was where we lived, where we slept. There were no blankets, no mattresses, no closets, no furniture of any kind. My barracks was filled to capacity, bodies touching bodies on the sleeping shelves. A Japanese officer with some command of English came by and gave us a short lecture, short and to the point. He told us that we had to remain inside our barracks. There was a latrine a hundred feet from the barracks, but only one man at a time was allowed out of the barracks to use it. If two men went out, one would be shot. Finally he told us that we must obey all rules, all orders from Japanese soldiers. Any prisoner who disobeyed an order would be severely punished until dead. Our orientation lecture was over. So much for human rights and the Geneva Convention.

I made it through the night. Nobody wanted to be "severely punished until dead." Next morning there was food. The Japanese gave us some rice, some huge cauldrons, and an open shed to use as a kitchen. We had to cook the rice ourselves. We set up a kitchen detail and by noon had our first home-cooked meal. Rice, unsalted, unseasoned, and not very much of it. Unsalted rice was to be our food staple for the next three-and-a-half years. Occasional additions, occasional variations, of course, but not much. On a good day we might get six chickens for three thousand men, or the head of a carabao, horns, eyes, teeth and all, boiled in a cauldron until the flesh fell from the skull. Sometimes it would be the skin of a pig with the hair still on, or the blood of a slaughtered carabao, poured into boiling water to form small gritty clots. There is nothing so unappetizing as to walk past the kitchen and see the head of a carabao, horns extending over the edge of the cauldron, eyes staring at you just above the boiling water.

The Japanese relaxed their strict rules a little. I could leave the barracks, actually walk about the camp in the late afternoon. We had spent the previous night in this camp, and this was our first full day. In the late afternoon there was a great hustle of activity in the Japanese guardhouse. Squads of Japanese soldiers stationed themselves at intervals through the camp. There was a lot of chatter in Japanese, but we didn't know what it was about. Something was up, something big.

A truck pulled up to the guardhouse and unloaded some Japanese soldiers and the four men who had remained hidden in the weeds at the schoolhouse. All four were there, Turman, Burlon, Garland, and Law. My God! They had been badly beaten. Their arms were tied behind them, tied at the wrists and elbows. They had to be helped from the truck. Then they were hustled into the guardhouse, and we were ordered back to barracks. There were guards everywhere. Security was strict during the night.

The guardhouse was not a guardhouse in the real sense of the word. It was just a one-room building in the center of camp that the Japanese guard detail used as an office or headquarters. It was built of thatch and palm leaves like the rest of the buildings. The only difference was that it had a wooden floor. Guardhouse was our name for it.

There were no lights in the barracks. We sat in the dark and talked. The four men had disappeared into the guardhouse, and we were confined to barracks. Two different worlds. Japanese guards were everywhere. We were still new at this business of being prisoners of war and all we could do was speculate. A fellow prisoner asked me what I thought the Japs would do to them. I didn't know. I figured that at the very least the Japs would beat the living hell out of them. Poor bastards. I knew for sure that the Japs would be rough on them. Hate like hell to be in their shoes.

Daylight. The Japs let us move about the camp again. The first order of business was to appoint a mess sergeant who sent four men to the kitchen. They brought back buckets of lugao, wet rice. There was no salt, no sugar, no milk, no coffee, just wet rice. Our mess sergeant divided it as fairly as he could. A cupful of wet lugao, this was breakfast.

As soon as the Japanese soldiers left the barracks I walked as close as I could to the guardhouse. I wanted to know what was happening to the four men from Fort Drum. The place was ringed with bayonets. I got close enough to see my friends but could do nothing to help them. Everything was out in the open. It was obvious that this was to be an object lesson for the rest of the camp. The Japanese wanted us to see, wanted us to know what was happening.

The four Americans were in front of the guardhouse, tied to poles that supported the roof of the small porch. They were tied in such a way as to make their position as painful as possible. Their wrists were tied behind their backs and then tied to the posts at almost shoulder level. To get their hands this high behind their backs the prisoners had to bend over, their upper bodies nearly parallel to the ground. Tied in this manner they could neither stand upright nor sit down. It had to be painful from the beginning, terribly so after a few hours, and after days, pure hell. This was what the Japanese wanted. They didn't want to just lock the four men in a cell, didn't want to execute them immediately. They wanted to make them suffer, suffer publicly. And they did, they made them suffer terribly. The four prisoners were hatless and shirtless, exposed to the sun. They were given neither food nor water. They weren't taken to a toilet and they were beaten, severely, every time the Japanese guards changed, about every four hours. For the beatings the Japanese were careful not to use rifle butts or clubs. Instead they used a piece of green bamboo about four feet long and as thick as your thumb. Green bamboo is pliable, heavy with water, doesn't break bones, but leaves welts that ooze blood and hurt terribly.

Between beatings the prisoners were left alone to suffer in the sun. When conscious they could talk to men in the nearest barracks, which was only fifty or sixty feet away. That's when we got the full story.

A truckload of Japanese soldiers had found the four walking along the road toward camp, just a half mile from the gate. There was a scuffle and the four were badly beaten. One of the four, Law, was a big man and very strong. They said it took five Japanese soldiers to subdue Law and load him into the truck. The four were brought to the camp, beaten again and tied to the poles in front of the guardhouse. I thanked my lucky stars I had decided not to hide in the weeds with them or there would have been five men tied to the poles instead of four.

The afternoon of the second day, barely conscious, terribly beaten, and suffering untold agonies, they asked the Japanese commander to execute them.

The Japanese dug four graves on the crest of a small hill just outside the barracks area. It was chow time because I already had rice in my tin plate. The four doomed men were untied from their poles and marched through camp ahead of a Japanese firing squad. Obviously hurting, they walked stiffly but unaided, hands tied behind their backs. They passed within a few feet of me. Hugh Garland, a small fellow with a thick shock of curly black hair, tried to grin and mumbled something, but I couldn't understand what he was trying to say. I didn't see the slightest sign of fear in their faces. If anything they seemed relieved that their suffering was almost over. They walked to the hill and stood by the graves. We watched. There was a little shelf a foot below the ground in each grave. The Japanese soldiers stepped them down onto the shelves, blindfolded them, and gave each man a cigarette. The four were facing the camp. The firing squad didn't wait for the Americans to finish their cigarettes. A sharp command in Japanese, the crackling volley of rifle fire, and the four tumbled forward into the graves. Law, the big fellow, attempted to climb out of his grave. The Japanese officer shot him through the head and he fell backwards. A single pistol shot at close range into each of the other three graves and it was over. The firing squad didn't look at us as they marched back through camp. They seemed ashamed of their work.

We were already into a world where survival became paramount. I went back to barracks and didn't see a single man throw away his rice. I ate mine, lay down, and eventually slept a very troubled sleep. I kept thinking about the four dead men, about how quickly their lives had been cut short. And I wondered vaguely if their loved ones would ever know how they died or that they were buried on this remote Philippine hillside.

Fort Drum had surrendered a little more than two hundred men to the Japanese. We had been prisoners for only eighteen days and already we had lost thirty-one men. Eighteen days, thirty-one men. I didn't know it yet, thank God, but we still had more than twelve hundred days to go.

June–October 1942:
Cabanatuan Prison Camp #3

Following the execution of the four men from Fort Drum there was a period of relative calm. We got to know each other, the Japanese captors and the American prisoners. I think, at that time, the Japanese did not know what they wanted to do with us. They were learning to be captors, we were learning to be prisoners. We settled into a dull routine.

Little by little, day by day, there emerged a semblance of organization. Our officers took charge, set up an informal but distinguishable chain of command. We were a conglomeration of Army, Marines, Navy, and Air Force, all thrown together by the act of becoming prisoners. We were assigned to a barracks and given a specific place to sleep. The barracks leader, usually an old sergeant or master sergeant, appointed one man as mess sergeant and assigned the rest of us to whatever details were requested by the officers. Our only work was camp maintenance, taking care of the camp and ourselves. Men were chosen to work in the kitchen, to do the cooking, and they became the elite. The kitchen detail lived in a separate barracks because they had to get up in the middle of the night to start cooking the morning meal, and of course, they got more food than the rest of us. There was a wood choppers detail, men who split logs into firewood for the kitchen, a detail to go out of camp and carry back heavy logs for the woodcutters, a detail to dig latrines, and yes, often, a burial detail. We lost a lot of good men in those early months, men who had been wounded, men who had malaria, men who were simply sick and exhausted from five months of fighting. Most of these deaths were unnecessary, could have easily been prevented with even a crude hospital, medicine, and decent food. The Japanese gave us none of these and so good men died.

It was during these early months that the basic tenet of survival, the dog-eat-dog, survival of the fittest, became apparent. It was every man for himself. Every prisoner had to live or die on his own. It wasn't that we didn't try to help one another. God knows, we did. It was simply that there was very little, almost nothing, a man could do to help. I could carry a man's food if he was too weak to stand in the chow line. I could help him walk to the latrine. I could give him sympathy.

All of this contributed absolutely nothing toward keeping a man alive. We needed medicine, a hospital, decent food. When a prisoner became sick we could only watch him die.

Food was in short supply. There was never enough. The Japanese fed us regularly, three times a day, but I could put two complete meals, rice and soup, in one canteen cup. When I was taken prisoner in May, I weighed two hundred twenty pounds. The following December, seven months later, I weighed exactly one hundred pounds.

Let me describe for you a man who has lost more than half his normal body weight. First the head. The head seems abnormally large for the body. It retains most of its size because the skull doesn't shrink. The face is cadaverous. The eyes and cheeks are sunken and the cheekbones become prominent. Ears seem unusually large. Collarbones protrude forward, but there are deep hollows above and below them where the flesh has melted away. Every rib is plainly visible, can be easily counted even from a distance, and there is an arch in front where the ribs taper up to the breastbone. Under this arch is a great hollow where the stomach should be. The spinal cord sticks out, each vertebra like a walnut under taut skin. The waist is small, necessarily so, but below the waistline there is almost a flat shelf where the hipbones jut out on each side. He is flat-assed. The buttocks are gone. Sometimes a loose fold of skin hangs down behind. Arms and legs are thin, of course, but it is the legs you notice most. I could take my two hands and touch my thumbs and fingers around the largest part of my thigh. At the top of the inner thighs, where the thighs usually touch, there is a square open space. You could take a two-by-four, flat side up, and not touch the thigh on either side. A starving man is not a pretty sight.

It was at Camp #3 that I really began to adapt to life as a prisoner of war. Not that life became easier — it didn't. It was just that some of the anxieties, some of the not knowing what to expect was gone. But from beginning to end, for three-and-a-half years, my life was a continuing series of adjustments. Prison life got rougher, I got tougher. Living conditions grew worse, I learned new ways to cope. Becoming a prisoner of war only took an instant, but learning to live as one took a long time. It was much like getting a sun tan. Had I gone naked into the tropical sun all at once, I would have burned, blistered, probably died, but minute by minute, a little exposure at a time, and I could tan to the point where I could spend all day in the same hot sun. I think it was the same for all of us. Those who adapted lived, those who didn't died.

The physical part of my adjustment was easiest. I could learn to live in a world without enough food, in a world without beds or tables or chairs or furniture of any kind. I could learn to live without clothing, without lights, without water to wash my body, without toilet paper, without any of the niceties we take for granted as the normal necessities of life. My body learned to do without these things. It was the mental, the psychological changes that were the most difficult. You cannot take an American boy and suddenly drop him into a situation where he has absolutely no rights, not the slightest, where other persons have full control over every aspect of his life, including the unconditional power of life and death, and not expect some tremendous psychological upheaval. I get slapped in the face by a Japanese guard, slapped in the face in front of everybody. The blow stings but the physical hurt is nothing; the psychological hurt is much worse. I have uncontrollable dysentery and crap my blanket in my sleep. It stinks and the whole damn barracks knows it. I feel humiliated, ashamed. I take a psychological brick and place it, psychologically, so that if this particular incident happens again, my psychological brick will give me something to hide behind, to protect myself from the hurt. And as time passes, incident by incident, psychological brick by psychological brick, I build a wall that I can hide behind, that will protect my inner self from these hurts, that will let me go on living with myself. The crux of it is that fifty years later the wall is still there. I have never been able to completely tear it down.

Though they were treated badly, all of the American prisoners were not treated as badly as the men from Fort Drum. Some of the men from Corregidor managed to get into camp with whatever they were able to carry. Not that it amounted to much. At best it was damn little, but it was something. The Japanese had the men from Fort Drum practically bare-assed and barefooted. I came into camp with shirt, pants, shoes, and a jagged piece of tin to eat from, nothing else. I found a Marine in another barracks with four blankets, and I stole one. Maybe I didn't actually steal it, but I took it. The Marine was nice enough about it. He knew that he had four and I had none. I don't know what I would have done if he had objected. I was desperate. And in the prison camp there was no way in hell a man could hang on to four blankets while half the men around him had none. Sleeping on the bamboo was hard, like sleeping on a flat picket fence without a mattress. Even with a blanket beneath me the bamboo strips pressed through, pressed deep into my flesh. My space was on the bottom shelf. I found some pieces of strong cord and tied the corners of my blanket to the upper shelf to make a hammock. It was great, comfortable, it kept me up off the shelf. It was great for three days; then a corner ripped off the blanket and I was back on the bamboo again.

Life was hard and such simple pleasures as we found became magnified out of all proportion. There were no lights, so after the sun went down we usually talked quietly until we fell asleep. One night I lay in the dark and whistled softly, some tune that I remembered from before the war. Just thinking my own thoughts, whistling for myself.

A voice out of the dark told me that someone was listening. The voice in the dark asked me to whistle some more.

I whistled another, and yet another. I whistled every song, every tune I could remember. When we broke it up to fall asleep, an hour later, there were twenty or thirty prisoners standing around listening, in absolute silence. You'd think they were at a concert, listening to a symphony. When you have nothing, something, even a little something, can seem like a lot.

It was at Camp #3 that I met Floyd Buckner. It happened like so many other things that took place in my life during the prison years. I had a sleeping space on a shelf, Floyd slept next to me, and through proximity we became friends. Our lives touched briefly for a few short months, then circumstances took Buckner in one direction, me in another. We never really got together again.

Buckner was a big man, tall, muscular, and eight or ten years old than I. His mother was Indian, his father Mexican. Buckner could have passed for either. His skin was dark like a deep tan. He had straight, coal-black hair, black eyes, high prominent cheekbones, and a mustache that came down around both sides of his mouth to the bottom of his jaw. He looked exactly like a movie version of a Mexican bandit. We talked. We talked because life had thrown us together and we both needed someone to talk to. It made POW life easier if there was a friend to bare your soul to, and we were good sounding boards for one another. I spent six months in Camp #3, mostly in the shakedown stage. Hadn't settled into the POW groove yet. Unconsciously I was learning to adjust to this new life-style.

I don't know what the Filipinos had in mind when they built this camp just before the war. Maybe it was never finished. At any rate there was almost no water, a couple of single faucets for the entire camp. There were no showers, no washbasins, no places to clean either my body or my clothes. I was grimy, dirty, smelly. A week or two without washing and my body sweat mixed with the dust and dirt to form a grime that I could scrape with my fingernails. I bathed when it rained, if you could call it that. Day or night, when it rained we ran outside the barracks, stripped off our clothes and scrubbed like hell. Without soap. Most of the time at least some of the dirt came off. In two-and-a-half years as a POW in the Philippines, just before the Japs shipped me to Japan, I never saw a shower or a washbasin. On rare occasions I managed to borrow a bucket, stand in line at night to fill it, and leave it beside my barracks to warm in the sun while I was away on work detail. If it wasn't stolen while I was away I could take a sponge bath.

Buckner went on work detail to dig a latrine for the Japanese. He worked his tail off and one of the guards gave him a small piece of yellow laundry soap. When he came back to barracks we took a bath. We used a canteen cup for a bathtub, two small rags for washcloths, and sunshine for a towel. And we had soap. We took turns, Floyd first because it was his soap, and then me. I held the cup while he carefully dipped one small rag, squeezed the excess water back into the cup, rubbed soap on the rag, and scrubbed as far as it would go. Then he dipped the clean rag into the cup, squeezed the excess, and wiped off the soap. Done with care, one canteen cup of water will wash a man's whole body. Floyd finished. Then it was my turn. It was great. The soap was gone but we both felt better. And we were the envy of the barracks.

Surprise inspection. The Japs loved surprise inspections. A squad of Japanese soldiers would march through camp and select a barracks at random.

Everybody out. Bring all your gear, lay it on the ground, and stand behind it.

Don't know what they expected to find. What the hell did I have? A blanket, the piece of tin that I ate from, a spoon. A few people in the camp had contraband. Some of the officers kept diaries, rosters, lists of the dead. These items were

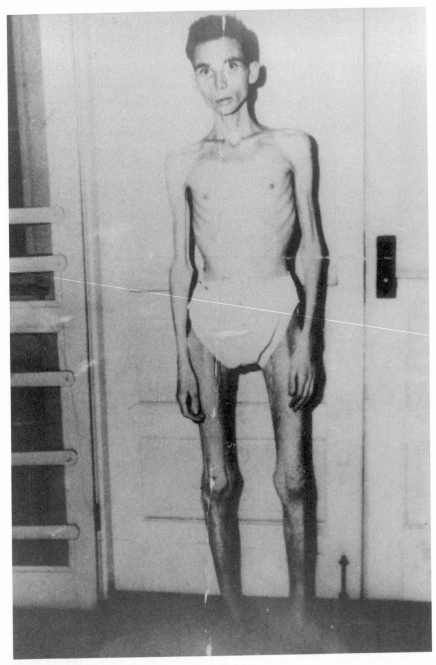

Prisoner showing the typical effects of starvation. He is wearing the "G-string" or one-piece clothing worn daily by most prisoners at Cabanatuan. (Photo courtesy of American Ex-Prisoners of War, Arlington, Texas.)

usually in a glass jar, concealed deep in a latrine, hung on a string. The Japs never looked closely at the latrines. Approached them with surgical masks over mouth and nose. I could see the clash of cultures in these inspections. They were just different from us. In earlier days as a POW I had seen a Japanese officer completely at a loss with a roll of toilet paper. He carefully unrolled it, examined it square by square for secret messages. In the early days they looked under bloody bandages to see what might be hidden there. Smart Americans were careful, dumb ones got caught. If you displayed everything openly, the Japs might take it from you, but they usually left your person alone. Get caught hiding something and you caught hell. They took anything, everything, watches, jewelry, mementos, American dollars, Philippine pesos. If they found anything Japanese you were either beaten or shot. They assumed you had taken it from a dead Japanese.

Lieutenant Folley, my battery commander, was in charge of the wood-chopper detail. He was a hell of a good guy and whenever he could do it without hurting someone else, he tried to look out for his own men. I wangled a job on the wood-choppers detail for Buckner and me. It was a deluxe assignment, cream o' the crop. There were ten of us. All we had to do was chop enough firewood for the kitchen. We got up at four thirty every morning and worked steadily until after dark. We worked long hours and we worked hard, but the Japs left us alone and we were excused from all the shitty details like latrine digging and the burial detail. Because we did work very hard the Japs allowed us a little extra rice. And the ten wood choppers could eat whenever they felt like it. I don't mean that we ate more often than the rest, only that when the food was ready in the kitchen and was being ladled into buckets for the individual barracks, the wood choppers could stop work at any time and send one man, with their bucket, to the head of the line. This was a great advantage. We weren't cheating because the rest of the camp had set up the rules, but our man would wait until a big cauldron of soup was almost empty, then rush up and get the good stuff that had settled to the bottom.

There were carabao loose in the heavy brushland across the road from camp. Once in a while the Japs would send a hunting party to shoot one. A squad of Japanese soldiers and a dozen volunteer POWs made up the party. We always managed to include one volunteer wood chopper.

It was my turn. Together with the soldiers we passed through the camp gate, crossed the road, climbed through a fence, and we were in wild brushland. No more fences for miles. We walked for miles, for hours, then the Japs shot a carabao. We skinned and dressed it where it fell. First we caught as much blood as we could in a five-gallon can, cut off the head, and skinned the carcass. It was a messy job. We dismembered the carcass, cut it into six pieces, four legs and two rib sections. Each of these was skewered on a pole to be carried back to camp between two prisoners. The head was also carried into camp with two prisoners holding it by the horns. Heart, liver, spleen and lungs were tossed into one gunnysack, the entrails in another and we were ready to go. We saved everything. All of the good meat went to the Japanese, but they gave our kitchen the parts they wouldn't touch themselves. The Japs got the meat; we got the head, the lungs and spleen, the can of blood, and the entrails. We carried the meat back to camp in single file, winding through the brush. The Japs divided themselves, four or five at the head of a column, four or five at the rear. I picked a spot in the middle of the line, the second man on a two-man team with a big chunk of raw, bloody meat dangling between us. As we twisted and turned through the brush I was sometimes out of sight from the guards, both those in the front and those in the rear. I had a small knife made from a broken-off table knife, and passed on to me from someone who died. The handle was wrapped with black electrician's tape and the short blade had been shaped by lots of rubbing on a flat rock. The Japs passed by it on inspections, considered it an eating utensil because it wasn't sharp and the blade was too short to be a weapon.

This day it came in handy. On the way back to camp, during those times when a twist in the trail put me out of sight of the guards, I hacked off a sizable chunk of meat from the large piece dangling in front of me and concealed the chunk in my shirt. My clothes were already bloody so a little additional blood wouldn't give me away. When we got into camp we had to pass two or three prisoner barracks on the way to the Japanese kitchen. Carefully prearranged, one of the wood choppers was supposed to be waiting by the first prisoner barracks. I was scared as hell. I was committed and there was no way to back out. Our plan had to work or my ass was mud. As we passed through the gate I began to limp badly as though I had a pebble in my shoe. I really put on an act. My eyes scanned the barracks. Where in hell was the other wood chopper? I prayed to God he was there, that I wouldn't be left holding the bag. I damn near died from relief when he ran forward and took the pole from my shoulder. The Jap guard nodded understandingly and motioned me over to the barracks. Relief flooded over me as I limped away.

We wood choppers drew our evening ration of soup and saved it. After dark we built a small fire and boiled my chunk of meat in the soup. Real meat in the mess kit. It was heavenly.

Fifty years later I still shudder at the sheer stupidity of my actions. So much was at stake, and so much depended on chance. First, the guards must not see me when I hacked off the chunk of meat and hid it in my shirt, the relief wood chopper had to be in exactly the right place at exactly the right time, and the guards had to be in a good mood to let him take my place, to let me drop out and go to the barracks. Had I been caught I might very well have been shot or at the very least beaten unmercifully. But things went well, everything meshed. The gods probably looked down and smiled at our feeble efforts to beat the system.

A work detail went out of camp under guard every day to cut and carry in logs, logs we wood choppers would later split into firewood. And through this log gathering detail a POW cottage industry was born. Our shoes were wearing out, falling to pieces. Many POWs were already barefoot. On the log detail a POW found a balsa wood log. Because it was extremely light for its size he decided to fool the Japs, make them think he was working hard, and carried it back to camp. We had sharp axes to split the firewood and saws to cut the logs into firewood lengths. With the balsa wood we had a ready-made shoe factory, and because we had the only sharp tools in camp we had a monopoly on the business. After our day's work was done we sat around and cut three-inch thick chunks of balsa wood. We hewed them to the shape of a man's foot, nailed a strip of leather across the instep and we had shoes. We called them skivies. They were light, durable, and beat the hell out of walking barefooted on the rocky ground. Everybody wanted a pair. We couldn't meet the demand. Dog eat dog. We traded skivies for anything we could get. Not that there was much available, but I got a beat-up old rain hat, another man got a few cigarettes, and a third got a mess kit. We were rich. But if a man needed a pair of skivies and had nothing to trade, we gave him a pair anyway. We made good skivies. I had a pair that lasted me for a couple of years.

Once in a while the guards would requisition a POW to drive a truck into San Fernando and pick up a load of rice or whatever they needed. If the guard was in a good mood and the American had a few Philippine pesos, the guard might let him buy fruit, raw tobacco, cheap candy, whatever was still available in the Philippine economy. Of course, the POW had to share his purchase with the guards. Medicine was the ultimate purchase, the aim of every truck driver that went into town, principally quinine for malaria. There was no medicine in camp and the Japs gave us none. Men were dying of dysentery and malaria, dying every day. When a driver did get his hands on some quinine it brought out the darker side of POW life. If ten men were dying, the man with the most to trade got the quinine; the rest were out of luck. Something to trade, a few cigarettes or a stale candy bar frequently meant the difference between life and death.

One afternoon a Japanese sentry came to the wood choppers' work area, looked us over carefully, and motioned for me to follow him. Instantly my mental alarm went off. Why me? I hadn't done anything, hadn't broken any rules. What did he want with me? Apprehensive, worried as hell, I followed the sentry to the Japanese headquarters building. Probably going to get the hell beat out of me and I didn't even know what for. I didn't like it one bit. I wanted to run, but there was nowhere to run to, no way to get out of whatever the Japs had in mind. Reluctantly I walked behind the sentry. A handful of Japanese noncoms and the camp commander, a colonel, were waiting. Outside it was raining hard, one of those tropical downpours that had a sheet of water running across the ground in just a few minutes. I was soaked and I dripped water all over the floor. I had never been summoned to the Jap guardhouse before and I fully expected the worst, but it never came. Instead, Colonel Mori, who spoke a little English but understood more than he spoke, told me that there was a hunting party in the field and it was raining too hard. He wanted me to find them and tell them to come back. I saluted and waited. I wasn't quite sure I understood him correctly, and I didn't want to make a mistake. Colonel Mori waved his hand, motioned toward the perimeter fence and the open field. I still hesitated because I was confused. Once again he motioned me toward the door, told me to go. I looked at the sentry standing on the porch. He made no move to go with me. The colonel's voice again, louder, more insistent. He shouted as he told me to get out, to go now. There was no mistaking the urgency in his voice. Dutifully, I went.

I took my time climbing through the fence, walked slowly across the road and into the underbrush. I was still uncertain, didn't want those damned guards to think I was running, didn't want a bullet in the back. This was unheard of, unbelievable. The Japanese would never let a prisoner wander off into the brush all by himself, but there I was, all alone.

I walked in the direction I thought the hunting party might have taken and as I walked I shouted my head off. It was still raining hard, visibility was poor, and I didn't want to surprise the hunters and maybe get shot because they thought I was trying to escape. So I shouted, loud and often. I thought about escape. This was my chance. I was alone, two or three miles from camp with a good head start. With the coming darkness I could be many miles away before the Japs even started to look for me. But damn it, the Japanese rule of thumb was that if one prisoner escaped they would shoot ten other prisoners chosen at random. Reluctantly, I turned back toward camp.

It was still raining and well after dark when I climbed through the fence and approached the Japanese guardhouse. On the porch the sentry blocked my way, motioned me to go on into camp. I stood fast, hoping he wouldn't slug me with his rifle. I was afraid to stay and more afraid to leave. I wanted to make damned sure the Japanese commander knew I was back, to make sure he didn't use me as an excuse to execute ten innocent men. The sentry shouted in Japanese. I thought he was shouting at me, but no, Colonel Mori came out onto the porch. I saluted in my most military POW manner and told him that I couldn't find the hunting party. Surprisingly he casually returned my salute and motioned for me to go. I turned away but Mori stopped me with a question. He asked me why I had come back when I was so far away and alone. I stood silently, saying nothing. Colonel Mori smiled and waved me on with his hand. He knew, damn it. He knew his strategy of executing ten for one was working, that his way of preventing prisoner escapes was effective. I'm sure the bastard knew.

For all prisoners these first six months were a series of highs and lows with long periods of doldrums in between. It was like a shakedown cruise on a ship. We learned what worked and what didn't. I found a groove that worked for me and stayed with it. A Japanese prisoner-of-war camp was no place to experiment with interactional behavior between guards and prisoners. A bad result could be devastating.

We ten wood choppers were in on everything. The guards knew who we were and where we were. When they needed one or two men for some special project of their own, they just grunted, pointed, and took us along. Our officers did the same. Big work details were rotated through the barracks, but the little ones came to us. One morning I was tagged to help move a latrine at the hospital. This was a regular barracks detail, but two of the men who reported were too weak to handle the job and a couple of wood choppers were taken to replace them. I took a good look around and what I saw horrified me.

Our hospital was a hospital only because we called it that. It was a string of four or five tiny one-room shacks a little apart from the main camp. The shacks were raw, unfinished. There were no windows or doors, no lights, no water, no toilets. There was no furniture of any kind, and the rooms were filthy. They had wooden floors. Each room was filled to bursting with our sick. Sick? These were doomed men who just hadn't quite died yet. They were body-to-body on the wooden floor. The lucky ones had a blanket under them; the rest lay on bare wood. There was no separation among the sick. There were men with raging fevers, men shivering with malaria. There were emaciated skeletons dying from dysentery and men with swollen, bloated bodies from wet beri-beri. The odor was sickening. I thought my barracks smelled bad and I hated the stink of our latrines, but this made me want to vomit. I could smell death in the air. The sick and the dying lay still on the floor. They didn't move, didn't bother to speak, but they followed my every move with their eyes. A couple of Army corpsmen did what they could to make them comfortable. The Japanese let us die without medicine. Maybe the guys in the hospital got a little extra rice, a little extra soup, but it was too little, too late. I have seen some of our doctors cry in futility, feeling helpless because they were unable to do what they knew could be done, what they had been trained to do.

The latrine we came to move was a six-holer, an eighteen-inch-high box with six holes cut in the top. It was out in the open, surrounded by mud and exposed to the rain. We picked it up and moved it from over a full hole to over an empty one.

I went back to my wood-cutting job. I felt unclean, a different kind of dirty. It may have been my imagination, but I thought the stench of death clung to my body for days. No matter what I did I couldn't get away from it.

Our sanitation system was awful. Latrines were deep rectangular pits dug in the ground with a six-holer over the top. When one hole was full we covered it with a layer of dirt and shifted it to another location. But the holes took days, weeks, to fill, and in the meantime they drew flies, big green flies, half an inch long with fat clumsy bodies. we called them blowflies. They came by the millions. Every damn blowfly in the Philippines came to our camp. And they bred in the warm filth of the latrines. They laid eggs, the eggs became maggots, the maggots became blowflies. Long before a latrine pit was full to the top there would be whitish yellow maggots crawling up the sides and over the ground. If you walked to the latrine barefooted you had to step on the little bastards, feel their slimy bodies crush under your feet. If you sat too long, one might crawl out from under the seat and wriggle across your ass. The camp was clearly in danger of an epidemic. Blowflies were everywhere. They literally covered the camp like a cloud. Sometimes they darted about; sometimes they just hung like fat little blimps, almost motionless in the air. There were so many that I actually had blowflies dart into my mouth while I was eating. Even the Japs were afraid of the flies. They took to wearing surgical masks all the time. They even developed an incentive plan to help us get rid of the blowflies. They came up with a bunch of empty tin cans about the size of a Campbell's tomato soup can. Any prisoner who turned in a full can of dead blowflies got a small biscuit as a reward. Prisoners made fly swatters out of palm leaves, out of strips of canvas, out of pieces of old shoe leather.

I made mine out of tiny woven strips of bamboo tied together with bits of thread. I tried, I really tried, but the flies were quick and I was slow, and it took an ungodly amount of flies to fill a can. After a couple of cans and a couple of tasteless biscuits I gave up the hunt. I was burning up a lot more energy chasing flies than I was getting from the biscuit. Lots of cans of dead flies were turned in every day, but it made little difference. The flies bred faster than we could kill them.

Here again though, American ingenuity came to the fore. Two POWs saw an opportunity the rest of us missed and cornered the market. Seems like there's always room for a little free enterprise, even in a POW camp. These two guys had an old piece of mosquito netting and with a little mechanical genius, built a flytrap. When I saw it, all I could think of was, why didn't I think of that?

They tied sticks together with string to form a cage shaped something like a beekeeper's hat and covered it with mosquito net. They left the bottom open but rigged it so it could be closed quickly with a drawstring. Then they went around to all the latrines, the six-holers, closed all the lids but one, set their trap over the one open hole and pounded on the sides of the box with clubs. All the blowflies under the six-holer, hundreds, perhaps thousands, of them would buzz through the open hole and into their trap. They pulled the drawstring, immersed the trap in a bucket of water and drowned the flies. No chasing flies with a flyswatter, the flies came to them, and in droves. These two guys not only had biscuits to eat, they had biscuits to trade. For a couple of months they monopolized the fly-catching business, but they still didn't get rid of the flies. Blowflies were everywhere, into everything. The most disgusting thing was that flies, attracted by the smells of the kitchen, would hover over the cauldrons, be overcome by the heat, and fall into the soup. At chowtime I was very suspicious of anything I found floating in my soup.

The blowflies controlled the camp, continued to make us miserable, until suddenly one morning literally hundreds of swallows appeared out of nowhere. Nobody could explain their sudden appearance; nobody knew where the swallows came from. They were just there. The swallows darted about, could change direction in a flash, and could snap up a clumsy blowfly in midair. The clicking of their beaks was like music. Within a week the flies were gone and so were most of the swallows, but a few of the birds stayed around camp and the flies were never a problem again. Some people swear by the miracles at Lourdes; I swear by the swallows.

I got tagged for another strange work detail. We wood choppers were always being called out by the guards for something or other. This day four guards and about fifteen POWs came by the wood-chopping lot where I worked. One of the guards motioned me to join the work detail. Now wood chopping was my job. I was supposed to split logs into firewood from before daylight until after dark. However, an American POW does not say no to a Japanese soldier with a bayonet.

I dropped my axe and fell in with the work party. We walked single file along a narrow path by a river, guards ahead, guards behind, POWs in the middle. We walked for three or four miles, turned around and came back. Never did find out where we were supposed to go or what we were supposed to do: Communication with the Japanese was mostly by unintelligible shouts, grunts, and hand signals. We never learned their language and they never learned ours. Anyway, we started back along the same narrow winding trail. Somewhere along the way a Filipino woman came out of the brush on one side of the path, walked through the line of POWs and disappeared into the brush on the other side. She never spoke, never looked at us, kept her eyes fixed on the ground. The guards ignored her. After all, what harm could she do? She was a woman, very tiny, very fragile, and very, very old. She must have been seventy or eighty, but my God, she looked a thousand. As she passed through the line of prisoners she stooped and laid a bundle of dry tobacco leaves in the path. The next POW picked it up. God bless her.

The Japanese guards were for the most part unpredictable. Beat the hell out of you one day, smile at you the next. They weren't all mean sons-a-bitches though, only most of them. Once in a while you came across a guard who treated you decently. At the time I'm thinking of, we had been without any means of keeping clean for months. We were dirty. We washed our bodies, without soap, whenever it rained. When it forgot to rain we stunk up the place. Maybe the Japs tired of the smell of unwashed bodies. One morning they ordered all men out of my barracks, surrounded us and marched us away. We didn't know if we were being transferred to another camp, if we were going on work detail, or if we were about to be shot. Not a damn word. The Japs were funny that way. We marched a mile to a small river and the guards motioned for us to take off our clothes and jump in. No, they weren't kidding. It was unbelievable. These guards were treating us like humans. My only shirt and pants had long since been used for bandages and I was wearing only a Japanese G-string, Japanese underwear, so I jumped in, G-string and all. The Japanese ringed us with rifles, sat down and smoked while we cavorted like a bunch of kids. The water was clean, warm, and wet. It was wonderful. Can you imagine five months without a bath?

Some Japanese with an eye for security had chosen this spot carefully. We bathed in a quiet pool in a small river, maybe only a large creek. Above the pool the river came through a narrow spot only four or five feet wide. Below the pool was a shallow spot the width of the river. I had thoughts about holding my breath, swimming under water with the current until I was out of sight around the bend. Then I saw a guard walk across the river in six-inch deep water and stopped thinking such foolish thoughts. Besides, there was always that "shoot ten if one escapes" to keep us honest.

Fifteen minutes and everybody was out, but God, it was a wonderful fifteen minutes. I felt better, cleaner, for days afterward. The Japs rotated the deal. Every day or two another barracks went to the river. Nobody escaped. I got to go a second time before I was transferred to a different camp.

Time began to run out for me. I had been a prisoner for five months, and I was getting sick. My body was failing, and there seemed nothing I could do about it. And I was deathly afraid of that filthy pigsty the Japs called a hospital. First of all I came down with dysentery. I began hitting the latrine ten, fifteen, sometimes twenty times a day. My bodily strength was draining out of my rear end. There was no medicine. The worst cases, men who were near dying, got a handful of charcoal to eat, black burned rice, scrapings from the cooking pots. Never could figure out what medicinal effect charcoal rice could have on a man's insides, but it didn't matter. Never got any anyway.

Damn near everybody in camp had dysentery to one degree or another. The only good thing that came out of it was that dysentery helped keep the camp clean. The Japanese never issued any toilet paper. We were on our own. Scraps of paper, any kind of paper, and rags soon disappeared from camp. Smart POWs hung on to their rags. If they could manage two, they tried to rinse out one and let it dry while the other one was in use. Even the grass was kept neatly trimmed. A POW hustling toward the latrine would dart off the path, grab a handful of tall grass, and continue on his way without breaking step. When the grass was gone we just stayed dirty. There was one small blessing. One of our chaplains had a supply of New Testament tracts. Everybody wanted one. Prisoners sat on the latrines and read the Bible, some of them for the first time in their lives, read each page studiously before using it for toilet paper.

Along with the dysentery my feet began to hurt. They hurt all the time. Not the kind of hurting you get when you step barefooted on a rock, or when your shoes are too tight. This was a constant burning sensation that could almost drive a man crazy. The doctors called it dry beri-beri. I noticed it mostly as a burning sensation in my feet. Full blown beri-beri can be bad. It hurts a lot. I have seen grown men cry because of the constant pain. Worse, beri-beri affects other parts of the body. Surviving POWs are still dying from what has come to be known as beri-beri heart.

For me, the combination of dysentery and beri-beri was almost my undoing. I was seriously ill, losing weight rapidly, and soon got to where I couldn't stand on my feet. Had to give up my job on the wood-chopping detail, couldn't stand on my feet long enough to do the work. So many prisoners developed beri-beri that our limping gait became known as the beri-beri shuffle. It became almost a normal, accepted part of POW life. Especially at night my feet hurt so badly that I couldn't bear to have anything touch them, not even my blanket. I tried sleeping with my feet extending past the edge of the shelf and into the aisle, but people going to the latrine at night brushed against them. I couldn't stand the pain. I stuck my feet through a loop of rope suspended from the rafters but the rope cut off my circulation. It didn't work. Eventually I learned to lie on my back, knees drawn up under my chin, arms wrapped around my knees, feet in midair. I could snatch a few minutes sleep before something slipped and the pain woke me again.

When I became sick and was taken off the wood-chopping detail I had to transfer to another barracks. Funny, but it was like moving to another country. A new place to sleep. Same kind of bamboo shelf to sleep on, but here I was an outsider. The prisoner whose sleeping space I had moved into had died, and the men on either side of me had lost a friend, someone they knew and were comfortable with. To them I was an intruder. They resented me because I reminded them of the loss of their friend and because having a new man sleep between them constantly reminded them just how close death was, all the time. Of course things changed. They weren't mad at me; they were reacting to the pressures of life as POWs.

This barracks was full of strangers, Army, Navy, Marines, all mixed together. Not a single man that I knew. E Battery as a unit no longer existed. We had between one hundred seventy and one hundred eighty men still alive, but they were scattered so thoroughly among the three thousand prisoners in camp that we ceased to function as a unit.

Moving to a new barracks began a period of semi-isolation for me. Not that there weren't other people around. There were. The barracks was filled to bursting. But I was so wrapped up in my own illness, my own pain, my own particular miseries that I withdrew, mentally, into a sort of protective cocoon. It was like living in my own tiny fishbowl. I was fully aware of other prisoners, other activity, but I cannot remember a single name, a single face, from the month or six weeks I lived in that barracks. All my thoughts, all my energies were focused, like a ray of sunlight through a magnifying glass, on just keeping myself alive. I think it was here that I made my determination never to become a "bedpatient." To me, becoming a bedpatient was synonymous with dying. Bedpatients died. "Bedpatient" was a term we invented. It didn't mean a sick man got a bed; there were no beds. It didn't even mean he got a mattress on the floor; there were none of these either. "Bedpatient" meant that a man lay on the bamboo, on a blanket if he had one, on bare bamboo if he didn't, and waited to die. Someone would bring him food, bring him water. The occasional medic, heroes all, would slip a bedpan under him if they had one, try to clean him up if they didn't.

Living or dying was often a matter of willpower, of determination. We had only been prisoners of war for six months, and I had already seen a lot of men die. True, most men died because a raging illness simply swept them away, but a lot of men just gave up. By "gave up" I mean that these were men who, though starved and brutalized, had no medical reason for dying. They just grew tired of the starvation, the degradation, the despair, lay down on the bamboo and in a week or so were dead. It was so easy. Just stop pushing back for an instant, relax and let go, and you could die.

On the other extreme I remember a Lieutenant Zackerman (I'll tell you more about Lieutenant Zackerman later). When I first met Zacky, as we called him, Zacky had survived a bout with diphtheria. He had lain helpless, curled up on his side, for so long that the tendons in his legs had shortened and he was permanently fixed in a fetal position. And Zacky weighed less than seventy pounds. Can you imagine a fully grown man weighing seventy pounds? Zacky had to be hand-fed, couldn't hold a mess kit, couldn't raise a spoon to his lips. He slept naked on a board across the frame of an iron cot. Medics had cut a hole in the board and rigged a pan underneath, so Zacky had his own personal bathroom without getting out of bed. When I looked at Zacky I saw the body of a terribly emaciated ten-year-old boy. He was that small, but there was fire in those bulging black eyes. Zacky made his own personal deal with the medics, told them what he wanted and made them swear not to stop no matter what he said or did. They agreed. Every afternoon two medics, still fairly big, fairly healthy, men, came into the barracks and stretched Zacky's shrunken tendons. One man on each side of the cot, one hand under an ankle, the other hand on top of a knee, and they pressed down hard with all their weight. Zacky would scream in agony. In between screams he would curse the medics, call them every vile name he could think of, then more screams, but he never told them to quit. This agreed-upon torture went on for months. Eventually Zacky, Lieutenant Zackerman, recovered, went back to the duty side of camp and took command of a barracks.

So I developed a phobia about "bedpatients," made up my mind never to be one. And I walked. My feet hurt like hell and it was terribly painful but I walked to the chow line, walked to roll call outside the barracks, and took as much as thirty minutes to walk the short distance to the latrines and back, but I kept on my feet, kept walking.

Any soldier who has been in sustained close combat, any solder who has survived a sustained ordeal as a prisoner of war, is scarred. Some of these scars, a missing arm or leg, can be seen. But there are other scars, equally deep, equally long lasting, that are invisible. To this day, fifty years later, I have this phobia about being a bedpatient. Since the war I have had a number of surgeries at VA hospitals, heavy surgeries, life-threatening surgeries. I won't sign the papers until I have made my deal with my doctors and the staff. Before I go to sleep I want a coatrack with wheels standing beside my bed. All the bottles and gadgets and the tubes they stick in me have to hang from that rack. No bedpans, no bullshit from the nurses or orderlies. When I wake up I get up. Maybe I just walk across the room, maybe to the toilet, maybe a few feet down the hall. After I've satisfied myself that I'm not a bedpatient I can lie down and start to get well. To date, fourteen surgeries and not a single bedpan.

Floyd Buckner used to drop by every day, talk a few minutes, see how I was getting along. Once when I was asleep, bare feet hanging over the shelf, he was afraid to touch me, so he blew his breath on my bare toes to wake me up. I screamed and he was embarrassed. Floyd was a good guy, big, rough, uneducated, but foursquare with the world. Once in another barracks, we were having trouble with our appointed mess sergeant. The sarg was cheating on the food. He controlled the mess, picked up our five-gallon bucket of rice from the kitchen, and decided how much to put in each prisoner's mess kit. He always managed to have a little left, and he secretly divided it between himself and a few cronies. We protested, but especially after the evening meal, after dark, we couldn't tell what he was doing. One evening after dark, Buckner pulled him aside and grabbed his shirt front to get his attention. Floyd told him that if he didn't stop cheating he was going to stomp a mudhole in his ass and then walk it dry. Flowery language but Sarg got the message.

From that day on, leftover rice, if there was any, was divided equally among all men on a rotating basis.

Once on a special work detail a guard gave Floyd a small ear of corn on the cob. I knew he was hungry, as hungry as I was, but he saved the ear of corn, came down to my barracks after dark, broke the ear of corn in two and gave me half. Together we enjoyed a rare treat.

A body was brought into camp, an American body, dropped on the ground and left there as an object lesson to the rest of us. Probably an escaped prisoner from some other camp because none of our men were missing. The Japanese let the doctors examine the body. I didn't go look, the body was far from my barracks, but I heard all about it. The guy was one hell of a mess. Arms and legs broken, some in more than one place, ribs caved in, and eyes put out. He had been bayonetted through the face and his jaw was broken and there were two bayonet wounds in his chest. But our doctors said he died from a crushing blow to the head ... after all the rest had been done.

We're moving. No warning, just grab your gear and be ready to go. I rolled up my blanket, picked up the tin that I ate from, the tin can I drank from, and I was ready. This was the Japanese way. I didn't know which way I was headed or why, only that I was being moved and that I had to go.

Prisoners marched out of camp until there were only a handful of us left, prisoners too crippled or too ill to walk. It was scary as hell. I hoped to God the commander was in a good mood because I knew the Japanese wouldn't put up with any bullshit. They'd just as soon shoot us as look at us. I was still sweating it out when they rolled two trucks into the yard and loaded us aboard. Thank God. This wasn't my day to die, not yet.

I was in the rear truck and got a final look at the camp as we rolled through the gate. It was dead, lifeless, empty. Strange, but somehow the barracks looked naked in their loneliness.

Cabanatuan Prison Camp #1: Life and Death in the Prison-Camp Hospital

This was the new camp. I had been here only a month or so, and already things were going badly. My health was failing rapidly. It was frightening, and I didn't know what to do. One day at a time the daily struggle went on.

I awakened with pain, pain in my feet, pain in my shoulders, pain in my hip. It happened several times every night. The bamboo strips I slept on pressed deep into my flesh, deep grooves that hurt and forced me to wake up and turn over. I grunted out loud when I rolled over, couldn't help grunting. The damned bamboo strips hurt. I explored the furrows in my flesh with my fingers. Better now, more comfortable, but I knew in a little while new pain would make me wake up and roll over again. My one thin blanket just wasn't enough to pad the bamboo. I slept with half the blanket under me, the other half over my body for protection from the bedbugs. It wasn't much, but at least it kept the bedbugs away from my body for the first hour or so after I fell asleep. After that, sleep was a series of short naps frequently interrupted either by the pain of the slats or the bedbugs. God, how I hated the bedbugs. They were always there. Daytimes they mostly hid between the bamboo strips and the framework. At night, as soon as they sensed body heat, they crawled out from their hiding places and began their voracious attack. Sometimes, half asleep, I tried to ignore the bedbugs crawling over my body, but sooner or later the burning, itching sting of their bites would make me scratch or slap at the little bastards. When I managed to kill one, the awful stink they exuded made me sick to my stomach.

I had to urinate. This was my alarm clock, and I knew it was time to get up. In the clear light of early dawn other figures were beginning to stir. Slowly, carefully, I got to my hands and knees and crawled to the end of the sleeping shelf. I didn't want to wake everybody. There was no way to climb over the man sleeping crossways at the end without bumping him. I got a muffled "Ah, for Christ sakes" as I stumbled into the aisle.

I found my balsa-wood skivies, slipped my feet into the straps, and clumped stiffly along the path that led to the latrine. My skivies made little scraping sounds as I walked. The urinal was just a hole in the ground about five feet across and perhaps eight feet deep. It was filled with urine to within three feet of the top. There was no guard rail, nothing to hang on to, and none of us wanted to drown, especially in a hole full of urine. To be absolutely safe, to keep from falling in, we stood back a little and urinated, mostly in the hole, but partly on the ground. For a distance of three or four feet around the urinal there was an inch deep mixture of urine and mud. My skivies were clumsy to walk in, but at least they kept my feet out of the mud. I felt sorry for the guys that that had to walk to the urinal in bare feet. It was a little thing but a daily thing, and I always found the morning piss call demoralizing as hell.

A bugle sounded the beginning of a new day and Cabanatuan began to come to life. Not much conversation this early, not much to talk about, but even though everyone was already awake, if we spoke we spoke in lowered voices.

I think it was in these early morning hours that I first began to notice the occasional prisoner whom I knew was going to die. No raging illness, just little things that gave them away. Listlessness, expressionless faces, eyes that became dull. It seemed as though they had lost hope, as if they no longer cared. Often they would isolate themselves, take their blanket and sleep in the weeds or in the mud beside the latrine. We knew, and perhaps they knew, that they were going to die. It was uncanny, this premonition of someone else's death.

I pulled my blanket from the sleeping shelf. This is the day, I remember thinking, this is the goddamn day I have to go to the prison hospital. The thought of the prison hospital area made my stomach tighten, brought up a feeling of fear that filled by body from my bowels up through my chest. In my mind I tried to shrug it off. Was it really fear? Was I really afraid? More likely the feeling in my belly was just the rumbling of the ever-present dysentery telling me it was time to take another crap. Still, the hospital area was a fearsome place. Separated from the duty side by a quarter mile of open ground, the hospital area was the place where men were sent to die. Hundreds of the desperately ill either walked or were carried across. Damn few ever came back.

As part of my morning ritual I walked outside the barracks and shook hell out of my blanket, shook it hard enough to make the edges pop. Hard enough, I hoped, to shake off any loose bedbugs and give me a little time to sleep undisturbed when I first fell asleep that night. Shaking completed, I folded the blanket in half, lengthwise, and spread it carefully across my sleeping place. This was my space, my turf, my territory. This tiny area of bamboo covered by the folded blanket represented the only place in camp, in the whole damn world, that belonged to me. I brushed out the wrinkles and placed my mess kit at the head of my blanket. Just my eating gear, nothing else. I didn't own anything else.

My single article of clothing was a piece of Japanese underwear that barely covered my ass. I wore it on my body. I worked in it by day and slept in it by night. Once every couple of weeks I stood naked while I rinsed it in cold water without soap, then let it dry on my body.

Everybody up, everybody out. Line up for roll call. Loud and clear the command rang through the barracks. With grunts and groans nearly a hundred prisoners turned their backs on a miserable night to face the prospect of yet another wholly miserable day. The barracks leader was already out in front waiting. Every barracks had a leader, usually a master sergeant, a lifer, a much older man. In charge, these older noncoms, ancient from my twenty-year-old point of view, still carried their authority as though their stripes were indelibly, invisibly, imprinted on the bare flesh of their arms. Like mother hens they looked out for the rest of us. For heading up a barracks they were usually excused from the brutality and hard labor on the farm. These old-timers, barefooted, naked except for a pair of ragged shorts, called the roll from a very dirty, very tattered roster, but not in alphabetical order. When a man died or was transferred, the barracks leader drew a line through that name. When a new man came in, his name was added at the bottom. Names didn't matter much. The guards who made the head count each morning didn't know our names. What mattered was to be sure our head count corresponded with theirs. If it didn't, there was hell to pay. The Japanese rule, "shoot ten if one escapes," was in effect and this caused a lot of trouble. We were still losing thirty or forty men a day from various illnesses, mostly dysentery and malaria. By far, the majority of deaths happened on the hospital side of camp, but not always. Men died on the duty side too.

For some reason that I cannot explain, prisoners often had a premonition of death. They knew when they were going to die. And sometimes a man elected to die alone. When the morning head count came up short, there would be a flurry of activity. We had to find the missing man before the guards made their count. We learned to look everywhere, and we found dead men in the damndest places. Sometimes in the weeds in the unused areas inside the perimeter fence, sometimes in the shallow ditches that bordered the paths between barracks, dead under a dirty brown blanket, indistinguishable from the dirty brown earth around them, sometimes wedged tightly into an inches-high crawl space beneath a barracks. Once found, the dead man would be included in the morning head count, then carried to the camp gate, later to be picked up by a burial detail and dumped into a common grave in the camp cemetery.

I dreaded the thought of going to the hospital. Hospital? Sending men to the hospital was just a way to segregate the dying from the living. I hadn't seen it yet, but I had heard about it. A damn cesspool, that's what it was. There weren't enough men on their feet in the hospital to bury the dead, and the duty side sent a burial detail over every day. Because I could barely walk I had been excused from these burial details, but I talked with men who went over, buried the dead, and came back. It was common gossip throughout the camp. The hospital was hell.

It's a hell of a thing to say, but the burial details regularly took advantage of the hospital patients. Prisoners on the duty side who worked the farm got ten Japanese cigarettes a week. Hospital patients got none. For a few cigarettes a dying man would trade a ration of rice, a ragged piece of clothing, a mess kit, even a blanket. What the hell, a dying man didn't need the stuff, and a healthier man might survive better with it. Dog eat dog, but both sides considered it fair trade.

After roll call the sergeant told me to take my gear and go down to the assembly area. New men going to the hospital would go across with the burial detail. He scratched my name off the roster.

Packing was easy. I didn't have much in the way of personal possessions. I rolled up my blanket, took the piece of tin I ate from and the tin can I drank from and my spoon, hung them on my G-string, and I was ready. I had only been in this new camp, this new barracks for a few weeks, but a lot of the fellows said good-bye, wished me luck. I knew they were sincerely sorry to see me go yet glad they didn't have to go with me. Glad that they were privileged to remain in this hellhole because it was still a little better than the hospital. The sun was already warm on my bare back. It was going to be a hot day. It took me a long time to limp down to the center of camp. It wasn't really down, but that was the way we called it. Barracks in Cabanatuan were numbered sequentially from one end of the camp to the other. Men in low-numbered barracks walked up to the center of camp, men in high-numbered barracks walked down.

Doctor Bush was there. I had talked with him a couple of days earlier. Doc Bush was the one who put me in the hospital. He knew me, knew me from before the surrender. He had come to us, on Fort Drum, when his gun battery on Corregidor had been blown all to hell and had seen me when I was in good condition. Two days ago he had weighed me on an old balance scale, his only piece of medical equipment. He seemed startled when I weighed in at exactly one hundred pounds. Quietly he let me know that I was dying, that I was already damn near dead. Then he told me that he could transfer me to the hospital, where I would be excused from work detail, where I could rest, and where the food might be a little better. He hesitated, then told me it was my only chance to live. I trusted Doctor Bush, knew he wouldn't steer me wrong, so I went.

When the medics asked me if I could walk, if I wanted to be carried over on a stretcher, I knew they didn't really want to carry me. Besides, the four-handled bamboo stretchers were the same ones the burial detail used to carry bodies out to the cemetery, and I didn't want anything to do with them. So, to hell with the stretchers. I walked.

I was the last one to make it across. The rest of the detail got to the hospital ten or fifteen minutes before I did. I limped along, slow as molasses, but I had a good guard. He could see I was hurting and didn't try to hurry me. Some of the guards would have whipped my ass all the way over.

I was put in a barracks near the gate, on the upper shelf. I didn't like the top shelf because it was hard for me to get up there. The shelf was only five or six feet off the ground, but the ladder was a couple of boards nailed to an upright post in the aisle. Made my feet hurt to climb it. I didn't like it at first, but it didn't take me long to realize that the guys on the top shelf had the best of it and the guys on the bottom shelf caught all the crap, literally. We all had dysentery, some worse than others. It was a fact of life. Especially at night, when a prisoner lost control of his bowels, the crap dropped through the slats onto the guys below. We could tell when a prisoner on the top shelf let loose, even if he was at the other end of the barracks. Lots of screaming, shouting, cursing. It was filthy, sickening, but this was the way life was lived in the hospital.

An American doctor came through the barracks every morning, held sick call. He'd stop briefly, talk with me, make little notes on scratch paper. He'd always ask how I was feeling, if I felt any better this morning, and how many times I went to the latrine yesterday. Then he'd tell me to hang on, that I was doing all right. And I know he did his best to get me a little extra rice or soup.

Sometimes the doctor would ask medics to help a man clean an open wound, a lesion or a dollar-sized ulcer on a leg. No medicine, no bandages, but at least they could wash it with water. Occasionally, the medics would carry a man outside on a stretcher, get a five-gallon can of water, and help him wash his dirty body. What else could the doctors do? They had no medicines, no bandages, nothing. If a prisoner crapped in his blanket the laundry was a five-gallon can of cold water, provided he could get the overworked medics to carry it. And the hospital barracks were just like all the other barracks, bamboo sleeping shelves with thatch roofs, no windows, no doors, no floor, open to the elements, the wind, the dust, the flies, the bedbugs, and the lice. Yes, before I had been in the hospital a week I was lousy with body lice. Like the bedbugs, lice were everywhere. Everybody had them and there was absolutely no way to get rid of them.

I became a member of the club, the hunting club. We called the body lice "seam squirrels." They hid and bred in the seams of our clothing, in our blankets, in our G-strings, and we hunted them assiduously. Best time for hunting "seam squirrels" was right after breakfast, early midmorning before the sun got too high or too hot. Even with dysentery, it was pleasant to sit for a half hour in the early morning sun. Most of the latrines were out in the open by now, and it was the usual thing to see three or four men sitting together on the latrine, buck naked, going inch by inch through their clothes looking for lice. The lice were little bugs, or big bugs, depending on how you thought about them, little gray bugs about an eighth of an inch long. They looked something like a tiny gray scorpion, with a tiny head, six or so tiny legs near the head, and a fat, bloated body that dragged behind. Wasn't enough to just find them, then you had to kill them. They were tough little buggers. Wasn't enough to squeeze them between thumb and forefinger, they were too tough for that. And if you threw them on the ground they just crawled around till they found something else to latch on to. No, hunting seam squirrels was an art. You had to find the little bastard, catch him between your two thumbnails, and squeeze until you heard a distinct pop. Then you knew you had him.

There was a rat in my barracks. Maybe a lot of them, but at least one particular rat that got on my nerves. I never saw him but I heard him and I knew he was there. He lived in the heavy thatch roof somewhere above my head. There was a small board that ran lengthwise through the barracks just above where I slept. Every night I would hear this rat running along this board on some ratty midnight mission. My buddies and I, the two men who slept on either side of me, talked it over and decided to put an end to it. We borrowed a saw from the wood choppers and cut off the board over our heads. Guess that'll fix the little bastard. Every night for at least a week that stupid little rat fell off the end of that board and down onto our beds. Then a mad scuffling, the rat squealing, running for his life, the three of us trying to pull our blankets tight so he wouldn't get underneath. The Padre came over from the duty side of the camp. He went from barracks to barracks with an announcement. This was the first day since the surrender that nobody had died. Didn't mean we were out of the woods yet, the dying would go on for nearly three more years, but for one glorious day there were no deaths and it was important enough for Padre to tell us about it. There was a second part to the Padre's announcement. Just a rumor but we grabbed at it. The Japs had brought in a truckload of food parcels, food parcels from home. It was ten days until Christmas and the Japs were going to distribute them, one to each man, on Christmas day. Was it true? Padre said he had talked with somebody who had actually seen them. Individual boxes about the size of a shoe box filled with food from home. We talked about nothing else for ten whole days. What was in them, what could it be? What would fit in a shoe box? Mentally we filled and emptied the parcels a hundred times over. If you liked candy they were filled with candy. If you liked cookies, it was cookies. Whatever you liked best, whatever you dreamed of, would be in that box. Visions of sugar plums danced in our heads.

For days now I hadn't been able to eat. I was what we termed "burned out" on rice. Even though I was starving to death, I could chew a mouthful of rice for ten minutes and not work up enough saliva to swallow it. Had to wash every mouthful down with a gulp of water. I was eating my soup, giving most of my rice away.

Today Doc sent me to another barracks. Farther down the line. I didn't like the move. I had only been in the prison hospital a short time, but I had already learned the hospital code. The healthier men, the better-off men, were in the higher numbered barracks. The farther down the numbers you went, the sicker you were, the more likely to die. I had been dropped about three barracks. I didn't like it at all.

In the new barracks the talk was the same, talk about nothing but Christmas food parcels. We were like little kids, filled with anticipation, hope. I couldn't wait.

Tragedy. Sickening, mind numbing tragedy. I woke up in the morning and couldn't move. I was pinned down. The guy next to me was dead. He had thrown an arm and a leg over me during the night, and I wasn't strong enough to move him. I hollered like hell till the medics came and removed the body. I was shaken. My first night in this barracks and the guy next to me was dead. I didn't even know his name, and the poor bastard hadn't lived long enough to get his Christmas parcel.

Christmas Eve, 1942. I had been a prisoner of war for almost eight months. A horrible time. A new guy had moved in next to me, but I didn't want to get to know him. A dead stranger is easier to take than a dead friend. What in hell is that? I thought I was hallucinating. Couldn't believe my ears, couldn't believe what I was hearing. Christmas carols. A group of eight or ten Japanese soldiers were walking through the hospital singing Christmas carols. No rifles, no bayonets, just singing carols. Outside my window they sang "Silent Night." They were off key, they mispronounced the words, but they sang it beautifully. Not a sound, dead silence in the barracks. Then someone managed a soft thank you. The Japs hollered, "Melly Clismas Amelicans," and moved on to the next barracks. I heard them singing far into the night, far down the line. Strange relationship, these Japanese captors and their American POWs. Beat hell out of us, let us rot from disease, starve us to death, treat us like animals, and sing carols to us on Christmas Eve.

Christmas day. The usual breakfast of lugao, wet rice, a messy glob in the bottom of my rusty tin plate, unsalted, unappetizing. To wash it down there was a cup of hot chocolate. Not the sweet creamy chocolate mother used to make, just a little cocoa in a lot of water, no milk, no sugar. I gave my rice away, couldn't stomach it, but I drank the chocolate. I didn't like the taste, but it was warm and comforting. Chocolate, cocoa and hot water, became a regular addition to the breakfast lugao, at least for a while.

Christmas day and every prisoner in the hospital was holding his breath, waiting, hoping that the rumor about the Red Cross food parcels was true. We had all had the experience, as little children, of going to bed on Christmas Eve filled with excitement and anticipation, waiting for the morning that seemed never to come. Although we were prisoners of the Japanese, somewhere in each of us there was still the little kid who was filled with excitement and anticipation. So we lay awake, hardly daring to speak about what we hoped the morning would bring.

Before noon the food parcels arrived. A truck drove into the hospital and prisoners from the duty side unloaded. This was really Christmas. Every prisoner in the hospital got his own individual parcel. I took mine at the tailgate of the truck and the healthier POWs hand-delivered to those too weak to get up and walk. There were tears. A wasted skeleton on a bamboo shelf could cry because he got a package of goodies from home. The guy who handed it to him could cry because he knew the wasted skeleton wouldn't live long enough to eat it.

What to do? I had my food parcel and didn't know what to do with it. I hadn't opened the package yet but I knew it was precious, and I wanted to hide it away. I had no cupboard, no dresser drawer, nothing. Like a squirrel hiding a nut in a hollow tree, I retreated to the safest place I knew, my sleeping place. I held a box on my lap a long time, then used it as a pillow. Other POWs were opening theirs, but I wanted to wait, to prolong the joy, the anticipation, to fantasize about what was inside. It was late afternoon before I opened it.

All the food parcels were Canadian, packed by the Canadian Red Cross. They weren't large, like a shoe box and weighed about ten or eleven pounds. And they were crammed with food, wonderful, wonderful food. Right on top was an eight-ounce bar of Hershey's chocolate. I knew it was Hershey's chocolate because it was shaped like Hershey's, looked like Hershey's, and tasted like Hershey's. Hershey's, but in a different wrapper with a Canadian brand name. There was a can of corned beef, a can of fish, large sardines in tomato sauce, a box of prunes and a can of powdered milk with a cutesie brand name, KLIM, "milk" spelled backwards. There was a can of Nescafe, not instant coffee but the first soluble coffee, quarter-sized wafers that you could drop into a cup of hot water, stir like hell and make coffee. There was a can of pork and beans, a can of sweetened condensed milk, and three packs of American cigarettes. Every box was a treasure trove. I remember the words of one POW who summed it up for all of us. Smiling like the Cheshire cat he told us that he was like a blind dog in a butcher shop, couldn't decide which one to eat first.

I unpacked my box and arranged the items on my blanket, examined each item carefully, then repacked everything. I repeated this two or three times, then I decided. At the evening meal I opened my can of sweetened condensed milk and mixed some of it with my rice. I hadn't been able to eat for days. Burnt out. A bit or two and give the rest away. But this evening, with the sweetened condensed milk mixed with my rice, I ate my ration and could have eaten more. The food parcel may have broken the logjam, may have saved my life. At any rate, for the first time in days I was able to eat my whole ration. Then, after dark, I made a damn fool of myself. I ate like a pig. Spoonful by spoonful I finished the can of sweetened condensed milk. It was sickening sweet and I loved it. I wiped the can clean with my finger and licked the finger, didn't waste a drop. I went to sleep stuffed, bloated, and as far as one can be so in a prison camp, happy.

It was well after midnight, maybe three or four in the morning when my sins caught up with me. I became terribly sick to my stomach. The overeating and the overly sweet and rich condensed milk was too much too soon and my whole system rebelled. Nausea came on so quickly and so strong that I didn't have time to move. I did, instinctively think of the men sleeping on the bamboo shelf beneath me and ducked my head under the top half of my blanket. I threw up everything I had eaten, threw up underneath my blanket and all over myself. God, was I sick. For a time I was too weak to move and I lay under my blanket in a puddle of vomit. When I stopped vomiting and recovered a little strength I crawled into the aisle and dragged my blanket after me, trying my best not to let my vomit drip through the slats to the men sleeping below. I was ashamed, humiliated, felt like I wanted to die. The stench was sickening and I hoped no one else would wake up, and if they did, in the darkness, maybe they wouldn't know who I was. Wishful thinking. In my heart I realized they already knew and were probably swearing under their blankets, cursing me all to hell. I dragged my vomit-soaked blanket outside the barracks and found a puddle of rainwater. I took off my G-string, dipped it in the puddle and tried to wash my body. The nausea came again and I grew weak and collapsed in the dirt. I was still lying there, naked in the dirt, when medics found me in the morning. One of them got a bucket of water and helped me wash up, the other rinsed my G-string and tied it, wet, around my loins so that I wasn't completely naked. I sat on the edge of the shelf, visibly shaking, and waited for the doctor.

Doc didn't even ask what happened, just told the medics to take me to another barracks. I was despairing. I knew I was sick as hell, very weak, near death. Any little shove could push me over the edge. I started to argue, figured that if I was going to die I might as well die here. Why go to the trouble of moving again? I was bitching pretty loudly when the medic told me I was going to Sammy Mayer's barracks. That was enough to shut me up. They got me on my feet, one of them carried my food parcel, and I walked on my own to Sammy's barracks.

Samuel D. Mayer had been the senior medical officer on Fort Drum, my outfit. He was a little fellow, short, plump, and with a face like a cherub. Dr. Mayer was a regular guy. He wasn't a stuffed shirt and didn't throw his weight around as an officer. After the war started he often sat in a darkened casemate at night and talked with us enlisted men. He told us about his boyhood in a strict Jewish family, about going to medical school the hard way, occasionally skipping meals because he was short on funds, told us how shocked he was on joining the Army, to find he was expected to take a shower in a room with twenty other naked men. But Dr. Samuel Mayer knew his business and he inspired men with confidence, with trust. He gave us hope in some pretty dark times.

Wonder if he knew we called him Sammy? We did. Not to his face, of course. Person-to-person it was always "Dr. Mayer," or "yes sir" and "no sir." Enlisted men, among themselves, often express great irreverence for their superiors. Nicknames. You can tell from the nicknames who enlisted men like or dislike. Skinny Wainwright and Dugout Doug are two extremes. When a gun battery on Corregidor was blown to hell, Skinny Wainwright would be up at the batter to see what he could do. His ass was exposed to the Jap guns just like everyone else's. He was good for us. On the other hand, General Douglas MacArthur, Dugout Doug to us, was bad for us. He gave morale a kick in the pants when he left for Australia. Whatever his reasons, when your commanding officer takes a hike and leaves you surrounded by your enemy, you know you're in deep trouble.

So, in Doctor Mayer's case we called him Sammy. Not with irreverence, hell no, with love and trust. In the prison camp at Cabanatuan I had seen men absolutely defy authority and refuse to go over to the hospital, preferring to die where they were rather than be sent to that stinking hole. However, assurance that they were being sent to Sammy Mayer's barracks often changed their mind.

Be sure to ask for Sammy's barracks. The word spread not just through his own men, the men from Fort Drum, but through the whole camp. Get me into Sammy's barracks and I'll go. I don't know how, maybe by some unspoken code, but enlisted men know things. We knew Sammy's barracks was a refuge, a place of hope. We knew, once there, we'd get the best care that was available in the prison camp. We knew if extra food was to be had, Sammy would wrangle it. We knew if medicine was ever to be found, Sammy would find it.

I arrived at his barracks nearly naked, shaking with chills, and dirty. Sammy took one look, told his medics to give me a bath and find me a place to lie down. He brought me an extra ration of soup for supper. Always suspected it might have been his own. Next morning I was feeling better. With a medic's help I walked back to my old barracks to find my blanket. If it was gone it would be a terrible loss to me. But it was there, clean, dry, and hanging on a rope line. Someone had washed the vomit off and hung it out to dry. God bless those unsung heroes, those medics.

I began to feel better, stronger. I ate. I supplemented my rice and soup with bits of food from my Christmas parcel carefully this time, a little at a time.

Cabanatuan was in a trading frenzy. Every prisoner had his Christmas parcel and every man wanted to trade something he didn't like for something he did like. I was one of the lucky ones. I was on cloud nine. My guardian angel was watching over me. A pack of American cigarettes traded for an eight-ounce bar of chocolate. I had three packs of cigarettes and I didn't smoke. A can of Nescafe bought any item in the food parcel and I didn't drink coffee. A box of prunes bought a can of corned beef and I didn't like prunes. Stretched out, nursed along, saved, most of the food parcels were gone in a couple of weeks but I was stronger and had actually gained a couple of pounds.

Just a note here. In Europe, prisoners of war got a supplementary food package once a week. In the Philippines and Japan we got three parcels in three and a half years.

Sammy, Dr. Mayer when we were face-to-face, was proud of me. I was one of his success stories. Once I had moved into his barracks I sort of settled down and took stock of my situation. I knew I had made a fool of myself the night I ate the whole can of sweetened condensed milk. I had damn near killed myself with that food binge, and I couldn't risk having the same thing happen again. I reasoned, correctly, that even if I ate everything in the box, over a period of time there wasn't enough to really make a difference. Short term, yes, long term, no. Therefore I decided to get all the enjoyment I could from my little box of food and not be too concerned with the health benefits. But even with this approach there were problems, problems that were the same for every prisoner in camp. One of them I had gone head-to-head with Christmas night. We were in the tropics and we had no refrigeration. Once a can was opened it had to be eaten right away or it would spoil, and I had already proven to myself that my starved body would not tolerate my eating a whole can of sweetened condensed milk or a can of corned beef or a can of fish all at once. What to do, how to handle it? I waited, looked around to see what other prisoners would do. There were some really creative solutions but they didn't always work.

Six guys sleeping and living in close proximity might decide to open my can of corned beef tonight, divide it up and we can mix it with our rice. Tomorrow we'll open Joe's can and the next day we can open Bill's. That way it'll last longer and won't spoil.

Great idea but it was flawed. Too often when they got around to the fifth or sixth man I would hear, "Jeez guys, I'm sorry, but some son of a bitch stole my corned beef last night and I don't have any left." Nothing anyone could do, but they all knew the "some son of a bitch" was the man himself who had probably eaten the whole can in the dark. Near death starvation puts a great strain on a man's integrity, and we all probably did a thing or two we would rather not talk about.

For me, I decided to go the chocolate-bar route. I traded my three packs of cigarettes for three bars of chocolate. I already had dysentery so it seemed logical to get rid of the prunes. There was no food value in the Nescafe, and I didn't care for the taste of coffee anyway. Not all at once, but an item at a time over a couple of weeks, I traded the things I didn't want for things that gave me both nourishment and pleasure. Even as a kid I had an almost uncontrollable sweet tooth. Hand me a bag of jelly beans and I could sit in a Saturday movie and pick away until the last jelly bean was gone. It took a lot of self control to break off a few squares and put the rest away for another time, but I did it, forced myself to stretch things out and make one chocolate bar last several days.

Days, weeks, time groaned past very slowly. I was holding my own but barely. Things must be getting better. The burial passed near my barracks. The "parade" as we called it used to pass by every single day. Now they skipped days. Used to be thirty or forty burials a day; now it's three or six or ten. Sometimes for a few days none at all. The burial details always came over from the duty side of the camp. They hated it, but most men in the hospitals were too weak to handle the job. The detail picked up the bodies mostly from the dysentery area, a separate part of the hospital, put them on wooden stretchers, covered them with grass, and then carried them through camp to the cemetery. It wasn't a fancy funeral. Bodies were buried in common graves. During the rainy season the graves filled with water and the bodies floated. Prisoners had to climb into the grave and hold the corpses down till they were covered with dirt. If they were buried too close to the surface wild dogs got at them and they had to be buried again. It was a nasty detail and everybody hated it. Three thousand good men died at Cabanatuan. That made for a lot of burial details. Men don't always die with hands folded across their chests. The dead went past with eyes staring, mouths open and clawlike hands reaching up. The dry grass didn't hide a hell of a lot.

We had been prisoners for ten months and the first rush of dying was over. Men who came into the camp wounded or sick with malaria and fevers, these were the men who died early on. Others, simply exhausted from five months of continuous combat never recovered but took longer to die. From this time on the death rate would be steady but slower. Malaria claimed a lot of victims from the men who had fought in the jungles of Bataan, but in Cabanatuan, away from the jungles and the mosquitoes, malaria deaths dropped off. Dysentery, on the other hand, stayed with us forever. Ten, fifteen, twenty or more times a day, barracks to the latrine, take a crap, back to the barracks. Coupled with weakness from malnutrition, this was both physically and spiritually exhausting. A few miserable souls took their blankets and slept in the mud beside the latrine. It was easier than repeatedly hobbling back and forth. Ready to die, these men usually declined to eat. They just lay in the mud and rain completely covered with a wet muddy blanket. After two or three days they were indistinguishable from the mud around them. Medics would nudge the shapeless lump under a blanket. If it moved the man was still alive and they would try to offer him food. If the lump didn't move the man was probably dead.

Dr. Mayer was good for me. I thrived under his care, thought I might get out of the hospital and back to the duty side of camp. Doc stopped by and talked with me a few minutes every day.

We had a priest in our barracks, a Catholic priest who lay on his blanket utterly helpless. Couldn't do a thing for himself. And we had two medics who lived in another barracks but spent their days with us. Both of the medics were gentle, patient, very kind, that is, with everyone except the Catholic priest. One of them rode the priest unmercifully. Always wondered if Doc Mayer put him up to it. When the medic got to the priest he would deliberately start an argument. Usually the medic would act surprised, ask the priest what he was still doing here, tell him he ought to be dead and buried by now. Then he would begin a long harangue, ask the priest why he wasn't up there with that God he was always talking about. The medic would pretend that he didn't believe in God, that all that God talk was just plain bullshit, and that the priest had found an easy way to make a living without going to work. The medic would ask him why God didn't come down and feed him, why God let him lie there like a stinking-assed vegetable and rot.

The priest would argue and shout and always take the bait. At times he would swear and almost become apoplectic, and the medic would call him every vile name he could think of. The priest survived. I'm sure pure hate kept him alive. And the medic never spoke another unkind word as long as I was in his barracks.

One day I got a duck egg, a hardboiled duck egg. I was the envy of the barracks. Dr. Mayer brought it to me, told me that it might do me some good. Doc was as hungry as the rest of us and he could have kept the egg, eaten it himself, but Sammy Mayer wasn't that kind of a guy. I thanked him for the egg, took it carefully in both hands, and told the Doc I'd take good care of it.

Both Doc and I knew that one egg wasn't going to make a difference, at least not physically, but psychologically it might have a greater impact. I hadn't seen an egg since I surrendered, a long time. Doc got me one more duck egg about a week later and then there were no more, ever. Two eggs a week apart. Seems like such a little thing to be writing about. But look at it from the other end of the telescope. Two eggs in three and a half years. That's about one egg every two years. From the POW point of view it was a memorable occasion, memorable enough for me to remember over these last fifty years.

I had an egg in my hand, now what to do with it? Believe it or not, it was a hard decision to make. Once eaten, the egg would be gone, and my body would hardly know the difference. On the other hand, if I saved it too long it would spoil and be unfit to eat at all.

I had plenty of help, plenty of advice from all sides. One man told me to eat the damn thing, to get rid of it so he wouldn't have to look at it and wish it was his. Another stated that if the egg belonged to him he would certainly know what to do with it. And a third man offered to trade for the egg, offered to trade his next meal, his whole ration of rice and soup just for that one duck egg.

Down the middle of the road, strike a happy medium, that was my decision. I saved the egg for a day, watched it, savored the thought of it and ate it a dozen times in anticipation. Then I cracked the egg, peeled it ever so carefully, and ate it with the supper meal. Big deal over nothing? Maybe, but try going that many months without an egg to eat.

Life was hard in those days, or to put it more concisely, it was hard to stay alive. For my first two years as a prisoner I walked a thin line between life and death. Life was simple but very hard. Most of the trappings of what we call civilization were gone. What remained were the basic necessities for sustaining life at an animal level. Food was minimal, a starvation diet, and the rice was usually wormy. Mixed into the cooked rice were a lot of tiny worms with short white threadlike bodies. Couldn't tell the worms from the rice except for a pinpoint of black that was the head. It was impossible to pick the worms out so we gobbled the rice without looking at it too closely. Even made jokes about the worms being the only protein in the meal.

Wormy rice and blowgun soup, these were the staples of our diet. The occasional scraps of real meat in the soup were the parts of the carabao that the Japanese themselves threw away, parts they considered garbage and would not eat.

Dr. Mayer told me that I was dying, that we were all dying, slowly, inevitably, a little at a time. Though I had gained a couple of pounds, I was plagued with sickness. My feet hurt. I had dysentery. My body was swollen and bloated with edema and I was going blind. Short of death, what else could have happened?

As I reread these pages it seemed incredible that anyone could have remained alive under the living conditions in the Japanese prison camps. It seemed that my life was a continual progression of illnesses, one to another, sometimes in multiples. But I want to emphasize, though this is my personal story, with a change of name, location, and sequence of illnesses, it could be the story of any man, every man, who survived the camps. Though it was a terribly difficult three-and-a-half years, my life was in no way different, no better and no worse, than the lives of the majority of the other prisoners.

I was somewhat used to dysentery. It was there every day as an almost normal, accepted part of my life. I didn't mention dysentery to the doctor unless I was going to the latrine more than a dozen times a day. I had learned to cope with burning feet. My main concern now was the swelling, the bloating in my legs and body. Though my medical knowledge was limited to being sick or being well, it was my understanding that edema, or wet beri-beri as we called it, was caused by a vitamin deficiency. Kidneys ceased to function properly and the cells of the body began to absorb and retain body fluids. I thought my case was extreme, but it wasn't because the extreme cases died. I lived. Nevertheless, for me, it was a rough time. My feet swelled until the skin cracked and fluid oozed from the cracks. Just to try it I borrowed a pair of trousers. Couldn't get them on. My feet wouldn't pass through the legs. Farther up, my legs grew big, big, big. Doc Mayer could press his thumb into the flesh at least an inch, sometimes more, and the flesh was dead. The dent would remain for half an hour. My scrotum filled with fluid and hung halfway to my knees like a big melon attached to my body. To walk to the latrine I had to interlace my fingers, cup my hands under my scrotum to hold it up. Eventually I made a hammock-like affair out of the flap of my G-string, rigged it under my scrotum and tied it with string around my waist. It worked. I could walk. At night when I was lying prone the fluid receded from my legs and into the body cavity. Daytimes gravity pulled it down into my legs again. Prisoners began to die at night, drowned in their own body fluids. I spent lots of nights sleeping sitting up, afraid to lie down.

Doctor Mayer came up with an idea. It didn't work but it was a hell of a good idea. First thing in the morning when my legs were down to normal, medics would wrap me like a mummy, feet, ankles, and lower leg to just below the knee. Don't know where they found the bandages. Supposedly, with my legs tightly wrapped, the fluid would have no place to go and my kidneys would be forced to function properly. Didn't work worth a damn. By noon my upper legs would be swollen like riding breeches with huge folds hanging down over my tightly wrapped lower legs. I felt ridiculous, must have looked ridiculous, clumping along the path to the latrine or to the chow line looking like a half-dressed mummy.

In the hospital, in the prison camp hospital at Cabanatuan, life was deceptively simple. Real life, down to the basics of eating, sleeping, and staying alive. There were no frills, no distractions, just basics. When I moved into Doctor's Mayer's barracks I was barely able to walk and sick as a poisoned pup. And though the leg wrapping didn't work, prisoners like myself, and good doctors like Sammy Mayer, were always ready to try out a new idea. Desperate situations require desperate measures, and who knows, the next idea just might work.

Somewhere along about this time I consumed the last smidgen of food from the Christmas parcel. It was gone, finally and irrevocably gone. I remember that when I ate that last bite of whatever it was, I felt a little sad. Looking back from today when I can walk into a supermarket and take my pick from thousands and thousands of food items, it seems unbelievable to realize that there was a time in my life when just opening a can of corned beef required a momentous decision. I could hold the unopened tin in my hand and treasure it. I looked at it and my mouth watered as I thought how good it would taste. I wanted desperately to open the tin and gobble it down, savoring every last morsel and even licking the tin to get any shred of corned beef or bit of grease that might cling to the inside. And so I did. I ate it and it was good. Yet even the memory is bittersweet because at the time I knew that once a can of food was eaten, there might never be another. And thus, in spite of the delicious taste and the joy of eating, the disappearance of each item from the food parcel was like a small death.

Proximity makes strange bedfellows. I bunked between a soldier from Wisconsin and a sailor from a little town near New York. Crossways at our feet was a soldier from Minnesota. The structure of the barracks and our sleeping space threw us together and forced us to share our lives. We slept together, ate together, went to the latrine together, and because we were too weak and sick to do much moving around, spent most of every day resting, sitting on our blankets and sleeping or talking. We formed a little group, identical to hundreds of other groups in the camp, a little group with nothing in common except our existence in this prison camp. That in some strange way bonded us together, and we became friends. Our little group in our sleeping bay in our barracks became the center of our universe. The rest of the camp were strangers. Prison camp was like that.

I'm not at all sure that I can explain this particular facet of prison-camp life, but I'd like to give it a try. I think a psychiatrist might find the American POW in the Philippines a study in isolation. I do not speak of solitary confinement; there was nothing of the sort. The isolation I am trying to describe was self imposed.

The physical aspects of prison camp life, the continual sickness, the starvation, the absolute lack of the basic necessities for living, even the brutality — after a couple of years these became the norm. This was our reality and we learned to handle it. As conditions grew worse we grew tougher. Conditions the reader might consider terrible, even horrifying, became a normal part of our everyday life. Simply put, we adapted. Those prisoners who could not adapt, who did not learn to bend with the wind, those prisoners died. Our adaptation was so complete that none of us realized how badly we were treated until we were repatriated at the end of the war and re-entered civilized society.

The psychological changes we had to undergo were much more difficult than the physical. For the most part we were young, uneducated, and completely unprepared for the psychological and emotional whirlpool we were thrown into. The stresses were enormous. The psychological change we were forced to undergo took place in the deepest recesses of our minds, in our very souls, changes we could not see, could not feel, which we were not even aware of. What does an American kid do when he finds himself in a world where the Judeo-Christian ethic is set aside, where his moral values no longer are valid, where the enemy does not think in terms of right or wrong? We had just about the same rights, got the same consideration, as the ancient Christians in the arena at Rome. Except that here the animals had two legs and carried a club or bayonet instead of claws and fangs.

The prison camp at Cabanatuan was a world of its own. We had no communication with the outside. We knew nothing of the progress of the war and nothing of what was going on beyond the perimeter of the camp. Inside the camp we tended to withdraw into our barracks, a smaller world, and within the barracks, into the still smaller world of our sleeping bay, and eventually, I suppose, within ourselves.

In Cabanatuan rules of conduct among the prisoners evolved, were accepted, understood, but were never written down. In my three-and-a-half years as a prisoner I never once walked into a barracks other than my own. It just wasn't done. A stranger was any prisoner from another barracks. A stranger who wanted to talk to me would stop at the entrance to my barracks and ask someone to call me to the door. The only exceptions I can remember were a couple of times when I was unable to walk, a couple of times when Floyd Buckner dropped by to see how I was getting along. And those times he stood in the aisle and talked, never climbing up on the sleeping shelf. And our sleeping spaces, my sleeping space, that little bit of bamboo shelf that belonged to me was almost sacred. It was inviolate. It was unthinkable that I come in from a work detail and find another man sitting in my space, and I never, never infringed upon the personal space of another. Thus we formed temporary alliances. I knew the names and faces of most of the men in my barracks, knew a little better the men in adjoining bays or across the aisle, but my real friends were the three or four men who slept and lived within touching distance in my sleeping bay. When I moved to another barracks or to another camp or to the prison hospital, these men disappeared from my life and I often never saw them again. Then, in a new barracks, in a new situation, out of sheer desperation and necessity I found myself a member of a new tiny group and the whole process began all over again.

Time passed slowly in the hospital area. There was nothing to do. Of course, just staying alive was a full-time job, but there was no busy work to occupy the time, nothing to stimulate the mind. A typical day went like this. Wake to a Japanese bugle call early in the morning. Most everybody trudged to the latrine, at least to urinate. This relieved the pressure and got the day started. Roll call, a daily morning ritual. In the hospital we were allowed to remain in barracks, to answer roll call from our beds. If a voice did not answer to roll call we assumed the man was either stuck on the latrine or dead. Either one could be checked out quickly. After that there was breakfast. Breakfast never varied. A ladle of thin watery rice without salt or seasoning, and a cup of unsweetened tea or very weak unsweetened chocolate. Shortly after breakfast, not every day, but almost every day, the burial detail would pass by my barracks. Objectively I saw them, was fully aware of the pitiful skeletal cadavers under the little mounds of grass, but emotionally I kept them at a distance. I didn't want to see their faces, to hear their names. Death was something that happened to other people, to the other guy. I think I avoided coming face-to-face with the fact that I was already in line and moving steadily toward the door through which these dead men had just passed.

Doc Mayer came through the barracks about ten o'clock every day. He usually had a word or two for everyone. Without fail he would ask me how I was feeling, tell me that I looked a little better. Always the optimist, he encouraged me by saying that if I kept making progress I could be out of the hospital in a few weeks.

I know practicing medicine must have been frustrating, almost impossible, for all the doctors, but especially for Doctor Mayer. He was so damned conscientious. But with no medicines he was helpless. Must have been like trying to type a letter with boxing gloves on. On the other hand, Doc Mayer gave us hope, and there were times when hope was the only thing we had going for us, the only thing that kept us alive.

Dinner came about noon every day, dry rice and blowgun soup. Sometimes a spoonful of pudding, water thickened with cornstarch. Supper was a repeat of the noon meal, and the day ended when the sun went down.

I was always hungry, always, and to me mealtimes were the most important times of the day. My first thought on awakening was, get to the latrine, and get there in a hurry. Then, how long before we eat? Time was measured not in hours but in how long it would be till the next meal. The time after breakfast and before lunch was usually a good time to get things done. If I had any energy at all, morning was when I felt it.

In Sammy Mayer's barracks, Semore, Wilkins, and I slept side by side and thus formed our little support group. Frequently, immediately after breakfast, we would go out along the path to the latrine together. Now this might sound like some weird kind of perversion, but it wasn't. Dysentery was pervasive. We all had it. Because of this, and second only to the long hours in my sleeping space, I spent more time on the latrine than any other place in camp. A half hour on the latrine soaking in the warmth of the early morning sun, talking, casually picking lice from my G-string, was probably the equivalent of the lady's bridge club, an afternoon tea, or church bingo. Inadvertently, I think I set the schedule for the three of us. We would draw our breakfast ration and sit in our bunks to eat. (In the hospital area we were allowed to eat in barracks because so many prisoners were too sick and weak to get up and out.) I would eat my lugao first, save my cup of watery chocolate or bitter tea until last. Never could resist drinking the chocolate or the tea. Although there was little or no nourishment in either the chocolate or the tea, I think I found some feeling of comfort from the warmth of the liquid, or perhaps I just enjoyed the temporary sense of fullness in my stomach. At any rate, as soon as I drank the hot liquid this ridiculous rumbling would start in my intestines. You know how when you are thirsty and take a drink of cold water you can actually feel the coldness of the water all the way down into your stomach? Well in my case I felt the hot chocolate rumble all the way down, through my stomach, through my intestines, through my bowels. It reminded me of a little kid's ball bouncing down several flights of tenement stairs. I could feel the liquid in my body rumbling down, hesitating, going around the corners, rumbling downward, ever downward. And I knew, from sad experience, when the rumbling got to the bottom I had better be at the latrine. So, as soon as I drank my chocolate I would head down the path, and Semore and Wilkins often went with me. After my little emergency, perhaps *our* little emergency, had passed, we would continue to sit on the latrine and talk, and bask in the early morning sun, and hunt "seam squirrels," body lice. This almost daily ritual somehow developed into a few moments of peaceful tranquility, a few brief moments of almost complete emotional escape from the harsh reality of everyday prison-camp life.

Semore, the kid who slept to one side of me, was from just outside New York. He came from a poor family, never had anything materially, probably never would have a hell of a lot. But Semore had a dream. Hell, we all had a dream, a little fantasy room in our minds where we could withdraw from the pain and the misery and play the game of "someday." Someday I'll get out of here, someday I'll go home, someday I'll do this and someday I'll do that. We all knew that these dreams were merely flights of the imagination that would most likely never come to pass, but like little kids who want to grow up and be policemen or firemen, we at least pretended to take them seriously, and I think, in their own way, these dreams, these hopes for the future, helped drag us through the days.

Semore's dream was to survive the camps, to go home, and to start a tour service around New York City. He had it all worked out. First, he was going to buy a bus. Not an ordinary bus but the kind of bus they have in London: a two-decker with an enclosed deck on the bottom and an open deck on top so the passengers could ride down below on rainy days and sit on the open upper deck on the good days. It was going to be bright red with shiny black fenders and lots of brass for trim. And on each side (here Semore always drew his open hand across the side of an imaginary bus), on each side in bold yellow letters the company motto, "SEE MORE WITH SEMORE." There would be a tour to the Statue of Liberty, to the Empire State Building, along the bright lights of Broadway at night, and escorted tours to the best Broadway plays or Radio City Music Hall. This was going to be the best tour service in the whole damn world.

I heard the story, Semore's dream, a hundred times, on the latrine, in the chow line, lying on my blanket in the dark of night. Always the same but with slight variations as Semore thought of some new wrinkle. Yet for the hundredth time it was as if he had never told it before, as if we had never heard it before. We all knew, Semore, who told it, and the rest of our little circle who listened, that it was just a fantasy, a mirage that would disappear if we examined it too closely. We all had a dream, a hope for the future, and we nursed it, cultivated it, kept it in the front of our minds.

Admittedly these were dreams, wide-awake daydreams, and knowingly we sometimes became totally immersed in them. Thank God we did. In retrospect I realize these daydreams served a purpose. In a medicinal sense they were the best, the only, medicine available to us. In a psychological sense becoming totally absorbed in a daydream helped ease the pangs of hunger, made my hard bamboo bed seem a little softer, blocked out, for a time, the fear, the despair, the hopelessness that always lurked in the back of my mind.

I would like the reader to keep in mind that from the moment of surrender until we were released, the world outside the prison camp ceased to exist. I was never in solitary confinement. I always lived among hundreds, sometimes thousands, of other POWs. Nevertheless, the fence around the camp became the perimeter of my world, the fence was the line where the ancient mariners would have dropped off the edge of the world. Beyond the fence there was nothing. For three-and-a-half years I never saw a newspaper, never heard a radio, never had the slightest communication with anyone except another POW or a Japanese guard. Our camp might as well have been in outer space.

In this context our daydreams were the only way we had to reach out, to contact, to keep alive the world we remembered. In this strange POW world these early-morning sessions on the latrine took the place of the proverbial quilting party or the cracker barrel in the general store. It was a place where at the same time, and very casually, we could evacuate our bowels, crack lice between our thumbnails, gossip, and bare our souls as well as our bodies.

In the dark of the night among the bedbugs and the unforgiving bamboo slats, and on the latrine with dysentery tearing at his guts, Semore built his bus line. And with little changes here and there it grew more beautiful day by day.

Wilkins, a soldier from Wisconsin, slept on one side of me. Wilkins and his sister had won first place in a statewide skatedance contest just before the war. What could be more natural? Wilkins was going to build a skating rink. It would be big and it would be beautiful. There would be organ music and colored lights, and a revolving mirrored chandelier to cast colored reflections all around the room. Castles in the air? Maybe, but they helped keep some of us alive. Sometimes, but not always. I don't know if Semore ever got his bus line, but I do know Wilkins never got his skating rink. Dysentery got him first. He was tossed into a hole with ten or fifteen other bodies and covered with Philippine dirt.

In Doctor Mayer's barracks Semore, Wilkins and I slept side by side. Blake, the fourth man in our group slept crossways at our feet. When we had conversations in the dark his voice seemed disembodied.

Blake let us know that before the war, in Minnesota, he had worked in a German bakery. His voice would come softly out of the darkness. He told us that he used to get up at four o'clock every morning to make pfeffernüsse, a loaf-shaped cookie that was the German equivalent of our donut. He bragged just a little, told us he made it all by himself and that it was damned good too. (None of us knew how to spell "pfeffernüsse" so we just guessed at it.)

Blake invited all of us to come to Minnesota after the war and get all the pfferneuse we could eat. Free too. Because he was such an experienced baker, Blake became our authority on baking, and with his help and guidance we created, in our imaginations, the most wonderful pies and cakes in the world.

We imagined a peanut-butter pie with a layer of peanut butter and a layer of strawberry jam and then a layer of whipped cream on the very top. Blake agreed that he could make it, but he's have to be extra careful with the whipped cream. Had to beat the cream just right. If he beat it too long it would turn into butter and nobody wanted butter on top of a peanut-butter pie.

I think, in a way, we POWs all lived a double life. On the reality side there were the Japanese guards, the barbed-wire fences, and the always subnormal living conditions, but in our imaginations we could slip through the fence, evade the guards, and go anywhere, do anything we wanted to do, be free.

Anyway, after long and serious discussion, and always under Blake's expert guidance, we would go on to the next concoction. Perhaps one time it might be a layer of white cake and then a layer of chocolate icing, then a layer of chocolate cake and a layer of vanilla icing, and a layer of … sometimes the cake got six or seven layers high.

Then cover the whole darn thing with coconut cream topping. A real thick layer with lots of red Maraschino cherries on top. Blake never said no, and we were convinced that he could bake anything. We'd create imaginary pies and cakes and puddings till we fell asleep.

Even in sleep, food, or the lack of it, was in the front of my mind. I dreamed of food. Not Blake's bakery creations but real solid food like meat and potatoes, dreamed of food so real I could actually taste it. Many many times I awakened in the morning, my blanket wet with saliva where I had drooled during the night.

Blake had two loves, his bakery, and a black nineteen-twenty-eight model A Ford sedan, which he had stored in his sister's garage. The bakery we took seriously. The bakery was a matter of food and nothing about food was taken lightly. But his car was fair game; we kidded him about his car.

Blake spoke lovingly about his prized possession, his "black nineteen-twenty-eight model A Ford sedan. We made a little joke about it among ourselves because he never, never spoke of it any other way. Blake never once said "car" or "automobile" or "my Ford" or "my sedan." He always used the full nomenclature, "my black nineteen-twenty-eight model A Ford sedan."

Damndest thing about the prison-camp hospital, the Japanese left us alone. There was a low, simple, three- or four-strand barbed-wire fence with guard towers around the perimeter and they did furnish us a minimum of food. But inside the hospital, except for an occasional patrol that made a surprise quick inspection, they left us strictly on our own. Once we passed through the hospital gate the Japanese didn't give a damn what happened to us. If we survived and got strong enough we walked out through the same gate and went to work on the farm. If we didn't, a burial detail carried us through the gate to the cemetery. Two ways out and they didn't care which.

The cemetery was a hated option for us of course. I tried not to think about it, tried not to talk about it, but I had my nose rubbed in it every morning when the burial detail carried the day's quota of bodies past my barracks. I don't think it was fear of death, for by this time I had come to accept death as a casual companion. It was more likely that I felt a tremendous repugnance at the way it was likely to happen. I didn't want to die of starvation and disease like some dirty two-legged animal. And what passed as a cemetery was a horror. Bodies weren't wrapped in shrouds, and they were not buried in coffins. They were buried naked because we couldn't afford to throw away even a G-string. The usual procedure was for the stretcher bearers to walk alongside the grave, tip the stretcher and let the corpse fall into the hole. The next body was dumped beside or on top of the first and so on until the grave was filled, then the bodies were covered with dirt. If there were not enough bodies to fill a particular grave, those bodies would be left uncovered until the next day when a couple more might be added. Even in death space was at a premium.

Nineteen forty-three was the most critical year for me. For months I lingered somewhere between life and death. I thought I was doing well when I could make it to the latrine and back without being completely tired out, poorly when I was reduced to having my food brought to me. All at the same time I had dysentery, burning feet, grossly swollen legs and body, scurvy and pellagra. I was truly a mess. I think it was Doctor Mayer, Sammy, who kept me alive. Not with medication, he didn't have any. Sammy talked with me every day. Not much because there were too many of us, but he inspired confidence, trust. He became like a father figure and we relied on his support. His concern was so obviously real that with just a couple of sentences he could leave me hopeful, reassured that I could get stronger, feel better, that I was going to make it. With typical soldierly irreverence we prisoners joked about our little one line prayers. Dear God, just help me over this next hurdle and I'll go the rest of the way by myself. However he managed it, Sammy Mayer was good for me. He helped me over one hell of a hurdle.

I had already been afflicted with almost every illness or pain except childbirth and leprosy. Thought nothing more could possibly happen to me but it did. One morning Sammy stopped by for his usual chat.

He always asked the same questions, asked how I was feeling, how many times did I go to the latrine yesterday, why didn't I help him by keeping count?

I really didn't know, guess at ten, maybe twelve. Doctor Mayer took my foot in his hands and firmly pressed his thumb hard against my shin. It made a deep, ugly depression that remained in the swollen flesh after he took his thumb away. (The inside of the shin just above the ankle was the best place to check for wet beri-beri because there is not a lot of fat or muscle to get in the way.)

Doc commented that I looked a little better, looked like I was coming along OK. He advised me to take things easy, to stay off my feet and rest and maybe tomorrow I'd be better yet. Doc Mayer spoke softly but with a confident air that somehow transferred to his patients. Maybe that was why so many prisoners wanted to be under his care. If there were a pound of bad and an ounce of good, Sammy Mayer always managed to find the ounce of good and bring it to the fore. Without medicine and under the worst circumstances Sammy managed to encourage a man, lift his spirits and leave him feeling better about himself. He turned to leave and I shouted after him. I was embarrassed. Doc was right in front of me and I shouted like he was a block away. I remember that my own voice was higher and sounded strange, even to my own ears. I must have been scared.

Doc turned back and sat on the edge of the shelf. I confided to him that I wasn't seeing so good lately, that he was all blurry. Blurry hell, he almost wasn't there. I could see him, but close enough to talk with him, couldn't tell if his eyes were open or shut. Doc raised my upper eyelid with his finger, looked at my eye, prodded a little bit here and there. He asked me if I had any pain. I told him that it didn't hurt but I just couldn't see too good anymore. Couldn't even find the lice in my G-string. Those little bastards were getting away with murder. Doc smiled. He liked a little banter to liven things up. I had only myself to worry about but he carried the weight of a hundred sick men on his mind all the time. He looked at my eye again. No infection, no pain, couldn't see anything wrong. He was thinking out loud, almost talking to himself. He asked me how long it had been going on. I wasn't able to answer, had to do a lot of guessing. I took my best shot at it, guessed it had been at least four months, maybe five, maybe six. Didn't happen all at once, sort of sneaks up on a guy. Doc wanted to know why I didn't tell him sooner. I couldn't answer that question either. Just didn't seem important until now. I thought I had some real troubles to worry about. I had dysentery, my feet hurt, and my legs were all swollen up. Besides, nobody ever died from poor eyesight.

He agreed. So far nobody had died from poor eyesight. Then I popped the real question, asked him if he thought I was going blind. I blurted it out because I had been afraid to say the word "blind." It was a word I had avoided, even to myself, but at last it was out in the open. Doc was noncommittal. In his opinion maybe yes, maybe no. There were several prisoners with the very same problem and nobody had gone totally blind yet.

I wanted to know how come. It was the simplest of questions but probably the hardest to answer. How come? He tried to explain that the medical profession wasn't sure just why this sort of illness happened, that they thought it was a thing called nutritional blindness. It happens when a person doesn't get enough of the right things to eat. Bodies react to starvation by setting up their own defense mechanisms, by shutting down some of the nonessential functions so the other can keep on going. I wasn't satisfied, I wanted to know more. I wanted to understand what was happening to my eyes. How come?

I'll bet Doc Mayer hated the question, how come?, but he tried his best to explain. Doc tried to put things in simple terms so I could understand them. His explanation went something like this. He told me that I could see the dysentery, that I could feel my burning feet, and that I could see my swollen legs. If I could see all these things happening on the outside, there must be a lot of things going on inside by body that I wasn't able to see. So your brain, aware of what's going on both inside and out, decides what you need and what you can get along without. Already your fingernails don't grow. Your hair doesn't grow very fast and you probably don't feel about sex the way you used to. Doc went on to explain that it was like living in a big house in the wintertime and not having enough fuel to heat the whole house. Maybe you shut the doors and let the bedroom get cold while everybody stays warm in the living room. Everybody's different. In your case your body is turning off your eyes. Doc went on to tell me that my brain knew I needed my eyes, so not to worry too much. Doc felt that I probably would not go completely blind, and when the food got better and I regained my health my brain would turn my eyes on again. He thought I would see as well as I used to. As he left he offered to see what he could do about getting me a little extra food; then he suggested that I go down to the medical shack and see if the doctors there could do anything for me.

The medical shack was a hundred yards from our barracks, but I figured I could make it on my own. As Doc went through the barracks I heard him ask a man what the good word was today. A half dozen voices told him that we'd be free in forty-three.

We'll be free in forty-three. It was getting too late in the year for that. Guys were already predicting a friendly shore in forty-four.

Next morning I made my way to the medical shack. It was a small one-room building the doctors used for an office. It was a place they used for special sick call, where they kept whatever medical records they had, where they performed an occasional autopsy, and where now and then they had to perform crude surgery on a wooden table without anesthetic.

I didn't expect much because I knew all of our doctors worked under the same conditions. They had years of training, were full of excellent advice, but had nothing at all to work with.

Took me a long time to walk that hundred yards but I finally got there. For me there was no other choice. I had to do whatever I could for myself or risk becoming a bedpatient, and I dreaded becoming a bedpatient. To me that was the kiss of death.

There were two young doctors in the medical shack. They didn't look a hell of a lot better off than I did.

One looked up as I walked in, mentioned to the other that I was a good-looking soldier and asked what he could do for me.

I think I straightened up a little. The casual comment made me feel good. I had almost forgotten that I was a soldier, felt more like an animal in a slaughter-house.

I gave them Doctor Mayer's name, Dr. Mayer this time, not Sammy, and told them I was having trouble with my eyes.

The first doctor took a long look, moved me closer to the window and asked if I could see his hand. He waved his hand in front of my face.

Sure, I could see his hand, but when it came to counting fingers I didn't do so good. He waved his hand again. I could make out the shape of the hand but couldn't distinguish the fingers. When he asked how many I guessed at three, maybe four. The doctors put their heads together for a short conference, then told me that in their opinion my vision wouldn't get any better unless the food improved, but that it probably wouldn't get any worse. I was relieved. At least I wasn't going to be cold-stony blind. I started to leave, but Doc asked me to wait a minute while he looked for something that might help. He fumbled around in a cardboard box and brought out a small bottle with an eyedropper cap. He tipped my head back and carefully squeezed a drop of something into each eye. Arghh, it was terrible. In three seconds I could *taste it*. Cod-liver oil. God only knows how long it had been lying around in the heat without refrigeration, but it was rancid and stronger than I was.

The doctor smiled when he saw the look on my face. He knew it was strong stuff but it was all he had. Thought it might help and told me to come back in the morning and do it again.

I began getting the deluxe medical treatment for my eyes. For ten days I got one drop of very rancid cod-liver oil in each eye. Then it ran out, and there was no more, never any more. I was on my own again.

True to his word, Doctor Mayer tried to get me extra food, but like the cod-liver oil, there simply wasn't any more. Doc continued to talk with me, to commiserate with me, to urge me not to give up. No matter how bad things became, and they became pretty bad, Sammy Mayer always left me with the feeling that whatever came my way, I could handle it. No medicine at all, just hope, yet that hope was probably the thing that kept me going.

A week or so after my twenty drops of cod-liver oil ran out Doctor Mayer came up with a minor miracle. He found a bottle of plasma. Don't know where or how he found it, never thought to ask. Probably a leftover, hidden away by the defeated Philippine army a couple of years ago and overlooked by the Japanese. However it came about, it was certainly the only bottle of plasma I saw or even heard about during my three-and-a-half years as a POW, and I got it.

Doc came down the aisle holding the bottle like it was pure gold. I could tell he was pleased with himself. Smiling broadly he announced that he had something for me, a surprise in the bottle that would give me a lift, "make you feel better." I had never been in a real hospital, never seen a transfusion, had no idea what plasma was or how it was used. Stupidly I asked Doc how he wanted me to take it. Should I drink it all at once or take it a little at a time. He overlooked my ignorance and told me I didn't have to drink it. He was going to put it in my arm with a needle, and afterwards I would feel better. Doc showed me a small package wrapped in a dirty rag that contained a piece of rubber tubing and a hypodermic needle. He fitted one end of the tubing to the needle, the other to the plasma bottle, then told me he was going to put the needle into a vein.

I lay flat on the lower bamboo shelf and Doc hung the plasma from the shelf above. There was no bed, no clean sheets, no nurses, no rubber gloves, no sterile equipment. I got my transfusion in the usual prison-camp style. A bamboo shelf in a barracks with a dirt floor and lots of flies. It boiled down to Doc Mayer and myself, a dirty arm, a dirty needle, and a hundred other sick guys lying around.

Doc probed my arm, found a vein, and inserted the needle. Damn, that needle was sure dull. I'll bet it had already punctured a hundred arms.

Doc showed me how to hold the needle in with my free hand, carefully so that it doesn't slip out, then told me that when the bottle was empty I should pull the needle out and put my finger over the hole so it wouldn't bleed. He told me that I'd feel better and that he'd see me in the morning. Doc moved on. He had other barracks to visit, other patients to see.

My trouble started within a few minutes. I felt strange. I got cold. It was a hot day and I thought I would freeze to death. My body quivered and shook uncontrollably, and I began to experience difficulty breathing. I curled up in my blanket, wrapped up so my head and feet were under cover and shook. Doc was gone and there was no one to help me. I had to ride it out myself. Half an hour, forty-five minutes, and the chill passed. Then I got hot. I threw off the blanket and lay on top of it in my G-string and began sweating. I passed out. When I came to, I was wet and my blanket was soaked through. I was frightened because I thought it was my time to die and there was no one I could ask for help. For hours I vacillated between chills and fever, between consciousness and unconsciousness. I had to go to the toilet, knew I couldn't wait, and was more afraid of using a bedpan than dying. Had it fixed in the back of my mind that as long as I was able to walk I was OK, but the moment I became a bedpatient I was as good as dead.

I have no clear recollection of exactly what happened to me in those two or three hours after Doctor Mayer gave me the plasma transfusion. I only have memory of raging fevers and chills, a brief few moments when I was neither hot nor cold, just limp with exhaustion and relief. I think it was during one of these brief respites that I tried to walk to the latrine. Made it too, but the exertion made me sick to my stomach. Sat on one hole and threw up in another. On the way back to barracks I began to shake again, to feel cold. My vision narrowed until I seemed to be looking down a long round tube. I stood still for what seemed a long time, cold as hell in the hot Philippine sun, then I remember going gently to my knees, not hard, but slowly, softly, as in a dream. I crawled for a short distance on hands and knees, then must have fallen asleep. The last thing I remembered was the pleasant warmth of the hot earth against my chest and belly.

In the camp hospital there was nothing in the medical sense that we could do for one another, but we looked after each other in humanitarian ways. The strong took care of the weak, carried their food, helped them keep clean, covered them with a blanket. They did the little things that blunted the harshness of everyday existence, little things that made life more bearable. When I didn't return to barracks, a couple of guys thought I might be in trouble and went looking for me. Somehow they got me back to barracks and got in touch with Doctor Mayer. I came out of the fog to find Doc sitting on the sleeping shelf beside me.

He asked me what the hell had happened, told me that I was supposed to be feeling better, not worse. I told him all that I remembered. Patients nearby chipped in their two cents' worth, filled in the blanks, described the chills and fevers.

Doc put his hand up and felt my forehead. The fever was gone. Doc looked stricken. I think it hurt him as much as it hurt me. He hadn't made a mistake. The plasma was probably just too old to be any good, but Doc acted as if it was his fault. It wasn't. In Doc's opinion I had suffered a bad reaction, but he thought the worst was over. He borrowed a blanket and wrapped me from head to toe. There was nothing else he could do. He told me to keep covered up and rest, that if it happened again I should send for him immediately; otherwise he would see me again in the morning.

I slept heavily through the night. Doc Mayer came by early the next day, came straight to my bunk. He was blunt, asked me how I felt, told me I looked terrible.

I felt OK, weak as a kitten but the chills and fever were gone. I felt OK, but I could hardly speak to tell him. My lips, from below my lower lip to above my upper lip, all the way to my nose and all around my nose was one big mass of fever blisters. I could look down and see my upper lip sticking out. The whole front of my face was one big scab. Doc looked at my eyes, took my pulse with his finger, felt my forehead. That was it. There was nothing more he could do. A finger on the wrist, a hand on the forehead, that was the full medical treatment at Cabanatuan. Doc stood up, started to leave, then told me to get some rest, that he would see me again in a little while.

I called him back and asked him if he thought we were going to make it. Unconsciously I avoided the direct question, am I going to die? Doc caught it. I could tell from his eyes that he understood, that he knew the question I was afraid to ask.

Doc hesitated, almost too long, then patted me on the shoulder and quietly told me that he thought we would make it OK.

Semore brought my breakfast, but I waved it away, knew I couldn't stomach it. No use letting it turn sour in the heat. Nothing was ever wasted. Semore and Wilkins divided it between them. I fell asleep.

I couldn't have been asleep long, maybe half an hour, then Doctor Mayer was back, shaking me awake. I started to protest but he silenced me with a wave of his hand. Without raising his voice he told me that he had arranged for me to move down to the dysentery area. I was fully awake by now and didn't like what I was hearing.

Quiet but firm. I knew Doc Mayer meant business. He told me that he couldn't do anything more for me there but that he had made a deal for me to stay in the first barracks inside the dysentery area fence with Doctor Roger until a space opened up for me to move on down to the Zero Ward. He told me that he had already spoken to Dr. Schwartz, a good friend of his, and that Schwartzie would take good care of me. Doc Mayer thought food might be a little better in Zero Ward, and besides, Schwartzie lived right in the barracks.

Frankly, Dr. Mayer's words scared the hell out of me. As bad as the prison-camp hospital was, I knew dysentery area was worse. And Zero Ward, that was like death row. I knew that for a space to open up in Zero Ward some poor bastard would have to die first. When his body was carried out to the cemetery there would be room for me.

At Cabanatuan there was little or no formality. Doctor Mayer said he would like me to move to another barracks and I moved. Not this afternoon, not tomorrow, not in a few days, but now. I folded my blanket, picked up my mess gear and moved. It was as simple as that. With a medic to steady me because I was pretty shaky on my feet, I walked out of Doctor Mayer's barracks, and in the way of the prison camp, walked out of his life. I never spoke to Doctor Mayer again. I saw him once at a distance after I recovered and went back to what we termed the duty side of the camp. He was on a work detail, heading out to do stoop labor on the farm. Doc had a hoe over his shoulder and was dressed in ragged fatigues that were at least ten sizes too large for his small body. He looked like a little kid playing "daddy" in his father's work clothes. He seemed dwarfed by the other prisoners on the work detail. No matter that Doctor Mayer was possibly the smallest man in the Army, it has always been my firm belief that when God made Sammy Mayer he put a big man in a small package.

It's been nearly fifty years since I last saw Doctor Mayer trudging off to do slave labor on the farm. In those years I've survived the camps, married my childhood sweetheart, raised seven children and now have twenty-three grandchildren. It's been a good life. Doctor Mayer made it through too. He's retired now, still living somewhere back east.

Wonder if he knew how the ripples spread out from the lives he touched, from the lives he saved?

Wonder if he knew we called him "Sammy"?

Like so many others whose paths he crossed, I never had a chance to tell him just how much his care and his kindness meant to me. So to Samuel M. Mayer, M.D., I offer my heartfelt thanks. And to "Sammy," Shalom, Sammy, and God bless.

Zero Ward:
The Dying Place

The prison camp at Cabanatuan was divided into two separate living areas, the duty side and the hospital side. On the duty side were the prisoners who were still capable of doing hard physical labor, of working on the farm, or building an airfield. Duty side was completely fenced in, a world unto itself.

Next to the duty side, but outside the fence, were the living quarters for the Japanese troops who guarded the camp. A good hundred years from the duty side, and beyond the Japanese barracks, was the hospital, also fenced off by itself. In appearance the hospital looked exactly like the duty side, same crude barracks, same crude outdoor latrines, absolutely no washing or bathing facilities. The only difference was that the hospital was where we sent the men whom even the Japanese considered too ill to perform any useful labor.

And in one end of the hospital, completely fenced off even from the hospital itself, was the dysentery area. The second I left the main hospital area and walked through the gate into the dysentery area I knew I was entering a different world. It was strangely quiet, nobody talking, nobody moving about. I could smell death in the air. My heart was heavy. Fear, despair, resignation, whatever, I felt down in the dumps because I knew there were only two ways I would ever go back through the dysentery area gate. Either I would walk through on my own two feet and return to duty, or I would be carried through and dumped in a hole in the cemetery.

I found my place in the first barracks inside the fence. There was a spot waiting for me and I crawled in. My medic escort wished me luck and left. I was on my own again.

Two new friends, the guys who were going to sleep on either side of me. One called Smitty, the other, by coincidence, another guy named Williams. They were friendly, considerate, didn't mention the fellow whose space I had moved into. They didn't have to; I knew I was taking a dead man's place.

My new doctor's name was Roger. I thought it odd that he had a first name for a last name but that was it, Dr. Roger. Doctor Roger was a young fellow, but nice. He made a standing offer to all of his patients. Any former POW who came to him after the war would get free medical treatment for the rest of his life. Doctor Roger gave me the once over, noted my blistered face, my waterlogged legs. He told me to rest up and stay in my sleeping space, that I needed to get some strength back. Someone else would have to carry my food.

Smitty and Williams took turns bringing me my meals. They were both still ambulatory. I could go for that because I really didn't have the strength to stand in the chow line. But become a bedpatient and use a bedpan, no way. There were a number of bedpatients in the barracks. I looked on them as dead men. I knew they were goners. It was hard but I struggled through my numerous day and night trips to the latrine.

After a couple of days I was able to sit up and eat. There was an open window at the head of my sleeping space, and I could look out on a small nipa hut about forty feet away. One day there were two bodies lying on litters on the ground in front of it. What the hell is that? I wondered to myself. Smitty noted the direction of my gaze. He told me that I was looking at the morgue, that when a man died in a barracks they carried him to the morgue right away. It didn't hold very many bodies and when it was full they lined 'em up on the ground until the burial detail picked them up next morning. We were eating and I hesitated. Smitty told me that if I didn't look I wouldn't know they were there, and anyway I'd soon get used to it.

I tried hard not to look but I still remember. Ribs seem to stick out, and bodies look skinnier when they're dead. I had trouble sleeping. Same old bamboo slats, same thin blanket, same food, and same climate, but I couldn't go to sleep. I twisted and turned and sat up and lay down, kept everybody awake. I knew it was the morgue just outside my window. It was too darned close. I thought I was toughened up to the possibility of death, even my own, and to some extent this was true. To survive at all I had to convince myself that death was something that could only happen to the other guy, to someone who lived in the far end of the hospital, or at least in a barracks other than my own. Life had been easier for me before I was moved to this barracks. Then, I had known about the morgue; its existence was no secret, everybody knew. Before, in my mind I thought of the morgue as being off in never-never land, somewhere else, somewhere where I didn't have to confront it directly. Now it was right under my nose. I couldn't avoid it. Burial detail picked up the bodies about nine each morning. If a prisoner died at ten his body was carried to the morgue to wait for the next day's burial detail. The hot Philippine sun worked on the bodies all day and they rapidly began to smell. Even after the bodies were taken away the smell still remained. It clung to the area, to my barracks like some insidious reminder that for me, death was close. At this stage I knew there was not a great deal of difference between my being alive and inside the barracks, or being dead and on the ground outside.

In terms of physical illness, the month or so I spent in this particular barracks was perhaps the most critical period of my entire time as a POW. I was nearly blind, could walk to the latrine only with the greatest difficulty, and was close to becoming one of the dreaded bedpatients.

Smitty, who slept next to me, took me under his wing during this critical time. He made it his business to carry my food and to rinse my rusty tin dish when I was finished. One night in the pitch blackness when I was quietly bitching about not being able to fall asleep, Smitty's voice came out of the dark.

He told me that when he was a little kid he used to have terrible headaches, and that his mother used to rub the back of his neck until the headaches went away, then he would fall asleep. Without any more ado Smitty reached over and began rubbing the back of my neck, at the bottom of my skull just behind the ears. My God, it worked. I relaxed and fell asleep within a few minutes. Such a little thing to remember almost fifty years, yet when I think back I realize that the only gentle touching I received during those three-and-a-half years was the time I was having chills and Doctor Mayer wrapped me in a blanket and the times Smitty rubbed my neck. Emotionally it was a barren existence.

By this time, those of us who still survived were mentally tough. We had to be. We could look at life and not think about how hard it was, look at death and not think about how close it was. I had adapted to the harshness of POW life as well as anyone, but now and then, quite unexpectedly, I found there would be a chink in my armor. The casual mention of something back home, a song, a movie, a place that I had been, would bring a sudden rush of emotional memories, sometimes good, sometimes bad. At these moments I was emotionally vulnerable.

We had to be terrible careful about what we said, how we talked around Smitty. In his soul Smitty carried an unhealed open wound and though we knew what it was about, it was sometimes hard not to inadvertently twist a knife in it. Smitty had a brother. They had enlisted together, served in the same outfit. After capture they had been taken together on a work detail to rebuild a bridge. One prisoner escaped. True to their word, the Japanese picked ten men at random and executed them on the spot. Smitty was forced to stand and watch his brother being shot.

The Japanese pulled a surprise inspection today. It was a surprise because nobody knew it was coming. On the other hand it didn't really matter. We had almost nothing to hide. There were no secret tunnels because even outside the fence there was nowhere to go. We had no clandestine radio to hide, no cache of weapons or food, nothing. Besides, the Japanese always telegraphed their punches. The Japanese barracks were well outside the hospital area, and there was only a single road, a single gate that led into the hospital. Whether they came on foot or by truck, by twos or threes or a hundred, they came along the same road and entered through the single gate. As soon as a truck approached or a platoon formed on the road a buzz swept through the hospital. The pitifully few things anyone might want to hide, like a diary written in pencil on ragged scraps of paper, were quickly passed along to the dysentery area where they were relatively safe. A small glass bottle with a tight lid, tied to a string and dropped deep into a latrine, was as secure as a safe deposit box in a bank. A platoon of armed Japanese soldiers might walk through the hospital, quickly and reluctantly, but I never saw a single Japanese enter the dysentery area. The guards would tie a surgical mask over mouth and nose, march to the little fence that separated dysentery from the main hospital, stop and look across. No more. The routine never varied. The guards would approach the three strands of barbed wire, stare across, chatter among themselves for a couple of minutes, then march away. They seemed deathly afraid of catching dysentery or whatever else we had on our side of the fence.

The five or six weeks I spent in Dr. Roger's barracks were critical to me. I was close to death and knew it. I moved through the days slowly, dreamlike. Like tunnel vision, my world narrowed down to eating and sleeping and talking to Smitty and Williams. Other men in the barracks were distant figures, shadows that walked in and out, passed by my bunk, but that had no place in my reality. It was a frightening time, yet in some ways it was a good time.

We talked, Smitty and I and Williams. We talked constantly. We reminisced, sometimes about the war, but mostly about home. It was important that we talk about home. Time and distance and our total isolation were beginning to play tricks with our minds. The danger was that prison camp might become the reality and home just a fantasy. We had nothing to work with but memories so we played mind games. We would try to recall the slogans from the various brands of American cigarettes.

I remembered the little uniformed bellhop with the flat round hat cocked on the side of his head, the bellhop with the high childish voice who used to walk through the hotel lobby announcing a call for Phillip Morris.

Smitty recalls Old Golds, whose slogan had been, "Not a cough in a carload." And Williams came up with Camels and the guy who said he'd walk a mile for a Camel.

To anyone at home these prison-camp conversations would have seemed idiotic mindless chatter, yet it was important to us that we remember even the tiniest detail. Talk dwindled and died away as we fell asleep but might pick up on awakening as though there had been no interruptions. Someone might ask if we remembered Lucky Strikes, the ones that came in a green pack with the big red dot on the front. And Chesterfields were white and Pall Malls came in a red wrapper. Kools were big too, the menthol cigarettes that advertised with the black and white penguin that went "Cool, cool, cool."

Radio programs were big too. We had all listened to radio before the war. We remembered "Amos 'n' Andy." That was a good program. And what about "Fibber McGee and Molly," or George Burns and Gracie Allen? We had liked them because they made us laugh.

Maybe a voice would chip in from another part of the barracks and tell us how he and his parents would sit up and listen to Jack Benny and Rochester on Sunday night, and after that they'd listen to Walter Winchell and the news. Walter Winchell sent his news program to Mr. and Mrs. North America and all the ships at sea. Winchell always started like that.

The guy with the disembodied voice might not have anything more to say for the rest of the night, but he was listening and he had made contact, even to this small extent, made contact with home.

We weren't smart; we weren't good conversationalists, but we talked about things that had been common denominators for all American kids. Joe Louis, "the Brown Bomber," and his second fight with Max Baer. Babe Ruth. Joe DiMaggio and the Yankees. I remembered sitting in front of the radio on Saturdays and listening to college football and falling asleep in the easy chair.

Somehow, during this period I began to get better. The swelling in my legs began to go down, not much, but noticeably. My sight began to get better. I could see people's faces, could see where I was going without stumbling around. Dr. Roger got me to the medical office where there was an old balance scale. I weighed one hundred ten pounds. I had gained ten pounds. Now I weighed exactly half what I had weighed before the war. Doc Roger was enthusiastic. It was a good sign. I was getting better. I was going to live. Maybe the food was a little better in the dysentery area, but if it was I couldn't tell it. It was the same old stuff and there was certainly no more of it. I think rather, that because I was young my body had figured out a way to use my own natural resources, to slow down my metabolism and to make better use of what food was available. I think that my body had finally decided to shut down such unnecessary functions as sexual urges and growing fingernails and hair, and concentrate on fighting off dysentery and edema and beri-beri.

Little things come back when I jog my memory, little things that were inconsequential yet must have had meaning. On the duty side we referred to barracks by number. I lived in barracks number three or nine or twelve. In the hospital we referred to barracks by name. I lived in Sammy Mayer's barracks, or Dr. Roger's or Dr. Schwartz's barracks. The only exception was the Zero Ward, the dying place, and we spoke of it in whispers.

Somebody had a book, a thin hardcover so dull and so boring that I cannot remember the name or a single word of what it was about. I borrowed it and laboriously read it from cover to cover, every single word. Word by word by meaningless word, it was like a ritual that celebrated my return to life. I could see again.

I could sit up now, sit up in my sleeping space and talk my head off. Familiarity and close proximity can dull many sharp emotional edges. Perhaps I had grown used to the sight, perhaps I had grown used to the smell, but now that I was not going to be one of them, the bodies outside my window were not so abhorrent.

Smitty was a farm boy, and he loved to talk about going out to his garden just at sunup and eating a ripe tomato right off the vine. I could taste those tomatoes. Or an ear of corn, fresh picked, tender, juicy, sweet, right off the cob. Smitty's chore, as a kid, had been to gather and bring in the eggs. We talked a lot about this and spent a lot of time wondering, if the chickens were left alone and nobody ate any eggs or chickens, and the chickens hatched all the eggs they laid, how long would it be before chickens took over the earth? Not deep philosophy but it helped keep us alive.

When we spoke of the war, about our short five months in the war, we spoke of the funny things, the unusual. I remembered a time when our little fort had been under attack by enemy bombers. We had two antiaircraft guns on deck, each surrounded by a parapet of sandbags. We would commence firing as soon as the enemy planes were within range and our range finders would closely watch the release of the bombs. If they thought the bombs were going to miss we would continue firing, uninterruptedly as the bombers passed overhead. If our range finders thought the bombs were going to score a direct hit they would call out, "Take cover!" and we would fall flat on deck inside the parapet. On this occasion the bombs were zeroed in and we were all hugging the deck, arms shielding our heads. There was no cursing, no praying, just fright and deathly quiet. Then one lone, loud complaining voice. "Take your damn feet outa my face."

Smitty had been in the infantry. He recalled an instance when the Japanese attacked his regiment with tanks and there were no tanks on our side to defend. Philippine scouts, Philippine cavalry had charged the Japanese tanks on horseback and with terrible losses had driven them back. He recounted other occasions when he had seen Igorots, Philippine tribesmen from the Northern mountains, sitting on top of our tanks, armed only with spears and bow and arrow, guiding our tanks into battle by pounding on the sides of the turret with sticks. The funny stories were the best. We didn't talk much about the blood and guts.

I got a chuckle when I told of the time when we were firing our three-inch gun at a Japanese ship. We had scored a direct hit and we wanted more. Then we had a misfire. The usual procedure with a misfire is to wait ten minutes, see if the damned thing goes off, then if it doesn't, eject the shell and dispose of it. On this occasion we needed the gun, couldn't afford to wait ten minutes. We ejected the live shell and one of the handlers cradled it in his arms. We continued firing at the enemy. When I looked around, the handler was running around the deck in circles, still holding the live shell and wondering what he was supposed to do with it, where he was supposed to go with it. An old sergeant urged him to "throw the damned thing over the side before it blows us all to hell."

I recalled a couple of instances of my own. Once, I came up through the casemate, up a vertical ladder to reach my machine-gun nest on deck. When I stuck my head out of the casemate I saw an unexploded Japanese artillery shell not eighteen inches from my nose. It was big, two hundred forty-five pounds of high explosive. We couldn't leave it there. We had to get on deck and man our machine guns and the damn thing might explode at any second. I was sweating blood and trembling with fear as we rolled it to the edge of the deck and dropped it into the water.

In another instance, not so dramatic, I had figured in advance what I was going to do if I got trapped on deck during a shelling. Behind my sandbag machine-gun emplacement was a series of concrete blocks, eighteen inches high and eighteen inches apart that in peacetime had supported our water tank. My thought was to lie down between these blocks, use them for protection and wait out the shelling. I thought it made pretty good sense.

Japanese shore batteries opened up and I was knocked flat, unharmed, but somewhat stunned by concussion. By the time I recovered the Japanese had scored several direct hits on my concrete blocks. They were blackened, seared by fire and shredded by shrapnel, as I surely would have been had I tried to hide between them. Sometimes staying alive was like winning the lottery.

It's moving day again. My time with Dr. Roger is up. There is space for me in Zero Ward. The very thought sickens me. Not in a physical sense. I already have all the physical ailments I can stand, but moving to the ward is like falling off an emotional cliff. Just for a place in the ward to open up for me somebody else had to die. Prisoners didn't walk out of Zero; they died and were carried out. I think everyone has an aversion toward taking a dead man's place, and for me, this was always difficult.

I had seen Zero Ward twice in those earlier days when I was still living on the duty side of camp, before I had been admitted to the hospital. Both times I had been on work detail, sent over with a group to lend a hand in cleaning the place up. A nasty job, but like burial details, a job that had to be done. On those occasions I thanked God that I was just on work detail, that I wasn't one of the patients.

In those months immediately following the surrender there were a lot of prisoners who were sick or wounded, already near death. The Japanese offered no medical care and made no distinction between the well and the wounded, just lumped all prisoners together and shoved us into barbed-wire enclosures to settle down and sort things out. This settling in period was bad. It became literally survival of the fittest. The strong lived, and the sick and wounded, the weaker ones, died. Again, I was one of the lucky ones.

It was in those earlier days that I had been sent on work details to clean up the ward. On those days I had been given a glimpse of hell. At that time Zero was just a place to separate the dying from the living, a place to get the dying out of sight. Men sent to Zero weren't expected to live more than a week or ten days, and conditions there were horrible, not fit for animals. I saw sick men lying on the bare wooden floor with no beds, no mattresses, many without even a blanket, men just waiting to die. The odor was awful. Sick men were lying in puddles of their own excrement. These were men who were too sick, too weak to crawl to the latrine and with no one to help them were already candidates for the burial detail. Of course they died. What the hell would you expect? I saw men who hadn't been moved for days, men still alive with maggots crawling over their bodies.

On the days I was there on work detail medics loaded patients on crude stretchers, carried them outside and washed them down with a hose. It wasn't much but it was the best that could be done under the circumstances. If not clean, they were certainly a little cleaner than before. Meanwhile I helped scrub filth from the floor. No disinfectant, not even soap, but with buckets, mops, and cold water we tried to leave it clean, not sanitary by any means, but temporarily clean. When the patients were carried back inside the whole dirty process started over again.

At Cabanatuan we thought of the Zero Ward as the dying place. We didn't like to talk about it, didn't like to think about it. Zero Ward was like an insane relative that had to be kept hidden from neighbors behind locked doors. Like the bodies stinking in the sun outside the morgue, like the common graves in the cemetery, Zero Ward was part of POW life that we didn't want to look at, that we didn't want to admit was there.

One thing about moving to Zero Ward, or any move I made as a prisoner: I never had to worry about what to take or what to leave behind. I owned nothing. Just pick up my blanket and go. For me, the worst part of moving, whether to another camp or just to another barracks, was the uncertainty and the feeling of depression that usually accompanied the move. There was the fear of possibly going from bad to worse. I think it was during these times of depression that a man was most likely to give up the struggle, to relax and let down his guard, to say the hell with it and die.

For any prisoner of war, moving from one place to another was traumatic. Not that it was physically difficult — it wasn't. Just pick up and go. The difficulty lay in the fact that every camp, every barracks, every work detail was different, and I knew that somehow I would have to make an adjustment for these differences. It must be hard for the reader, who has not walked in my shoes, to fully understand how these sometimes minuscule changes in my lifestyle became so important, important because I knew I was living life like a circus performer on a high wire and a little tilt in the wrong direction could make the difference between life or death.

Consider, for instance, such a simple thing as my sleeping space. To the unaccustomed eye all sleeping spaces looked pretty much alike, space for a body on a shelf made of bamboo slats. To me, because I had to sleep there, my space was different. As a matter of expediency I slept on my side, knees drawn up, one arm folded under my head as a pillow. The bamboo was hard, unforgiving, but somewhere among the strips, the spaces and the bumps on the bamboo, I tried to find a space wider than the others, a sort of hole or cavity where the point of my hip bone would fit more comfortably. This was the most important spot in my "comfort zone" because my hip bone protruded, carried most of my body weight while I slept. Hopefully, no matter how contorted my body, I could find another such "soft" spot for my shoulder. Once established, I always slept in this same position. When I turned over I wriggled and squirmed until I found the same spots with my other hip and shoulder. Without this so-called "comfort zone" sleep was miserable, almost impossible. Once the best position was found, it became habitual and though never comfortable, sleep became at least a little less miserable. Applying this same approach to every tiny facet of prison life, it is easier to see how survival became a matter of constant luck, adaptation, and endurance.

My move from Dr. Roger's barracks to Zero Ward was uneventful, an easy hundred yards. Dr. Roger offered to get a detail of four men from the duty side to carry me down on a stretcher.

Hell no. I had made a number of moves since coming to Cabanatuan, barracks to barracks, duty side to hospital, hospital area to dysentery area, and so far I had made them all on my own two feet. I was determined that this one would be no different. My "hell no," refusal to lie down on a stretcher, wasn't a matter of pride; pride had long since given way to the emaciation, the nakedness, the physical dirtiness of the camp. Saying "hell no" was simply a way of keeping a psychological wall between myself and the awful fear of admitting that I was close to being a bedpatient. This was an invisible line that I knew I must not cross, that once I crossed there would be, for me, no returning. Stretchers were for carrying bodies to the cemetery and bedpatients, though still living, had already accepted death. Dr. Roger understood that I was desperately hanging on to a mental crutch and asked a medic to walk along with me to show me the way. I carried my own blanket and hung my tin plate, my can, and my spoon on the back of my G-string. Independence? Self-determination? I don't know, more like fear of the bogey man, irrational to most people but very real to me. I walked to Zero Ward on my own two feet.

The distance from one end of the dysentery area to the other was more or less the length of a football field. A good athlete can run this distance in about ten seconds. As I was a strong contender for the title of "worst physical specimen," I covered the distance in about forty minutes. My medic/escort walked slowly, patiently, beside me. We talked. We didn't talk about death or sickness or the misery of the prison camp; we talked about home. We talked about home as though it was just over the next hill or just around the corner. No matter that we were from different parts of the country. Home was in our heads, in our memories. It was important that we talk about home just to keep the images sharp; otherwise home might become a fantasy and this damn prisoner-of-war life might become our reality.

It was a clear day. Anywhere else in the world it would have been a nice day. The sun was warm, not yet reaching the burning heat of midafternoon. The sky was a brilliant blue, and the wind was soft against my body. Cabanatuan was in the country, surrounded by pasturelands with lots of high grass and brush and trees. There were mountains in the near distance. When the breeze was right I could smell the green from the countryside. The earth inside the camp was devoid of vegetation, bare, brown, and dusty. My wooden skivies kicked up little clouds of dust as I scuffed along. Cabanatuan was always either muddy or dusty. There seemed to be no middle ground.

My friend told me about the "swimmin' hole" on his farm back in the Midwest. His father had dammed a small creek with rocks until the backed-up water had spread out and formed a sizable pond. My friend had played in it, summertimes when he was a kid. He talked about it as if it had happened in another lifetime. Hell, he had been a big kid just a couple of years ago. I remembered a fishing trip with my father. I must have been only six or seven years old at the time, but I remembered being in a rowboat with my father and another man. We were on a very calm, slow moving river and the water was just like glass. We fished for hours with no luck and then, miraculously, I felt a tug on my line. After much ado I hauled in a small pickerel. It was too small to eat and pickerel are full of bones anyway, but it was the only fish of the day and I was proud, little-boy proud.

My father always said that it didn't matter how many fish he caught, it was the fishin' that counted. In my heart I knew better; it was the little pickerel that really counted.

The medic who walked to Zero Ward with me was patient, understanding. He was a little older than I, maybe twenty-three instead of twenty-one, but I could sense that he was already burned out with the death, the sickness, the absolute misery that surrounded him. We walked down the path chatting as though the prison camp didn't exist. He didn't try to hurry me, didn't try to help, acted as though it was quite the usual thing to take forty minutes to walk a hundred yards. He said good-bye at the entrance to Zero Ward, wished me luck, and went back to his frustrating job, without the least bit of medication, of easing the way for the sick and dying.

I stood outside Zero Ward for maybe ten minutes. I didn't want to go in; I wanted to go back. I wanted to go back to Doctor Roger's barracks or to Sammy Mayer's barracks. Hell, I wanted to go all the way back to the duty side. I wanted to go anywhere except through the door in front of me.

Funny thing about Cabanatuan. There was an absolute hierarchy of status. At the top of the ladder were the prisoners of the duty side of the camp, the men who daily performed hard physical labor for the Japanese. Quite a ways down the ladder were the prisoners in the hospital, the men whom even the Japanese considered too sick to work. Farther down, segregated by barbed wire from the rest of the hospital, were the men in the dysentery area. At the very bottom of this dung heap were the handful of men in Zero Ward. For them the choice was basic: get better or get dead.

There was a great deal of contrast in the treatment of prisoners between the hospital area and the duty side. On the work details from the duty side there was a lot of brutality. There was hard physical labor from dawn until dusk, daily beatings and a tremendous amount of unnecessary humiliation and degradation. These men caught hell from the Japanese almost every day.

In the hospital area the Japanese left us pretty much alone. The Japanese hated the hospital area; they were afraid of it. They came into it as little as possible. They guarded the perimeter, fed us a reduced ration, gave us absolutely no medication, and left us to live or die as best we could. And the dysentery area was inviolate. The Japanese only approached it with surgical masks tied over their faces, and they never came past the fence.

Those of us in the hospital were fully aware of what was happening on the duty side. We knew about the hard labor, the daily beatings, the brutality, yet we considered it a privilege to return to duty. Not that we weren't fearful of the hard labor and the beatings and the mistreatment. We were, but we felt it a privilege to take one foot out of the grave and to be physically able to go back to duty.

I was still hesitating when a man appeared at the door. He was wearing skivies, very short, very ragged trousers, and a wide-brimmed campaign hat, nothing else. The minute he opened his mouth I knew from his accent that he was from the Deep South.

He asked if I was the new guy. He waited until I nodded, then told me they had a bunk ready. He put out a hand to help me up the two steps into the building, then dropped it and stepped back. He paused while I climbed the steps, then pointed to an empty bunk on the far side of the barracks, my new sleeping place. I dropped my gear and waited for the doc to come around.

I moved into Zero Ward with all the expectations of a man being sent to death row. I knew I was expected to die, didn't want to, didn't intend to, but I knew that almost no one left Zero Ward except by the cemetery route. It was not a pleasant prospect, and I was determined to be an exception to the general rule.

I was amazed and pleasantly surprised at the change that had taken place in the ward since I had been there on cleanup detail a few months earlier. Dying prisoners were no longer sleeping on the floor, no longer jammed body-to-body in puddles of excrement. The terrible smell, the stench of death was gone. It was no longer the charnel house I had visited during the big surge of early deaths.

Make no mistake, Zero Ward was still the dying place, still the place where the most hopeless cases lived out their last few days, but the conditions of their dying had improved. Now, instead of more than a hundred men jammed together on the floor, there were only thirty sick prisoners on the ward. And they had beds. Good God Almighty! I hadn't so much as seen a bed since the surrender, had almost forgotten that such things still existed somewhere in the world. They weren't fancy beds. They weren't hospital beds, no white sheets, no fluffy pillows, but they were places to sleep and they were raised up off the floor. Some were rusty iron cots with flat wire springs laced between the side rails. Some were just wooden racks raised off the floor with a hole cut through the boards so a man dying of dysentery could lie naked on the rack and empty his bowels through the hole into a pail underneath. But crude and old and rusty as they were, they were still beds and a big improvement over the bamboo slats.

My bed, the only empty one in the barracks, was a very rusty iron cot, but it was off the floor and it looked good to me. And my bed had a mattress, lumpy, bumpy, and paper thin. Still, it was a mattress and by far the best thing I had seen since the Japs took over.

I sat gingerly on the edge of the cot and tested the mattress with my hands. It was incredibly dirty. Every inch was stained yellow from urine, brown from feces, and in between, just dirty gray from sweat and grime. Still, it was a mattress and it was the best thing that had come my way since the surrender. I sat on the cot and looked at the mattress and tried not to think about the guy who had died on it yesterday, or the guy who had died on it the week before, or the guy who had died on it... I could see the stains on the mattress, could touch them, could smell them, but I had to block out thoughts of the agonies that had put them there. These weren't the stains from bedwetting, these were the stains of death. They were gruesome reminders of how close death really was. I shivered a little, uncontrollably. I didn't want to lie on them, to rub my body against them, even thought of sleeping on the floor, but the lure of the mattress was too strong. Like it or not the stains were there and I had to live with them. The mattress had been wiped somewhat clean with a wet rag, the best the medics could do. I spread my blanket so as to cover it completely. I slept on top of the blanket, never turned it over, always kept the same side down.

A voice from the next bed advised me to relax and get comfortable. The guy that was in that bunk before I arrived checked out of the hotel yesterday. Gallows humor.

I stretched out on the cot, felt strange, alone, isolated, but I knew that in a few days the strangeness would pass. I'd adjust, adapt, accept. In a few days, provided I lived that long, I would feel out this new barracks and learn its ways, become comfortable with it, and this space, this bunk, this barracks would become mine. I got up and rolled one end of the mattress under to make a sort of pillow for my head. Never mind that my feet hung out over the other end, I felt better about it. Already I was easing in, trying to establish some control over this new phase in my life.

The first three weeks in Zero Ward passed, quickly if you look at the whole three weeks, slowly if you reflect on the minute-to-minute struggle. When you are very close to death the totality of life becomes concentrated like tunnel vision. For me it was like being in the recovery room in a modern hospital after heavy surgery. There is a period of time when nothing exists but a blur of consciousness and every sense is focused upon the next breath, the next instant. There is a time when every second is an eternity, when every breath is a herculean effort and every muscle twitch an agony. Then a voice says that it's OK now Mr. Carson, we're taking you back to your room. When you hear that voice you realize, however dimly, that you have passed through an ordeal and come out on the other side.

Life was like that, for me, during those first weeks in Zero Ward. I was aware that bunks emptied and bunks filled. Men came into the ward, died, were carried out and other men replaced them. I ate my meals, somehow managed trips to the latrine, and either slept or was only half conscious most of the time. Then one day I knew that three weeks had passed and I was still there. I was an old-timer on the ward. The worst was over.

Once the crisis had passed I settled into the routine of the barracks. I had no thoughts, no plan for the future, just stay alive, try to get better and try to get the hell out of here.

Life on the ward was amazingly basic, amazingly simple. I had no duties, no responsibilities. My only job was to stay alive. The medic who had met me at the barracks door, the one with the campaign hat and the deep-southern drawl, was named Cowboy. Don't think he ever had another name. We called him Cowboy, he answered to Cowboy, and that was the end of it. Every morning while we lay in our bunks, Cowboy and Dr. Schwartz walked the length of the room and made a head count. On a good day there were thirty patients on the ward. If someone died during the night there were twenty-nine or twenty-eight. Didn't matter. Could have been ten or could have been fifty; the Japs never came to check. They accepted the morning report from the other side of the dysentery area fence. They were terribly careful not to expose themselves to the diseases we carried.

Cowboy, another medic, and Doctor Schwartz lived in a small room at one end of the barracks. In all the months I lived in Zero Ward I never saw into that room. My world had narrowed down to my bunk, the path to the barracks door, and the latrine outside, maybe thirty feet away. The next dysentery barracks was only a hundred feet from Zero Ward, but I never managed to get over that far.

There was no kitchen in the dysentery area. Three times a day Cowboy and another medic would walk to the kitchen in the main hospital compound and bring back our rations in tin buckets. They brought the pails into the barracks and walked from bunk to bunk, serving each man his ration at his bedside. Breakfast was always the same, lugao, wet rice, a sometimes-warm, sometimes-cold, unsalted watery gruel. Usually there was something hot to drink, bitter tea, bitter watery chocolate, or just hot water. The one cupful of rice was never enough, so I drank the whatever just to get the momentary feeling of fullness. Mess kits were washed in a single bucket of cold water in the middle of the barracks floor. Eat fast kid, better to gobble it down and rinse your mess kit early before the water gets thick with the other guys' slop.

After breakfast, the sanitation detail. Another bucket of cold water, the same bucket we had used to rinse our mess kits, and a long stick with a burlap sack tied to one end. The bucket and the mop were passed from bed to bed, from one end of the room to the other. Every man who could get out of his bunk took the mop and swabbed under and around his own bunk. The medics helped the worst cases. No soap, no antiseptic, but at least some measure of cleanliness.

This day I moved a step higher in the POW world. I became a *bon vivant*, a man of substance. Cowboy came by and gave me a mess kit bottom and a canteen cup. Now I owned a blanket, a real mess kit bottom, a real canteen cup, and a spoon. I also owned a pair of wooden skivies and a G-string. In my POW world I was fairly well off. No matter that some poor bastard had to die before his mess kit could be passed on to me — I was glad to get it. I had been eating from a very rusty bent piece of tin and drinking from the same rusty tomato can for more than a year. The mess kit and canteen cup were treasures. When you have almost nothing, every little addition makes a world of difference. I dropped my old tin dish and my tomato can into the nearest latrine. I wish I had somehow managed to hang on to that rusty bent-up piece of tin. I could hang it on the wall, maybe show my grandkids, maybe remind myself that I now have a pretty good life. As they say in the Virginia Slims ads, "You've come a long way, baby."

Doc Schwartz was a good doctor and a regular guy. He cared deeply about every one of his patients. I remember the way he dressed, the way he looked. Ragged khaki shorts, ragged shirt, and he always wore a soft, wide-brimmed straw hat. He was a little short, a little plump, and wore a neatly trimmed black mustache. He would have looked right in place on a sunny street in a little village in the Bavarian Alps. I could see why they gave him Zero Ward, the dirtiest job of all. He was cheerful, projected a jaunty, devil-may-care attitude, yet he was a no-nonsense kind of doctor. On one occasion a prisoner with diphtheria was dying, unable to breathe, already turning blue. In less than thirty seconds Doctor Schwartz performed a prison camp tracheotomy. He threw the dying man on the floor, stuck a pocket knife into the man's throat and twisted the blade sideways. The prisoner breathed through the hole in his throat and he lived.

Surgery in the camps was crude. Sometimes, with no anesthetic, the only alternative was a couple of strong men to hold the patient down. Doc Schwartz had to remove an impacted wisdom tooth with nothing but a pair of forceps and a small bone-cutting chisel. The roots were crossed deep in the bone and Doc had to chip away at the jawbone to free the tooth. The patient fainted, was out of it at least part of the time, but I swear, I think it was harder on Doc than it was on the patient. Schwartz was visibly shaken. When he finished he was ashen, soaked with sweat, and his hands were trembling. If he had been in the States he probably would have gotten roaring drunk that night.

Time passed slowly, one monotonous day after another. I slept a lot. Daytime, nighttime, it didn't matter. My body demanded that I sleep. In my awake periods I began to take an interest in my surroundings, to become more than a collection of flesh and bones waiting to die. I had already outlived my allotted time, the usual week or ten days of life expectancy on the ward, and I was feeling better, getting stronger. Things were looking up.

My new lease on life was like waking slowly from a long deep sleep. My body gained strength, my mind became active, and my world expanded. Not that I suddenly became hale and hearty and started running around; of course not, but at least I began to relate to more than my own bunk and the path to the latrine. My bubble now took in a couple of beds on either side of mine, and four or five beds directly across the room. Mine was a small world, and I think, in some sort of mental self defense, I deliberately kept it that way. I had to know the people who lived and slept close to me; circumstances forced them into my life. Perhaps I didn't want to look at what went on outside my bubble; perhaps it was too painful. Men walked into Zero Ward and bodies were carried out. My own sanity required that I keep some things at a distance, that I not become too much involved. Somehow, as a component of survival, I think each of us encapsulated ourselves in a small world and distanced ourselves from the greater miseries that surrounded us. It sort of reminds me of when I was a little kid. When I didn't clean my plate my mother used to lecture me about the starving children in Africa. I listened, I understood, but I couldn't really connect because they were just too far away.

There was a window near the end of my bunk. No glass, just a square hole in the barracks wall. On a clear night I could lie on my bunk and look up at the stars, thousands of stars, bright points of light in a blue-black sky. They were beautiful in their quiet way, and gazing up at them I found a few rare moments of contemplative peace in a world that was otherwise quite insane. It was such a contrast, the beauty of the stars above, and the misery of the camp below.

I watched the stars for weeks without really being aware that I was watching; then gradually, I began to distinguish one from another. We became friends. Low in the sky, in the far distance, I picked out a constellation called the Southern Cross. I was thrilled because I had never before known one star from another.

And as I watched I became aware that the Southern Cross moves across the sky. In the early evening it would be tilted to one side and as the night progressed it would straighten up and before dawn be tilted to the other side. One night I put two and two together and began to use the Cross as a rough timepiece. Nobody had a watch and our days were governed by sunup, sundown, and the Japanese bugle. I learned that if I got up in the night to go to the latrine and the Cross was on one side it might be near ten o'clock, on the other side maybe three in the morning. It wasn't much of an accomplishment, but I think I felt a little smug about it.

Food, or the lack of it, became the most important thing in my life. I was always hungry. There was never enough to eat, and in the hospital there was no way to supplement my diet, no way. Meals were the same day after monotonous day, wet rice and tea in the morning, dry rice and soup for noon and evening. For me the morning meal was the worst. Watery rice, usually cold by the time it got to us, and tea. No salt or pepper, no sugar or milk, just a cupful of cold, starchy, wormy rice.

Noon and evening meals were the same, rice and soup, the big difference being that the rice was steamed until there were individual grains. We termed the morning meal wet rice, noon and evening meals dry rice. Along with the cup of rice, for the noon and evening meals we got a cup of soup. The rice was always the same, but the soup varied from day to day. Some days the soup would be made from blowguns or pigweed. Some days it would taste of tomatoes or meat or chicken. Blowgun or pigweed soup was made from weeds that grew wild on the farm, often from the tips of sweet potato vines, just weeds boiled in water. Tomato or meat or chicken soup was usually thickened with cornstarch and was more filling than the weed soup. Make no mistake, when I speak of tomato or meat or chicken soup I am not describing soup like mother used to make. Prison-camp soups were mostly water with just enough ingredients so that we could identify them by color or taste. In my cup of tomato soup I usually found three or four tiny pieces of tomato, mostly skins rolled up tightly like little paper cones. It didn't pay to look too closely at the soup. For meat we got only the parts of the animal the Japanese refused to eat. We got the head, the blood, the spleen, lungs, and entrails. Whatever tiny pieces of meat I found in my soup, they all looked pretty much alike. I could never tell what part of the animal they came from. Maybe it was better not to know. I learned not to question my food, just to eat it. Chicken soup, the name implies more than it delivered. There is no way to translate six chickens for three thousand men into a drumstick for each man.

Food never changed much. Can you imagine eating unsalted, unseasoned rice three times a day for three-and-a-half years? Still, I think that some mechanism in my body recognized that survival required adapting to this starvation diet, perhaps slowing down my metabolism. Eventually I recovered my strength, gained weight to a maximum of one hundred twenty-seven pounds, and was able to perform a hard day's work.

Comedy one day, tragedy the next. Today two prisoners, both patients on

Zero Ward, got into an argument. They were separated by a couple of beds and yelling at the top of their lungs. It seemed humorous at the time, even ridiculous, because in our circumstances it really didn't matter a damn whether or not Joe Louis was the greatest boxer of all time. Both prisoners got off their beds and staggered to the aisle. The insanity was that neither was strong enough to stand without holding onto the end of a bed. When they drew close they flailed at one another with the only weapons they had, one with a mess kit, the other with a canteen cup. No damage was done to either fighter. There was no blood, not even a bruise. After a minute or so of ineffective swings, a few hits and a lot of near misses, both were exhausted. They stood in the aisle, holding a bed end for support and glared at each other. Cowboy came out of the back room, raised a little hell and got them both into bed. The irony was that the argument was never settled. Both men died from dysentery within the week.

Dysentery made no distinction between officers and enlisted men. There were two lieutenants and a major within my immediate group of eight or ten beds. They were naked, half starved and racked with disease just like the rest of us. Lieutenant Hall was a Princeton graduate, had been a member of the varsity rowing team. I could tell that Hall had once had a magnificent body, but dysentery had ravaged it, had torn it to shreds. Hall was older than I, maybe twenty-six or twenty-seven, whereas I was twenty-one. I felt that he was a very old man. He was a nice guy, talkative, friendly, cooperative, but there was always some sort of barrier between us. Neither of us was really comfortable in the other's presence. I am sure the fault was mine. It wasn't a question of age; in our circumstances six or seven years wasn't important. Rather, it was a matter of maturity, a matter of education and social background. We were never able to comfortably bridge the gap between Princeton and a high school dropout. I sometimes think the enforced isolation of the Japanese prison camps tended to blur the line between imagination and reality. More so in the hospital area than on the duty side because in the hospital, and especially in Zero Ward I was continually close to death. I am not speaking of a combat situation where death can come in the blink of an eye, but rather of my debilitated state where for months on end I half expected just to quietly die in my sleep and where my body was weakened to the extent that my mind could play tricks on me. There was an evening when four of us, all hospital patients on Zero Ward, were sitting on our bunks talking. We were in the dark and could barely see one another, but it was a warm night and we preferred the companionship of conversation to the isolation of sleep. Somehow the conversation turned to religion. God knows, none of us were religious. None of us had attended Sunday services before the war and certainly none of us had attended a service since the surrender. However, we were all Catholic, at least nominal Catholics. We talked about the Church in general, about schools we had attended, and mentioned a couple of tough old nuns that had cracked knuckles with rulers in the good old days. With the wisdom of young adults who had dutifully memorized their grade school catechism we tossed our ideas about religion back and forth. Here we were, four kids near death in a Japanese prisoner-of-war camp trying to sort out the meaning of life, and our combined knowledge of religion would have made a loud rattling noise had it been encased in a peanut shell.

For my part, I was raised in a religiously divided family. My father was a Mason, an avowed atheist, my mother Catholic. She had me secretly baptized when the two of us visited her relatives in Boston, and it was always, "Don't mention religion in front of your father." With the innocence of childhood I had dutifully memorized and repeated the prayers. I still remember the last line from the Hail Mary, "Pray for us sinners, now and at the hour of our death, Amen." I prayed for us "cinders." I wasn't sure what a sinner was, but the street in front of our house was paved with "cinders," so I knew what a cinder was, and I prayed for us cinders. Some years later in Tampa, Florida, I was still in grade school and we lived directly across the street from the Catholic school and a convent. My mother's cousin, a kindly yet fearsome old nun, was the mother superior. My chief memory is that whenever I got into trouble at school, no matter how fast I ran across the street, my mother would be waiting at the door. Damned Alexander Graham Bell, his telephone was always faster than me.

Anyway, in the darkness of this prison-camp night our talk turned to confession. Now we all knew, or at least thought we knew, that when you confess your sins to a priest, and do the penance assigned by the priest, your sins are forgiven, you are in a state of grace, and if you die you go straight to heaven. On the other hand, if you die with a mortal sin on your soul you go straight to hell. It had been years. I couldn't remember my last confession. None of us could. And mortal sin, missing Mass on Sunday was a mortal sin and missing Mass just once was enough to send you straight to hell. And hell, my concept of hell, was still that of a place filled with fire and lots of little red devils with long pointed tails jabbing three-pronged spears into bare-bottomed sufferers. However vague my concept, hell was a place I didn't want to go.

Suddenly we were afraid. However it happened, however it spread from one to another, we were all afraid, afraid that if we died we would go to hell. I was terrified. I wasn't afraid of death — I had seen too much of that — I was afraid of hell. I was afraid to go to sleep.

Ridiculous, certainly, but ridiculous or not, the fear was nevertheless real. Remember, there were three thousand deaths at Cabanatuan, and most of these deaths occurred at night. Most of these deaths were from a combination of malnutrition and disease. Men didn't die kicking and screaming; they simply went to sleep and when, during the night, some part of mind or body said, "I've had enough," they expired. All of us had had the experience of waking up next to a dead man, or with a dead man a few spaces down the aisle, and all of us were afraid that if we went to sleep we too might die and go to hell. This was not a normal fear. It was the kind of unreasonable fear I remembered from childhood, when as a child of five or six I stood next to an old steam locomotive and the engineer blew the whistle. I knew where the whistle was coming from, knew I was in no danger, yet the noise was so loud that it struck terror to the bone.

Ridiculous or not, the four of us sat silently, staring at one another all through the night, afraid to go to sleep, afraid to die and go to hell. That night had remained sharp in my memory because, I suppose, I think religion, man's connection with God, should be comforting, not terrifying.

It was during my last months on Zero Ward, a time when I was gradually regaining a modicum of health and strength, that I began to hear, through camp scuttlebutt, about a most unusual person in the distant civilian world outside our prison. This man was a Catholic bishop in Manila, and more importantly, I think, he was also a German citizen. Because Germany and Japan were allies in the war, this German bishop of the Catholic Church was accorded limited privileged status. Now I must admit that I never saw this man, this bishop, never even heard the mention of his name, but I can attest to his validity because I, personally, enjoyed what we considered to be some of his minor miracles.

It seems that from time to time he would appear at the camp gate in a rickety carabao cart, and always with something for the prisoners. Foodstuffs, no, he didn't have any. Medicines, they were nonexistent. Food and medicine, basic necessities for the human body, were things he could not find. Instead, the little miracles the bishop managed to deliver became food for the spirit, sustenance for the soul. First of all one of our Catholic padres received a small black suitcase containing the basic necessities for saying Mass. There were the simplest of vestments, a chalice, a paten, a missal, and a small altar stone. With these any outdoor table, any nipa hut, any barracks could become an altar and a chapel. Later the bishop brought in a piano. I had never seen anything like it. It was a tiny thing, almost a toy, thirty-six inches wide and about thirty inches high, but it was a real piano and it made music. We had musicians who could play, and to us it sounded like a concert grand. At different intervals the bishop brought in a trumpet, a slide trombone, and a guitar. By the end of the second year, by the time I got out of Zero Ward and back to the duty side of camp, we had a band, a combo, a four-piece symphony orchestra.

Near the end of the duty side there was an open area with a small wooden platform stage. Before the war when Cabanatuan was built as a training site for the Philippine army, the stage had probably been intended as some sort of reviewing stand. The Japanese permitted us to rig two small lightbulbs on poles, one at either end of the stage.

About once every week or ten days word of mouth would announce an evening program. After dark, after the day's work was done, prisoners would assemble in complete blackness and sit on the bare ground in front of the stage. I remember the scuffling of feet, the rustling of bodies, the quiet conversation. There would be the sound of footsteps on the wooden stage, the scraping of a chair. From the audience, absolute silence. The two lightbulbs would come on and our four-piece orchestra would be on stage. The piano would begin to tinkle, the guitar and the trumpet and the trombone would join in soft accompaniment, and suddenly, in this desolate prisoner-of-war camp, in the midst of the starvation and brutality and death, we would be in Carnegie Hall. The band would play the music of our time, love songs, ballads, light classics. Two POW comedians, a comic and a straight man, would perform their same silly slapstick routines, and Paul Brisco would sing. Paul was a member of the Fourth Marines, and one of a dozen or so that had been assigned to Fort Drum during our war. He had a rich, beautiful voice, had in fact been a cabaret singer before the war. I can still see Paul, clad in no more than a campaign hat and a G-string, belting out "On the Road to Mandalay" with gestures.

All through the performance the POW audience would remain silent, no talking, no scuffling about. Here and there among the audience there would be a Japanese soldier, uniformed but unarmed. The Japanese soldiers would quietly appear in the darkness, take a seat on the ground among the POWs, take in the performance, and just as quietly disappear when the show was over.

Back to Zero Ward. I've been rambling, getting ahead of myself. After that night of stupid, unreasoning terror, when I sat through the night with three other men, all of us afraid to go to sleep because we might die in our sleep and wake up in hell, I became obsessed with the thought that if I could just get a little stronger, just gain a little weight, get out of Zero Ward and back to the duty side of camp, then I would be all right. I wanted desperately to get out of the hospital, to get away from the smell of dysentery, to escape from the stench of death.

The fear of dying in my sleep bothered me for a while. I slept uneasily; I found myself acting foolishly. I would wake in the dark and lie perfectly still, holding my body immobile, holding my breath for those first few seconds of semi-consciousness, while my mind slowly focused on my surroundings, recognized the texture of my blanket, or began to perceive the familiar dim outline of the barracks. It was as though some part of my subconscious was sitting precariously on the edge of an abyss and the slightest motion of my body would send me hurtling over the edge. Scary.

I had one thousand two hundred thirty-one nights as a prisoner of war. Don't know why these few nights were different from all the others unless it was that bit of religion, that fear of dying and going to hell. The possibility of dying in my sleep had been with me for months, especially so since I had been in the hospital area. Most of the prisoners who died at Cabanatuan died in their sleep. Sleep was seductive, a sedative, a magic potion that could embrace a man, hold him, wash away the pain and the misery until he awakened. On the other hand, it was during sleep that a man was most vulnerable. It was during sleep that a man relaxed and let his defenses down. It was during sleep that death was most likely to slip in and whisk him away.

I often thought, during those difficult days, that it would be nice to be able to go to sleep and to sleep in total oblivion, without any pain or suffering, until the POW days were over. When I thought like this, I thought in terms of, "Until this damn business is over." The time frame was elusive but always short, until tomorrow, until next week, until next month. I am not sure that I could have survived had I been able to project ahead for three-and-a-half years.

As for the four of us, the four silly prisoners who sat up all night, afraid to go to sleep because they might die and go to hell, Joe died within the week, Tom and Ed six months and a year later. I was the only one of the four to live to come home.

Across the aisle and down a couple of beds was a Major Rodney. Rodney was an Army dentist in the last stages of dysentery. He was from the Midwest, Indiana maybe. He was close enough to have heard our religious discussion but didn't join in the conversation because he had troubles of his own. Rodney came into Zero Ward ravaged by dysentery and coincidentally, at about the same time our German bishop brought in a small amount of ipecac, as I remember it, a strong purgative. Rodney was chosen, as a sort of guinea pig, to see if the ipecac would help his dysentery. Cowboy mixed the ipecac with water and administered it rectally through a crude enema. The only problem was that Cowboy misread the zeroes in the directions and gave Rodney a huge dose instead of a tiny one. The cure was worse than the illness; Rodney damn near died. For a couple of days and nights he lived on a bedpan beside his bunk. Poor guy never got into his bunk, spent the time throwing up at one end and defecating at the other. I don't know if the medication helped Rodney's dysentery, but it sure cleaned him out.

When he was able to talk, to move about again, Major Rodney came to my bedside. He got right to the point, letting me know what he had overheard our discussion about religion the other night. He knew I was Catholic and asked if I would volunteer to help Padre say the mass, if I would serve as an altar boy.

Me an altar boy? I had never given it a thought. Sure, when I was in the fourth grade a couple of kids used to stay after school and study with the priests in the rectory. Eventually they became altar boys and served Mass, but they were only nine years old.

Being Catholic, I felt obliged to say yes, but I thought I was off the hook when I told him I didn't know a thing about serving Mass. Besides, I was too old. Rodney knew he had cornered me somewhere between embarrassment and religious duty and he was ready. He offered to teach me.

The major produced a ragged missal. He read the priest's lines, and I read and memorized the altar boy's responses. Line by line, verse by verse, we worked through the Litany. In a few weeks I had it mastered. It was a good couple of weeks because it gave me something to think about besides food and disease and misery and death. Finally the Sunday came and Major Rodney and I served Mass together.

Just outside Zero Ward there were two thatched roofs, both open on all four sides. One covered the latrine; the other we used as a chapel. The altar was a chest-high table covered with woven palm leaves. Padre said Mass in his vestments, but underneath the vestments there were bare feet, a pair of ragged shorts, and a lot of bare skin. Rodney wore a pair of shorts, I had my G-string; otherwise we were naked. The congregation, nine or ten nearly naked, emaciated bodies, sat on the bare earth or on benches behind us.

I hope God has a sense of humor. If He has He must have chuckled or maybe even shed a tear or two if He happened to look down and notice our little congregation. Primitive, unreal, but in that hut amidst all the hell of a prisoner-of-war camp I was probably closer to God than I have ever been in a magnificent Cathedral.

It's been more than forty-five years since I attended a Catholic school or entered a Catholic church, but it's funny how some things remain burned into one's mind. From my ninth grade Latin class, Gallia omnes en tres partes divisa est. All Gaul is divided into three parts.... And from a little hut in a prison camp, Introibo ad altare Dei, I will go unto the altar of God. And the response, Ad Deum qui laetificat juventutem meam, Unto God who gives joy to my youth....

Here is another example of the type of isolation that was possible in Cabanatuan. Padre came to our thatched roof chapel every Sunday morning at ten o'clock. He donned his vestments, set up the altar, nodded to the altar boys, and began the Mass. When the Mass was over Padre packed up his gear into a black suitcase and left. I never learned his name and I don't believe he ever learned mine. I never spoke with him, never a single word outside of the responses during the Mass. I never learned where he came from before the Mass, never knew where he lived, never knew where he went after Mass was over. Perhaps, somewhere he heard confessions, but I knew he never heard mine. I suppose it was enough that he volunteered to come into the dysentery area, that he dared to come down to the hellhole that was Zero Ward. My memories of Zero Ward are somewhat ambivalent. On the one hand there was a good side. There was the quiet knowledge that we were safe from the brutality of the Japanese guards. They were afraid of the dysentery area, afraid of our diseases and left us strictly alone. It seemed almost a fair exchange: our illness and near death as a shield against their brutality. And there was the inescapable beauty of the stars at night, more noticeable because there were no lights in camp. This was especially true on the quiet nights when the breeze that blew through the open windows was gentle, yet still warm enough so that I could lie comfortable on top of my blanket. Nights were usually quiet — some moaning and groaning but on the whole pretty quiet. Prisoners on Zero Ward were too weak to do much screaming or thrashing about. Those who died usually died in their sleep, and we wouldn't know they were dead until we found them in the morning.

Daytimes I remember the early morning sun streaming through my window and making a bright spot on the floor beside my bed. As the day progressed the sun would rotate across my bed and off to the other side. I seemed to gain strength from the sun. My body needed its warmth, its comfort.

On the bad side there was the continual starvation, the sickness, the squalor we lived in. My mind became compartmentalized, indifferent to the misery, the stench, the death around me. I ate many a meal with the man on either side of me sitting on a bedpan. I learned to ignore the sound of a bowel movement, the smell of warm feces. And I was not alone in this. While I was thus eating my meal the men on the bedpans would be eating theirs, food simultaneously going in one end and coming out the other. Sordid perhaps, but nevertheless true. Survival as a prisoner of war meant learning to live without the amenities of civilization, concentrating instead on filling just the most basic needs of body and soul.

My life took an odd turn for a while. Another soldier moved into the ward, took a dead man's place way down at the far end of the room, too far away for him to be in my inner circle. We never talked, he was too far away for that, but I overheard Doc Schwartz questioning him when he first moved in. Doc liked to get a little background information on new arrivals. I think, maybe, it helped him decide just how close they were to either living or dying.

Doc usually started by asking a man how he was feeling. The soldier wasn't feeling so good because the damn dysentery had him running day and night.

Everybody had dysentery, so Doc ignored the obvious and asked the man his age. We were all young, this one was twenty-two, going on twenty-three. The kid sat on the end of the bunk to rest. I listened with half an ear as Doc asked the kid about his height and weight. The new arrival answered quickly. He sounded sort of despairing as he told Doc Schwartz that he was six foot two and "about a hun-nerd'n fifteen, hunnerd'n eighteen pounds." The kid brightened up a little when he recalled that he had weighed two twenty before the war.

I listened with both ears now, became curious, interested. Just about my age, I thought to myself. Just about my size. Without any conscious effort I began to run his statistics through my mind. A soldier, twenty-two years old, six foot two, a hundred and fifteen pounds, used to weigh two twenty. Hell, this was me. This guy looks like me.

The thought intrigued me, gave my mind a little busy work, something to do. There were no mirrors at Cabanatuan, no way for me to stand outside myself and look at the real me, to objectively see what I really looked like. I saw others but I never saw me. I saw men so bloated with wet beri-beri that their eyes were swollen shut, faces grossly distorted, features hidden in puffy flesh, bellies distended like long dead corpses rotting in the sun. The sight sickened me, made me want to throw up. I saw living skeletons, no, dying skeletons, too weak to move but still alive and waiting for death. Whenever I could, whenever I was able, I helped them, fed them, comforted them, but I did no more nor no less than what others did for me. I know, during those first years as POW I allowed my mind to play tricks on me. I lived, physically in one world, mentally in another. Physically I was just like so many others, a bag of bones in a tight skin with all the air sucked out, a walking skeleton that had lost a hundred and twenty pounds of solid body weight. But in my mind I was still the same kid who weighed two hundred twenty pounds, the same kid who could run and swim and left weights and play basketball. Now, suddenly, I became aware for the first time that I was looking at another prisoner who had been, and who was, very much like me. Though we never spoke I became deeply conscious of this other prisoner who looked like me. It was the darndest thing. Here was a kid who was completely different from me. Different features, different voice, different mannerisms, another person. Yet subconsciously, because our physical characteristics were similar, I could look at him and see me. He became a sort of alter ego. Looking back over the years I honestly believe that when he was up and around I felt better, stronger. When he had a bad day or a bad week I reacted, worried about my own mortality. As I said, we never spoke,

I never knew the guy. It is just another POW memory that I thought I ought to share. But I am thankful that I recovered, got stronger, got out of Zero Ward and back to the working side of camp before it happened. I never knew, never found out for sure, just when the other guy died.

Life as a POW was hard, unbelievably hard, but now and then some individual incident would occur that was contrary to the usual Japanese behavior. And when something nice did happen the incident became memorable, something like the single ray of sunlight that broke through the clouds on a gloomy day. The sunlight may appear for just a brief instant, but the memory remains long after it is gone.

One such incident occurred just before I moved out of the dysentery area and back to duty.

Zero Ward was situated in a remote corner of the dysentery area. Several feet from one side of the ward was an ordinary three- or four-strand barbed-wire fence, then a narrow dirt road, then another fence. On the other side of the road, beyond the second fence was a mostly open field with the Japanese barracks in the far distance. Across the road and just beyond the second fence was the only building for a quarter of a mile. It was just a shack, maybe fifteen or twenty feet square. As patients in the hospital we had no idea what this shack was used for. We saw it, knew it was there, and dismissed it from our minds. As far as I was concerned the building might as well have been on the moon. It was on the other side of the fence, and the fence was the absolute limit of my world.

One morning four POWs and a Japanese officer came to the shack. I knew it was not an ordinary work detail because there were no guards, no rifles with bayonets, just an unarmed Japanese officer and four prisoners. We shouted back and forth. Naturally, we asked them what they were doing in our part of the camp. They didn't know what they were going to do, only that they had been lined up for work on the farm and this officer had pulled four men from the detail. Whatever it was, it would be better than working on the farm.

I wanted to know what it was like on the duty side, what life was like on the farm. I'd been isolated in Zero Ward for months and was eager to talk about anything with someone outside. He told us the farm was rough as hell, that somebody got their ass beat every day out there. Then he asked how it was with us. They already knew the answer but I told them anyway. With us it was the same old crap. Food was no better, no worse, but there was no ass whipping in the hospital. The Japs leave us alone but there's guys dyin' over here every day.

I tried a little humor, told them they oughta stay out of the hospital because it was full of sick people. They laughed at my little joke, then seriously advised us to just hang on, that the war would be over someday and we'd all get to go home.

The Japanese officer broke up the chatter with a loud shout. While telling them not to talk, he unlocked the door and took the four men into the building.

Several of us stood at the fence on our side of the road and watched with interest. Nothing happened. I could hear the mutter of voices, the sound of things being moved about, but nothing else. An hour passed, maybe two. We still stood at the fence, wanting to know everything that was going on.

The Japanese officer came out of the shack and stopped. He was only thirty or forty feet away. He stared back at us silently for a full minute. We said nothing, stared back. Don't know what went through his mind but I know we were a deplorable sight. Big heads, big eyes, skeletal bodies nearly naked, some only days from death.

After staring at us for a long while the Japanese officer turned away and called the four prisoners out of the building. I was surprised when he spoke in English, very broken but understandable English. He told them to stop work. It was yoshime time. They could rest, they could smoke. Nobody moved. None of the four had a cigarette. Rest yes, smoke no.

The officer noticed and growled to himself, a growl that seemed to come half from his throat, half from his nose. Arrrgh. It was a sound typical of the Japanese. The officer looked at us again, half a dozen skeletons staring at him mutely over a barbed-wire fence. He took a pack of Japanese cigarettes from his pocket and very carefully laid four cigarettes and a box of matches on the doorsill. The four prisoners on the work detail stood silent, waiting.

He told them that it was OK to smoke, OK to rest. The four prisoners nodded agreement, wakaru, they understood. Each one took a cigarette, bowed and thanked him with a polite arigatou. The Japanese officer held up his hand, a signal to wait. He pulled a knife from his pocket, picked up a stick from the ground, opened the blade and made a series of whittling motions with the knife.

For a second time the Japanese assured the prisoners that they could smoke, that they had his permission to yoshime, to rest. Apparently he was satisfied with the work they were doing and had decided to reward them with a little break. He strode to the side of the shack, sat on a small box, and began whittling on the end of his stick. His back was toward the prisoners, toward us. His voice drifted over his shoulder as he cautioned them. When they finished their cigarettes they would go.

All four prisoners lit up, appeared to be enjoying their smokes. It took a full minute for realization to set in. This Japanese officer had set a time frame, they had until they finished smoking, and the officer was sitting, whittling, with his back toward them.

One prisoner went into the building, the other three formed a human chain to the fence. Objects appeared, were passed from hand to hand, the last man tossing them across the road to us. Gauze bandages, a bottle of pills, a pair of surgical scissors, all came flying across the fence. God damn! The shack was full of medical supplies. Thousands of us had died and the bastards were sitting on a building full of medical supplies, American medical supplies, medication that could have saved a lot of lives. Incomprehensible, but true.

The four prisoners on the work detail moved quickly but carefully. One item at a time was passed along and tossed to us. The four had to be cautious. They were understandably scared. They knew that if they had guessed wrongly, that if the Japanese turned around, they would surely be beaten, tortured, then executed.

On our side of the fence we absorbed the stolen medicines like a sponge. We picked them off the ground and tossed them through the barracks window. Everything. Everything was out of sight. The action went on for a full five minutes. Bandages, bottles, came across the fence and disappeared into Zero Ward. The officer stood up, his back still toward us.

Without turning he called the detail to attention, told them smoke time was over, that it was time to close the door and go. He led the work detail away without ever looking back.

We gathered up our loot. There wasn't a hell of a lot. Mostly gauze bandages, some sulfa pills, a little quinine, all together enough to fill a couple of shopping bags. Not much, but nevertheless the only medical supplies I saw in two-and-a-half years at Cabanatuan. Among thousands of sick POWs in desperate need, not much. It was like a teaspoon of water to a man dying of thirst, not enough to do any good but damn well appreciated.

No one will ever know the name of that Japanese officer, but there are a few ex–POWs who will always remember his small gesture of humanity.

November 1942–July 1944:
Brutality of Work
on the Farm

I was feeling better. Not good, but better. Things had changed for me. I was stronger both physically and emotionally. Somehow, without any medical intervention, my body had adapted to the rigors of POW life, to the starvation diet, to the dysentery, beri-beri, malaria. My weight was up to a hundred and twenty pounds. Not the picture of health, but I knew that I wasn't going to die.

I was restless, I wanted out. I felt I had survived the worst and now I wanted to get out of Zero Ward, out of dysentery area, out of the hospital. I wanted to breathe air that didn't stink of dysentery and death. It was November. At least I thought it was November. We had no calendar and no contact with the outside world. There were times when I wasn't quite sure even what year it was, much less the month or the day. But my birthday was in November, and if I was right, if this was really November, I would turn twenty-two on the sixteenth.

I put it up to Doc Schwartz when he made his morning rounds. I caught him as he stood at the foot of my bed and told him I wanted to go back to duty.

Doc didn't seem surprised at my request. He acted as if it was the most normal thing in the world for me to say. Of course he asked me how I was feeling, how my dysentery was getting along. And of course I lied, told him I was down to seven or eight times a day. That wasn't too bad, now was it? I really wanted out. I saw the trace of a smile. Doc Schwartz was nobody's fool. He probably knew better than I just how I felt, just how many times I went to the latrine, just how I was getting along.

He lifted my foot and pressed his thumb hard against my shin. When he took his thumb away the flesh didn't spring back. A half-inch depression showed in the flesh, stayed there. I saw the hesitation in his eyes so I beat him to the punch, talked fast to convince him, didn't give him a chance to voice an objection. I argued that my beri-beri was lots better, almost gone, used to be much worse. Reminded him how my feet used to swell up till the skin split. That doesn't happen any more.

Schwartzie was one hell of a good doctor. He knew medicine, and more importantly, he knew men. He knew I was not well, far from it. But I think he realized that I had crossed the line that separated those who were apathetically just waiting to die from those who were determined to live. I assured him I could make it on the duty side. I was certain that I could.

Doc told me he would fix things so I could go over when the burial detail went back in the morning. He called me son. Doc called every patient son. He turned away, then came back and held out his hand, wished me good luck, told me to take care of myself over there.

I didn't sleep much that night. I lay awake thinking, trying to project into the future, a confused mess of thoughts tumbling through my mind. My night was filled with typical POW thinking, filled with apprehension, anxiety, antici-pation. It was as though I had made a long exhausting climb up an impossible hill. I knew things would get better once I reached the top and started down the other side. If only I didn't reach the top and find yet another hill just beyond.

Morning came and with it the usual morning meal of cold watery rice, a good cupful, no less, no more. I gulped it down, rinsed my mess kit, rolled my blan-ket, and was ready to go. There was no fanfare; nobody tried to make a big deal out of it. Just the usual good-bye, good luck, take care of yourself over there, that sort of thing. "Zacky," Lieutenant Zackerman, made a joke. He tried to sound like a parent talking to a kid going out on his own for the first time.

In his high thin voice he told me not to worry. If I couldn't make it in the big world outside I could always come back to Zero Ward and have my old bunk back.

I had to smile. Zacky had less to joke about than any man on the ward. Sure, he had survived diphtheria, but he still lay in a fetal position and the tendons in his legs still would not straighten out. He still screamed aloud every day when the medics tried to straighten his legs, and he still weighed less than seventy pounds. He was nothing more than a tight skin over a skeleton, broomstick arms, broom-stick legs, and a big skeletal head. He had nothing at all going for him except a damn strong determination to live. Yet Zacky still made jokes.

It was awkward. I felt ashamed, guilty because I was leaving. I knew it was good for me, that it was right that I should leave, but we had shared so much, these mostly dying men whose names I didn't even know. We had shared so much, and now I was the lucky one that was walking out.

Cowboy, our medic, came to my bed. He was going to walk with me to the hospital area gate. Zacky's bed was by the door. His body didn't move, but his eyes followed me as I left the ward. I remember how his dark eyes seemed so big in that skeletal head.

Cowboy and I walked through the gate, the gate that separated dysentery area from the main hospital. Damn, I felt good when I passed through that gate. Dur-ing my months in Zero Ward a lot of good men had come and gone, but those who left, all of them, had been carried out to the cemetery. To my knowledge I was the first to walk out on my own two feet.

The daily burial detail had finished their grisly job of dumping naked bodies into a common grave. I joined them as they walked the quarter of a mile from the hospital area to the duty side of the camp. Cowboy stayed behind, a corpsman whose job was to tend to the sick and dying. He didn't have to stay, to go back to the misery of Zero Ward, but I think he was bound by a sense of duty in a place where duty no longer existed, constrained by his own moral values in a place where moral values no longer applied. Our medics, our corpsmen, were a strange breed. In the confusion of the camps no one would have known they were corpsmen had they not volunteered. Yet volunteer they did and they performed their dirty job under the most difficult conditions. As bad as things were in the hospital, life there would have been much, much worse had it not been for our dedicated corpsmen.

When I left the hospital with the burial detail I never looked back. That door slammed shut in my mind, and I never wanted to open it again. My thoughts raced ahead, trying to project into the future. Could I make it on the duty side of camp? How would I fare on the farm? Could I survive the brutality of the guards? A jumble of thoughts raged through my mind, one pushing another out of the way before I had time to absorb the first. What would the farm be like? Was I strong enough, well enough, to make it? What barracks was I going to be in? What work detail would I be on? Was I jumping out of the frying pan into the fire?

Once inside the gate the burial detail disappeared, each man going to his own barracks. I was left standing alone. A man approached. Enlisted man or officer, I couldn't tell. He was just another sunburned body in a G-string.

He asked if I was Carson, said he was waiting there to meet me. I nodded assent. Of course I was Carson, who else could I be? The sunburned prisoner in the G-string pointed the way to a barracks in the far corner of the camp, told me it was my new home, and left without another word. I was on my own. I was finally on the duty side and not sure that I was going to like it.

Barracks twelve was empty, or almost empty. Most of the men were on work detail on the farm. Joe Ross, the first sergeant, was there because being barracks leader excused him from work on the farm. Two or three prisoners lay stretched out on the bamboo, prisoners unable to work but not sick enough to be sent to the hospital.

Joe looked up as I entered through the doorless end of the building, asked me if I was the new guy, and without waiting for an answer asked me my name. I gave him my name and told him I was just out of the hospital. Joe looked at me curiously, then gave me some fatherly advice. He told me to fall in with the work detail the following morning and that the farm was rough as hell. I was to pick one guy, stick with him, do what he did till I learned the ropes. He told me to watch out for the guards because some of them were mean as hell, to keep my head down, work hard, and don't do anything to attract the guard's attention. He paused and looked at me squarely for the first time, then said that I'd probably be all right if I did what the other guys did and watched my ass. He stood up, shook my hand, led me down the aisle and showed me where I was to sleep.

Joe Ross was a master sergeant, a typical Army career man. During the pre-war depression years he had found his niche in life, settled into the military routing, and had fully intended to remain in the military until he retired. In his late forties, Joe was a fatherly figure who mothered the men under his command. He called every soldier boy. He patted an empty space on the upper shelf, said that was where I was supposed to sleep, and told me to throw my gear up there and take it easy until the work detail was called out in the morning. He looked at me quizzically and asked me if I owned a hat.

I didn't. The Japanese had taken it away in the first week. He went back to his sleeping space near the front of the building, fished around for a moment, and came back with something in his hand. He thrust it toward me. He said for me to take it because it was hot as hell on the farm and I would need to have something on my head. The last guy in my sleeping space had left it behind and I might as well have it.

The shapeless rag in Joe's hand was a hat, a battered, nondescript rain hat. Wasn't much but I knew it would serve to keep the sun off my head and I was glad to get it. Joe handed me the hat and turned away. It was a small hat and very old, just big enough to sit on top of my head with a two-inch brim all around for a little shade. Once it had been a good rain hat, but the rubberized material had long since disintegrated and peeled away. What was left were three layers of dirty brown cloth that flopped limply in all directions, but it was a hat of sorts and it would keep the sun off my head. I tried it on and it fit.

Lordy me, did I feel well dressed. One floppy hat and a G-string. I was ready for the farm.

I climbed to the upper shelf, spread my blanket and staked out my sleeping space. It was small enough, just enough room to take my lengthwise doubled blanket. I was back on the bamboo. My precious thin mattress had stayed behind in Zero Ward. For the next few months this small rectangular space on the bamboo slats, this area covered by my folded blanket, would be home. I stretched out, tested the bamboo to find a place to put my hip bone, found it, and waited. The work detail would be coming in around sundown, and then I would meet my new bunkmates.

I was worried, scared, filled with apprehension. Any move, any change in the prison camp was filled with tension, misgivings. When you have absolutely no control over your life or the conditions you live in, no matter how bad your present situation is, it is familiar and any move from the familiar into the unfamiliar is emotionally stressful. I wasn't really fearful, it was just that I was filled with uncertainty about tomorrow, about my first day on the farm. Fear is what you feel when you stand at attention while a Japanese soldier places a bayonet at your throat and you know the next command means life or death. Fear is what you feel when the bombs are on their way down, when you are running for cover and aren't sure you'll make it before the explosions tear your body to shreds. Fear, uncontrollable bowel-emptying fear, is what you feel when an artillery shell passes between you and your partner, destroys your sandbag gun emplacement, and doesn't go off, when you realize that six inches to one side and it would have taken off your head, and had it exploded, little or nothing of your body would have ever been found. Apprehension, on the other hand, is when you fully expect to take an ass whipping on the farm and just hope that somehow you won't have to.

Late in the afternoon the workers came in from the farm. I watched as they came through the gate. They didn't march; nobody marched in prison camp. They simply trudged along in close-knit groups of about a hundred men each. They didn't march, but each work detail came through the gate as a unit. There were no stragglers; the guards with their clubs saw to that.

I could see that the men were tired, hungry, bedraggled. All were barefoot and many were limping. A few had to be helped along by their fellow prisoners. These last were men who had either become exhausted from the heat and hard work or men who had been badly beaten by the guards. Almost without exception their faces, their naked bodies, had been burned to a deep walnut brown by the sun. Fresh from the hospital, I was going to stand out like a white bandage on a sore thumb.

The Japanese made no attempt to segregate prisoners by service. Army, Navy, Marines, Air Force, even a couple of civilians, we were all lumped together in one homogeneous mass, and barefooted in a G-string we all looked pretty much alike. Life in the POW camps was a great leveler and quickly reduced all of us to a common denominator, a Japanese POW. Aside from facial features, hair color, and body build we were indistinguishable one from another. Army, Navy, Marines, when they bled their blood was the same color. While they lived they endured the same deprivations, the same hardships, the same brutalities. When they died the common graves at Cabanatuan made no distinction between branch of service.

The work details came in, we lined up for supper, and I met my new bunkmates. Johnson, Clifton Johnson, a tall, very skinny soldier, would live and sleep in the space on one side of me. Mahoney, just Mahoney, a not-so-tall but just as skinny sailor, would sleep on the other. We were complete strangers but the prison camp had thrown us together, and together we would share our trials, our sufferings, our most intimate thoughts, our very lives for the next several months.

Johnson and Mahoney knew I was fresh from the hospital area so they asked about the hospital, about dysentery area, about Zero Ward. Burial details had come back with horror stories, and these guys were scared of the hospital. Me, I was comfortable with the hospital. It was familiar, I had been there. I was scared of the farm. That was one thing I learned from the prison camps. A man is most at ease with whatever he knows best. Johnson and Mahoney were afraid of the hospital. I was afraid of the farm. In the camps I met infantrymen who would not consider flying a combat mission in an airplane, who thought it was sheer idiocy to fight from a sealed gun turret in a battleship.

Another rather sleepless night. Whenever I woke up my thoughts turned to the next day, my first day on the farm. Dawn arrived, was announced by a bugle call in the distance. The barracks began to hum with quiet activity.

Johnson told me to get up. It was time for breakfast.

I climbed down in my single G-string, would go to work in the same G-string. I was ready for work. Life was so simple because the Japs had made it that way. The barracks was a place to sleep. There were no facilities for washing or shaving, therefore no need to wash my face or shave. My only piece of clothing was the G-string I slept in, so I didn't need to get dressed.

There was a steady flow of men to and from the latrine. Johnson and I and Mahoney joined in. Rule number one every morning: Unload. Take a leak, take a crap if you need to. Get rid of everything before you go out on the farm because there aren't any latrines out there. And take a drink of water just before you go because there ain't no water out there either.

I did. In any new situation in camp there was a period of quick adjustment. The trick was to watch the other guys who had been there before me, to see what the old-timers were doing and copy them. It was wise not to attract the attention of the guards by doing something stupid.

Breakfast was the usual — wet rice and bitter tea. We ate sitting on the ground outside the barracks. Eating inside attracted too many flies and bugs. After eating we lined up for work. Johnson was full of good advice. He told me to do whatever he did and I'd probably get by OK. He also told me that the best thing to do was to keep my head down and my ass up, to keep moving and always look busy. The guards didn't like to see anyone standing up and looking around.

The day's work details lined up in hundred-man groups. Johnson and I and Mahoney stayed together. For better or worse we were a trio.

Mahoney and Johnson seemed calm enough but they were old-timers. They did this every day. I was the new kid on the block and I was nervous. I wanted to learn the ropes quickly, not to make any damn fool mistakes.

I didn't have to worry about the guards with guns. I knew they wouldn't bother me. It was the guards with the clubs that I had to watch. They were the honchos, the guards in charge. The ones with the guns were just along to see that nobody escaped.

The Jap guards took over just inside the gate. One honcho, the guy in charge, and a handful of guards armed with rifles and bayonets took over each group of prisoners. It was the luck of the draw. No way to know in advance which guard was going to take charge of a detail. No way to know in advance where we were going or what kind of work we were going to do.

There were stacks of tools just outside the gate. Here a pile of hoes, there a pile of picks and shovels, a stack of litters, another of tin water buckets. Mine was the third detail to go through the gate. The first picked up hoes, marched off with hoes over their shoulders. The second took litters, wooden platforms about six feet long and four feet wide with long handles at each corner so they could be carried on the shoulders of four men. My detail walked right on by. No tools for us today.

Mahoney thought it was a good detail. We'd probably spend the day pulling weeds or planting. The whole detail seemed to lighten up and breathe easier.

An unseen voice from back in the ranks happily announced that there would be no idiot sticks for us today. I learned later that the prisoners themselves called the heavy, awkward Japanese hoes idiot sticks.

We walked for a good quarter of a mile onto the farm. I was barefooted and the sharp rocks that surfaced the path cut into my feet. We were all barefooted but I was just out of the hospital and my feet hadn't toughened up yet. The rocks hurt like hell and I knew my feet were bleeding. I learned there were two reasons why the Japs made us leave our wooden skivies inside the gate. First, they were useless once we got off the paths and into the soft dirt and mud of the fields, and second, a barefoot prisoner wouldn't get far if he tried to escape.

The guards spread us out along the edge of a planted field — long rows of plants with furrows between the rows. The honcho shouted and waved his club. None of us knew what he said but we all understood his meaning. Go to work.

I was no farmer but I could see that we were here to pull weeds. I bent over and got busy. Our guard that first day was "Air Raid," the head honcho on the farm. Air Raid was older than most of the guards and he outranked everybody, told them all what to do.

All the guards had names, Japanese names. I doubt that we ever heard them and if we did we didn't understand, so we named them. Air Raid got his name as a sort of hangover from the war. While we were still fighting, whenever a lookout saw a plane approaching he would call out "air raid." The alarm would be passed from man to man and everybody would take cover. On the farm, whenever this particular guard approached, the first prisoner to see him would whisper, "Air Raid," and the alert would be passed on from man to man. On the farm it simply meant that trouble was on the way. Don't talk, don't look up, keep busy, work like hell and maybe avoid a beating. So the name stuck and the head guard became "Air Raid."

This was my first good look at Air Raid. I watched him as we marched out on the farm, glanced at him whenever I could while I was working. He was an average-sized Japanese, shorter than most of the prisoners but huskier because we were half-starved skeletons. On that day I thought Air Raid had no distinguishing features except big black-rimmed glasses and one gold tooth. That was the first day. Within weeks I was able to identify each of the guards, even at a distance, by their body shapes, voice, or by the way they moved. I could be working on the farm, head down, hear a footstep and see a leg out of the corner of my eye, and know immediately which guard the leg belonged to. Air Raid didn't like us but he tolerated us. It was his job to see that we worked the farm, and he did. He treated us with a no-nonsense, businesslike attitude, always severe, often brutal. Once in a great while he showed a sense of humor. I didn't know it that first day on the farm, but Air Raid was to become an important part of my life for the next several months.

It seemed a simple enough job, pulling weeds. I thought any damn fool could do it. I was wrong. At first things went easily, not too many weeds in a row. I bent over and pulled them with my fingers. No dice. Within fifteen minutes my back gave out. There was no way I could work bent over all day. I tried squatting on my haunches, pulling weeds as I duck-waddled along the row. This didn't work either. In less than ten minutes my thighs and calves were screaming. I spent the day crawling on my hands and knees. Things went easily for a while. I crawled along my row, worked hard, and pulled every weed clean as a whistle. I watched the other prisoners and kept up. Then I ran into trouble. I hit a spot where it seemed that every weed in the Philippines had decided to grow in my row. I gradually fell behind. Even the weeds seemed against me. The grass pulled easily, but some of the weeds had roots that went deep and clung tenaciously to the ground. I had to dig these out with my fingers. I paused for an instant to rest, wiped the sweat from my eyes with the back of a dirty hand. Whop! I felt the impact of a heavy blow across my buttocks. I was still on my hands and knees and the force of the blow almost put me face down on the ground. Damn, it hurt. Instinctively I turned to see what had hit me. It was Air Raid. I recognized the big black-rimmed glasses and the one gold tooth. I took another lick across the shoulders and Air Raid shouted angrily in Japanese. Hyaku, hyaku, hurry, hurry. He pointed with his stick. I hustled to work faster, began pulling weeds with both hands. Air Raid watched for a moment, then apparently satisfied, moved on down the line of prisoners.

It was my fault. I had been careless and had allowed Air Raid to sneak up behind me. But it was my first day on the farm and I had much to learn. Basic. Know where the guards are at all times. Be alert. Be wary. Protect your ass. It would happen again, over and over again, but as I became more "farm wise" hopefully it would happen less frequently.

Working the farm was like learning to drive a car. All the book learning, all the fatherly advice aside, nothing could substitute for the actual experience of sitting behind the wheel. Likewise on the farm. My bunkmates, Mahoney and Johnson, gave me lots of free advice. Don't do this. Be sure and do that. Watch me, do what I do. This was great advice, these were great tips, but the real learning came under the clubs of the guards on the farm.

I thought the day would never end, but it did. Air Raid blew a referee's whistle. We wearily straightened up, formed on the path, and marched back to camp. I was exhausted, dog tired, sunburned to the point of blistering. My knees were raw, my fingers bloody and I had taken two terrific wallops across the back, but I had made it through my first day on the farm. Chowtime. Rice and weed soup. I was almost too tired to eat. Still wearing the dirt from the farm I crawled onto my blanket, found a space between the slats for my hip, and dropped off to sleep. Deep heavy sleep proved a sedative, blanked out the throbbing hurt across my back.

There would be other days, lots of other days on the farm, and there would be other beatings, but I felt I could toughen up to the work, become "farm wise" and as the saying went in the camp, learn to cover my ass. True, there would be lots of other days on the farm, but there would never again be a first day. I felt relieved; in a sense I had won a small victory. Tomorrow would be a better day.

After two or three weeks, work on the farm became routine. I did become "farm wise," and I did learn to "cover my ass."

Beatings, usually painful but not life threatening, were a daily occurrence. Not that I got beaten every day; I didn't. I could not have lived through it. But a few guys, sometimes in my group, sometimes elsewhere on the farm, got the hell beat out of them every day. I think the beatings were a sort of Japanese incentive program, the Japanese way of getting the maximum effort out of a recalcitrant labor force.

The farm at Cabanatuan seemed huge, maybe as much as a hundred or even a hundred fifty acres. There was no machinery, not a single tractor. The closest approach to mechanization was a POW with a pick or shovel or hoe. Every square inch of the farm was torn out of virgin soil by hand. And the farm at Cabanatuan was not like the farms at home in the Salinas Valley, where cabbages and celery and strawberries stretch in beautiful even rows as far as the eye can see. Our farm at Cabanatuan had dry spots and wet spots, rocky spots and soft spots. On the farm I quickly learned that though all men are supposed to be created equal, all rows on the farm were not. When the Japanese spread a hundred men across a field to pull weeds, some would face patches where the ground was hard and there would be few weeds. Some would find patches where the ground was soft, moist, and where weeds and grass grew in abundance. The problem was to keep things balanced out, to keep a hundred men working across a field in a reasonable straight line, because the men who fell behind, for whatever reason, usually got an ass whipping. This Japanese way of looking at the work ethic resulted in maximum effort from the prisoners. Sure, occasionally some guy with an easy row would slow down and give the others a chance to catch up, but a man could get walloped for that too. The usual result was a dog-eat-dog attitude, POW pitted against POW. Hope for an easy row, put your head down and work like hell, and cover your own ass.

Air Raid was a tough guard to work for. He was a hard taskmaster, a strict disciplinarian, but he wasn't vicious. When things went right, when he got the level of production he expected, he actually seemed pleasant, affable. And little by little he developed his own unique sense of humor. One day when we had finished the day's work, when we were forming on the path and waiting to march back to camp, Air Raid struck up a conversation with one of our officers. Now Air Raid didn't understand our language. His English was limited to such phrases as "hurry, hurry," or "work faster, work faster." Our officer complained about the lack of food, that what little food there was was sadly lacking in vitamins. Air Raid listened attentively, but I think, with little or no understanding. Perhaps he understood a little, perhaps not, but it was plain that the word vitamins was completely new to him. He kept repeating it over and over, vitamins, vitamins. His pronunciation was atrocious. The American officer patiently and slowly explained to Air Raid that vitamins would make the prisoners stronger, healthier, that vitamins would make them work harder, faster. Air Raid seemed to dimly comprehend and went away repeating to himself, vitamins, vitamins, vitamins. A few days later Air Raid appeared on the farm with a hardwood stick, thicker and heavier, but shaped like a Samurai sword. On the side in large black letters were the words, "vitamin stick." Air Raid laughed uproariously as he explained to the officer that a swat across a prisoner's backside with his "vitamin stick" would also make a man work harder, faster.

Food was abominable. Rice and soup, day after day after day. Never enough of it and almost never any variety. Our rice was most often old and wormy, the dregs of whatever the Japanese had, and our soup, "blowgun soup," made from the boiled tips of camote vines. Camotes are an inferior type of sweet potato. We planted a lot of camotes on the farm, but the Japanese took most of the crop away from us. Occasionally we would get a few to put in the soup. Camotes, like sweet potatoes, grow deep in the earth, but the vines, growing on top spread out in all directions. It was the tips of these vines, the last ten or twelve inches, that we regularly broke off and boiled into soup.

We supplemented this meager diet whenever we could. I scuffled for extra food just like everyone else. Pigweed grew wild on the farm. The Japanese considered it a weed to be pulled and thrown away. They didn't seem to mind if I carried a pigweed bush into camp. Pigweed is crisp, tender, edible, and has a bland taste, something like lettuce. Whenever I could manage, I would bring in a small bush from the farm, and after my rice and soup, a few mouthfuls of raw pigweed helped to fill in the hollows.

Hunger, constant prolonged hunger, makes almost anything edible seem palatable. Food, or the lack of it, became a driving force in my life. I ate anything and everything that I could put in my mouth and swallow. For me, I can remember only two exceptions. When I first came to the working side of camp I noticed that at first light I would see a number of what we called "night crawlers" lying on the ground. Night crawlers were huge dead worms. They looked exactly like the worms I used as fish bait when I was a kid except that these were huge, maybe seven or eight inches long and as big around as my finger. During the night these worms came up out of the ground and when I saw them they appeared already dead. Disgusting creatures. I paid them little attention until I realized that by sunup they had all disappeared. How could dead worms crawl back into the ground? They couldn't. Actually some of the prisoners with very strong stomachs were gathering the night crawlers, slitting them open, removing the single strand of gut, boiling and eating them. I toyed with the idea. I was sorely tempted, even picked up a couple, weighed them in my hands, kept them in my canteen cup all day, and threw them away that night. I just couldn't quite bring myself to eat the slimy creatures. I heard that they were tough, tasteless, and chewed up like soft gristle. But for those with the intestinal fortitude to eat them they were probably a good source of protein.

My second exception was snails. Now and then I worked near or in the shallow irrigation ditches that crisscrossed the farm. Occasionally I managed to grab three or four snails that clung to the weeds in the ditches. The kitchen crew would let me put them in a tomato can full of water and set it next to the cooking fires.

When boiled the snails pulled out of their shells quite easily, and they were palatable, tough but palatable. There were, however, some snails that were off limits even to my stomach. Immediately bordering the cemetery and only a few feet from the graves was a long pond, and just below the cemetery was an irrigation ditch. Once in a while it was my job to stand waist deep in the pond and fill buckets for the rest of the detail to carry out for irrigation. Snails here were plentiful but I couldn't rid myself of the idea that they had fattened on water that had seeped through the thousands of rotting corpses in the cemetery. I couldn't stand to even touch the damned things.

Life as a prisoner of war affects men differently. Though all of us, officers and enlisted men alike, ate the same food, lived under identical conditions, endured the same brutalities, most managed to hang on to a modicum of dignity and self respect, but a few men lost it altogether. The Japanese, perhaps even unintentionally, had reduced us to the status of animals. Outright resistance was impossible, but we fought back in more subtle, more personal ways. Case in point. I'll use myself as an example. I was barefooted, nearly naked. My only article of clothing was a single G-string which barely covered my genitals. I was skin and bones, at least a hundred pounds below my normal weight. There were no facilities for taking a shower, not even for washing my face. I had not taken a bath, had not shaved, had not cut my hair for months. I was a dirty filthy stinking mess. I slept with a single blanket between my body and the bamboo slats. Everything I owned lay at the head of my sleeping space, a spoon, a mess kit bottom, and a canteen cup. The Japanese had stripped me of almost everything that gave me my identity, but short of killing me they could not take away my mind. My mind was my secret weapon, my last line of resistance. Whenever I was forced to bow to show politeness and respect to a Japanese guard I kept this thought running through my mind: "You little son of a bitch. You think I'm bowing out of respect. I'm really thinking just how much I'd like to kill you with my bare hands." Not much, you think, but for me it was a toehold on sanity that kept me from falling into the abyss.

In my barracks we had a little problem. Its solution was both heartless and humorous. The barracks was a stark bare place. There was absolutely no furniture, just a thatched framework with a dirt floor and two bamboo shelves along opposite sides of a long aisle. Each of us had a sleeping space on one of these shelves. We were overcrowded, slept four men in each ten-foot bay, but if we slept with our heads close to the wall there was room for a fifth man to lie lengthwise across our feet and next to the aisle. We did our best to keep the barracks reasonably clean and ate our food sitting on the ground outside to avoid attracting more flies, bedbugs, and other vermin into the building.

The bottom bamboo sleeping shelf was a foot off the ground, bare earth underneath. On the bottom shelf directly below my sleeping space a fifth man slept lengthwise next to the aisle. He was too lazy to get up in the night and walk outside to the hole in the ground we used as a urinal. Instead he would simply roll over, stick his penis through the bamboo slats, and urinate on the ground beneath.

In a few days the barracks smelled just like the latrine. The air was filled with hundreds of fat green blowflies and we even found maggots crawling on the ground. We begged, pleaded, even threatened, but the guy still urinated on the ground under his bed. One night I heard the now-familiar splash, smelled the stench of warm urine. I started to scream at the man, to ask him for Christ's sake guy, get up and go out to the latrine. Then it happened. Somebody on the shelf below, it could have been any one of four men, kicked hard against the bamboo slats. The bamboo went together like scissors and pinched the offender's penis hard between two bamboo strips.

It must have hurt like hell because the man screamed out loud. In an anguished cry the man screamed that they were hurting him, that they were killing him, begged them to turn him loose.

Except for the screaming and cursing there was silence in the barracks. Old Joe Ross, our barracks leader, came stumbling down the aisle rubbing his eyes. Joe asked the screamer what the hell was going on, asked him what the fuss was all about. The screaming and cursing slowed long enough for the man to tell Joe that they had him caught between the slats, they're cutting it off. He pleaded with Joe to make them let him go. Trapped face down the man couldn't look up at Joe.

The old sergeant took in the situation, reflected for a moment, told the man that he got it in there by himself and he was going to have to get it out by himself.

The screaming went on for a good ten minutes, alternately cursing, pleading, threatening, then someone relented. The foot relaxed, the bamboo strips separated, and the man pulled his penis out. No, his penis wasn't cut off, just badly bruised, sore as hell for a few days. But he never again urinated between the slats.

Our Japanese captors, in a fit of generosity, began paying us ten cents a day, Japanese script, for every day we worked on the farm. A magnificent gesture. Now I would have money to buy anything I wanted. Except, there was nothing to buy. A pack of American cigarettes, holdouts from last year's Christmas package, sold for ten dollars. A cup of raw brown sugar, when it was available, also went for ten dollars. This meant that if I worked every day on the farm, if I didn't get sick, if I didn't take a beating that required me to lie in barracks for a couple of days, if all went well, in just a little more than four months I could buy a cup of raw sugar. If it was available.

About the same time the Japanese started giving the farm workers ten cigarettes a week. These were Japanese cigarettes, "green deaths" we called them. Horrible tobacco. I didn't smoke and always traded mine to my advantage. Lastly, the Japanese set up a quota system, a required number of workers a day on the farm. On a good day, if we had no sick men in the barracks, one man, never more than two, could stay in barracks and have a day off. Rotated through the barracks, it meant that I might get three, maybe four, days off in a year.

Doesn't sound like much, ten cents a day, ten cigarettes a week, three days off in a year, but taken together these things became commodities that were worth something, commodities that could be traded. Around these things, the ten cents a day, the ten cigarettes a week, and the rare day off, a small racket sprang up, a racket dominated by a group of seven or eight sharpies that I likened to a POW mafia. Not that they did anything wrong, they didn't. It was just that these seven or eight guys were hustlers — smarter, cleverer, more sophisticated, more worldly wise than the rest of us — and thus they were able to take advantage of us.

Somewhere these sharpies got their hands on a deck of cards and started a poker game. Nobody had to play but the game was open to everybody. Most of the POWs were just kids, uneducated kids, dummies just like me. At the end of the month, what the hell could I do with my two dollars and twenty or thirty cents in Japanese money? In about four months I might be able to buy a cup of sugar. But with a little luck, if I could just win a couple of hands at poker, I could buy that same cup of sugar right now. Bingo! There went my two dollars and twenty cents Japanese.

I wasn't the only sucker with grandiose dreams. Almost everyone had the same get-rich-quick idea, and almost everyone chipped in their pittance to the ever-growing wad of money in the hustlers' pockets. In a matter of days each of the sharpies had accumulated three or four hundred dollars in Japanese script. The racket, as I called it, started when one of the hustlers walked through a barracks waving a fistful of money, asking if there was anyone there with a day off who would be willing to take his place on a farm work detail for a day in exchange for a cash payment of ten dollars.

There were always takers. After all, what can a guy do with one day off every three or four months? And ten dollars would buy instant gratification, a pack of cigarettes or a cup of sugar right now. Some of these sharpies never had to work a day on the farm for months on end. The Japanese didn't give a damn who worked on the farm; all they wanted was the right head count. I knew that when my day off came I could make a deal.

I worked for Smiley today and got a new lesson in brutality. Not brutality to me, thank God, but to another man on the work detail. I don't think I could have taken it. Smiley was one of our regular farm guards. He got his name because he always seemed to be smiling. Not that it meant anything. Smiley could beat a man to a pulp with a green bamboo stick and never lose his smile. My job this day, my detail's job, was to clear and prepare new ground for planting. We picked up tools outside the gate. Hoes, picks, and shovels. Hoes were for clearing away grass and weeds, picks for turning the soil, and shovels for leveling, for breaking up the clods and getting it ready for planting. There was a scramble for tools, every man trying to find a tool that would work to his advantage. I grabbed a hoe, one of those "idiot sticks" that were so damned awkward to use. Most of the hoes had big heavy blades, seven inches wide, fourteen or fifteen inches long, and all hanging on one side of the handle. There were a few small, light, American-style hoes, but if you took one you were suspect. To the Japanese mind, little hoe meant little work. If you took a little hoe you had to work especially fast to keep the stick off your backside.

Our work site was a field of Cogon grass, tough grass with serrated edges that grew as high as a man's head. Just brushing against Cogon grass could draw blood; working through it, naked, was a nightmare. The field was virgin soil, never touched before, never tilled. Today we had an unusually large number of guards. One honcho, Smiley, and lots of soldiers with rifles and fixed bayonets. Perhaps they thought it too easy for a prisoner to slip away in the tall grass.

We started across the field, hoers cutting grass and weeds, behind them prisoners with picks turning the soil, behind them the shovelers breaking up clods, leveling. For me, what worked was to place my left foot against a clump of saw grass, carefully push it over, then cut off the roots with the hoe. If my foot didn't slip on the saw grass I wouldn't get cut. It was hot. I was sweating heavily. If there was a breeze it didn't get down below the tops of the Cogon grass.

The day went well enough until the middle of the afternoon when we came across an anthill. The minute I saw it I knew we had a problem, wished I was somewhere else. Anthills were nothing new. We had leveled a lot of them while clearing the farm, but we hated them. They were big, big conical piles of earth, four or five feet high, and like beehives are full of bees, these hills were full of ants. Usually, in every anthill we found one, sometimes two cobras that came out fighting mad. We knew the cobras were poisonous, and they were scary. On the other hand, if we killed one, Smiley would be pleased. He considered cobra meat a delicacy.

Best way to handle an anthill was for a dozen prisoners with picks and hoes to surround it, barefooted, of course. At a given signal we would all start hacking away, picks and hoes, doing our very best to cut it down, level it in a couple of minutes, and run like hell before the ants knew what was going on. Believe me, when we leveled an anthill the Japs got maximum effort. We worked hard, we worked fast, and with a lot of dancing and jumping about, got in and out as fast as we could. Smiley was something of a sadist. He liked anthills. He liked the cobras we flushed out. He liked the excitement. He liked to see us jump and swear and slap at our feet. Smiley liked to see us suffer, and all the while he wore his perpetual smile.

All my life I had thought of ants as little nuisances, tiny black things that marched in long solemn lines across the countertop to gather round a drop of maple syrup. Sometimes they were the larger red ants, fire ants that stung and tried to ruin a picnic. But these Philippine ants were like nothing I had ever imagined. In the first place they were monstrous, a good half to three quarters of an inch long with fat heavy bodies like a large honeybee. And they were mean. They came at you like the fierce little warriors that they were, warriors dressed in black and yellow stripes. And when they bit they drew blood. They didn't "sting," they *bit*. Each time they bit, their pincers took out a round piece of flesh about the size of the head of a straight pin, and you bled. We called them "tiger ants."

On this particular day we had almost leveled the anthill and the tiger ants were swarming. I was bitten again and again. Joe, one of our crew, broke, dropped his hoe and ran away from the anthill, slapping at his legs. Smiley went berserk. Smiley made Joe stand at attention while he gave him a half dozen heavy blows with a green bamboo stick. Joe's mouth twisted in a grimace every time he got hit. Smiley wasn't satisfied. He shoved Joe toward the anthill and shouted in Japanese. Joe hesitated and Smiley motioned for Joe to do pushups in the middle of the swarming ants. Smiley struck him again and again, beat him to his knees, beat him into a prone position. Every blow with the bamboo left a white mark across Joe's back. The guards held the rest of us at bayonet point while Joe did pushups. It didn't take long. A few pushups and the tiger ants were all over Joe's body. Joe gave a low groan, almost a sigh, and fainted, collapsed face down on the ground. Ants were all over him. Little rivulets of blood oozed down from his arms, his shoulders, his legs, his body. After a few seconds Smiley let us drag him off the anthill, let us brush off the ants. Joe swelled up like a poisoned pup and got a few days off. And Smiley? May he rest uncomfortably in hell for a long, long time.

Master Sergeant Joe Ross came to me after dark. Hot damn! My turn for a day off. Won't have to work the farm tomorrow. It was a lovely thought, a day of rest, but I had been there once before and I knew it wold be boring as hell. This was Cabanatuan, a Japanese prisoner-of-war camp. Couldn't wash my clothes, I had no clothes to wash. Couldn't wash my body, there was no way to take a bath. No movies to see, no stores to shop in, no books to read, no errands to run. Nothing. My friends, if I had any, would all be working on the farm. Nothing to do but sit alone in an empty barracks and wait for the farm detail to come in.

I walked down to the poker game and announced that I had the next day off and was willing to take someone's place on the farm. It didn't take long to get a response as one of the sharpies immediately offered me ten Japanese dollars to take his place and started counting out the money. He told me to be inside the gate when the morning work details formed, and he would step out and I could take his place. He pushed the money toward me but I didn't pick it up, not yet. I could see he was eager to make a deal and so was I, but I didn't want to let on. I wanted more.

I let the money lie on the bamboo. I didn't want his ten dollars, what I really wanted was a canteen cup full of raw brown sugar. I told him so. We started to argue, deadly serious. The stakes were a cup of sugar for me and a day off the farm for him. He started by telling me that I could buy a cup of sugar from someone else with ten dollars. I knew this was a bad deal for me. Maybe yes, maybe no. Maybe there would never be any more sugar. Maybe all I could do was wipe my ass with his ten dollars. I knew I couldn't beat these guys at poker, that was their game, but the farm was mine so I played my trump card. I told him that the guards had been on the warpath lately and they had been beating hell out of everybody on the farm. For me, it wasn't worth chancin' a beating for a lousy ten dollars, but a cup of sugar was worth taking a chance on. I waited, waited to see if I had pushed the right button. I could see the sharpie weighing the possibilities in his mind. He had a cup of sugar, but he damn well didn't want to part with it. On the other hand, he wouldn't enjoy it so much if he went on the farm and took an ass whipping. Reluctantly he made his decision. He agreed to give me the sugar but told me that I had damn well better be there to take his place when the workers lined up in the morning. I grinned to myself. I had won.

The sharpie went back into his barracks, came back with a small cloth sack. Very carefully he poured sugar into my canteen cup. I tapped it on the wood to make the sugar settle. He cautioned me not to tap it so hard. He was willing to fill it full but it wasn't supposed to be hard packed. Packed or not, any way he filled it I had won.

It was almost dark. I climbed to the upper shelf and hid the sugar under my blanket. I tasted it with my finger, dipped my finger in the sugar and licked it. Golly! It was good. First taste of anything sweet since the chocolate from last year's Christmas package ran out. I slept on my side with my knees drawn up, cup of sugar tucked tightly against my belly. During the night I carefully ate two spoonfuls of sugar. I held each spoonful in my mouth till it melted, then swallowed it a tiny bit at a time. Made it last as long as I could. It was hard to stop. I wanted to hog it down, to eat every deliciously sweet grain, to make myself sick to the point of throwing up. Wanted to eat the whole cupful even though I knew it would go right through me, make my dysentery worse. Common sense prevailed. I was going to take another man's place on the farm tomorrow. For what? Was I willing to chance a beating for this momentary satisfaction? Not yet. I had more important things in mind for this cup of sugar.

Morning came. Same old wet rice for breakfast. I gave Johnson and Mahoney a spoonful each to put on their rice, took another spoonful for myself. The cup was half empty. No more sugar on the rice, no more fooling around. Time now to get some serious mileage out of what sugar I had left.

Johnson and I and Mahoney and the fourth man in our sleeping bay stripped the bamboo shelf, took everything we owned outside and spread it on the ground. Now for the important part.

In the daytime hundreds of bedbugs and body lice hid in the crevices where the bamboo strips crossed the two-by-fours. Underneath the strips made ideal hiding places because we couldn't get to them. At night, alerted by our body heat they crawled out and feasted on our flesh. They made the nights miserable. Now was our chance to get even with the little bastards, to actually get rid of them for a few days.

Carefully, so as not to waste a single grain, we spread the sugar along the two-by-four framework, a few grains of sugar in each space between the bamboo strips. It took all the rest of the sugar to do a good job. I knew I'd be disappointed as hell if my idea didn't work.

Sounds crazy, doesn't it? Feeding precious sugar to the bedbugs. But it wasn't. At Cabanatuan, bedbugs were as much our enemy as the Japanese. And we were using POW strategy to lay a trap for the enemy. Satisfied with our preparations we fell in with the farm detail and went to work. All day long on the farm I was thinking about that half cup of raw sugar, thought about it so much I darn near let Air Raid sneak up on me.

In the afternoon when work details came in off the farm, first thing I did was rush to my sleeping bay and check it out. Had our plan worked or had I thrown away half a cup of precious sugar? Johnson came in from another detail and we checked it out together. The sugar was still there, little piles between the bamboo strips, but it was white instead of brown. Swarms of tiny black ants, attracted by the sickly sweet smell of raw sugar, had eaten away the syrup and left stacks of little white grains that were tasteless and looked exactly like salt. Suddenly Johnson laughed out loud and slapped me on the shoulder.

I didn't know why he was laughing. He pointed his finger. I followed his pointing finger with my eyes. There was a long trail of little black ants going back to their nest. I grinned with elation. We had won. Our stupid little strategy had worked. Here and there along the trail of ants I saw an ant dragging a bedbug. I watched one little ant in particular. He had a bedbug firmly by the leg. The bedbug was ten times bigger than the ant, but the ant was dragging it in a very businesslike way toward the nest. Seems like the ants had found the sugar, and while scouting the cracks and crevices to see if there was more, had found the bedbugs in their hiding places. If the ants had cleaned out all the bedbugs we could sleep without the biting and scratching for two or three weeks before a new plague of bugs migrated in from other parts of the barracks. I felt smug, happy, self-satisfied. This was a victory, a small one to be sure, but in a world where even small victories were few and far between, it really made us feel good.

One day in camp is little different from another. First, days, weeks, even months merge into a monotony of hunger, misery, and brutality. There is no end in sight and death seems the final solution. The big surge of dying is over. We no longer lose twenty, thirty, or forty men in a single day, but burial details, much smaller burial details, still go over to the hospital. Darwin was right. It has been survival of the fittest. It has taken almost two years but the weeding-out process is over. The weak and the wounded have passed away. Death is still with us but from now on the death rate will be slower, more constant. The men who are left are those who were physically strong, mentally strong, and above all, lucky as hell. Personally, I feel that death is no longer tapping me on the shoulder, beckoning, but that he is still lurking in the darkness a little distance away.

Hunger is always with me. The only time my belly is full is when I drink lots of water. Everybody does it, at least, everybody tries it, but some are better than others. At first I thought all farm work details were the same, work hard and watch out for the guards. As I became more "farm wise" I began to prefer some farm jobs over others. Harvesting details were the best. We regularly harvested string beans, camotes, and pechi, a kind of Japanese cabbage. Not that we got much of it; the Japs took almost everything we grew for themselves. But at least the harvesting details gave me a chance to grab a bite or two of raw vegetable now and then. Camotes were the best. We dug camotes out of the ground with picks then carried them to litters at the edge of the plot. When things were just right, when I was at the far end of the field and away from the guards, and when I found a small piece of camote that had been broken off by a pick in the digging, I could pop a bite into my mouth, dirt and all, and chew it and swallow it before I got back with my armful. Had to be careful though. Guards would accept a camote that had been broken by a pick, but a camote with an obvious tooth mark could bring a severe beating. Mornings were best for this kind of scrounging. In the afternoons, with the hard work, the hot sun, and no drinking water, my throat often became too dry to swallow. Careful, careful, careful, that was the watchword. The Japanese were hell on even the slightest infraction of their rules, and to them, this was the worst kind of thievery. A prisoner caught with three or four hot peppers in the lining of his hat was beaten unmercifully, then forced to eat a canteen cupful of peppers. The peppers were worse than the beating. Big blisters on his mouth and lips and the peppers must have burned all the way through. Another prisoner caught stealing from the farm was beaten with clubbed rifles until they crushed one of his kidneys. He lived but he did a lot of screaming at night for a while. Bad medicine, stealing from the farm.

The guards were unpredictable. One day I killed a small snake with my hoe. A little fellow, big around as my finger and about fifteen inches long. Too small for the guards. They only liked the cobras, the big fat snakes. I carried my little snake openly in my hand, and I think, because I didn't try to hide it, they let me keep it. Inside camp I cut off the head, skinned it, removed the single strand of gut and coiled it up in a small tin can. The cooks let me shove the can close to the cooking fire. That night I had boiled snake with my rice. It was just like eating a long, long chicken neck.

A new peril on the farm today. Many Many, our honcho, no longer carries a green bamboo stick. He had replaced it with a pick handle. Much heavier, much more dangerous. Most of the other guards will follow his lead. Many Many is so named because these words seem to be all he has learned of the English language. He rages in Japanese, then with gestures tries his English, many many. Translate it any way you please, but when he says "many many," it means many many work, work harder, work faster, and he is liable to punctuate his words with blows from the pick handle.

Many Many loved to walk behind the row of prisoners as we worked our way across a field. I hated to see him coming down the line, dreaded the moment when he passed behind me. Most of the time Many Many passed me by, but once in a while I would get a wallop with his pick handle. God damn, but it hurt. The lick across my buttocks or the back of my legs hurt like hell for a moment, then everything would go numb. The real hurting came later when the numbness wore off and the burning and throbbing began. A pick handle across bare flesh sounds exactly like an overripe tomato dropped on a cement floor.

Even with something as fundamental as Many Many and his pick handle there was a right way and a wrong way to handle it. From experience I learned that even when I knew Many Many was behind me, even when I steeled myself for a blow, I couldn't help giving out with a whoosh of air, a gasp, or a grunt of pain. But if I kept on working, working faster if possible, he would pass on by. To show protest in any way was to guarantee further beating. To cry out in pain, Many Many liked that and would pursue it further. Best way was to learn to ignore the impact and pain of the first blow and to go on working as though it never happened. Hope Many Many would pass on by. Don't give him an excuse to stand you at attention and give you a tongue lashing because he would surely give you more blows before he put you back to work. Talk about survival techniques, we learned them and learned them well.

Fight back? How in hell do you fight back when resistance means death? How do you fight back against an enemy who holds all the aces, the food, the guns, the absolute power of life and death? I found a way. It wasn't mine alone, many prisoners used it, but I like to think of it as mine because I used it whenever I could and because I got tremendous inner satisfaction whenever I worked it successfully.

The first time it happened it was an accident. The second and third and numerous times after, it was as deliberate as I could make it. Dysentery was still with me. Not death threatening any more, but bad enough to require seven or eight bowel movements a day. When nature called I had to answer, whenever and wherever the call came. Inevitably, some of nature's calls came while I was working on the farm. There were no latrines on the farm, nothing. The only possible solution was to scrape a hole in the earth between the furrows, squat in place in front of the guards and a hundred prisoners, perform in public, scrape a little dirt over everything, and go on with my work. Painful because it was dysentery, degrading because it had to be done in public. Psychologically, I suppose, all in my mind, but I found it more embarrassing to have a bowel movement in the field than to have one sitting on the latrine even though both were in full view of anyone who happened to be near. Anyway, the first time I was close to one of the guards, not the honcho who supervised the work, but close to one of the guards who stood around the perimeter of the field. I got the guard's attention, bowed, and indicated that I had to go to the toilet. The guard nodded and motioned me farther into the field. He kept motioning me to go farther until I was a good fifty or sixty yards away. Satisfied that he was satisfied, I took off my G-string and squatted. My little guard let out a roar in Japanese that had me standing at attention in a split second. I couldn't understand the words, but I knew from the tone of his voice that I had done something wrong. I was facing the guard. I didn't want a beating and I didn't know what I had done to cause this outburst. The guard motioned with his hand, arm extended palm down, hand fluttering up and down. I turned and squatted again. Another roar in Japanese. Plainly I was confused. I didn't know yet that when a Japanese extends his arm and waves his hand toward the ground he doesn't mean sit down, he means come here. Thank God my little guard wasn't one of the mean ones. He stomped angrily into the field and I stood naked, facing him. I expected the worst. The guard took me by the shoulders and pushed me down into a squatting position. He nodded his head affirmatively, up and down, and told me this was joto. I knew joto meant OK. He turned me around so I faced away from him and shook his head negatively, told me this was not joto, that this was not OK.

I must have looked either terribly confused or terribly stupid because the guard patiently went through the whole thing again.

Now I understood. Squatting, facing the guard was OK. Squatting with my backside toward him was not OK. I understood that he didn't want to be mooned.

I could have my bowel movement if I squatted facing the guard. It was an insult to make him look at my backside while I was doing it. It took a few days but gradually I determined three things. First, the Japanese guards did not want to look at my backside. Second, they hated to leave the dry perimeter path and walk into a muddy field. Third, they were reluctant to hit a man while he was having a bowel movement. Maybe it was too messy, beneath their dignity.

It was a situation made to order. Every once in a while I would drop my G-string and squat with my bottom facing a guard. I usually got the desired response, shouts of anger, protest. I pretended ignorance until the last possible moment. I had to be careful not to pull this too frequently, and to spread it out amongst different guards. Most of the time I got away with it, but even when I got a harangue and a couple of licks at the end of a work day it was damn well worth it.

Big work detail today, maybe a hundred fifty or two hundred men. Can't figure this one out. We're not going out on the farm, going instead toward the Japanese Army barracks. Whatever it is it will be a dirty job, something the Japs can't do or don't want to do themselves. We have lots of company. Guards with rifles behind and four honchos, Air Raid, Charlie, Many Many, and Smiley walking in front. We have an officer with us too, a Japanese officer who is new to me. Must be something important. I hear a rumor that we're going to move a building. That's why we have so many men. I have visions of two hundred prisoners dismantling the building, carrying it piece by piece to another site and putting it back together again. Sounds reasonable to an American mind. Two hundred men just might be able to pull it off in a day.

Shows how little I knew of the Japanese mind, of the Japanese way of thinking. I saw the building. About seventy feet long and thirty feet wide. It was made of wood and it looked big. There was a pile of logs beside the building, long thin logs like long thin telephone poles. Maybe we could use these logs as rollers, put them under the building and push it, roll it from one place to another. I was wrong again.

The Japanese had cut small holes along each side of the building, small holes four feet apart and about thirty inches off the ground. We shoved the long poles through these holes, all the way through the building, and out the other side. I began to catch on. The officer who figured this one out must have been a mechanical genius. Through the door and into the building. There was no floor. Two hundred prisoners spread out across twenty long poles. Everybody lift. Nothing moved. The building was too damn heavy. A few clubs across a few backsides and the building got lighter. We grunted, groaned, picked the building off the ground and moved it a hundred yards. Must be how the ancient Egyptians built the pyramids.

Back in barracks the bedbugs have taken over our bamboo shelf once more. I spent the nights scratching, slapping, stinking up the place with their sickening odor. Sergeant Ross, our barracks leader, came up with a brilliant idea. We dismantled the bamboo shelves and carried them outside the barracks a section at a time. We laid them flat on bare ground, left them out all day while we worked the farm. The ground was flat, hard, and the sun was hot as hell. By midafternoon the bedbugs were crawling out from under the bamboo slats and running for cover. A few yards on the burning hot earth and they were dead. The little black ants hauled them away. No, we didn't get them all. No such luck. There had to be cracks and crevices where they could hide, where the heat of the sun couldn't reach them. But we did get a lot of them and life at night was a little better.

The guards have figured out a new way to punish us. Demoralizing and degrading to us, somehow enjoyable to them. They pull this whenever we don't do enough work on the farm. Doesn't mean we didn't do a good day's work, just means they were looking for an excuse to hurt us. At the end of the work day, if they aren't satisfied with production, the guards will line a work detail up in two rows, one row facing the other. Then they order us to slap one another. The guards walk up and down behind the lines with clubs. If you aren't slapping hard enough they let you know with a club across your back.

Another routine day at Cabanatuan. I wake to the sound of a bugle in the half light of early dawn. I slept poorly. My night was a series of short naps punctuated by twisting and turning. The damn bedbugs and the lice are back in full force. I can feel the lice crawling over my body, but they are only an irritant. I can ignore them, tolerate them, in general pay no attention to them except when I am sitting on the latrine with my G-string in my hands hunting seam squirrels, cracking their fat little bodies between my thumbnails. Bedbugs are the worst. How I hate the little bastards.

First thing I do in the morning is head for the latrine. I bypass the muddy urinal if I see an open hole on the six-holer. More comfortable and more efficient. On the six-holer I can urinate, defecate, and hunt seam squirrels at the same time.

Toilet paper is something of a luxury. Luckily I do not smoke so when the Japanese issue our weekly ration of ten cigarettes, green deaths, I trade mine for toilet paper. I feel rich when I have a little stack hidden under my blanket.

We line up for work just inside the gate. This is butterfly time, butterflies in my stomach. These moments before work are filled with worry and apprehension. No matter how many times I got out on the farm these first few moments are always the same. We form up on one side of the fence; the guards are waiting for us on the other.

This is pot luck. I never know which guard is going to pick up my detail. If I'm back in the crowd I may not know till we start to work. I have my preferences. I like to stay away from Smiley and Charlie. They're both mean bastards. Love to hurt us just for the hell of it. Best guard to work for is Webfoot. He's big for a Japanese, the biggest of the lot, maybe five foot nine and a hundred ninety pounds. We call him Webfoot because his feet are big, spread out like little snowshoes. Webfoot is right off the farm and doesn't seem to give a damn for traditional Japanese discipline. With us his favorite words are speedo, speedo, but he says it with a grin. Webfoot never hurts anyone. He carries a club but seems reluctant to use it. As long as we do a reasonable amount of work he seems satisfied. If a Japanese officer comes around Webfoot will begin hollering speedo, speedo, and he'll whack a few backsides with his club, but it's all for show. There's never much force behind his blows. Smiley and Charlie are at the bottom of my list, Webfoot at the top. Air Raid, Donald Duck, and Many Many are somewhere in the middle, neither gentle nor vicious, just somewhere in between.

My details picks up litters, flat four-handled contraptions about the size of a double bed. We're going to do a little harvesting today. The litters are for carrying in whatever we pick up from the fields. And our head guard is Air Raid. I don't worry much about the guards with rifles and fixed bayonets. They mostly stand around the perimeter and act bored as hell. Air Raid is different, unpredictable. If he's in a good mood we may have a good day. If not, some of us will surely catch hell before the day is over.

My bare feet hurt and I am limping badly before we get to the plot we're going to harvest. The paths on the farm were originally surfaced with large sharp gravel. Most of this has worked down into the paths, but there are still a lot of sharp points that stick up to cut and bruise the flesh.

Air Raid gives us a talking-to in Japanese. None of us understand a word of what he says. He spreads us out along the rows and we begin harvesting pechi, a Japanese cabbage that grows tall and thin like celery. We begin picking and Air Raid roars his displeasure. I stop in my tracks and wait. I've heard that roar before. Air Raid walks along the line swinging indiscriminately with his vitamin stick. I get more than my fair share of blows. I can tell in advance, this is my day on the cross. The licks across my backside and the back of my legs hurt, but at least I have a little flesh, a little padding there. When I get hit across the back and shoulders there's nothing but a taut layer of skin, and I bruise right to the bone.

Air Raid motions us back to work, but he stands by the litter and watches me. I pick a good armful of pechi and carry it back to the litter. More blows. Air Raid isn't satisfied and I don't know what in hell I'm doing wrong. Air Raid walks me into the field and points with his stick to a pechi. I pick it and he seems pleased. I pick the next plant and he wallops me again. What the hell? After another harangue in Japanese, Air Raid picks an armful for me, loads me up and motions me back to the litter. I begin to vaguely understand that he wants me to pick only pechi that has gone to seed, but I honestly can't tell one pechi from another. Air Raid goes off to another part of the field, leaving me with the armful he himself picked. I am getting desperate and still don't know which pechi is right or wrong. In big trouble I do the only thing I can think of. I stay as far away from Air Raid as I can, pretend to pick pechi, and hang on to the armful Air Raid picked for me. Time to go home. The litters are loaded. Triumphantly I bring in the very armful that Air Raid himself picked for me earlier. No good. He was just in a helluva bad temper, and I was the goat for the day. He took off a wooden clog and began hitting me on the head. Three or four licks and my head was cut. Blood ran down my face and neck. When he saw the blood Air Raid relented, put on his wooden slipper and went off grumbling. I had to help carry a loaded litter. Eight men lifted it shoulder high, then the four men on the handles had to carry it into camp. The sharp rocks cut into my bare feet and Air Raid walked beside me all the way in.

When I got into camp I found a puddle of rain water and washed the dirt out of the cuts on my feet. The cuts on my head would heal and the bruises on my back would go away, but if my feet got infected I could be in real trouble. One bad day that sort of merges into three-and-a-half years of good and bad days. Should have been better, but could have been a heck of a lot worse. That night I slept an exhausted sleep. Bedbugs be damned.

When I get back home.... The most frequently heard phrase in the prison camp was "when I get back home." Fantasy, pure fantasy, like a little kid saying that when I grow up I'm going to be a fireman. Fantasies, they were impractical, impossible flights of the mind that extended a ray of hope, that helped to block out the grim reality of our daily life.

Conversation among prisoners tended to follow a somewhat regular pattern, governed for the most part by the tough routine of camp life. Early mornings, wake up chit chat, was mostly filled with meaningless utterances. If I said good morning, I had at least tried to make verbal contact, maybe to the guy sleeping next to me, maybe to the world in general. If there was a reply, it might not be a direct answer, more likely just an acknowledgment that I had reached someone.

My favorite way to start the day was to complain about my aches and pains. I never got used to sleeping in bamboo slats. I complained but nobody listened. Mahoney would bitch about the bedbugs that had kept him awake all night, and Johnson usually wanted to go to the latrine right away.

At the urinal, nothing. Six men standing in stinking slippery mud and urinating in the same hole in the ground will tend to ignore one another. In a place where all bodily functions are done in public, the only possible privacy is in silence.

Early every morning without fail Joe Ross's voice calls us to the front of the barracks. Joe went through the daily routine of calling every man's name from a ragged sheet of paper. Didn't know why he bothered. Everybody was there. Nobody had a weekend pass. Nobody stayed out all night. Unless a man was dead he would be out front of barracks for roll call. Don't see why, but that's the military way. If Joe Ross and nine other guys were locked in a cell he'd still hold roll call every morning.

After roll call, chowtime. Wet rice and bitter chocolate made with just chocolate and water. My God, why can't they give us a little salt for the rice? Plain unseasoned rice. A little salt wouldn't be too much to ask. For chow we break into our little groups. Johnson and Mahoney and I have a table now, and a crude bench to sit on. Rough, but it beats sitting on the ground. Mahoney found a couple of old boards in some tall grass behind the latrine and we rigged this bench under the eaves, under our window. Crude, a board to sit on and a board to eat from, but we have come up in the world. From now on this will be our place to sit and talk and eat, our territory.

Talk at breakfast is limited to bitching. Bitching about the food, bitching about a poor night's sleep, bitching about the guards. Doesn't take long. Very little food and tasteless. I gulp it down. We finish eating at the same time. Not that we have good table manners, but just in case. On those rare occasions when I am sick or for any reason cannot eat all of my rice there is always someone to help. Nothing is wasted, nothing thrown away. If I leave a spoonful, even half a spoonful, there is always someone to scrape my mess kit clean. Me too. I am not squeamish, have no false modesty. I'll gladly scrape the last bit of rice from another man's plate.

Not much time between breakfast and line up for work details. I hurry to the latrine, urinate, vacate my bowels and kill a couple of seam squirrels. Again, not much time but this is a necessity. By this ritual of going to the latrine right after breakfast I may eliminate a later conflict with the guards. I use my tin can and take a big drink of water. There is no drinking water on the farm. Johnson has a canteen but I don't have one. If we stick close together he will share his water with me, but if we get separated it will be eight or nine or ten hours before I can get any more water.

I am ready for the farm. Johnson and I and Mahoney move up to where work details are forming. This is butterfly time. We try to appear nonchalant, but in reality we are full of nervous apprehension. Inside the gate the Japanese leave us pretty much alone. Outside the gate is another world. Outside the gate I will be under the close scrutiny of the guards, completely at their mercy, under their clubs. A good day on the farm is a day of hard work, naked, under a blistering sun, but without brutality. A so-so day is the same but with a little hell raising and a few licks from a club thrown in. A so-so day is when someone else gets badly beaten and I only get a couple of licks. A bad day on the farm is when I am the goat, when I get a beating, when the guard focuses his attention on me.

It helped to know what detail I was going on, or to know that Air Raid was on the warpath yesterday, to hope he might be in a better mood today. Whenever I heard that a guard had struck a man for no reason at all, or that Webfoot's detail was pulling weeds or that Smiley was a real son of a bitch, I stored these tidbits of information away and used them to help me get ready for my own work day.

In a bitter world, POWs embrace the lighter moments, look for a reason to laugh. We occasionally found such a reason during the rainy season during the morning lineup. In the Philippines it rains heavily during the summer months. Lots of rain, lots of wind, now and then a typhoon. On those rare days when it rained so hard that work on the farm was impossible we got a day off. The Japanese canceled the work details and we remained huddled in our barracks. When we lined up for work detail on a day when a storm was threatening, the POWs would, in their own way, pray for rain.

A voice would implore J.C. to send it down, to give us a day off. A second and third voice would take up the call, look longingly at the sky and ask J.C. to please let it rain. Soon the whole formation would echo with shouts asking J.C. to send it down, to please send it down.

All of this, of course, done in a way that would not antagonize the guards. We lined up quickly, correctly, and had the right head count. So we laughed and we shouted and we played our little joke for all it was worth. A couple of times J.C. heard our prayers and we went back to barracks. Most days He wasn't listening and we trudged on out to work the farm.

The Japanese always looked puzzled. It was plain they didn't have the slightest idea who J.C. was or what we were shouting about. It was our own private joke and it gave us occasion to laugh. Sacrilege, maybe. Blasphemy, possibly. But if J.C. heard I don't think he would have minded.

Not much chance for conversation on the farm. Low mutterings to the man on the next row or short sentences as I walked past, but guardedly, carefully. Too much conversation brought the wrath of the guards down on our heads.

The real time for talking came after the day's work was done, in those two or three hours between coming in off the farm and going to sleep. Once inside the gate we were safe. The Japs were outside, we were inside. We could relax, commiserate with one another, openly bitch against the guards, lick our wounds. The kitchen had chow ready when we came in from the farm. Dry rice, weed soup, and on a good day a spoonful of hominy. I carried mine to our board table and took my time eating. The pressure was off until lineup time next day. This was the time we could talk. Mostly we reminisced.

One kid swore that his mom made the best chocolate cake in town. When we got home he'd have her make one up for us. Another invited us all up to his place where we could use his boat and go fishing on the lake. Promises, solemn promises and plans for the future. We talked as though we had a future.

We made a pact among ourselves and decided that we would get together once a year and have a meal where everything was made from rice. There would be wet rice and dry rice and rice ground into flour to make bread and hotcakes. And we would roast some rice in the oven and grind it up to make coffee. There would even be rice pudding for dessert.

We made it sound like a great reunion that we could all look forward to. But just that one time each year. After that, none of us ever wanted to see or taste or smell rice again. We didn't even want to hear about it.

It was talk, just idle talk, yet we were sincere. We really intended to get together. Talk, lots of idle talk and empty promises. Meaningless perhaps, yet it was our way of spanning the gap between what used to be and what we wanted things to be like in the future. And it helped avoid the awful reality of what was now.

We were four men whom the circumstances of war and surrender and Japanese captivity had decreed would sleep together on a bamboo shelf in a prison camp in the Philippines. Because we slept together we worked together, ate together, talked together. Simple proximity forced us to share our lives. We were a solid support group, almost like a little family, yet we were a fluid group in the sense that if one man moved out, another prisoner would of necessity take his place. The fourth man, I don't remember his name, was transferred to another barracks and disappeared from our lives. Mahoney died of dysentery, slowly crapped his life away on the latrine. Johnson and I went together on a hell ship to Japan.

As I said, aside from bitching about the guards our talk was mainly about what we had done before the war and what we were going to do when we got out. Of course, if we stayed in the Army we were all going to be cooks, stay close to the food, never be hungry again. On the other hand we all had our dream project. Mahoney was going to be a sailor. Naturally, when he got home he was going to build a boat and sail it around the world. And it was a beautiful boat, and he built it all in his head. No paper and no plans and Mahoney had never built anything, let alone a boat. Yet he knew the length and breadth and depth of it. He knew how many sails it would have and their size and shape and just where he would place them on the deck. He knew what kind of wood he would use for the hull, a different kind for the deck, and the hull would be painted a glistening white with red trim and shiny brass letters across the stern for the name. Mahoney furnished the inside of his boat too. So many bunks, so many sheets, so many blankets. A table that would fold up out of the way after meals, and a kitchen and a shower and a toilet. Believe me, that boat had everything. Mahoney even stocked it with food. He knew precisely how many cans of corned beef, how many jars of jam, how many pounds of coffee it would take to sail around the world. Fantasy, pure fantasy, yet we listened intently, took him seriously, made little suggestions that we thought would help him along. I heard every tiny detail of Mahoney's boat a hundred times over, heard it until I could build his boat in my own head. We became so involved that we often became upset, disagreed with him when he proposed making a change.

Mahoney was continually changing, rearranging the food supply on his imaginary boat. For instance, one evening he decided he had too many cans of corned beef and thought he might take out a few cans and replace them with a few tins of condensed milk. His suggestion disturbed us, caught us by surprise like a thunderclap from a clear blue sky, and we didn't like it. We argued that we'd already worked out the food supply. He needed all the corned beef he could stow aboard, and besides, canned milk might go sour because there was no refrigeration on his boat. Also, we didn't want him to carry canned sardines because he would probably be able to catch all the fish he could eat. Mahoney finally agreed to take more chocolate, less sardines.

For myself, I was going to build a car. Not just any old car. Mine was going to be the best car in the world, every part made by hand, by me. Didn't matter that I knew almost nothing about cars, that I didn't know how to build anything. I was just going to do it. Before the war, before I enlisted in the Army, I used to ride the streetcar to high school. On the way I passed a used car lot, and on that lot was a 1928 Packard, a convertible coupe with a rumble seat. It was a beautiful car, big, gray, lots of chrome on the headlights and radiator. Oh, how I wanted that car, but the price was forty dollars and I never had forty dollars in my life. I never got that car, but it was the model for my dream car, the car I was going to build. Aside from our dream projects none of us thought about what we would do for a living when we got home. Vaguely, we would get a job. What job? Didn't matter, any job. Pump gas in a filling station. None of us had ever had a real job, just kid stuff. None of us had ever made a living. Maybe that's why we joined the Army. Before the war I had jobs, odd jobs. One summer I worked as night watchman in a downtown garage. I checked autos in and out. Bing Crosby's car was there, a big late-model sedan. Used to sit in it and start the motor and listen to the power under the hood. Got a dollar that night. Nothing as formal as a paycheck. The owner just handed me a dollar bill when he took over in the morning. Once a carpenter, a friend of my father, hired me to help him build a house. I cut boards to length, drove nails where he told me to, fetched this and handed him that. Together we put up a four-room house, frame, floors, windows, doors, and roof. Finally we painted it white with cherry red trim around the doors and windows. For a thousand dollars my carpenter friend bought the materials, furnished the labor, and built that four-room house. I earned a dollar a day. Anyway, what little money I earned went into the family kitty. We needed food for the table. I never saved forty dollars and never bought the old Packard. But it was still my dream car, and when I got home I was going to build one just like it, only better. Like Mahoney with his boat, I built my dream car entirely in my head, every wheel, every nut and bolt. The motor, a twelve-cylinder V-8, was going to be hand crafted by me. Mentally I worked on my car for months, dreamed about it, talked about it. One day someone pointed out to me that there was no such thing as a twelve-cylinder V-8. A V-8 motor only had eight cylinders. Somewhat crushed, I abandoned my car and decided to concentrate on Mahoney's boat. None of us were stupid. Uneducated, ignorant, but not lacking in intelligence. Had I been asked outright, I would have answered truthfully and admitted that my dream car was just a bunch of crap, that it would never happen. On the other hand I think we deliberately cultivated these fantasies as a coping device to keep from facing the reality of our day-to-day existence.

Talk about cars and boats and mother's cake was just a cover-up for our deeper feelings. It was on the bamboo shelf, in our sleeping spaces, in the darkness of the night that we really let our hair down. Sometimes in the darkness of the night a voice would come from the blanket-covered form beside me.

The voice might ask me if I was awake, an indirect way of asking if I wanted to talk. If I answered yes, the talk was on. Or more seriously he might ask me if I was scared. Scared of what? Hell no, I wasn't scared. Just another damn lie; I was always scared. Three thousand bodies that were buried on the farm told me I had something to be scared about.

Mahoney said that he'd hate to die out here. My folks might never know what happened to me. Maybe they wouldn't even know where I was buried. He asked if I was scared of dying.

Sure, I was scared of dying. I didn't want to die. But death was no big thing, and death meant peace and rest. There were lots of nights when I went to sleep not wanting to get up and face another day. On the other hand, the key to survival was in the mind. I think it was mental attitude that let some men live and let other men die. And truly, I always felt that if just two of us were left, and one of us died, I would be left to bury the other fellow.

They say that laughter is good for the soul. It is good for the body too. In a world delineated by hunger and misery and sickness and brutality, a good belly laugh can lift the despair, make the living a little easier. Even the recollection of a good laugh can be pleasantly stimulating, can rekindle a warm glow. One of our guards, the one we called Donald Duck, was a continual source of amusement. So much so that after fifty years I still recall the Duck fondly. Let me tell you about him.

The Duck was a regular prison-camp guard, one of the honchos that supervised work details on the farm. He was a little fellow, small even for a Japanese, with sharp features, thin lips, and a high-pitched voice. The Duck was a perfectionist and like the character for whom he was named, subject to sudden fits of rage in which his voice got higher, his face got redder, and his behavior became comical. As a Japanese guard I hated him but as the Duck I think I was actually fond of him.

The first time I worked for the Duck, this was before he had earned his name, we were planting camotes. The field had been prepared for planting, the dark earth piled in long even furrows. As a work detail we had spent the morning picking litter loads of camote vines, just the foot-long tender tips, the same kind we used for soup. In the afternoon we were going to plant them.

The Duck chose me for his first pupil. He dug a furrow with his hand, laid a camote vine in the hole, and covered the stem with dirt. Then he motioned me to do likewise. This was going to be easy. Any damn fool could see that. I scooped out a hole, placed a camote vine in the hole, and covered it up.

Wakaru nigh, you don't understand. Donald planted another vine, gave me another demonstration. This time I dug the hole a little deeper, placed the vine carefully, and covered it with dirt. Donald flew into a rage. It was plain that he thought I was stupid and just as plain that I didn't know what he was raging about. Another demonstration by Donald, another hole in the ground by me. I was trying, but I got it wrong again. The Duck was screaming, screaming at my obvious stupidity, and screaming at his own inability to communicate something obviously simple. I tried a fourth time. I was on hands and knees digging the hole. This time the Duck dropped to his knees beside me, took my hand in his, and patted the soil around the vine. Three times he patted the soil with my hand. Wakaru, understand. I still didn't wakaru. It must have shown on my face. Donald took my hand, patted the ground twice, shook his hand negatively and screamed in rage. He patted the ground four times and screamed again. Then, still holding my hand, patted the soil three times, nodded approvingly and smiled. I began to understand. The Duck wanted the soil around the new planting to be patted three times. Two wasn't enough, and four was too many. Three was just right and the Duck was pleased. It was a strange trade-off. Donald Duck was pleased because he had been able to communicate with me, because he was getting what he wanted from us. We were pleased because in spite of his frequent outbursts of temper nobody had been beaten. And in barracks, talking about the happenings of the day, we thought the Duck's temper tantrums comical.

The story doesn't end here. Let me tell you how Donald Duck got his name. The Duck spoke a few words of English. He spoke English about like I spoke Japanese. A word for "I need to go to the toilet," a word for "I understand," (or "I don't understand"), for "attention," "good morning," "hurry," "work," "rest." When the Duck couldn't communicate he became frustrated and flew into a rage. The angrier he got the faster he talked and the shriller his voice became.

Like all the guards the Duck carried a stick to hit us with, but it wasn't a big stick, nothing like Charlie's pick handle or Smiley's green bamboo. When the Duck used his stick, and he didn't use it often, it was without the usual Japanese brutality. The Duck didn't pick out one man and beat him to the ground; he spread the bad news around, a lick here, a couple of licks there, different prisoners up and down the line. Our feelings toward the Duck were ambivalent. We hated him as we hated all the guards, yet we preferred to work for him because we didn't fear him.

Once, twice, even three or four times a day, whenever we thought we could get away with it, we quack quack quacked behind Donald's back. Occasionally the entire detail would join in with a thunderous quack quack quack. It was our private joke. Nobody got hurt and it gave us tremendous satisfaction.

The meaning of the quack quack, like the supplication for J.C. to send down the rain, was rooted in the American culture. Donald Duck didn't understand but he knew something was going on. He became suspicious. A line of sixty or seventy prisoners stretched across a field, the Duck at one end of the line, a loud quack quack at the other. The Duck would rush to the spot, select a prisoner, any prisoner, and stand him at attention. The Duck would ask if this man was the one who went quack quack. The prisoner gave a negative shake of his head, a solemn denial. The Duck grunted in disgust, gave the prisoner a whack or two with his stick and moved on. Donald skipped a couple of men and tried again. Same fierce question, same solemn denial. Donald would ask the man if he quack quacked and give him a sharp poke with the stick to emphasize the question. Two, three, four times the Duck confronted different prisoners. He asked the same question, got the same answer, a negative shake of the head.

Stand firm. Don't smile, don't look Donald Duck in the eye. Thank God it was the Duck. Smiley would have taken the first man in line and beaten him to a writhing pulp to get the right answer.

This went on for several days. The Duck was clearly perplexed but not angry because he didn't realize that he was involved. One sunny afternoon the Duck walked back and forth behind the line of farm workers whacking every third or fourth backside and repeating to himself the words quack quack over and over. I took my licks and they stung my backside, they hurt, but damn it, it was worth it. Even as my ass was stinging from the blow, I smiled. Not outwardly, not with my face, that would have been disastrous, but deep in my chest, in my heart, I know I smiled.

Then the unthinkable happened. We grew careless. A prisoner with an urge to quack quack failed to check on the Duck's whereabouts, and when he gave out his quack quack the Duck was standing directly behind him. The Duck gave a triumphant yelp and pounced. At last he had his man. He ordered the prisoner to the edge of the field and followed him, punctuating each step with a blow from his stick. Donald threw away the stick and picked up a real club, a heavy one. Then he called two of the perimeter guards who came running in, rifles and bayonets at the ready. This was going to be a real beating. The Duck hit the hapless prisoner with the club. This time it was a statement of fact, not a question. Donald knew he had his man. The prisoner stood stiffly at attention. Donald hit him again. He held a short conference in Japanese. One of the perimeter guards spoke to the prisoner in very broken English and asked him why, why did he go quack quack?

Again and again the guard asked the same question. The Duck waved his club menacingly. The poor prisoner, still standing at attention under the threat of Donald's club, must have been listening to his guardian angel because he blurted out the right answer: "I went quack quack because we think you look like Donald Duck and Donald Duck is a great American movie star."

Word must have gotten around among the Japanese guards, for they seemed to show deference to our Donald, and our Duck enjoyed the added prestige. He seemed to grow in stature, to swell his chest out, to stride about with more authority. Why not? After all, he looked like an American movie star. And we prisoners, no more quack quack. We didn't dare. We didn't want to push our luck. If you put your hand in the friendly lion's mouth, you will surely be bitten.

For several weeks the Duck basked in his new-found glory. He was agreeable, even pleasant to work for, used his stick sparingly. Then fate decreed that a Japanese big shot, some general probably, should inspect the prison camp. In his honor the guards erected a canvas screen inside the camp and ordered all prisoners, under threat of severe punishment, to assemble for a movie. After dark we gathered in the designated area, Japanese soldiers in the front rows, American prisoners seated on the ground behind. The movie was awful. A documentary on the love life of the hummingbird. Entirely in Japanese. The voice droned on and on. The hummingbirds hovered and fluttered and sat on the nest and hovered some more. Truly, it was boring. So boring that even after two years in a prison camp I wanted to leave. Then it was over. We started to leave when the screen flashed on again. A real American Donald Duck cartoon, probably confiscated from a Filipino movie theater. We prisoners hollered and whistled like kids at a Saturday matinee. Then silence. Polite silence from the Japanese soldiers, stunned, despairing silence from the prisoners. We knew.

Inevitably, as the cartoon rolled on, the cartoon Donald Duck did his usual. His face grew bright red, he screamed, waved his arms, smashed the furniture, and flew into an apoplectic rage. The guards caught on immediately. This was Donald Duck, the American movie star. The guards roared with laughter. They pointed, clapped one another on the back, rolled on the ground. One of the guards, I knew it was our Donald Duck, stood up and ran screaming in Japanese through the American prisoners, striking indiscriminately with his stick, then disappeared toward the Japanese barracks. The show was over. The guards left together. I heard them laughing till they were out of earshot.

Poor Donald Duck. A week later I was shipped out to Japan. I never saw the Duck again, but when I think of that night I still smile in my heart.

How long has it been since man scratched his living from the earth without the aid of animals or machinery? A thousand, two thousand, maybe five thousand years. I feel we must have been pushed back in time. I live, but how? The cave man must have softened his bed with leaves and grass and skins. I sleep on hard bamboo. As far back as prebiblical times civilized people wore clothes. I wear only a loin cloth. Ancient peoples had clay pots to hold water, to cook in, to bathe from. I share a single faucet with hundreds of prisoners and have only a canteen cup. When I get water I drink it. I bathe when it rains or when I wade through a puddle on the farm. The Romans had physicians, healers who prescribed herbs and roots as remedies. We have doctors without medicine. Their knowledge is in their heads, but they have no way to use it. Early man could at least hunt for food. I must accept what little I am given. Where do we fit in the time frame of human progress?

There were two old men at Cabanatuan. I didn't know either personally, but I saw them about camp on an almost daily basis and I knew their stories. The first, a Negro, was in his middle sixties. He was noticeable partially because he was so old, partially because he was quite tall and stood erect, and partially because he had a thick shock of silvery white hair that contrasted sharply with his very black skin. He had been a soldier in the American Army in the Spanish-American War and had been discharged, in the Philippines, in eighteen ninety-eight. He stayed in the islands, married, and raised a family. When World War II came along, some forty-three years later, the old gentleman volunteered his services and was given command of a company of Filipino infantry composed of men from his own village. After the surrender the Japanese interned Filipino troops separately from the Americans and this old captain was thrown in with us.

Because of his age the old man was given the job of taking care of some ducks and chickens that belonged to the guards, and of tending a small garden. In a way the old man was lucky. The village where he had spent most of his life was not too far away. In the distance he could see the spire of the church where he had been married. And his little chicken ranch overlooked a Japanese checkpoint on the road that bordered our prison camp. At least once every couple of weeks members of the old man's family would walk past the camp, his wife, some of his children, some of his grandchildren. They didn't dare try to communicate, gave no sign of recognition, but at least he saw them, they saw him, and they knew he was still alive.

The majority of Philippine Army troops were interned for only a few months, then the Japanese released them to go back to their villages, to their farms. Survivors from the old man's infantry company were released as a unit to go back to their village. As they walked past the prison camp they recognized their captain, who was tending his garden. In front of the Japanese guardhouse this raggedy-assed bunch of Filipinos snapped to attention, saluted the old man, then turned and bowed to the guards. The Japanese soldiers were stunned, didn't know what to make of it. They slapped the Filipinos around for a few minutes and let them go.

The second old man in camp was a Jewish rabbi, maybe seventy or seventy-five years old. Then I didn't know, but I think now that he must have been Orthodox because he always kept his head covered with some kind of ragged hat, and he wore whiskers with a mustache and a full beard that reached almost to his waist. I never spoke with him, but I saw him often. He was a familiar figure as he walked slowly about the camp, clad only in shorts, a floppy hat, and wooden shoes. His body, above and below the shorts, was tanned by the sun to a deep, leathery, mahogany brown. Cabanatuan was a place of misery and brutality, and often, inhuman treatment and we prisoners were filled with hate and anger and bitterness. Yet of this old Jewish rabbi I remember the most blue eyes set deep in that mahogany face and the calmness that I could feel in him as he passed by. There was a man truly at peace with himself and with his God.

Rumors floated through the camp, wild rumors, crazy rumors, fantastic impossible rumors.

One was that we were going to be traded, that we'd be home by Christmas, that there was a ship on its way right now to take us home. Another was that the Japs were going to give us better food, move us to a better camp, with beds and showers and clothes and no more bullshit from the guards. Rumors, always rumors. Pie in the sky by and by. And I believed. We all believed because we wanted to believe. We talked about those rumors as if they were fact, as if they were actually going to come true. We talked about them during the day, took them to bed with us at night, kept them alive in our minds like children believing in Santa Claus or the tooth fairy. Better to believe in a fantasy, better to grasp at a wisp of smoke than to face the fact that the only way out of here was through the gate to the cemetery.

This time the rumor was about another food package. And why not believe? There had been a food parcel at Christmas in '42. This was the spring of '44. Of course there would be another. We talked and we waited. It's hard to explain the waiting for something like a food package. I want to believe; I truly want to believe. On the other hand something in my mind has learned to be wary. There have been other times when I allowed myself to be taken in by hope, and the disappointment can be terribly cruel.

Sure enough, one afternoon a Japanese Army truck rolls into camp loaded with parcels. Some prisoners get a package with their name on it, a package from home. Of course we try to match the name with the prisoner. There are lots of packages with names that belong to the three thousand guys out in the cemetery. It's sad. Folks at home have no way of knowing. They are still hoping, still praying for their loved ones. Unclaimed packages are passed out to guys who have no one at home to send a package. Everybody gets a package, one package. The Japanese take the rest away, and we never see them again.

The packages are small, about the size of a shoe box. They can't hold a hell of a lot, but at least they are a contact from home, a contact with the outside world. And they put to rest a question we all have been afraid to ask going into the third year. I am sure it was a question somewhere in the back of every prisoner's mind. Do the people in the United States even know we're here? And if they do, does anybody really give a damn?

I got a package from home. I knew it was from home the minute I saw it. It was a cardboard grocery-store box, wrapped in brown paper and tied with string. And hand lettered. Andrew D. Carson, 19056693. I didn't open mine right away. I wanted to think about it. Must have been on the way for at least a year. These parcels must have been shipped from all over the United States. Mailed from all over and assembled at some central place. They had to be assembled, sorted, loaded on a ship and taken to a neutral country, unloaded, put on another ship and taken to Japan. Unloaded, resorted, and trucked to our prison camp. A miracle that they got to us at all.

Mine was filled with simple things, not things from the store but things from the cupboard shelves at home. Some hard candy wrapped in waxed paper and secured with a rubber band, a box of raisins, a can of this and a package of that. Biggest item was a can of Hershey's chocolate, the bitter unsweetened kind. I could see my mother's hand in that. The bitter chocolate had been emptied out, mixed with sugar and replaced. I could have a few cups of hot cocoa. Next day we got letters. Must have come in the same truck with the food parcels. Mine had my name on it, Andrew Carson, 19056693, Prisoner of War, Japan. Only letter I got in three-and-a-half years, and it was from a distant relative of my mother's that I had seen only once when I was five years old. I was from California but my mother had taken me to visit her relatives in Boston when I was five years old. It was ironic. Of all the people in the world, I get a letter from a woman who met me once when we were both five years old. I still have a scar under my left eye where this kid jabbed me with a fork.

My food parcel was gone within a week and the letter, it was full of the usual stuff. How are you? I'm fine, hope you are fine. We remember you in our prayers. Still, maybe my letter wasn't so bad. One kid got an overdue bill from the telephone company.

Prison camp does strange things to a man, or conversely, prison camp caused a man to do strange things. I find myself living in a hostile alien world where my background, my culture, my traditional values mean nothing to my captors. When I was a kid we had rules and everybody understood them. Never hit a guy with glasses, two on one is not fair, my turn, cross my heart and hope to die, Scout's honor. Everybody knew the rules, and everybody played by them. I still remember, when I was about nine years old, playing cowboys. There was the traditional knock-down, drag-out fight in the saloon. Only with us it was a wrestling match on the front lawn. And when it was over, the plaintive, almost tearful protest from the little guy on the bottom, "You cheated. You're not supposed to win."

Here, life is still a game, but the Japs are the bad guys and they make all the rules. In age I am twelve or thirteen years away from the child who played cowboys and Indians on the front lawn, but I am a grown-up soldier now and a prisoner of war. The stakes are high. As we used to say when I was a kid, "You bet your life." Living, simply staying alive, is difficult. After more than two years of daily conflict with my captors I have toughened up, but I still have chinks in my psychological armor and the little bastards still find the sore spots. The hunger, the subhuman living conditions, the sickness and the pain of my day-to-day life are in themselves almost too much to bear, but I have learned to bend with the wind. Still, when I am struck in the face or beaten with a club there are moments when my brain almost explodes with the intensity of my emotions. Shame, humiliation, anger, hatred, merge in my mind in a psychological scream of anguish, and I want nothing more out of life than to smash my tormentor, to stomp him into the ground, to destroy him utterly. I endure, I suffer, I take the abuse. By my childhood standards I take the coward's way out. Still, I do not think of myself as a coward but as a winner in this diabolical game of life and death. Somewhere in the back of my mind a little voice whispers to me, and I listen. "Carson," the voice says, "if you strike back, if you hit this little son of a bitch, you're dead and you lose. If you can take all the crap he can dish out, then turn and walk away, in effect, he loses and you win." This is a lousy game, and I don't want to play anymore. I want to go home. But the choice is no longer mine. I am here and the enemy makes the rules and day by day, hour by hour, minute by minute, I do the best that I can.

Now and then I pause long enough to take a good look at myself. I am healthier now, stronger. I am tanned by the sun to such a deep brown that I no longer sunburn. The tops of my shoulders, my ears, and my nose get sore but I don't blister. I have to smile when I think of my first days on Corregidor, when it was a court-martial offense to be caught without a shirt between sunup and sunset. On the balance line between living and dying I have moved away from center, a little more toward the side of the living. In my mind I am still the young kid who stands six foot two and weighs two hundred and twenty pounds. In reality I am a hundred-and-twenty-pound skeleton that can barely drag his ass in off the farm after a minimal day's work.

Floyd Buckner came into my barracks today. We've been in opposite ends of the same camp for eighteen months but haven't seen each other because just staying alive has taken all of our time and energy. There is damn little visiting between barracks in Cabanatuan. This is a special day, a special reason for a visit. Fifteen hundred prisoners are being shipped out to Japan. Floyd is one of the fifteen hundred. He is apologetic but glad to be going. I can tell he feels guilty at leaving the rest of us. I don't blame him for going. Tried to go myself. I volunteered, offered to take another man's place, tried my damndest to get on the list but to no avail. The Japs would have none of it. All fifteen hundred men came from the other end of the camp. It's the same old POW syndrome. The grass is always greener in the next place. Maybe the food will be better. Maybe living conditions will be better. Maybe! Maybe! Maybe!

Fifteen hundred men going to Japan. At least that was the rumor going through camp. Was it true? God only knows. Like all the rumors that flashed through camp, might be true, might not. Rumors grew out of nowhere, usually meant nothing. Sit on the latrine long enough and you're bound to hear a new one.

Soon after the fifteen hundred left I was assigned to a new work detail. Johnson too. We lined up with the regular farm detail, drew picks and shovels as our tools for the day and marched off in a different direction, cross-country for about a mile. I could see at a glance that this was not going to be an ordinary farm detail. Nothing growing there but grass and weeds.

Japs put us to work unloading a couple of trucks that were already there waiting for us. The first truck was piled high with prefabricated sections of narrow gauge railroad track. The sections fit together, end to end, like pieces of track on a little kid's choo-choo train. Second truck was loaded with iron gondola cars with little iron wheels that fit the track we unloaded, cars small enough to be pushed by six or eight men yet large enough to hold a lot of dirt. Took a couple of days to lay the track and get the cars rolling; then we figured things out. We were going to build an airstrip, a landing field for Japanese warplanes. Dig the dirt from the high places, load the dirt into cars, push the loaded cars along the track, and dump the dirt into the low places. Slow, brutal, exhausting hand labor. Seemed like an impossible task, but from the Japanese viewpoint our labor came cheap, and we had the rest of our lives to finish the job.

Within a week work on the new airfield fell into a routine, developed a rhythm all its own. You could almost say the airfield had its own personality. Physically it was harder than the farm, heavier labor that demanded constant maximum exertion. On the good side, the guards for the most part stayed on the edge of the field and left us alone. There were fewer beatings.

I think the guards left us alone because we were doing their job for them. Unwittingly we began competing among ourselves to see which team could dig faster, fill their railcar faster. There were a couple of good reasons for this rush of work on our part, the first being that all the dirt cars were one behind the other on a single track. No one car could be moved until all the cars were full; then they were all pushed together along the track to the dumping point. And of course, if any one car was not filled quickly enough and held up the rest of the line, that team of workers was sure to catch hell. Secondly, if a team found a good spot to work where the dirt was not too hard and where it was not too far to carry the dirt to the car, that team could work like hell, fill their car to capacity, and rest a few precious minutes while the slower or less-fortunate teams caught up.

Dog eat dog and let the devil take the hindmost. In this case, fight for a good spot to dig, work with a rush till your car was filled to capacity, and rest a few minutes while the guards raised hell with somebody else.

Two men to a car. Johnson and I worked together. Our favorite spot was not too hard and there were not many rocks. There was a daily rush for the better work places and almost territorial rights were claimed for patches of dirt.

Two guys tried to take over our favorite working place, claimed that they had worked there yesterday, and by God they were going to work there again today. I told them to kiss off, that they had better get the hell out of there and find another place to work before the guards came down on us. They moved on.

Arguments were settled quickly lest the guards beat hell out of everybody involved. On the march from camp to the airfield there was a lot of jockeying for position at the head of the line. The first prisoners in line usually got the best places to work. New guys, slow guys, sick guys got the leftovers.

Johnson and I had our own system for digging. With picks we would under-cut the bank for twelve or fifteen inches, then with luck and a few heavy licks on top of the bank with a heavy pick the whole cut would tumble down. Big chunks we picked up by hand, little stuff with shovels. Hopefully, hopefully we could fill our car and rest those few minutes while the slower teams caught up.

I liked work on the airfield better than work on the farm, but as weeks went by I paid the price with my body. It was midsummer, rainy season in the Philip-pines, hot and wet. We followed a dirt path from the airfield back to camp, and two hundred pairs of bare feet turned it into a slimy, slippery morass. Generally I finished the day's work on the airfield exhausted but otherwise OK. But lately on the quick march back to camp I had slipped and fallen several times, heavy falls that knocked the wind out of me and left me shaken. My body was failing and I wondered just how long I could keep up. I was relieved when old Joe Ross, the master sergeant who led our barracks, announced that we were shipping out in the morning. Just like that. Work today, ship out tomorrow. Where to? Nobody knew and I didn't give a damn. I was ready to go.

Bet they never did finish that damn airfield.

Hell Ship:
The Voyage to Japan

I slept fitfully, in little snatches throughout the night, and long before the first touch of daylight appeared in the sky I was wide awake. Apprehension, fear, anticipation, myriad thoughts racing through my mind kept sleep away. I was being moved, shipped out, transferred to another camp, and the uncertainty preyed on my mind. All I knew was that fifteen hundred men were being taken from the camp, and I was to be one of them.

A soft breeze drifted through the open sides of the barracks, its gentle warmth hinting of the hot day to come. It had rained during the night, and the air smelled fresh and clean, as it usually did after a heavy downpour. Water still dripped from the thatched roof into the shallow ditch beneath the eaves, the ditch chiseled there by the endless dripping during the long rainy season. I was very familiar with that ditch. Because we had no tables or chairs, it was convenient, even comfortable, to sit on the ground with my feet in the ditch while I ate my meager ration of rice and soup.

Cabanatuan was alive with rumors. Fifteen hundred men were being shipped out, but to where, to what, only God knew. Our Japanese captors never let us in on anything.

For more than two years life in Cabanatuan had been a taste of hell, yet it was a familiar hell and I was used to it. I knew the routines, the work details; I knew the pitfalls and the dangers. I knew the guards and their individual personalities, their predictable as well as their unpredictable behavior. I knew what to seek out, what to avoid. In these two years I had become adapted to an entirely unnatural way of life. In short, I had learned to survive. Being transferred to another camp would mean different guards and a different living situation. Transferring to a new camp meant learning to survive all over again, and I wasn't sure I could handle it.

Dawn was breaking and the man who slept in the space to my right was already up and out. Johnson, who slept on my left, was still huddled under his blanket. He wasn't moving but I knew he was awake. Living in such close proximity, sleeping shoulder-to-shoulder, body-to-body, not always but sometimes inadvertently touching, we got to know a lot about one another. When you share your personal space with someone, anyone, almost twenty-four hours of every day, you have absolutely no privacy; there is no place to hide. I could not remember the last time I had been alone, but I knew it had been longer than two years. Living in Cabanatuan was to be forever in a crowd. We slept jammed together, lined up together for roll call, lined up together for chow. Whatever I did, it was always in the company of others. Even the latrines were public, wooden benches with multiple holes under a thatched roof without walls. If I walked from one barracks to the next there were always other eyes watching, and all around me were prisoners, walking, eating, resting, sleeping, urinating, having a bowel movement, prisoners busy with living and just staying alive, but prisoners whose most intimate acts were open to everyone.

Chowtime — breakfast, dinner, supper — was the most enjoyable, the most social time of any day. We lined up for chow by barracks, and it was dished into our mess kits as we walked single file past a common kitchen. We carried our ration back to the barracks, because there was nowhere else to go, and ate standing or sitting on the ground just outside. Except for prisoners near death, prisoners too weak to move, no one ate inside the barracks. Spilled or dropped scraps of food, no matter how minuscule, simply attracted ants and lice and bedbugs and other vermin and made an already inhospitable living area even less habitable. Even though we were terribly undernourished and there was never enough food to slake the ever-present hunger, eating our skimpy ration of rice and blowgun soup was the one thing we all did at the same time. If it can be so described, chowtime was the most comforting, most pleasurable moment of any prisoner's entire day. And it gave us a chance to gather in groups of two or three or four and to share a common experience. At chowtime we ate, usually very slowly, and we talked about the life we had known before the war or the life we were going to live after this hell was over. At chowtime, with the talking, I could sometimes forget the ass-whipping I had taken on the farm today, forget the dysentery tearing at my bowels, forget the monotony of years of unsalted rice and unsalted weed soup. At chowtime I could distance myself from the misery and the suffering and dare to hope that someday, today's reality would be a memory, and I could daydream that today's fantasy of the good life at home might someday in the future become reality.

Johnson was awake, but I hesitated to disturb him. I knew he was awake because I had learned to recognize a subtle difference in his breathing between consciousness and sleep. There were other little giveaways too, I suppose, differences in the structure of the prison camp culture that we all had learned to understand, to respect. For instance, in such close quarters there was unavoidable touching, body contact. When asleep, the thrust of a knee, the toss of an arm, the bumping of a shoulder, such actions were jerky, unrestrained. Awake, these same movements, though necessary, would be more tentative, less intrusive. On the one hand, survival as a prisoner of war under the Japanese demanded that I give up a part of my personal space, of my dignity, of myself, to the other fellow. On the other hand it was commonly understood that he go to great lengths not to take it away deliberately.

In the civilized world, take riding in a crowded elevator as an example. The shoving, the jostling, the touching of one's body, another's breath in your face, even if done impersonally these intrusions into your personal space are acceptable. On the open street or in your living room these same intrusions would be considered an insult. In my prison-camp existence the realities of life were more basic, more gut-wrenching, more down to earth. I didn't look at the man who clung to the corner of the barracks, face contorted, body quivering as he fought a losing battle with dysentery cramps. I didn't look at him as he staggered along the path with shit running down his legs because he hadn't been able to make it to the latrine in time. I didn't look at him as he stood naked, rinsing the crap out of his drawers. I didn't look at him because I knew he didn't want to be seen, because to look at him, to acknowledge his condition, might destroy that sense of anonymity behind which he wanted to hide, might destroy that last tiny shred of dignity, of self-respect he was clinging to so desperately. I did not look, I did not see because I had been there. I had shit my pants on the way to the latrine. I had vomited all over myself with my head under my blanket. I had fallen full length in the piss and mud beside the latrine and waited for the mud to dry so I could scrape it off with my fingernails because there was no water to wash. Yes, I had been there many, many times, and I knew without a doubt I would be there again. I had thanked God that no one had pointed a finger at me and taken notice of that poor son of a bitch. Yes, I had been in every shameful, humiliating, degrading situation imaginable; thus prison camp etiquette demanded that there were many things, plainly visible, that we did not look at, that we did not see.

I whispered, asked Johnson if he was awake. The question gave him the option of not answering if he wanted to remain with his own personal thoughts. He answered, softly, said that he had been awake for a long time. He grunted, a short involuntary gasp of pain as he shifted his weight on the bamboo slats. We lay quietly for a few minutes, each man with his own thoughts. There was no real need for conversation because we had talked things out at length in the darkness of the previous night.

Johnson's head appeared from beneath his blanket and I asked him if he was ready. My question was superfluous but it established a connection, a verbal touching with another person. He said that he was ready to go as soon as he rolled up his blanket.

Packing up, getting ready for the move was no big deal. Neither of us had much in the way of material possessions, nor did any other prisoner. With the exception of a single G-string for each prisoner the Japanese had given us nothing.

When the first fifteen hundred men were shipped out of Cabanatuan, we thought they were being shipped to Japan. That was the rumor and we believed it. And I had wanted to go with them. I wanted to go so badly that I offered to take another man's place, anything to get away from Cabanatuan, away from the farm. After they had been gone a month or so I realized that we really didn't know a damn thing about where they were going or what was going to happen to them.

Then I began to hear talk about another large detail leaving the camp. Was the rumor true? And if it was, would I be one of the prisoners chosen to go? My feelings were ambivalent — half of me wanted desperately to go; the other half, the more cautious half, warned me to be careful. Maybe it's better to confront a devil you know rather than take a chance on a devil you don't know. At any rate, I was on the list. I was going.

I rolled my blanket into a tight bundle and tied it with a string so I could carry it slung under one arm. My mess kit bottom, my canteen cup, and my spoon hung on the G-string that tied around my waist. I was packed and ready to go.

Master Sergeant Joe Ross, our barracks leader, was a career man. To us kids he seemed a very old man. He must have been at least forty, maybe even forty-one. We deferred to his age, his rank, and his judgment. On this particular morning he walked down the barracks aisle and placed a canteen in my hand. He told me he knew I didn't have a canteen, so he had managed to get one for me. He turned away, hesitated, then turned back, told me confidentially that he wished he was going along with us. Then old Joe Ross gave me one last bit of fatherly advice. He urged me to take care of myself because wherever I was going, it wasn't going to be a picnic. Like my mess kit bottom and canteen cup, I knew that this canteen had been handed down to me from some poor bastard who had died recently. Nevertheless, I was overjoyed to get it.

I knew people reading this chronicle may find it difficult to fully understand the importance of getting a canteen. For me it was a big step upward. It meant that for the first time in two years I could carry water on a work detail, that I didn't have to do slave labor from dawn to dusk without a drink and then stand in line for half an hour to get water from our single faucet. Having a canteen was important because it gave me an edge in the daily game of staying alive.

Ready to go, Johnson and I sat on the edge of the sleeping shelf with our feet in the center aisle. The whole damn barracks was just sitting and waiting. Chow was over. We had eaten our morning meal and now we waited for the word to go. There was no work detail for our barracks because most of us were being shipped out. Nothing to do but sit and wait. Sit and wait and worry.

Johnson was speaking, half to himself, half to no one in particular, wondering where they were going to take us. I didn't know. I answered without turning my head, too busy watching for the guards to come after us. I thought they might be sending us to another camp, maybe even to Japan, but I knew the Japs weren't going to tell us a damn thing until we got to wherever we were going. Other prisoners from different parts of the barracks voiced their own opinions. Some thought the food in the new place would surely be better. Others were hoping for medicine, something to fight off the dysentery and beri-beri, maybe better treatment with no more beatings, no more work details, even a place to take a shower bath. Nobody knew a damn thing, but everybody was eager to speculate. Any change had to be for the better. Surely, we were optimistic dreamers. We had to be.

Without that little ray of hope, that glimmer of light at the end of the tunnel, there was no reason to keep on struggling. In a Japanese camp, looking ahead to tomorrow was like trying to peek into the hereafter, quite impossible. But we could always dream, always hope that someday, tomorrow even, things would get better. In the sweet by-and-by, maybe.

I knew Johnson was scared and he knew I was scared, but neither of us spoke of it. Hell, every guy on the list was scared. As a group we pretended that this day was like any other, but the fear was there among us and that fear was very real. This type of fear, perhaps anxiety would be a better word to use, was a common denominator among all prisoners. It was not the surge of adrenaline, the breathtaking, heart-stopping response to sudden shock, for me, rather a cold visceral gut-wrenching tightening of the chest and stomach that I lived with day by day. I felt it every morning knowing I would be at the mercy of the guards on another work detail, felt it every time a guard with a club walked behind me as I labored, felt it every time I saw another naked body carried out to be dumped in a common grave.

Johnson uttered the words uppermost in everybody's mind when he asked me if I thought the next camp would really be better. I thought it had to be, that things couldn't get much worse. Trying to appear confident I tossed off a typical wise-guy answer. Truth was, things had never gotten better. Day by day, month by month, our conditions had steadily grown worse.

Corporal Stearman joined us while we waited, a good old southern boy from Lubbock, Texas. Soft-spoken, friendly as a hound pup, he was tough as old rawhide. Before the shooting war started, Stearman and I and a few other high school dropouts who had joined the Army lifted weights for recreation. Why weights? Because in those days every magazine, every dime western, carried an ad for Charles Atlas. The ads said he had developed from an eighty-seven-pound weakling into Mr. America just by exercising and lifting weights. No bull, had to be true. The ads said so. So we took good care of our bodies and struggled with the weights. And Stearman, though only middle-sized, was pound for pound the strongest man on the fort.

Stearman told us his mom used to say that the grass was greener on the other side of the fence. He wasn't sure what she meant back then but now he was beginning to understand. The next place, the next camp, always looked better to him. Wouldn't take much improvement to beat the hell out of this camp.

Even after the war started and the Japs lay siege to our tiny fort with almost continuous bombing and shelling and strafing, we kids thought we were going to live forever and we still tried to keep our bodies in shape. Defiantly, between bombings and artillery attacks, we would sneak onto the open deck behind the huge turrets of our fourteen-inch naval guns and exercise. We thought the Japs could not see us. When we saw one of their bombers or when they opened up with artillery, we'd run like hell for the nearest casemate. One afternoon the Japs put an artillery shell squarely in the middle of our set of weights and blew them all to hell. After that, in those rare moments when we weren't either shooting or being shot at, our little group of ex–weight lifters would gather in a casemate behind one of the six-inch guns and listen while Stearman strummed an old guitar. His favorite song was "What's New?" I lost track of Stearman when the Japs shipped me to Japan. Never saw him again. God, I hope he made it.

Johnson turned to me with a quizzical look and asked if I thought the grass would really be greener in the next camp. He was looking for reassurance, but I had none to give.

In my opinion we couldn't count on anything. It had been all downhill so far. It had been all downhill and thousands had died, but for me, though it was none of my own doing, things just seemed to work out right. My thoughts ran back over a number of times in the last two years, times when just by luck or chance I had avoided making a fatal mistake.

I remembered how at Nasugbu I had looked for a way to escape. I had been desperate to get away from what the Japanese termed "special severe punishment." We had been confined on a tiny finger of land surrounded on three sides by water, and had been heavily guarded. I had thought if I could slip into the water at night, unnoticed in the dark, I might swim quietly across the little bay and escape. I couldn't get out of sight of the guards, so I didn't try. Gardener and another prisoner had tried, though, and the Japs were waiting. Both escapees had been shot.

I thought about the time near the end of our two weeks of "severe punishment" when the Japs had selected one officer and fourteen enlisted men to work in a nearby sugar mill. Of course, I had volunteered. I would have done anything to escape the brutality of those two weeks. I had stepped forward but had been rejected in favor of Cy Allen, a big fellow standing next to me. My chance was gone. The fifteen selected men were marched away, worked a few days, and then put into a pit, doused with gasoline, and burned alive. There were other times when my luck had held. I remembered the night in the execution chamber in Bilibid prison and the unbelievable train ride to San Fernando with prisoners packed into the tiny boxcars so tightly the dead had no room to fall down.

I thought of the night when the Japanese had herded us like animals into an empty school yard and how there had been no shelter from the torrential rain that ran an inch deep across the ground. Cold, wet, sick, and utterly miserable, I had crawled under the schoolhouse to get partially out of the rain. I remembered how, in the morning, Turman, Burlon, Garland, and Law had hidden while the rest of us were herded off down the road, how I could have stayed with them, and how I didn't. But most of all I remembered how the four were caught, beaten savagely for two days, tortured, and then executed by firing squad.

And the Nicholas Field detail. I had again volunteered and been turned down for that one too. They were starved to death, worked to death, and sometimes beaten to death. Only a handful came back. What kept me alive? Was it luck, fate, or the hand of God? Maybe I'll never know.

I thought then we had better get to the latrine while we could. Never know when we'll get another chance.

Johnson merely grunted in assent. I stood in line and waited my turn at the hole in the ground that served as a urinal. Experience had taught me never to start anywhere with a full bladder. Not looking ahead was asking for trouble. Having to go later in a bad situation, possibly pissing on myself, would be humiliating and bad enough in itself. If it happened in a truck or in a crowded boxcar where the Jap guard might be offended by the sight or the stench, such an oversight could get me badly beaten or even killed. Survival as a prisoner, just staying alive, often depended on trivial decisions.

The men from my barracks moved to the camp gate in formless ragged clusters, a very unmilitary manner. We were counted and loaded into open trucks, as many as could be crowded into each truckbed. Johnson and I tried to keep together. Not that it made a hell of a lot of difference; it was simply more reassuring to be with a buddy than to be alone. Without putting it into words I knew the Japanese would stay at the rear of the truck to block any escape, and I didn't want to be standing next to a guard. Here again the natural instinct for self-preservation, the absolute necessity to make the best of every situation, came to the fore. I held back a little and when the truck ahead had room for only three or four more prisoners, moved toward the next empty one. Johnson followed. It was close enough that the guards didn't object and we were the first ones on and took our places just behind the cab. A tiny victory, perhaps meaningless, but in a hostile environment not meant to be lived in, I felt safer with even a little distance between me and the nearest guard.

A querulous voice repeated for the hundredth time that he didn't know where we were going. Asked if anyone else knew? The voice didn't expect an answer, knew there was no answer, but to speak, even into the air, sort of joined the man with the group, made him feel a little less helpless and alone.

The truck ride lasted most of the day with lots of fitful starts and stops, but with no food, no water, and no opportunity to relieve ourselves. The sun bore down, and the metal roof of the cab became too hot to touch. I could stand the heat, burned nearly black from months of working near naked on the farm, but thirst was harder to take. I held off till midafternoon, drank from my canteen, and shared the rest with four or five prisoners nearest me. Only with those nearest me. There had to be other water bottles in the truck, and besides, even empty, I didn't dare let my precious canteen out of my sight or reach.

Bored as hell, the two guards stood, one on each side at the tailgate. They talked, smoked, sometimes just stared at each other and tried to pretend that we prisoners didn't exist. Plainly, this was not a job to their liking. Not to worry about escape though, there were scout cars with infantry and machine guns at the front and rear of the convoy as well as at intervals between trucks.

The countryside, what I could see of it, looked peaceful and serene. The sun was bright, the sky a cloudless blue, and in every direction the fields and hills were green. Here and there we passed a wide-horned carabao lazily dragging a plow through the rich dark soil, usually with a nine- or ten-year-old Filipino child urging it on with a stick. Luzon is a lush, green, beautiful island with a superb climate. The land was there, the beauty was there, but something intangible was missing. Our convoy passed through a number of villages. Gone were the usual children playing in the streets. Gone were the broad smiles, the friendly waves, the staccato chatter of the Tagalog tongue. The peasants working the fields didn't even look up as we passed. It was obvious that this was no longer a happy land, that these were miserable people, that the foot of the oppressor lay heavy upon their necks.

Talk among the prisoners was limited to the usual inane crap. Except that we were being moved, this day was no different from any other. Nothing new to talk about. I heard the same, oft-repeated, meaningless utterances. "They say the food'll be better." Nobody knew who in the hell "they" referred to, but it didn't matter. It was tacitly understood that "they" indicated someone who had a connection, access to information, and whose word could be depended upon to be true. In the camps any statement prefaced by "they say" was accepted with the simple faith that a child has in Santa Claus. To question too closely, to ask for specifics, might shatter the illusion. Without this illusion, this self-deception, without believing that someday, somehow, this suffering would come to an end, a strong man could simply give up, lie down, and die within a week. We lost a good number of men, not for any medical reason, but just because they no longer had the will to live. There were already nearly three thousand bodies in the mass graves at Cabanatuan, and those who still lived had to believe that death was for the other fellow and not for them. A positive mental attitude seemed to be the best medicine available.

I turned to Johnson, jammed with me against the lurching, jolting side of the truck, said that it was the same old bullshit wherever we went. The truck rattled noisily as it hit another pothole. I asked Johnson if he remembered why we were still fighting, that the relief convoy was supposed to be just a few days away. He nodded his head in assent. Sure, he remembered. He was a believer too, but the damn convoy never came. Always pie in the sky ... maybe tomorrow. Horn blasting, our truck passed a two-wheeled farm cart drawn by a carabao. Cart and driver had to pull off the road and into the ditch to let the convoy go past. We talked about the prisoner exchange that was supposed to have happened at Christmastime in '42. It never happened. And "we'll be free in '43," that never happened either. Johnson grinned ruefully and grunted as the truck hit another bump and the siderail slammed into his ribs. He thought we were suckers to have believed in all that crap. Disappointments, sure, but they were in the past. Don't look back. Better instead to latch onto a new slogan for the future. "Friendly shore in '44," or "home alive in '45." Next month, next year, maybe. Both guards turned with angry looks. They didn't understand English and didn't like us talking. We knew it was time to knock it off.

I was thinking to myself. It was the same old bullshit every time. Unspoken, the same thought was in the back of each prisoner's mind. If I can just hang on, someday the United States will kick these little bastards in the ass and finally get us outta here.

Gone but not forgotten. Did the folks at home even know that we were still alive? And if they did, would they ever be able to find us? Was home just another memory and was this stinking prisoner life going to be ... forever?

We were coming into a big city. It had to be Manila. The voice was loud and there was an excited stirring in the truck. The guards reacted angrily and made threatening motions with their bayonets. The truck quieted down. The streets of Manila were deserted, no automobiles, no carabao carts, no people in sight. Perhaps the Japanese had cleared our route in advance so we wouldn't be seen.

After jolting through deserted streets for a few miles the truck drove directly onto a large pier. Prisoners, moving stiffly and awkwardly after the daylong ride, climbed from the truck. Closely guarded, we were allowed to move about within a small area. Through an open pier door I could see the gray iron side of a ship. I knew it was waiting to carry us to a still unknown destination. There was a toilet on the pier with holes over the water. An officer advised us to relieve ourselves. Impossible for fifteen hundred men to all use this two-holer. Again, luckily, I was close to the door. I heard my urine spatter into the water.

Ten minutes later the last truck was in the shed and with shouts of, "Hyaku, hyaku, hurry, hurry," the guards herded us like cattle, up the gangway and down a crude stairs into a hold in the after part of the ship. The square of the hatch was empty but along both sides, under the overhanging deck, rough wooden shelves had been built. There were three levels, each with just enough headroom for a small man to sit upright. One hatchboard over the next lower level had been left open and as we came down the stairs we were forced to throw everything we carried into the lower hold. I lost my blanket but managed to hang onto my utensils, my canteen cup, my mess kit bottom, and spoon.

I could see Johnson a few feet in front. By Cabanatuan standards he was dressed better than most. He still had his safari hat and a shirt. The shirt had two gaping holes where the sleeves had been, had been cut off about four inches above his belly button and all the buttons were missing. From the neck up he was well dressed. From neck to midbelly he was ragged as hell. From his belly button down, the loin cloth, the naked legs, the bare feet. The whole combination was ridiculous, laughable. The guards threw his hat into the hold but let him keep his shirt.

Johnson was tall, skinny, and walked with a stoop because he didn't have enough muscle left to hold his body upright. He was so skinny, so emaciated, that I daily expected him to fall down and never get up again. I could see his every rib, every vertebra through his shirt yet he still made the daily work details with the rest of us. Of course, we all had the same incentives to keep working. A pick handle across the ass is quite a motivating factor.

Weary, sick, nearly naked and incredibly dirty, skeletons of men continued to stream into the hold. The shelves filled to capacity and the remainder stood, jammed together in the open square. There was no more room but the impossible flood of bodies continued, pressing tighter, ever tighter together. The Jap guards became violent. It was obvious there was no more room, but they continued to force prisoners into the hold, prodding them with bayonets and beating them savagely with clubs and rifle butts.

When the last prisoner tumbled down the steps, fifteen hundred men were crammed into a steel-walled cargo hold with no room to move, hardly room to breathe. At first it was remarkably quiet. Curses, groans, cries of pain, even these were muffled. At first there was no panic. But here and there, especially among those in the very back of the press, a man broke and began screaming and cursing, cursing the bodies pressed against him, cursing the Japs who had put him there, cursing the God who had abandoned him. This screaming and cursing, sometimes just a meaningless babble of sounds and words and epithets, served no real purpose except that of a safety valve, an instinctive primeval way to relieve the fear. Fights broke out. Eyes were gouged, cheeks ripped, and bodies lacerated as men pushed and tore at each other in their struggle for the breath of life. On the whole the prisoners remained quiet. Aside from the purely physical, the psychological pressure was incredible.

I knew, we all knew, it was senseless and stupid to waste strength in struggle. We had long ago internalized the most basic concept of POW life. Conserve everything. Conserve your strength, conserve your energy, conserve your emotions. Use your will to shut out the fear, the horror, the pain. Teach yourself to bear the unbearable, to tolerate the intolerable, and when you must, try to accept the inevitable. Bow to the little bastard with the fixed bayonet, but always call him a son of a bitch in your mind. The Japanese could never take that bit of mental defiance away from you. Control hatred and leave room for hope in your innermost soul, for hope can sustain a man and keep him alive. Do whatever the enemy forces you to do; accept whatever you must, but survive, damn it, survive.

Daylight faded into dusk and there were no lights. The darkness became absolute. The long, long night began. Without the tiniest bit of light, even from the stars, the fetid air seemed thicker, heavier, harder to breathe. We waited in the blackness, fifteen hundred desperate men crammed body-to-body, sweaty flesh against sweaty flesh. We waited without knowing what we were waiting for.

Movement was out of the question. There were too many of us, too little room. Only the turning of a head, lifting of an arm from between sweaty bodies, shifting weight from one leg to another. Nothing else was possible. And for Christ's sake, don't fall down. Your space will be gone and you'll never get up again.

I had been one of the first two or three hundred to go aboard and had found a spot on an upper shelf, halfway back toward the side of the ship. The space filled so quickly that I had no time to change my mind or to move to another location. I was jammed in tightly and had to make the best of it. Within minutes I knew I had chosen badly. I had made a mistake. The steel deck was only inches above my head. It had been absorbing the heat from the tropical sun all day. The overhead deck was too hot to touch and the heat radiated downward like the blast from an open oven door.

I sat dripping with sweat, knees drawn up under my chin, arms wrapped around my legs. Bodies pressed against me, backs, arms, knees, hemming me in. I waited, unable to move, hardly able to breathe, able only to wait, endure, and try to stay alive.

Johnson was somewhere nearby. I could hear his voice but in the blackness couldn't tell where he was sitting. Next to me was a kid from a tank battalion, a young fellow from Salinas, California. I had talked with him, knew him by sight, but never learned his name. I knew his story though, liked him, and felt some little reassurance at having him near me. Like most of the tankers, those who were still alive, he had attacked until his tank ran out of gas, fought in it as a pill box till they ran out of ammunition, dropped a grenade down the hatch and ran like hell. He picked up a rifle and fought beside the infantry until the surrender. Just a kid, but a good man to have close by.

My eyes adjusted somewhat to the dark, and I could make out the faces closest to me. The ship began to vibrate, to pulsate, to throb with the beat of the engines. The ship was moving. I was on my way, but to where?

A little more light came into the hold. Maybe the ship had turned, maybe the moon had risen. Though faint, the light was better, and the ability to see a face, to recognize an expression, to make eye contact made me feel less isolated, less alone.

Body heat and moisture in the humid air combined and began to condense on the steel deck over my head. Large drops began to fall like a gentle rain. We had been given no food or water since we left Cabanatuan the previous morning and my canteen was empty. Hunger was bearable; it was with me all the time, but my thirst was immense.

A prisoner a few feet away, someone I didn't know, took a piece of cloth and sopped up the overhead condensation and squeezed the few drops of liquid into his mouth. His partner warned him to knock it off, to leave it alone. Said nobody knew what the hell was in that stuff. The prisoner with the rag continued to wipe and squeeze condensation into his mouth. We knew it was a stupid thing to do, but the man's thirst was stronger than the warning.

Half an hour later "stupid bastard" vomited all over himself and the two or three guys crowded around him. He was told in no uncertain terms that he was a no good son of a bitch and to go ahead and die. Not to be taken literally, these words gave emotional release to a man soaked in another man's vomit. Though his stomach was empty and nothing more would come up, "stupid bastard" continued to heave and retch throughout the night.

Slowly, very slowly, the hours dragged by. My knees, my ass, my entire body ached from sitting so long in one cramped position, yet I was held firmly by the press of bodies around me. At best I could only shift my ass a couple of inches. It didn't help. I wanted so badly to straighten out my legs, to unbend my knees. I began to be afraid. I began to lose control. It was the same panicky feeling I remembered from childhood, when I had foolishly dived deep into a lake, stayed down too long, and had run out of breath before I got back to the surface. I knew my body was trembling. I felt a surge of anger, partly at the Japs who put me in this hellhole and partly at myself because I couldn't control my body, my emotions. I didn't think it was the fear of death that I felt, that would come later. I had already seen so much of death that it had become commonplace. In these last two years as a prisoner I had on more than one occasion faced the possibility, even the probability, of my own death. I had more than once looked death squarely in the eye, known it for what it was, and slowly learned not to be too much afraid. This time was different. I didn't want to die here in this total blackness. Hell, I never wanted to die anywhere, but especially not now, not like some animal sealed below decks in the bowels of the ship. The fear I felt was the unreasoning fear of a child in the dark, afraid to look under the bed because the monster might be there. I closed my eyes and took a few deep breaths, dropped my head on my knees, and tried to calm myself.

I wanted to know where they were taking us and tried to start a conversation. Conversation would have been something positive to focus on, might have helped to get away from the fear. I didn't know, nobody knew, but the man next to me took the cue and joined in. He thought we might be going to Japan. For some unknown reason, possibly because it was the Japanese homeland, Japan seemed to offer the promise of better treatment. Maybe, just maybe, the food there would be better, and there might be medicine for the sick and some clothes, even a place to take a shower. We hadn't had a real bath in a couple of years.

We heard it was just a bunch of baloney, but there it was again, "I heard," or "they say," the usual indefinite sources from the rumor mill. Nobody protested because nobody wanted to ask directly, who said it? or where did you hear it?

I think that in desperate times men cling to hope. They try to believe because they need to believe, and through this mental self-deception they are able to translate the slimmest of possibilities into tomorrow's, always tomorrow's, probabilities. If I can just get through the hell that is today, then treatment will get better, food will get better, life will get better — but tomorrow, always tomorrow.

Personally, I couldn't see how things could get worse, but they did. The closed-in air became thick with the heavy smell of fifteen hundred hot, sweaty, unwashed bodies. Now the sharp acrid smell of fresh urine and the warm heavy smell of human feces thickened the air, adding to the olio of smells. Here and there among this horrible crush of human misery, men were reaching the breaking point, the point beyond which they could no longer control their basic bodily functions. Here and there a man had to urinate, and when he could no longer hold it in, he had to urinate on himself and whomever stood or sat next to him. When his diarrhea-infected bowels erupted, the press of bodies left him no choice but to crap on himself and anyone or everyone around him. Fights broke out, but there was really no room even to fight.

Cries of rage and anger, sounds of outrage and disgust, of shame, came from the darkness.

An agonized whisper, half apologizing, half pleading, "Oh God, I'm sorry, I can't help it."

An outraged, "Son of a bitch. Dirty little bastards, why don't they let us outta here?"

Anger, hatred, shame, disgust, but no recriminations. We all knew that if our situation didn't change, and damn soon, our time too would come.

In a tiny part of my mind I quietly thanked God that I had been able to relieve myself just before boarding ship. Though I knew there would be no blame, no condemnation, I also knew that if I broke, the shame and humiliation would be personal. For the time being I could probably hold out longer than most, yet I was thankful that I was surrounded by a bunch of strangers. Except for Johnson some distance away, almost no one near me knew my name or my face. To some small extent I could hide behind this anonymity. What a hell of a thing to be thankful for, that I might not crap my pants, and if I did, no one who knew me would know about it.

Very slowly, second by second, agony by agony, the torturous night dragged on. There was little talking. In the crush of bodies it was hard enough just to breathe and stay alive. Not much conversation, but the darkness was filled with moans and low cries of pain, and the heart-rending sobs of terrible mental agony. Now and then, out of the darkness, a few words of comfort or reassurance. In the dimness, when a man's head sagged to his knees, I couldn't tell if he was unconscious or had just fallen asleep from exhaustion. From the whispers and rumors that passed from man to man, I knew there already were dead among us — dead men still standing, trapped in the press of bodies with no room to fall down.

A trickle of warm liquid ran under my feet. I smelled the stench of hot, fresh urine and knew someone nearby had just let go. I couldn't move, there was no place to go, nothing I could do, so I just sat there clinging precariously to sanity and waited for morning, hoping as always that daylight would bring some relief.

Looking back over the years I can still remember the sounds, the fears, the emotions of that one awful night. I can still recall, quite vividly, the weight of slick sweaty bodies pressed against mine, jamming me in, holding me immobile. I can still feel the undercurrent of fear that filled the hold, the tightness in my chest, the difficulty in breathing. I remember, in the darkness of night, the low cries of pain, the soft moans of delirium, the cursing, the weeping. Sometimes I remember the contradictions, the incongruities. We were fifteen hundred American prisoners, mostly young kids, many of us not yet out of high school. We were fifteen hundred American fighting men, trained, disciplined, battle-tested, and we were tough. Tough because we had survived two years of brutal treatment at the hands of our captors. Yet underneath this veneer of toughness were typical American kids who, in their pain, their suffering, still cried in the dark for their mothers.

Morning came, and with the morning light came reality. We were in a hell of a tough situation. None of us could survive a voyage of any length under these conditions. The equation was simple and direct. There were only two alternatives, relief or death.

I was lucky in the sense that I had been one of the first into the hold and had found seating on one of the shelves. Life, or living, was more difficult for the poor devils with standing room only. I saw a limp form passed over heads and hoisted on deck with a rope. Dead or unconscious, I couldn't tell. More followed at intervals. How many, I don't know. The Japs allowed two very weak men to climb the vertical ladder to the deck where the cooler air might revive them. An atypical show of compassion. Half an hour later the two came back looking somewhat refreshed. I was too far away to hear the conversation, but it didn't take long for the word to pass. The guards threw a couple of buckets of sea water on him while he lay on deck. He thinks they tossed some bodies over the side.

Time crept by. The sun was midmorning high, high enough for the first of its rays to shine directly into one corner, adding to the already sweltering heat. I could feel its heat beginning to radiate from the steel plates over my head. It was unbearably hot and could only get worse. Since yesterday morning we had been given no food or water, especially water, and we were slowly dying. A day, three days, a week, how long could even a strong man last under these conditions? And none of us were strong. As a group we were exhausted, physically and mentally. We were terribly underweight, ill nourished, and overworked. In the States even the best among us would have been hospitalized on sight. In a word we were sick, walking on the edge, and probably closer to death than to life. We didn't need, couldn't stand, a shove in the wrong direction.

For myself, on looking back, I think I was somewhere in the middle of the pack, worse off than the best of them and better off than the worst of them. At that time I weighed about one hundred and twenty pounds, an even hundred pounds below my normal weight but a good twenty pounds more than I had weighed when I went into the camp hospital.

In my three-and-a-half years as a prisoner of war, there were a number of times when just staying alive became a question that I had the power to decide. It was as simple as, "Do I or don't I struggle for the next breath?" When I felt like a very weary man trying to keep his eyes open just a little while longer, when it would have been so easy just to close my eyes, relax, and go to sleep, or go to death. This was one of those times. However, the will to live, some primal instinct to survive, is strong in all of us, and the fact that I am writing this is proof enough that I always opted for the next breath. I think it would be disappointing to look back from the other side of death and have to say to myself, "Damn it, if I had just held on a little while longer things would have been all right."

About ten o'clock there was a bustle of activity on deck, and a stir of excitement ran through the hatch. The Japanese were up to something, but what? As usual, when the Japanese became interested in us I became apprehensive. What were they up to, what were they going to do? A partial answer came quickly. The Japs began taking men out of the hatch. From our position down below we could not see, but there was no shooting, no shouting, no cries of pain, and we assumed those prisoners who were leaving the hatch weren't being treated too badly. We later learned that the six hundred men taken from our hold were moved to another hold in the forward part of the ship. The engine room and superstructure were between us and we lost contact until we landed in Japan. Prisoners continued to climb the ladder, to disappear on deck until there were only nine hundred of us left in the hold. We had room to breathe. We could move about. Not that there was a lot of room, but like a theater lobby when the play is over, with a lot of bumping and touching and a little shoving I could move about.

My first thought was to get off my numb ass, to crawl down from that god-damn shelf and straighten my aching knees. After sitting scrunched up in a tight little ball for so many hours I wasn't able to stand so I tumbled down from the shelf and sat on the steel deck with my legs stretched out in front of me till feeling and circulation returned.

With our newfound freedom to move about, however limited, prisoners circulated throughout the hold, climbing onto the shelves, climbing down off the shelves, gradually coalescing into small groups of three or four or perhaps half a dozen. No matter the size, these little groups would band together, talk together, eat and sleep together, and in some small sense look out for one another. When this voyage was over, if it were ever to be over, they might be separated, sent to different camps, might never see or hear about one another again, but for now the common danger, the common suffering, the need not to be totally alone would bond them together like a small family.

I knew that the milling about would soon stop, that individuals and groups, like some species of animals, would begin staking out their territories. In a very short time a prisoner who slept in a particular place would be able to leave to get food, to urinate, or just to talk with someone, then return and find he had established a kind of residual ownership, a proprietary ownership that would go unchallenged.

Johnson and I and the kid from Salinas moved into the forward end of the hold, under the deck house, where we thought it might be a little cooler. Against the steel wall that formed the end of our compartment we found a space about six feet long between two huge vertical beams that supported the upper decks. Between these beams there was a steel shelf about fourteen inches from the floor. Empty now, in the ship's younger days it had probably held some piece of ship's machinery. We sat on the shelf, backs against the bulkhead, feet on the deck, and made it ours. For better or worse, this was to be our space for the rest of the voyage. It would be home to the three of us until we arrived wherever we were going.

Not that we had a lot of room, or even enough room. Quite the contrary. When the prisoners stopped milling about and the hold settled down for the voyage, no matter how tightly we squeezed together, only about two thirds of us could lie down. With nine hundred prisoners still in our compartment, I could lie on the iron deck for two nights but had to stand up on the third. Certainly not a good arrangement, but infinitely better than the first night.

In my space, our space, where Johnson and I and the guy from Salinas sat, we decided one would sleep on our shelf, one under it, and the third was on his own to stand, sit, or make the best of it. We rotated among ourselves, so I stood on my feet every third night.

It was comfortable under the shelf, as far as sleeping on a steel deck can ever be comfortable, but it was scary. The shelf was just high enough so a man flat on his back could slide under, but there was absolutely no room to turn over. Once under the shelf, the adjoining space was blocked off by other sleepers. There was no way out until one or two men directly in front stood up and made room. Something like sleeping in a coffin with the lid down.

Funny thing about the guy from Salinas. We were together for the entire voyage and I never learned his name. Don't think he knew mine either.

About noon the Japanese hung a wooden tub on a rope and lowered it into the hold. A ripple of excitement spread. The end of a fire hose followed the tub, and water, real fresh drinkable water gushed into the tub. Pandemonium! Nine hundred thirst-crazed prisoners rushed the tub, and the Japanese turned the water off. It was a mob scene. The tiny bit of water spilled on the floor, and nobody got any. Prisoners in the rear couldn't see that the water had been turned off, and they screamed and clawed and fought to get closer to the tub. From where I stood I couldn't see the damn tub, but crazy with thirst, I pushed and clawed and fought for water like the rest. I got nowhere.

A couple of sunshiners, old noncoms who had spent most of their lives in the Army, took over water distribution. They ordered us back to our places, told us that they would take one section at a time and everybody would get some water. "Get back, damn it! Get back or there won't be no goddamn water for nobody." The voice was loud, strident, angry, but it was a voice that had called a thousand formations to attention and it rang with authority. The shouting, crowding, surging mob began to lose focus, turned into groups, clusters, individuals who moved reluctantly back to their former places. Most of us were Army regulars, what in prewar days had been termed the Old Army, and even after two years as a prisoner of war, the tough Old Army discipline was still there. I moved back to my spot in the far end of the hold and waited.

Johnson told me his mouth was so dry he could spit cotton. He was almost mumbling. He was talking to me but his eyes never left the empty water tub.

I wondered if we were really going to get some water or if the little bastards were playing with us again. I felt rage at the Japanese. At that moment, if I had my way, I'd have killed every damn one of them.

I remember snatches of conversation, but nobody was listening. Every eye, every thought was on the empty water tub. I don't think I had anything more to say because I was so deeply involved in my own personal thoughts. I needed that water. I needed it badly, and I needed it right away. I knew the trouble signs. My mouth was fuzzy dry and my body craved water, but worse than that, I had stopped sweating. In the stifling heat of nine hundred bodies crowded together in a small compartment, I had stopped sweating. My skin was bone dry and I felt even weaker than usual. I had seen too many cases of sunstroke, of heat exhaustion, not to know that I was on the verge of serious trouble. The silliness of the thought struck me, and I laughed, a little chuckle just to myself, but Johnson heard. He asked me what the hell I was laughing at. Something he didn't know? He didn't expect an answer and I didn't offer one. My own personal joke. Unless I was dead, how could I be in more trouble? Humor aside, I knew death was a real possibility.

The old noncom sounded off again. First he selected four men at random, then he told us that when we got water, these four men would pass it out, as evenly as possible, one canteen cupful for everybody. Nobody offered an objection so he went on, outlined his plan.

He told us to pay attention and listen up good. He pointed to the men in the first section of wooden shelves and said that when we got water we'd start there and work through the hatch taking one section at a time. He ordered us to line up, get our ration of water and get back to our place as quick as possible, and he said that anybody who fucked up "don't get no water."

Satisfied that he had things under control and everybody in place, the old man placed his hands on his hips and stared defiantly up at the Japanese. They turned on the water.

Plainly, the Japanese had not prepared for our trip in advance. Either they had decided to move us out in one hell of a hurry, or they had given absolutely no thought to the matter. We were horribly overcrowded, there were no toilet facilities, no places to wash our dirty bodies, no places to sleep except wooden shelves and bare steel decks, and provisions of food and water was an afterthought. The old wooden slave ships couldn't have been much worse.

The water tub they gave us was part of a barrel that had been sawed in half. It had not been used for a long time because the wooden staves were not tight together and the tub leaked through every crack. We tried to place cups to catch the larger leaks but a good amount of water drained onto the floor, mixed with feces and urine and dirt, and was lost.

The four designated water servers knelt beside the tub, and each held a canteen cup to use as a ladle. When your turn in the water line came and you got to the tub, you held your container over the tub and the server poured your ration into it. Then you got out of the way, fast. Had to be fast, everyone was desperate for water and we had no way of knowing just when the unpredictable Japanese would turn off the supply.

If you had a canteen cup or a tin can the server would empty his cup into yours. If you had only a canteen you held it over the tub while the server tried to empty his ladle into your canteen. Difficult at best, but damn near impossible with the jostling and the hurry. Always some of the precious water missed the small opening of the canteen and splashed back into the tub. It was emotionally painful to lose even the tiniest mouthful, but that was the luck of the draw. There were no second chances, you took your ration and made room for the next guy.

People are somewhat like pictures in a kaleidoscope, each one is a little different. A few prisoners with their cup full to the brim tried to carry it back to their sleeping place, but in shoving through the crowd, stepping over reclining bodies, or climbing up on the wooden shelves, they spilled some. More cautious prisoners drank a part of their ration on the spot and then moved back, spilling less. Six of one, half a dozen of the other, but hard to choose between the desire to drink it all now and the need to make it last.

Looking back today, looking back from these United States, from this bounteous, almost unbelievable land of plenty, the disposition of a cup of water seems almost trivial, yet in those circumstances, what a man did with his cup of water was both an important and a difficult decision, another reminder that life as a prisoner of war was made up of countless such difficult decisions.

Look at it this way. I am suffering from thirst and I have been given a cup of water. I don't know when, if ever, I'll get another. Will I drink it all at once and try to satisfy my raging thirst, or will I nurse it along and make it last? Will I gulp it down here or will I carry it back to the place where I am among friends, where I feel a little more secure?

If I drink all of my water right now, then by God I've done it. It's in my belly, and I won't worry about it spilling, or worry about some bastard stealing it while I'm asleep. On the other hand, if I drink all of my water now, it's gone, and I've lost the comfort, the reassurance, the security of knowing I have some in reserve for later.

If I carry this cupful back to my place in the hold, I'll have to watch it all the time. We're so crowded there's no room to set it down. I can't risk getting my cup kicked over, and I can't hold a cup in my hands forever.

What if I fall asleep? Maybe, if I curl up on my side I can tuck my cup into the folds of my body and it won't spill. Maybe, lots of maybes. Such a little worry, such a trivial decision, often as not meant the difference between living or dying.

In my case, I was again one of the lucky ones. I was in clover, eatin' high on the hog. I had both a canteen and a canteen cup. When the server filled my cup I carefully made a funnel with my fist and poured my ration of water into my canteen. Now I could drink it, save it, nurse it along, even safely sleep with it. I took the cord that held up my G-string and passed it through the chain that fastened the screw cup to my canteen. Secured to my waist, my water would not be stolen in the dark, and I could sleep. In a miserable uncertain world, for the moment, my water was safe.

Water rationing went swiftly. The Japs pulled up the tub and it was over. We each had our ration and we could do any damn thing we wanted with it. Drink it, save it, or hold it and worry about it, but spill it and you were, in the Army vernacular, "just shit out of luck." No more till next time, whenever that might be. There was no cheating, however, no going twice to the water tub. There were too many eyes on the tub, and we had all heard old Sarge's warning, "Anybody fucks up don't get no water."

That first single ration of water probably saved my life. If it did not actually save it, it slowed down the process of losing it. On that first day of our voyage I drank my first ration of water within seconds. My body demanded it and I couldn't imagine doing it any other way. Later, as the days dragged into weeks, I managed to exert more self-control. I forced myself to take my ration and nurse it along, to make it last the full twenty-four hours. I would open my canteen, take a mouthful of water, and hold it in my mouth for minutes, letting only the smallest sip trickle down my throat.

When you are truly, desperately thirsty, a mouthful of water is not just something to be gulped down to quench your thirst. It is instead an experience, a delight to the senses, a relief that can be felt throughout your entire body. At such a time water has an ambrosial quality all its own, like a good wine that should be held in the mouth, rolled about the tongue, tasted and thoroughly enjoyed before swallowing. It became a daily personal challenge to keep a little water in my canteen, so that when the next day's water tub came down, when I was standing in line waiting for my next ration to be doled, when I knew for sure there would be more, I could stop sipping and drink the last of my water with abandon.

There was never enough water, not by any means. A canteen cup holds a good pint, not much more, and a pint of water a day is not nearly enough under the best of circumstances. In our case it was barely enough to sustain life.

Once a day, usually before noon, the water tub magically descended from above, and its appearance became one of the focal points of my existence. I no longer measured time by the hour; I didn't have a watch. I measured time by the amount of water left in my canteen, by how long I thought it had been since the last water tub was pulled up, by how long I thought it would be till the next water tub came down. My mental comfort level was directly proportionate to the amount of water remaining in my canteen. I enjoyed the feel of it, enjoyed the weight of the water sloshing around when I shook it, and occasionally, when my canteen was empty, I felt the loss of its comfort.

Water rationing was as fair as we could make it. Fair, but not always equal. The four servers worked at a furious pace because the Japs were impatient. They never left the tub down more than a few minutes.

The server scooped up a cup of water, I held my cup over the tub, and he emptied his into mine. The action was necessarily fast and if a little spilled, it couldn't be helped. Like everyone else, I took what I got, made the best of it, and got the hell out of the way. I wanted my canteen cup full to the brim, but if the water was down an inch from the top I had to take my ration and go. The loss of a few ounces of water was painful, but there was nothing I could do, nothing anyone could do. There were no arguments, no hesitations, no second dips, no second chances. Get it and go. That was the rule. Anybody fucks up don't get no water.

Dysentery is a terribly dehydrating illness and we all had dysentery to a greater or lesser degree. It is an enervating, weakening illness that literally drains the life from your body, that turns everything you eat into a thin watery slush that ten, fifteen, twenty or more times a day, along with agonizing cramps, uncontrollably spews forth.

Thus the all-consuming attention we paid to daily water ration. Under normal living conditions the small amount of water would have been barely sufficient to sustain life. In our hot, crowded, unsanitary hellhole it was simply not enough.

I was always thirsty, but with my canteen, a closable container, I had control. I could make my ration last throughout the day. A few prisoners with no cup at all were really in a bind. They had to borrow a cup, drink their ration on the spot, and then deal with a twenty-four-hour dry spell.

As the voyage dragged on, prisoners became crazed with thirst. Fights over water usually ended with the water being spilled and both parties losing out. Water left unguarded, even for the tiniest moment, was immediately stolen. Severe dysentery increased the bodily need for water and weaker men died. Terrible things happened in the blackness of night. Men were found dead with their throats torn open and we knew at least one of us had sustained his own life by drinking the blood of another. The crazy one, the blood drinker, was never caught, but the killing stopped. I can only assume that this one demented prisoner probably died in his own private hell.

Late in the afternoon of the first day at sea, food was lowered into the hold just as water had been given us earlier. A commotion on deck, then a tub lowered on a rope. This time I felt as if I had passed another milepost in my long trek to wherever.

There was another daily happening that was important to us, though not nearly as important as food and water.

Following the first drink of water and the first meal, the Japanese gave us two half-barrels to serve as toilets. We already had a thirty-six-hour accumulation of human feces and urine on the floor. We were standing in it, sleeping in it. The entire hold was a stinking, filthy mess, but the tubs were at least a step in the right direction. Unfortunately, the Japanese had rigged only one spot where they could raise or lower tubs from the hold. For the whole trip there were two shit buckets (our language was often crude but literal) within a couple of yards of the place where we dished out our food and water. During daylight hours, whenever the buckets were full, the Japanese would hoist them on deck and dump them over the side. When they came back empty but dirty (they never washed them out) there was always some poor bastard standing on the spot, shuffling from one foot to the other, waiting to hang his bare bottom over the tub and start filling it again. Not a single cupful of water or a single serving of barley was dished out without someone squatting over the shit bucket a few feet away.

After that first terrible night, after the Japanese took six hundred of the fifteen hundred prisoners out of our hold, we remaining nine hundred divided the available space among ourselves. Through trial and error we found that by utilizing the entire hold, including the open area of the hatch square, two thirds of us could lie down in some fashion while the remainder had to sit or stand. Thus we gradually coalesced into groups of three and rotated among the three, the sleeping, sitting, or standing. When the food or water tubs came down we crowded a little more tightly to make room for them to land on the floor. When the toilet buckets came down we did the same, crowded back to make room, but when full they were too heavy to be moved by hand so food buckets and toilet buckets were in the same place.

The tub contained cooked barley instead of water. I was relieved, reassured. At least the Japs weren't going to starve us to death. Not today anyway. The barley was doled out just as the water had been doled out earlier. Never enough, but at least a scant portion to each man. With the serving of this first meal of unsalted barley, a second benchmark was established. Water in the morning, barley in the afternoon. These were the only interruptions in the mind-blurring monotony of sitting, standing, sleeping, day after day in the same overcrowded space. Water in the morning, barley in the afternoon. These daily rituals quickly became the only moments that were in any way different from all the other moments of my day. When you have absolutely nothing but a precarious toehold on life itself, a little water, a little barley, can become synonymous with comfort, safety, security. Food and water became moments of reality in the mind-numbing fantasy of waiting, wondering, speculating. They become islands in an endless sea of fear, pain, apprehension and despair.

As the voyage continued, as the hours dragged into days and the days dragged into weeks, time as I had known it became meaningless. I could see better in daylight, in the dim light that penetrated to my place far back in the ship's hold, but other than that there was no difference between day and night. I no longer stayed awake by day and slept by night. I slept when exhausted. I stretched out in the coffin-like space under the shelf when it was my turn, sat down when I could, stood when I had to. There were no clocks, no bells, no jobs to do; there was no reason to sleep at one time, to stay awake at another, no reason to differentiate one minute from the next. One thing, however, did become obvious to me. Like a cow that wanders back to the barn at milking time, I developed a mental time clock. Mentally, emotionally, physically, I knew when it was time for the water tub or the barley tub to come down. If either of these was late I became fidgety, worried, apprehensive. I was always awake at these times and I watched the spot where the tubs were lowered. When the water or the barley came down I felt reassured.

Once darkness fell, the Japanese left the toilet buckets in the hold until full daylight. In the night the toilet buckets overflowed and the rolling motion of the ship sent streams of feces and urine sloshing across the floor. Except for the prisoners on the wooden shelves and a few men farthest from the toilet tubs, men literally lived and slept in puddles of filth. For weeks we lived in this filth with no water to wash our bodies, and of course, no water to wash the crap off the floor. It was a helluva way to live, even a helluva way to die.

I don't know how long I was on that ship. I don't know just how long the voyage took. Hours blurred into days and days blurred into weeks. Military records indicate that we left Cabanatuan on July 17, 1944, and I remember being in a new camp in Japan in September. In between I believe my mind and body turned off all functions except those necessary for survival.

Days passed into weeks. Water bucket, barley buckets, and shit buckets came in and out of the hold. Now and then a limp form was dragged to the square, hoisted on deck, and dumped over the side. We were no longer nine hundred. Some prisoners had died in the crush of that first brutal night. Some died of hunger, of thirst, of dysentery. Some died of despair.

Realistically, who in hell knew just what a man died from? Dead was dead. During the entire voyage no Japanese came into the hold. Probably couldn't stand the stench. There were no doctors among us, and had there been, we had no medicine, not so much as a single aspirin. We were just left to die. After more than two years in prison camps, after prolonged malnutrition, after repeated bouts of dysentery, beri-beri, edema, scurvy, malaria, pellagra, illnesses even our doctors couldn't name, resistance became so low that even a common cold could prove fatal. It was all so unnecessary because most of the deaths on the ships and in the camps could have been prevented with medicine and decent food.

Illness and death had become common denominators in all our lives. For me, I had already had all of the vitamin deficiency diseases, often in multiples, most of them more than once. Some of the nerves in my teeth had died, so now, instead of toothaches, I had pyorrhea and repeated abscesses of my gums. I had been almost totally blind for nearly a year and then, miraculously, recovered my sight. My feet had swollen to the point where the skin cracked and burst open, until my ankles were as thick as my thighs, until walking was a matter of clumping slowly along dragging huge, swollen, heavy feet. There had been days, weeks, when I was so bloated from edema that my scrotum hung nearly halfway to my knees, when I had to cup it in both hands to sustain the weight while I walked to the latrine; weeks when I sat upright all night, afraid to lie down because the accumulation of fluid in my body might stop my heart or collapse my lungs and cause me to suffocate. All this, and I still considered myself a middle-of-the-roader, no better, no worse off than the average prisoner.

Under what came to be considered "normal" conditions in a Japanese prison, bodily functions, those functions not absolutely necessary to sustain life, began to shut down. My fingernails stopped growing, I could go months without a haircut, sex was not even a dim memory. I worked, I slept, I ate, I went to the latrine, nothing more.

At times it seemed as if a man's internal systems, his heart, his lungs, his liver, got tired of the struggle, gave a sigh, and simply said no more, and the man died.

I remember one day some weeks into the voyage, I really don't know how long, I was sitting all crowded up on our shelf way in the back of the hold. It was sometime in the afternoon and lunch, breakfast, dinner, whatever we chose to call it, our one daily small ration of barley had just been doled out. I remember sitting there eating my barley slowly, very slowly. I always ate slowly, chewed every mouthful until it was slush in my mouth before swallowing because eating slowly somehow seemed to make the small serving larger in quantity. And while I was eating, something funny happened.

Like beauty, humor is in the eye of the beholder, and on rare occasions something happened that tickled my funny bone. And unlike humor on the stage, in the movies, or on the radio, POW humor was unplanned, unrehearsed. When it occurred it was usually by surprise and its spontaneity made it even more delightful, more delicious. One such event happened somewhere about midpoint in our voyage. I was sitting in the half-light of my personal space, my butt on the low steel shelf, my back against the iron bulkhead, intently scraping the last vestige of barley from my mess kit.

I heard someone ask a kid we called Swede what part of the country he was from. It was meaningless small talk. He didn't give a damn, he just wanted to start a conversation. I didn't look up from scraping my dish. Swede picked up the conversational ball, kept it rolling. He said that he was from Minnesota, that his old man was a farmer. Damn fine country up there, lots of trees and grass and cows. Our space grew quiet as Swede reminisced. He told us there was a little lake on their farm, warm enough to swim in during the summer, cold enough to skate on in winter. Freeze your goddamn balls off in winter.

Small talk, going nowhere. We all had a home, but sometimes it was so far in the past we almost forgot to think about it. Another prisoner ventured that he was from New York, East Side down by the river. Got hot as hell in New York in the summertime. Sometimes the city'd turn on the fire hydrant so the little kids could cool off by playing in the water. He said that the kids would run and scream and get their clothes all wet. They had one hell of a time. Grown-ups too, but they just stood and watched. Acted like they didn't care. Wanted to get in but too dignified to act like little kids. Said that he used to go down and jump into the East River. The water was dirty as hell but nobody ever got sick.

I was into the conversation now, mentally at least. A moment's hesitation, a minute of hush. Everybody had his own lake or fireplug or East River to think about. For a second, a minute, a single drop in an ocean of time, our spirits could break free from this stinking hole and soar in our imaginations through endless space to home, where the hell home was. "Visions of sugarplums danced in their heads"; nobody wanted to break the spell.

The next man to talk said he was from El Paso, told us he had been raised with one foot on either side of the border. American-Mexican or Mexican-American, he wasn't sure which one he was but he identified himself as Tex Mex. Tex Mex told us he had been raised on beans and tortillas and Texas chili and that his mother made the best chili in the whole state of Texas. He invited all us northern guys, after we got home, of course, to come down to his part of the country and eat. He said it didn't matter where we were from, we all looked like Mexicans anyway.

I looked and he was right. We all looked alike. For probably the first time during the voyage I really looked at someone else and in looking at them I saw myself. Good God! We had all been dirty when we boarded the ship, and for the past five or six weeks we had been unable to wash. Not one drop of water to wash our hands, our faces, our stinking bodies. I hadn't rinsed my mess kit or rinsed my G-string for the whole trip. The dirt and shit and urine from the first day and all successive days still lay caked on the floor. I was filthy. For five or six weeks I had been sleeping on the rusty iron floor, sitting on the iron shelf, leaning against a rusty bulkhead, and sweating, always sweating. Every time I moved, every time I wiped a hand across my forehead, every time I rubbed a dirty forearm across my face, I either added more dirt or smeared the dirt that was already there. I must have looked like an escapee from the pits of hell, and we were all the same dirty streaky brown color.

Somebody snickered, somebody chuckled. We all looked like a bunch of Mexicans. Tex Mex thought it hilarious. He looked at the rest of us and howled with glee. He rocked back and forth and pointed at the guys next to him. He gasped and tried to talk, but no words came, only laughter, gales of laughter. He paused, caught his breath, gurgled once or twice and laughed again. His laughing eased off, subsided to a chuckle, then rose again. Tex Mex had his own private joke.

He tried to explain. "If the folks..." he broke up again. "If the folks at home..." more deep chuckles. "If the folks at home could see us now, marchin' down Main Street, they'd run like hell."

It took a second for the thought to sink in, then in my mind I saw myself, saw the bunch of us through the eyes of a stranger. We would have been one helluva sight. Emaciated, unbelievably dirty, mostly naked, surely no sight like this had ever been seen in our United States. Tex was right. They would have run like hell. I could imagine blinds being pulled down, shopkeepers closing their doors, mothers picking up, running with their kids.

The same thought must have hit several of us at the same time. There was a chuckle, a laugh, then everybody was laughing. We laughed at ourselves, laughed at each other, laughed at the guy next to us. For a few fleeting moments we were transformed. We were like a bunch of little kids at the dinner table with the giggles. We couldn't look another man in the eye without starting to laugh all over again. The laughing was contagious. Prisoners on the fringe of our group, too far away to know what the laughing was about, began to laugh with us. It spread. Within a couple of minutes the whole damn bunch of prisoners was laughing uproariously. And most of them didn't give a damn that they didn't even know what they were laughing about.

The Japanese, from their vantage point on deck, must have thought we were crazy, and I suppose, for a moment we were. Deranged? Possibly. Pathetic? Perhaps. The whole thing was over more quickly than I can tell. It was like a brief flash of sunlight that for a moment warmed our hearts and moved on, but after it was gone some of the warmth remained. In that one moment we somehow regained a little bit of ourselves. We became a little more human, and in that moment, fear, apathy, anxiety, despair, one hell of a lot of pent-up emotions were released.

Time dragged on. There were no storms, the seas were calm, hours dragged into days, days dragged into weeks, and no given day was different from the day that went before or the day that followed. The routine never varied, water in the morning, barley in the afternoon, and shit buckets in the hold all around the clock. Occasionally another limp form was tied to the rope, hoisted to the deck and tossed over the side. This body disposal, this makeshift burial at sea, was done quietly, as inconspicuously as possible. We tried not to notice.

The days dragged on, the routine never varied, but a noticeable change had come over the prisoners. Where the first days in the ship had been pure hell, the following days and weeks had seemed a lesser hell, and finally, the impossible, the unbearable, had become the norm. We had learned to cope with the rigorous demands of this particular lifestyle. We had made the adjustment. By God, we were going to survive.

Although I was unaware at the time, I now realize that I, we, had made such adjustments many times before. The almost instantaneous transition from free American to prisoner of war had been one hell of a culture shock, had required one hell of an adjustment. As our months and then years as prisoners of war passed, our living conditions changed, never for the better, always for the worse, and we adjusted. We adjusted so that living conditions that would have killed us in the beginning, a year later had become the accepted norm. Hardship, deprivation, death, these things became so much a part of our daily life that at times, I believe, we were completely unaware of just how difficult life really was. Day by day, as the long ordeal dragged on, I observed whatever was going on around me, and subconsciously, I'm sure, made the physical, mental, and emotional adjustments that allowed me to survive. Those unfortunates who were too rigid, who could not make the necessary adjustments, who could not bend with the wind, they were the ones who died.

Toward the end of our voyage the Japanese built a little outhouse on deck, a one-holer that hung over the side of the ship so the crap fell directly into the ocean. Surely not out of any concern for our comfort, more likely because they could no longer tolerate the stench of our hold. During daylight hours one man at a time was permitted on deck to use the outhouse. The outhouse was there and thankfully, one man at a time used it, but it made no noticeable difference to the hundreds of us still straddling the shit buckets down below.

It was my turn to sleep under the low iron shelf. I had inched my way beneath the shelf, legs straight out, arms at my sides. Flat on my back with the steel deck beneath me, the bulkhead tight against my right side, the shelf an inch above my nose, and I was tucked in for the night. I was snuggled into my coffin-like space with no way to get out until the two or three men sleeping on the deck next to me got up and moved out of my way. Once under the shelf I was fixed in one position. I couldn't turn over, couldn't sleep on my side, couldn't bend my knees, couldn't scratch my nose. For the first little while I could stretch out full length, comfortably, then the hurting, the aching pain in my back, my shoulders, my buttocks would begin, the nightly price exacted from my bare flesh by the hard iron deck. Eventually though, my ass, my shoulders, the entire back side of me would become numb. Only after the numbness was I able to sleep. Uncomfortable, sure. A hard way to live, hell yes, but the prisoners sleeping next to the shit buckets would have traded places in an instant.

At any rate, on this particular occasion, it was dusk. What little daylight remained was fast fading into darkness. I was under the shelf, settled in for the night when it happened. It was unexpected so I don't know whether I felt it or heard the sound first, or possibly both at the same time. There was a bump, a thud that ran through the ship. I didn't think at all at the time, but on looking back it felt as though the ship had run into something like a dead whale or a huge log, a jolt like in an automobile when a wheel drops into a pothole. At the same time I heard an explosion, a booming that reminded me of the whooshing roar of our big naval guns. A red glow filled the sky and even from way back under my shelf I could see the redness filtering down into our compartment. There was a big commotion on deck and the Japanese began putting on the hatch covers, began sealing us in below decks. The last man to use the toilet on deck came tumbling down the ladder. The last hatch board was put in place, and we were in total darkness, sealed in like rats locked in a steel box.

I didn't know what was happening, didn't know what was going on, but it was the only time on the voyage that the hatch had been completely closed.

The last prisoner to come off the deck was talking. His voice was shrill, excited, almost unintelligible. He kept repeating that he had seen it, goddamn, goddamn, he had seen it. He had seen a ship with lots of black smoke coming out and another ship burnin' like the Fourth of July. Goddamn, goddamn, he had seen it.

I still didn't know what was going on. My dull half-numbed brain couldn't put two and two together. I'll admit I was slow on the uptake, but there were a few Navy men among us and I heard one of them speaking. He was telling everybody within earshot that it's got to be torpedoes, got to be that our Navy finally caught up with the little bastards, got to be that burning ship's a tanker. Good for our side, hope it burns all to hell. Pandemonium, hundreds of voices asking questions.

From the pitch blackness a dozen voices urged Uncle Sam to give 'em hell, shouting that our guys were finally here and guess this'll give the Japs something to think about. Another voice from the dark, impossible to locate but easy to hear, saying that we had been prisoners so damn long he was beginning to wonder if the USA was still there. The unseen voice quivered with emotion, broke a little. I heard a low half-sob as the man caught his breath, and I suspected that there might be a tear or two accompanying the quiver in his voice. It had been a long time, a long, long time, and in our isolation we had been told nothing about the progress of the war. Now, suddenly, there were Americans out there, Americans still free and close enough to blast the hated enemy. Maybe, just maybe, there were other Americans out there who, somewhere, somehow, someday, would get us out of here.

I felt the elation, the hope, the instantaneous surge of emotion that passed like an electrical charge from body to body in the darkness. We were transformed. In that split second of realization, of knowing there were fellow Americans, free Americans nearby, we again became participants in the war. Not on the battlefield, but by God we were surely in the bleachers cheering our team on.

For half an hour, maybe even an hour, the hold was alive with conversation. We couldn't see each other but everybody had something to say, everyone wanted to talk and, for the most part, all at once.

Our guys, our subs, our troops. Through the babble of voices I could pick out certain phrases, could hear them repeated endlessly, over and over again. Our guys, our troops, Americans.

Truly, we were guessing. We didn't know what was going on, didn't know what was happening. We were grabbing at straws, but a drowning man will grab at every straw that passes by, and for these past two years we had been drowning in isolation. Now, for the moment we once again had identity, we belonged. We weren't sure just what we belonged to, but it was American and that was enough. We belonged. America was still there, and we knew it was our America. Like the lowliest freshman at a big university, we could take pride in the feeling, "That's *my* team." So we talked in the darkness. We took strength from one another, encouraged one another, repeated the same words, the same phrases endlessly, over and over and over. We kept talking, because talking about it kept the dream, the illusion, alive, and subconsciously perhaps, we knew that if we stopped talking, this dream, like a thousand dreams before it, this dream too would die.

I heard a distant explosion and an instant later felt our ship quiver as the shock waves from the concussion reached its sides. Another Jap ship blown to hell. A cheer. Shouting. Exultation.

Give it to the little bastards. That was my first thought. Kill the sons a bitches. Hope they sink every goddamn one.

A moment's cheering, a moment of elation, and then silence, and with the silence a cold icy fear. Fear, an icy realization that spread through the prisoners as quickly as turning on a light. We were unmarked. Our ship was unmarked. When we boarded I remembered seeing the dirty gray sides of the ship, gray paint with rust spots showing through, and vertical rivers of rust where the scuppers drained over the side. I remember briefly glimpsing the red ball of the Japanese flag flying from the stern, but I had been so busy looking out for myself as we were driven, cattle-like, into the hold, that the thought of how the ship was marked never entered my mind. Now, with the sound of the last explosion echoing in my ears, the full realization hit me. We were unmarked. There was no red cross painted on the sides. The tanker was burning. At least two other ships had been hit, and we were in no way different from any other ship in the convoy. I was sealed below decks in a ship filled with American prisoners of war and there was a submarine out there that had already torpedoed three ships in our convoy. Jesus Christ, we were fair game for the next torpedo because nobody, nobody knew we were there.

In an emotional mob like our eight or nine hundred prisoners jammed together in the dark in an already untenable situation, fear, like anger or hope, can spread from man to man in a flash. And it did.

I do not know how to accurately describe the situation in the ship for the next half hour. Perhaps because it does not bear description. At best it was chaotic, at worst, sheer madness. Remember, we were in absolute blackness. We were almost nine hundred men crowded body-to-body in a confined space. The hatch was sealed shut, and there was no way out. We knew three ships in our convoy had been torpedoed and we might well be the fourth.

Fear swept through the hold like a blast of cold air across a frozen lake. Fear's icy fingers grabbed at our hearts, at our guts, at our minds. You could sense it, you could smell it, you could feel it. Fear was everywhere; it touched everyone. There was no escape.

I heard people swearing at the goddamn little bastards. The noise was unbelievable. Hundreds of men screaming at the top of their lungs. Screaming for the

Japs to "let us outta here!" Asking them to "open the hatch you sons a bitches, don't make us die here!" "Our Father who art in heaven ... Why in hell don't you help us?" Now and then, above the clamor of voices, a few words would come through.

In my coffin-like space under the shelf I went berserk. I was confined, I felt trapped, I suddenly found it difficult even to breathe in my tiny "safe place." I banged my head against the overhead shelf until it bled. I tried to turn over until my shoulders were raw. I couldn't. I wriggled and squirmed and struggled to inch my way out from under the shelf, struggled and pushed with all my strength against the wall of sweaty flesh that blocked my only way out from under. I shouted and cursed till my throat was sore, struggled till I was exhausted, but to no avail. In the clamor nobody heard, and if they did hear, nobody gave a damn. In the end, actually after only a very few minutes, weakened, strength used up, I lay in my own sweat and blood and waited. Waited with wrenching guts, a tight ass, and dread in my heart. I didn't want to die. I didn't want to die shut up in the hold of this goddamn prison ship. And most of all, I didn't want to die trapped like a rat in this coffin-like sleeping place.

The hold was full of movement, but really, there was no place to go. In the blackness a man could not see the man next to him. Move an inch in one direction or six inches in another and you pressed up against another body. Had I been alone in the hold I could only have run for fifty feet and smashed into a bulkhead, or perhaps run in circles, but I would still have been trapped in the hold, below decks, waiting for the next torpedo, waiting for death.

After an eternity, probably less than half an hour, the hubbub quieted down, bodies in front of me gave way, and I scooted out of my coffin. Actually, it made little difference. I had moved from my tiny coffin, my sleeping place under the shelf, to a larger coffin, the sealed hold of an endangered prison ship, but I was relieved.

Once the initial shouting, the outpouring of protest, of rage, of horror at the thing the Japanese had done by sealing us in below decks was over, an unreal silence blanketed the hold. Now we were listening, waiting, waiting for the sound of the next torpedo, waiting for the explosion, waiting for death. The noise was gone, the shouting was gone, but the fear was still with us.

I was afraid. Damn right I was afraid. And so was every prisoner on the ship. But fear is nothing to be ashamed of. It is simply the body's physical and emotional acknowledgment of impending danger. On looking back over my three-and-a-half years as a prisoner of war I now realize that fear was such a close and constant companion that, for the most part, I became unaware of it. Yet I know it was there, always there.

To make this account believable, I ask the reader to remember that in Europe, under those terrible Nazis, less than 1 percent of prisoners of war died in their prison camps. In the Pacific, under the Japanese, the death rate was slightly more than 50 percent.

Anyway, I have to admit that on this night, I was damn well afraid. I never,

at any time, wanted to die, but in times of crises the desire to live seems to inten-
sify, and this was one of those times. I stood up the whole damn night. Whether
I stood or sat didn't make a bit of difference. If the ship went down I was going
down with it, but somehow I had the idea fixed in my mind that I had a better
chance to survive if the explosion came while I was standing rather than while I
was sitting on my ass. So I stood and I waited in the dark. Goddamn, to this day
I still hate waiting.

One thing I remember, one thing that stands out from that hellish night:
there was almost no praying. An occasional "Our Father," "Hail Mary," "Lord
have mercy," or "God help us." Nothing more. At least not out loud. Even our
padre, and there was a priest among us, must have done his praying silently. It has
been my experience that when death is imminent the mind either goes blank, or
possibilities whirl through the brain like the spinning wheels of a slot machine and
when the spinning stops the three bars will spell out whether to run, hide, fight,
scream, or whatever. I think, when facing death, the mind is fully occupied just
with keeping the body alive. Prayer, giving thanks to God, these can come later
but not now. You can get your ass shot off if you stop to pray when you ought to
be running for cover.

Speaking for myself, I had long ago settled my accounts, made my peace with
God. I had been raised Catholic, but I was a nominal Catholic. I went to Mass
most of the time, skipped Mass if I had a chance to go fishing. I thought of myself
as a Catholic, always said my prayers, and gave very little thought to religion. In
the prison camps, precisely because I had paid so little attention to God before the
war, I felt He would think me hypocritical if I suddenly got down on my knees
and asked for His help. On the other hand, you don't have to get calluses on your
knees to pray. Communication with God can be instantaneous. All the feelings of
sorrow, atonement, repentance, forgiveness, love of God or love of fellow man,
can be expressed in a millisecond. This, basically, was my relationship with God.
Not superficial, not really, we just cut through all the crap and got right to the
nitty-gritty. I knew that God was always aware of my deepest feelings, of my innermost thoughts, of my motivations, of all the bad as well as the good there was
about me. I knew that His knowledge of me was always on the surface, always
ready between us, always up to date. I never had the feeling that I had fallen
behind, that I had to catch up, never had the feeling that I would wake up on the
other side of death thinking, Jesus, if I had just lived another ten minutes I might
have made God understand.

So, in the sense that prayer is conventionally understood, I did not pray. But
I felt, deeply and intensely. I felt, and I think my God understood those feelings.
And occasionally, when I could almost reach out and take death by the hand, there
was a lot of fast, sincere one-liners. "Oh God, get me through this day and I'll try
not to bother you again. I'll try to go the rest of the way by myself."

I stood there in the dark, barefooted, naked except for my G-string, and
waited. Every muscle was tense, or at least as tense as the muscles of a hundred-
twenty-pound skeleton could be. My G-string was soaking wet with sweat and

the sweat ran in rivulets down my back and legs, probably as much from fear as from the heat. The air was heavy with odors of crap and urine and stinking unwashed bodies, but added to that, I could smell the fear, mine and everyone else's. Authors write about it. Psychologists talk about it. I have smelled it. Fear has a sharp pungent odor all its own, different from any other smell. Dogs can recognize it instantly and in this case, so could I, and once having smelled fear you can never forget its odor.

I was afraid. We were all afraid. Have to be a damn fool not to be. That old stuff about men going calmly to their death is a bunch of horseshit. Unlike they show it in the movies, soldiers don't just fall down and die. They die violently, sometimes horribly, kicking, screaming, struggling. The proverbial death rattle is just some poor son of a bitch trying to take one more breath. When my turn comes, God, like a parent with a recalcitrant kid in tow, will have to drag me off, kicking and screaming and raising hell because I don't want to go.

There were more explosions, more concussions at varying intervals through the night, some close by, others a distance away. I never counted, so I don't know how many there were. Like the hours, they blended with time and became lost in the dark. I only know that after each explosion we waited for the next one, and we expected the next one to be ours. It was too dark to see the men around me, even the man next to me, yet with every new explosion I could feel bodies twitch and jerk as if they had been touched with a cattle prod. Mine too. I jumped with every concussion. Yet there was almost absolute silence. We wanted to hear, wanted to hear that damn torpedo coming. Why? I don't know. Maybe to have some tiny advantage, to be ready to grab at even the slightest opportunity for life that might present itself. Maybe just to have a split second to tighten your ass and wait for the final shock. My body trembled; every muscle ached. I found myself taking a breath, holding it as long as I could, letting it out softly, and taking another. Holding that breath too. The strain was beyond belief. I was so taut, hurt so badly, physically and emotionally, that I almost wanted the next torpedo to be ours, to end the goddamn waiting. Sometimes, I think, the suspense, the waiting, is harder than the dying.

It had been a couple of hours since the last explosion, since we heard or felt the last concussion. Daylight came and with daylight the Japanese opened one end of the hatch. Light streamed in and blinded me for an instant, but I was alive. We were all alive and damn glad of it.

With the coming of daylight, with the removal of the hatch covers, things changed. Tensions eased and my emotional level went down like air escaping from a punctured tire. I was as wet and limp as an old washrag that has been thoroughly chewed by a puppy. Sure, I knew the submarine might still be out there, but the last explosion had been hours ago. Maybe the submarine had run out of torpedoes, maybe it had lost us in the dark, maybe the convoy had scattered and the sub was chasing another ship in another direction. Maybe, maybe, maybe. I didn't know, might never know why we were still afloat, might never know why we had been spared, so maybe was the best I could do.

There was no cheering, no hurrahing, no wild bursts of excitement. Instead, a quiet realization that we had been taken to the brink and allowed to step back. Fate had smiled, had played her little joke, and once again, for the moment at least, death had passed us by.

Nothing much had changed. We were still filthy, emaciated, half-starved prisoners on an overcrowded prison ship bound for nowhere. But the daylight, the fresh air, the open hatch, the blue sky, had given us a new lease on life. Even in a cage it is better to be able to see out than to be completely sealed in.

The Japanese wasted no time at all. As soon as the hatch covers were off they took about twenty men out of the hold. What for? What were they up to? What the hell was going on? There was no shooting, no shouting in Japanese, no cries of pain. What the hell? We had our answers in half an hour. The first twenty men came back into the hold, dripping wet but unharmed, and clean. Well, not really clean but cleaner.

The Japanese had a fire hose on deck and were letting the prisoners wash themselves with clear, warm salt water pumped directly from the ocean. It must have felt good because the prisoners who came back were elated. The brief dousing with warm sea water had raised their spirits.

Twenty more men went on deck and when they came back, twenty more.

In the hold we questioned this sudden change of attitude on the part of the Japanese. They had given us nothing before, why now? Why are they being so nice all of a sudden? What's in it for them?

It didn't take long, didn't take a genius to figure this one out. Even the dumbest among us could put two and two together and come up with the answer. There had been no change of heart. They were not showing pity, or kindness, or compassion. And this was not "be kind to prisoners week." Our Japanese guards were afraid. Their asses were still twitching from the night before. American prisoners of war, on deck and in plain sight and being kindly treated might be their insurance against the next torpedo. The voyage lasted another four or five days and there was never a minute during daylight hours when the Japs didn't have their insurance policy, a bunch of prisoners, on deck under the fire hose.

My turn came in the afternoon and it was truly wonderful. The afternoon was hot, the salt water was comfortably warm, and there was plenty of it. We took turns, one prisoner holding the hose and spraying water on the rest. I scrubbed. God, how I scrubbed. No soap, just salt water and elbow grease, but it was great. I took water on my front, on my back, in my eyes, in my hair. I rubbed my hands across my face, my chest, my arms and legs, scrubbed with my hands and scratched my fingernails as fast as I could make them go. I even managed to rinse out my G-string for the first time in two months. Did I get clean? Hell no, no way, but I felt clean. I might never get clean gain, but for the moment I felt clean. I felt better.

That first few minutes under the water hose was like a glimpse into heaven. It was a real morale booster, a spirit lifter. The sheer luxury of clean, warm water, even salt water. I turned and twisted and bent and stooped so the hose could spray on every part of my body. I smiled at a fellow prisoner and he smiled back. I even laughed a little. I scrubbed the dirt off his back where he couldn't reach, turned, and he scrubbed mine. We milled about in front of the nozzle, slipping, sliding, shoving, but gently, always gently, trying to stay in the main flow as much as we could, but at the same time trying not to deprive the other fellow of his fair share. For a moment in time our troubles washed away with the dirt and we were little kids again, splashing in a rain puddle. Even the guards had an occasional smile and pleasant looks on their faces.

I went back into the hold. Nothing had changed. I was still a prisoner of war on a hell ship, caged like an animal, not enough food, not enough water, not enough room to lay my body down to rest. Nothing had changed, but I had changed. I felt better about myself, more a man, less an animal. I had a new outlook, a new lease on life, a fresh start. I knew I was going to live through this ordeal, going to beat these sons a bitches at their own game.

Can a little salt water make such a difference in a man's outlook on life? Damn right it can. Try, try it yourself. Try living for five or six or seven weeks, however, long it was, without a single drop of water to wash your face, your hands, your body. Try sleeping on a dirty floor without bedding with only a rag around your loins for clothing. Try going six weeks without toilet paper, without washing. Damn right a little water can make a difference.

Before I had the first salt-water bath my hair was matted so I couldn't run my fingers through it. My unshaven whiskers were stiff with dirt. My fingernails could scrape furrows in the dirt, the grime on my arms and legs and body. The creases in my groin were cracked, slimy, stinking. The cheeks of my ass were raw because there had been no toilet paper. Damn right. A little water can make a big difference in a man's life.

I went back into the hold feeling cleaner, feeling refreshed, feeling better about myself. The stink that rose from the hold was still horrible. In my mind I pictured a bird flying over our hatch, running into the stench, and falling dead among us. It never happened, of course, no seabird was that dumb.

The shit buckets were still there, slopping over on the deck, prisoners still sleeping beside them. Filth was still caked on the floor, and we were still crowded in, body-to-body, flesh-to-flesh. Nothing much was different except that some of us were cleaner, and those men who had not yet had their turn under the hose on deck had something to look forward to. Nothing much was different, but our attitude had changed, a lot of tension, a lot of psychological pressure had dissipated. Life was hard, but we had made it through this far, and of course, tomorrow would be better.

The Japanese kept their insurance policy in full force and a couple of days later I got a second turn on deck. This second time was as enjoyable as the first. I loved it. My mind was still muddled. Didn't know what day it was. Wasn't even sure of the month, but I rubbed and splashed and utilized every second of those precious few minutes. Sheer pleasure. Wonder if a man on death row gets the same enjoyment from his daily exercise period?

This time I made it a point to look around. The ship's superstructure was in the way. I couldn't see anything toward the front, but I could see to the sides and over the stern, and as far as the eye could see, we were alone. No other ship in sight.

Our guards no longer carried clubs or rifles with fixed bayonets. Oh, the guns were there all right, but hidden out of sight. Even their hatred was masked by an almost friendly cordiality. Who knows who might be watching through a periscope?

The voyage continued for two or three more days, our living conditions, our lifestyle pretty much unchanged, hell for those prisoners below decks, a few moments of relief for the twenty or so on deck under the water hose.

One afternoon the pulsing throbbing of the engines slowed to a whisper, then stopped. I was in a half-stupor and my mind was cloudy, but I sensed the change. When the engines stopped some part of me immediately went on the alert. The absence of the throbbing rhythmic beat, the silence of the engines, was itself a sensation that pounded against the ears and penetrated the brain.

What was happening to the ship? What was going on? I was sitting on the low iron shelf, feet on the deck. It was my turn to be under it, but no thanks. Since the night of the submarine attack I never slid under that damned shelf again.

I turned to Johnson, asked him what he thought the silence meant. He was sitting beside me with arms folded across his knees, head up, alert. He too had sensed the change. Both of us were aware that the engines had stopped. Hoped to Christ it didn't mean trouble.

We were all awake now, whispering softly to one another, but for the most part we listened and waited. We didn't wait long. The Japanese took off all the hatchboards exposing the hold to full daylight for the first time in weeks. I could see clearly now, and what I saw was revolting. We were in bad shape. Our bodies were a little cleaner because we all had been given at least one turn under the salt water hose on deck. My hair was still matted and I had several weeks' growth of whiskers on my face. My turn under the hose had been days ago. My G-string stank and my sweaty body was streaked with rust and grime.

The hold itself was beyond description. The floor was smeared with feces and urine and the vomit of those prisoners who had been seasick. The accumulated filth could have been scraped up with a shovel. Though we were used to it, the odor must have been terrible.

Prisoners were climbing out of the hold. We were being taken off the ship. I made it to the deck with some difficulty. My legs were shaky. Crowded together with others in the hold, I had not been able to move about. I followed the line of nearly naked prisoners down the gangway. We moved silently like dumb animals, not knowing where we were being taken, concerned only that we were escaping the misery of the last few weeks. This time it had to be true. Tomorrow would be better.

We had arrived, but where were we? Somewhere in Japan? Possibly. I stumbled along the pier to dry land, not caring a damn about where I was going, really conscious of where I had been. I never looked back at the ship.

Our guards were relaxed, seemingly at ease. They weren't screaming the usual unintelligible orders and they didn't try to hurry us. They seemed as happy as we to leave the ship. And why not? We were told that ours was the only ship in the convoy to make it through. It was a clear day, a few high white clouds, but a bright day with lots of sunshine. The smell of the air was fresh, clean, glorious. On the ship, even for those few minutes under the hose on deck, the awful stench of the hold had followed me. The pier, solid and unmoving, felt strange beneath my feet. My body was still used to the constant rolling, pitching motion of the ship.

I had little time to look about. Wherever we were, the area had been cleared of civilians before we got there. A half block from the pier we were ushered into a large empty building. It might have been an old warehouse, but more likely it was an auditorium or gymnasium because it had a clean wooden floor. The place was clean and well lighted with windows high in the sides, but there was no furniture of any kind. No chairs, no tables, nothing. But there was room, room to sit down, room to walk about, room to stretch out full length on the floor. Good God, for the first time in weeks there was no other body touching mine. The guards stayed outside, left us alone. Here I was, naked except for a G-string, owning only a mess kit bottom, a canteen, and a cup, and I thought it was great.

In a much smaller room at the end of the auditorium there was a toilet that would accommodate perhaps six or eight people at a time. The toilet was clean and there was running water. I scooped my hands under a faucet and drank until my stomach hurt, then splashed water on my hands and face. Thank God for water. After gorging on water I got my first look at a Japanese toilet. A strange contrivance to a westerner. The toilets were rectangular holes cut in the floor, maybe ten inches wide and eighteen inches long. There was a curved porcelain splash guard about eight inches high at one end of the hole, and that was it. Just a hole and a splash guard, nothing else. You use the damn thing by placing one foot on each side of the hole and squatting all the way down on your heels. So far so good. But we found it took three men for one man to use the toilet. Once squatted on our heels, most of us were too weak to get back up again. One prisoner to use the toilet, two prisoners to help him up again when he finished.

In the afternoon the Japanese gave us food, dry rice mixed with soybeans, shaped by hand into a round ball the size of a large orange. There were no stinking toilet tubs under my nose, no fighting to get to the rice bucket, no tangled mess of pushing, struggling, sweaty bodies. Just a ball of rice popped into my two hands. I ate, went to the toilet, drank my fill, stretched out on the bare wooden floor and slept.

Here again, I came face-to-face with one of the truisms of life as a prisoner of war. There were some things I could control, some decisions I could make that on occasion might make the difference between dying or staying alive, but there were other things, equally important, that were completely out of my hands. Johnson, Clifton S. Johnson (I never knew what the S stood for) and I had been buddies for almost a year. At Cabanatuan we slept in adjoining spaces on the bamboo slats, we commiserated with one another. Wrapped in our individual blankets we swore at the goddamn bedbugs, bitched because the same guard had kicked us both in the ass on the farm, complained about our aches and pains and bruises. We talked about our troubles, our hate, our fears. We shared our hopes, our dreams for the future. In short, we supported one another. We were close, in a sense, like family. Why? Because fate had thrown us together, two entirely different people who otherwise might never have met and who, in this unbelievably hard prison-camp life, both needed somebody. Clifton was there for me and I was there for Clifton.

And now that same fate was splitting us apart. When we left the auditorium the next day, we were loaded into different trucks. In our new camp we were assigned to different barracks, to different work details, to different shifts. Though we spent the next year in the same prison camp, a camp of only two hundred men, Clifton and I never saw each other for more than a few brief minutes at a time. My new life, such as it was, would center around new friends, new companions, the five men with whom I shared a room in the barracks and the nine men with whom I labored in an isolated shaft in a coal mine.

August or September 1944: Fukuoka, Japan, and Prison Camp #23

I slept the sleep of exhaustion, curled up, first on one side, then the other, bare flesh on a hardwood floor. Every little while the aches and pains, the discomfort, made me roll over, but in between rollovers I hugged that wooden floor like it was the softest mattress in the world. And however foggy my brain during these frequent half-awakenings, in the back of my mind there ran the constant thought, "I made it. I made it, by golly. I made it."

The rustle of bodies, the soft pad of bare feet moving across the floor, the grayness of the predawn sky through the high dormer windows told me it was morning, time to get up. I sat for a moment with my knees drawn up under my chin, more comfortable that way because there was still a little padding on my bottom. The floor of the large room was covered with prisoners, huddled lumps of humanity exhausted from their ordeal on the ship. Skinny, dirty, near-naked bodies, all knees and elbows and protruding ribs twisted into grotesque shapes, seeking the oblivion of sleep. We were truly a sorry-looking mess, but it didn't matter. We were alive. We were the lucky ones.

Just as the warm rays of the sun can be gathered with a magnifying glass and focused to a burning point, some events of life become focused into a moment of particular importance. This was one of them, the moment that I realized I was finally off that damned hell ship. Didn't matter that I was cold, near naked and sitting on a hardwood floor. Didn't matter that I was filthy dirty, hungry, and so weak that I could hardly stand. All that mattered was that once again, through luck, fate, or the grace of God, I had avoided death. I was off the hell ship and I was alive, and the certain death that had been staring me in the face had moved off into the distance. Life, such as it was, even this miserable bit of it, was sweet as hell, and I knew it and I was thankful for it.

While writing this and looking back over these many years, I still find it almost impossible to express in words the magnitude of the change that had taken place in my life in just a few hours. Physically, of course, that was easy. I was off

175

the ship and away from the filth and the thirst and the unspeakable living conditions. Physically the journey on the ship was already in the past. It was over, done with. Emotionally, now that was a different story. The scars from some wounds are plain to see, but I believe the POW was wounded in his soul in a place where the scars cannot be seen, and though not visible to the eye, those scars are still there. For myself, I find that I tremble as I write, and I still scream silent screams in the darkness of the night.

Perhaps it was just an instinctive form of psychological self defense, a kind of mental barrier that we place between ourselves and things that were really too horrible to face, but we rarely spoke of the hell ship or of beatings or of death. These things we probably placed in a little mental box and then hid the key. Instead we continually talked about home, about whatever we had done before the war and about whatever we were going to do after the war, and lightly skipped over the three-and-a-half years between the two.

Perhaps this strange ability not to dwell on the past was a necessary part of learning to survive. Yesterday was over. Once lived through, it couldn't hurt us anymore. Tomorrow was unpredictable. Today was the focus of our lives. The next meal, the next guard, the next work detail, these were the important things to worry about. Nothing else mattered.

The man next to me was up and awake. His voice was friendly, but he spoke to me only because I was next to him, because I was there. He asked me how I was getting along.

I was doing OK. Thought to myself that I was a lot better off than I was yesterday. He was sitting up, arms wrapped around his knees, not the picture of health but happy as hell to get off that ship alive. He wondered out loud about what they were going to do to us next.

Again, unconsciously, he voiced the thought that was always uppermost in my mind: not what are they going to do *with* us but what are they going to do *to* us?

Nobody knew. There was no scuttlebutt yet, not even a rumor, and the Japanese never told us anything.

Strange. This POW life was so strange. Here I was, talking casually to a man I had never seen before as though I had known him for a long time. Because fate had thrown us together, because we had gone through a life-threatening ordeal together, we were somehow already bonded together as friends. On the other hand, I knew that had I remained asleep and the fellow on the other side awakened first, this little conversation might never have taken place.

He posed the usual question about where I thought we were going. He spoke quietly, tossing the question into the air like a wisp of smoke that would disappear into the heavens. He didn't expect an answer. I think, instead, his question was just a reaching out to make contact with another human, a reaching out for a little reassurance that in this hostile world he was not completely alone.

He stood, reached out a hand to help me up. We decided to go to the head, get a drink of water, and maybe find out what other prisoners were doing.

The washroom was large and reminded me of the toilets in a Greyhound bus depot, a long trough for a urinal, seven or eight porcelain washbasins along one wall, and half a dozen toilets. And white tile everywhere, tile on the floor, tile on the walls. Such a beautiful toilet, such luxury. The toilet was a magnet for those few prisoners who were up and awake, and we tiptoed in and out with almost churchlike reverence. Frankly, I was ill at ease. For two-and-a-half years we had been without even a place to wash our hands, and now, suddenly, this tiled washroom with washbasins and toilets and an unlimited supply of water. It was too good to be true.

It was a thrill just to be there, to run my hands over the smooth white porcelain, the shiny chrome faucets. I made a minimal effort to wash up, splashed water on my hands and face, cupped my hand under the faucet and drank my fill, then moved on. No time for more, there were others waiting.

Took my place in line for one of those strange toilets. For once in my life I was glad there was a line. Gave me a chance to see how the darned thing worked. When I finished in the washroom, I stalled around. The change in my lifestyle, in my life expectancy, had been so abrupt that some part of me felt uneasy. Yesterday the filth, the stench, the horror of the ship; today, the cleanliness, the abundance, the safety of this washroom. The real world was waiting outside, and I was reluctant to go back to it. I still remember the feeling. The washroom was a place of refuge, like standing in a small doorway to get out of the rain. The doorway might be safe, might be comfortable, but sooner or later you had to leave.

When I came out, Japanese soldiers armed with the ever-present rifle and bayonet, had taken over the gym. They were passing out food at the door, baseball-sized balls of rice laced with soybeans. I got in line, was handed a rice ball, and followed the line through the door. The man ahead of me climbed into a canvas-covered truck. I followed. We drove off.

Simple but typical. Through the gym door and onto a truck. There was no selection process, no chance to pair up with a buddy. To the guards we were less than human, we had no personal identity, we were not names, not even numbers. More like loading animals out of a corral. The first ten or twenty or twenty-five prisoners through the door got into the first truck, the same with the second and so on. It was obvious that the guards neither knew nor cared who we were, that they weren't even sure how many of us were still alive until they counted us out of the gym and onto the trucks. They just didn't give a damn. And for that matter, neither did we. Getting off the ship was like bursting out of a totally black hole and finding the whole damn world spread out before you on a bright sunny day. We neither knew nor cared where we were going or what we were going to do when we got there. Just, please God, not back to the ship.

We jolted along country roads for half a day. From my place in the truck I got only an occasional glimpse of the countryside through clouds of dust. Nevertheless it was a nice day, hell, even a beautiful day. Yesterday I had been in the bowels of the hell ship waiting for death. Today, with food in my belly I was touring the Japanese countryside. Under the circumstances it was a wonderful day.

Anybody hear anything? Anybody know where we're goin'? I certainly didn't know. Didn't seem to matter a hell of a lot. I knew where I had been, and since to my mind nothing could be worse, the next place had to be better.

For two-and-a-half years I had been moving from prison camp to prison camp like a man walking through life backwards. I couldn't see where I was going but I could always look back and see where I had been. Every camp, so far, had been a place of pain and suffering and death. I knew what the past was like. On the other hand, precisely because I couldn't see ahead, every move held out at least the possibility, the hope, that the new camp might be better. Maybe yes, maybe no, but sight unseen I was always ready to try a new camp just to get away from the hell of the camp I was in, always ready to move just on the strength of a maybe.

We were quiet in the truck, unusually quiet because each of us was immersed in his own thoughts. Each of us carried inside a tremendous burden of fears, anxieties, and yes, even hope, that at moments like this overshadowed the need for conversation. Besides, what was there to say?

Personally, I was elated, overjoyed at just getting off the ship alive and in one piece. Putting it simply, I felt good. Physically I was still hurting. I was exhausted, weak, dirty and half starved, and my body hurt in a dozen different places, but emotionally I was riding on a high. How to explain it? Have you ever been out in bone-chilling cold, the kind of cold that turns your breath into ice around your mouth, where your hands and feet become useless lumps, where your entire body is shivering so violently that it becomes difficult to talk? And then have you ever stumbled into a warm room and bellied up to a hot stove and felt the heat and warmth flow over your entire body? Well, that's how I felt on that first day in Japan. Figuratively speaking, I had somehow clambered over a wall and the ship, and death, the monster that had been chasing me, was on the other side. For the time being I felt safe. My job now was to pick myself up, to brush off the dirt, and not to dwell on the past but to prepare myself for whatever was coming my way tomorrow.

Think they'll give us some clothes and maybe a decent place to sleep? The question was tentative, the usual reaching out for reassurance, for some kind of emotional support. Any answer would be meaningless, one guess was as good as another. Yet when the answer came in the affirmative, as it always did, I accepted it as gospel. We all accepted it because we needed something to hope for, something to daydream about. Better food, better treatment, the very thought was comforting, like the quiet hand of a stranger on the arm of a blind man crossing a busy street.

Sure they will. Now that we're in their own country they gotta treat us better, feed us better and all that.

This was an optimistic point of view. Realistically we ought to stop dreaming of the good life. Past experience warned me that it would probably be the same old crap. The Japs would work our asses off and wouldn't give a damn if we lived or died. They'd rather see us dead anyway.

Still, that clean washroom last night was great. A fellow could set up house-keeping in a place like that.

Quiet again. We were still too close to those horrible days on the ship, too exhausted physically and mentally to do more than just go along for the ride. And somewhere in the back of my mind was the certain knowledge that I was still held prisoner by an enemy who had thus far shown neither mercy nor compassion. Though once again hopeful, I had no reason to trust in the benevolence of the Japanese.

It was late afternoon when our little convoy stopped. The steady growl of the motor, the hum of the tires, the sense of motion, everything came to an abrupt halt. No one spoke. I looked at the man sitting across from me and waited. The silence was heavy and had I spoke it would have been in a whisper. The truck ride had been long and had given me the opportunity to sort out my own thoughts. It is still a strange recollection. To this day I don't know if my feelings were dictated by my thoughts or if my thoughts were governed by my feelings. I can only describe it as thinking and feeling on two or three different levels at the same time. I felt comfortable with life, self-satisfied, a little smug. This was because getting off the ship was such a tremendous relief. Being off the ship felt just plain good. On the other hand, there was anxiety and more than a little bit of fear. Where in hell were they taking me? What was going to happen to me? Anxiety, fear, under the circumstances, very normal feelings. Though my future was unknown, realistically, looking back over the last couple of years should have given me a pretty good idea of what lay ahead. Finally, anticipating the new camp was something like a little kid looking at an unopened package. Though it might contain nothing more than a utilitarian pair of socks, until it was opened it held the possibility of a pleasant surprise.

Guards hustled us off the truck. I stumbled, went to my knees. My legs were rubbery. Twenty-four hours off the ship wasn't long enough to regain strength. We were all shaky and we steadied one another. New guards, probably had never seen an American prisoner close up, and they weren't about to contaminate themselves by touching our smelly unwashed bodies.

Confusion, mental confusion. A rush of unconnected thoughts cramming themselves into my brain. A cluster of prisoners, movement, guards shouting in Japanese. A high wooden fence, an open gate, guard towers. I remember looking at some grass and thinking, "Looks like any other grass but this is Japan and this is Japanese grass." Tomorrow or the next day I would sort things out, try to make some sense of my new surroundings, but today, today be careful, keep alert, try to anticipate and don't do anything stupid. Such a mental blur, those first few minutes between off the truck and through the gate. I was at a new camp, in a new country, yet strangely, nothing had changed.

We walked through a gate, a ragged cluster of prisoners surrounded by Japanese soldiers, hesitant, apprehensive, hopeful, and I got my first look at my new home. It was a tiny camp, two hundred prisoners and twenty or thirty Japanese soldiers, but it would be the focal point of my existence for the duration of the war.

Guards pushed and shoved and shouted us into four ranks and then, for the first time, we met our new camp commander, Lieutenant Nakamura. He was tall for a Japanese, resplendent in his full dress uniform with the samurai sword at his side, sternly military in his bearing, and very, very young. He stood in front of us, feet apart, hands clasped behind his back, and stared at us silently for a full two minutes. Obviously, he had never seen an American prisoner, and just as obviously, he was totally unprepared for what he saw. Probably he had been told to receive two hundred Americans and to put them to work. But no one had told him that we were weak, dirty, naked, and half starved, and practically useless as a work force.

Surprise, disgust, hatred, nothing showed on Nakamura's face, but I got the feeling that whatever he had expected, we were not it. Then he spoke, in English. Though sometimes poorly phrased, Lieutenant Nakamura had a good command of the language and his English was quite understandable. Speaking sternly he gave us the usual welcoming speech.

He introduced himself as camp commander and told us that we must obey him, must obey all Japanese soldiers. He said that because we were prisoners of war we must work hard and obey all the rules. Any prisoner who does not obey all the rules would be punished severely until dead. He paused for a second and then continued in a softer voice, telling us that if we were good prisoners, if we worked hard and obeyed all the rules, then in just twenty years our parents would be allowed to visit us. Satisfied, he paused again to give his words time to sink in, then got quickly to the business at hand. He told us that we must now learn to count in Japanese. He held up one finger, that was "ichi," two fingers, that was "nee," three fingers was "san," and so on until ten. Dutifully we repeated the strange-sounding words. After three or four sequences of one through ten the lieutenant nodded to his sergeant, who stood in front of the first prisoner and counted. The prisoner successfully repeated the words. On to the second man and then to the third. The fourth prisoner made a mistake and a stinging slap dropped him to his backside. It wasn't a vicious blow, just an attention getter, but in our weakened condition it didn't take a hell of a lot to knock a man down. The lesson and the counting continued along the line. Happily, I was near the end of the rear rank. By the time they got to me I knew how to count. "Hayku nana ju san," one hundred seventy three. Now I had a number, an identity. For the next year, to my Japanese guards, this number would be the only thing that differentiated me from any other prisoner.

The lieutenant seemed highly pleased. His first attempt at teaching us had been a success. He could teach and we could learn. The lieutenant stood in front of us, counted to ten and made a sweeping gesture with his arm. He told everybody to count. In unison we counted to ten in Japanese. "Mo ichi do," Nakamura waited expectantly. "Mo ichi do," everybody count. We counted. Mo ichi do. We counted again and again. Finally we began to catch on. Loosely translated, mo icho do meant do it again, or, one more time. We listened, we understood, we learned to count, and then and there Lieutenant Nakamura got his new name.

Throughout the last year as prisoners few, if any, of us remembered the name Nakamura, but we all knew, and tried to understand, and eventually, even to like, Mo Ichi Do.

Before leaving us that first day, Mo Ichi Do made one final demand. He selected one wild-haired bearded prisoner and taking a pair of scissors from his pocket, trimmed the prisoner's hair to about three quarters of an inch, then trimmed his beard close to his face. He gave the scissors to an American officer and made a sweeping gesture that included all of us. Tomorrow, tomorrow. His gesture took in all prisoners. We were dismissed to settle into our new home, and we did a lot of hair cutting that night.

Uncertain as to what to do next, we milled about and I had a few minutes to look around the camp. Outside what I assumed to be our barracks there was a long structure that appeared to be an open-air washhouse. A double row of concrete tubs, roofed over but open on all four sides. Tentatively I turned on one of the faucets, drank from my cupped hand, then splashed cold water over my hands and face. A Japanese soldier stood watching, impassive, apparently unconcerned with the water I was wasting. Didn't want to press my luck so I drank my fill, turned off the faucet, and moved on. I was hesitant, suspicious, slow to believe that there may have been a positive change in my life. To go, in twenty-four hours, from the stink and filth and misery of the ship to a camp with clean running water was just too much for my mind to absorb all at once. Besides, I knew instinctively that once I believed things were getting better, it would hurt just that much more if the good changes were taken away. Better to wait and see.

First order of the day was to form a line and move toward what turned out to be a bathhouse. A bathhouse! Unbelievable. And with hot water. The most hot water I had seen for the past couple of years had been in a canteen cup.

Still not knowing what to expect I entered a starkly bare room, stripped naked, and hung my G-string on a peg on the wall. A guard handed me a small piece of yellow soap and I realized, for the first time, that I was really going to take a bath. I didn't know who was most eager, we prisoners to take our first hot bath or the guards to have us wash off the sickeningly heavy stench of our bodies, which surely must have offended them.

I got to the head of the line and a guard motioned me through a door. In the next room there were two community tubs, concrete tubs perhaps ten feet long and six feet wide. The water in both was a little more than knee deep, but one was filled to capacity with splashing prisoners, the other quite empty. A guard indicated that I was to get into the full one. I managed to squeeze in. God, the water was hot enough to make me gasp, and when I finally managed to sit down, deep enough to come up to my armpits. We were jammed tightly, squirming body to squirming body, so tightly that no one could really be sure whose foot he was washing but none of this mattered. The water was hot and I was in it, and it was a glorious feeling. Already the water was dirty and there was a heavy layer of soap scum floating on top, but nobody gave a damn. I dipped my piece of soap in the water and scrubbed to beat hell, scrubbed hard, hands, feet, face, everything. I even managed to get my head under water and scratched away with fingernails at my dirt-encrusted scalp. Good Lord, it was wonderful. You can't imagine how good it felt to take that first bath.

Monkey see, monkey do. I watched other prisoners and did what they did. I stepped out of the dirty tub into the clean one and poured pails of clean water over my head and body, rinsed until I was clean. Guards hustled me along and I stepped out. My bath was over, and it had been a wonderful, memorable experience.

No towels, we just stood around naked until we were dry. I tied my dirty, smelly G-string around my waist. Guards took us in groups of six to the barracks. There was little time for introspection. Changes kept coming hard and fast. There was a little shoving and pushing but no real violence. The guards were all business. These Japanese soldiers were new to us, and of course, we to them, and they viewed us with obvious disapproval. Clearly, guarding a bunch of skinny, half-naked American prisoners was not to their liking.

Six men to a room. No furniture, no beds, just a bare empty room, four walls, floor, and ceiling, but at least it was clean. Compared to Cabanatuan, this barracks was a luxury hotel. Six prisoners to a room. The guards herded us along like cattle in a stockyard. Six animals in the first pen, six in the second, six in the third, and so on till the barracks was full. In my room the six prisoners were strangers, yet already bonded by the common experience of having survived two-and-a-half years at Cabanatuan and having been together on the hell ship. Intuitively we already knew a lot about one another. I looked around the room. Small by most standards but palatial when compared to the bamboo shelves at Cabanatuan. The end walls were made of wood with a single wooden shelf, head high, extending the length of each wall. Both side walls were made of shoji screens, doorlike panels made of flimsy wooden squares covered with an opaque parchment-like paper. On each side, the two center shoji panels slid back to leave the room open to the outside. My mind was so filled with the pleasurable aftereffects of that first bath and the newfound cleanliness of my body that I overlooked the obvious. Soon there would be nothing between me and the ice and snow, the bitter cold of the fast-approaching Japanese winter, except these flimsy, paper-covered shojis.

Looking back, remembering, I can still feel the torrent of emotion that swept me along on that first day in Japan. Yesterday I had been on the hell ship with the filth, the stench, the degradation, with the uncertainty of life itself. Yesterday I didn't give a damn where I was going or what I was going to do, just as long as I got off the ship. Today, a new camp, that wonderful first bath, a clean place to sleep, what the hell, why worry about the coming winter? Fight that battle when it gets here. Today, God is smiling on us. Life is good.

The floor of my new room was made of tatami mats laid out and fitted together like huge dominos. Four mats side by side and two across the end filled the entire space. I chose one and sat down. This little rectangle, about the size of a twin bed, would be my sleeping space, my living space, my own private world for the next year.

Chowtime. The word was passed from room to room. I was hungry and ready to answer the call. Single file we went into the mess hall. Another miracle. One large room with wooden tables along each side wall. Eight men to a table. And eight small white porcelain bowls already filled with rice sitting on each table. No more sitting on the ground to eat. A real mess hall. Felt strange to sit at a table, kinda like going to a party.

Back to barracks, back to my room. The Japanese guards had placed a pile of clothing on each tatami mat. On my mat there was a well-worn Army blanket and a "pookow," a soft Japanese quilt. I got a pair of coarse white cotton pajamas, pants and jacket to work in, and pants and jacket to wear in camp. Also, a pair of leather Army shoes to wear in camp and a pair of Japanese tennis shoes to wear to work. The tennis shoes were Japanese style with a split between the big toe and the four little toes. A couple of caps, one for work and one for camp, and finally, an Army overcoat. Wasn't American, and couldn't tell from the buttons, but it might have been British or Canadian. I folded the clothing and put it on the shelf above my tatami mat. It would take a lot of swapping back and forth but I would eventually get everything in a reasonable fit. I felt rich, rich in clothing, rich in circumstances, rich in life. God had smiled on us today.

The general feeling was one of pleasant surprise, upbeat, like Jesus Christ, ain't this something? The Japanese had never treated us this well before, and I wondered what the little bastards would take out of our hides to make up for it.

There should have been a lot of conversation in our room that night but there wasn't. Our world was filled with magic and nobody wanted to break the spell.

It was dark. I put on the pajamas, folded my blanket lengthwise over my tatami mat, pulled the pookow over my head, and retreated into the blackness of my little private cave, head under the pookow. This would become a habitual way to sleep because the single electric light hanging from a wire in the center of the room never went out. I dozed off, clean, warm, comfortable, vaguely hoping that when I woke in the morning the dream would still be there.

Next morning I was roused from my state of semihibernation by a Japanese bugle call and commenced what was to become a regular routine, up with the bugle call, a few minutes to go to the latrine, roll call, a quick breakfast and then to work. Trouble was that we didn't know yet what our work was going to be.

First morning in the new camp and the warm afterglow of the first bath began to disappear. We had a problem, small to be sure, but nevertheless a critical one. Simply put, there wasn't enough time between the wake-up bugle and roll call for all of us to use the latrine. The latrine was built across one end of the barracks, three stalls with holes in the floor and a trough for a urinal. No running water, but just like an old fashioned outhouse, everything dropped into a pit under the floor and stayed there. Bad news for the guys in the room next to the stench. Dysentery was still prevalent among us. Some poor bastard would be in the stall crapping his guts out while a dozen men stood in line holding tight with their legs crossed and screaming for him to hurry up and get out. And the stalls were always dirty, filthy dirty. They were washed down once a day with water and a broom, but sooner rather than later some prisoner with the shits would miss the hole and spatter over the floor. The next guy would add to the mess and so on. My rule, wake up half an hour, even an hour early. Get there before the morning rush. And always, always wear shoes. At least I could leave them on the ground outside my room and wash the crap off later.

We stayed in camp. The guards put us to work digging a big hole in the center of camp. Sick prisoners, those who were damn near dead from the trip on the ship, were allowed to stay in barracks to rest up and try to regain a little strength.

Why were the Japanese making us dig this huge hole in the ground? Nobody knew. We figured they just wanted to keep us busy, that they couldn't stand to see us standing around doing nothing.

Tempers grew short. A little pushing and slapping around, lots of angry shouting, but no real brutality — not yet. We could tell that the guards weren't satisfied with the way we were working. Too slow. What the hell, what did they expect? I was one of the able-bodied, and twenty minutes with a pick or shovel left me exhausted. Incredible, but these Japanese had never seen an American soldier up close, and they thought these skinny, emaciated bodies were our natural condition. Equally incredible, we had no idea that we were digging an air-raid shelter. When the hole got too deep we thought the steps we built at one end were for our convenience in climbing in and out. When we finally roofed it over with timbers and piled dirt on top we thought the Japanese were going to use it for some kind of storage. It wasn't until the guards cranked up a hand-operated siren and shooed us in for a practice session that we realized we had actually built ourselves an air-raid shelter. But why? What for? Just to keep us busy, of course. The thought of American planes flying overhead never entered our minds. Too bad. It would have been a blessing, a real morale booster had we realized that our soldiers and sailors were getting close enough to cause the Japanese to prepare for an air attack.

As it was, the shelter was just a hole in the ground, some silly idea of our Japanese lieutenant. The reality was that we had been cut off from the outside world too long for us to relate to anything beyond the prison-camp fence. Being a prisoner of war had become too much a way of life for our expectations to soar beyond the borders of the camp. Happiness was a hot bath, a full belly, and a good night's sleep without trouble from the guards. We remembered the world outside, thought about it, talked about it, but like some faraway land we had never seen, sometimes it didn't really exist.

The honeymoon was over. Mo Icho Do had given us three or four days to settle into camp, to scrub the accumulated filth from our bodies, to perhaps gain a little strength after our ordeal on the hell ship, and to build an air raid shelter.

The short respite had been good for me. I felt better, stronger. Better is perhaps the word to use because my gain had been emotional, psychological, rather than physical. My spirits had lifted, and my whole outlook had changed for the better. That first hot bath had been a Godsend. After years of bathing only when it rained, after months of not bathing at all, that first hot bath stands out in my memory like my first day of school or my first bicycle, an occasion to be remembered forever. As a POW my first time to sit at a table, my first time to eat from a real porcelain bowl, my first time to have more than a G-string to wear, these, too, were memorable occasions, milestones along the road to recovery. I was a hell of a lot better off than I had been a year ago or even a week ago, but this was still a POW camp, and I was still a prisoner of war. Don't take anything for granted. Wait and see.

Rumors were flying, seemingly carried on the wind from barracks to barracks. I never learned how these rumors got started, but the latest one was that "we're goin' to work tomorrow. Gonna put us to work in a coal mine."

Even with my head under my pookow I knew the voice belonged to Roland Jollie. Jollie's voice was distinctive. He spoke with an accent that came from way back in the hill country of Kentucky or Tennessee, but when he spoke he usually knew what he was talking about. Jollie had heard from somewhere that the Japanese were going to put us to work in a coal mine.

We thought it was just another bunch of crap. Jollie insisted that it was the real scoop. He'd overheard the officers talking about it up on the hill, heard it while he was cleaning up the mess hall.

If the officers were talking about it they probably got it straight from Mo Ichi Do. Had to be true. Heads came out from under blankets. I'd never been in a coal mine, never so much as seen one. Two or three prisoners were all talking at once. Jollie volunteered that he had seen a mine in the movies. Couldn't tell much though, just a bunch of buys with dirty faces comin' out of a hole in the ground. Had some kind of an accident down underground.

We decided that it might be scary working in a hole way far down in the earth, but scary or not, we knew the Japs wouldn't give us much choice. Anyway, it couldn't be much worse than working on the farm, and it had to be a lot better than being on that damned ship. Looked like we were all going to learn to be coal miners.

I went to sleep worrying about the coal mine, wondering just what it would be like, thought about it every time I woke during the night. These first three or four days in the new camp had been good. A bath, a clean place to sleep, clothing to cover my body, this wasn't the usual Japanese way. What did they want from us? What were they after? Probably find out in the morning.

Wake-up call came a little before daylight, and the word passed quickly from room to room. Put on the work uniform for roll call. Wear the canvas split-toed tennis shoes and the canvas leggings when you fall in.

It was a quiet bunch of prisoners that lined up for roll call, quiet and apprehensive as hell. Nothing much good had come our way in the last couple of years. POW life had been brutally hard, and we had no reason to expect anything but more of the same.

Major Hogan, our senior officer and prisoner commander as well as our American doctor, gave us the scoop.

He said that we were all going to be working in a coal mine. The first hundred numbers were to go back to barracks and try to get some sleep. They would be on the night shift. The second hundred men were to stay in the lineup. The guards would escort us to work in the nearby mine. The major had the last word. He cautioned us to watch what we were doing, to try to learn the new job, and for Christ's sake, be careful. We marched to the mine under heavy guard.

Our three officers, the kitchen crew, a medic, one man to tend the boiler that heated the bath water, these few were excused from work in the mine. The rest of us were coal miners.

September–December 1944:
First Look at the Coal Mine

We were a subdued lot as we took that first walk from the camp to the mine, subdued in the sense that we were quiet, didn't talk, couldn't think of anything to say. Problem was that none of us knew, none of us knew a damn thing about where we were going, what we were going to find there, or what we were going to do when we got there.

I was immersed in my own thoughts, trying to make myself ready for whatever lay ahead. Of course I was worried, not afraid, just worried, apprehensive. My mouth was dry, my belly hurt, my ass was tight. It wasn't the guards or the thought of being forced to work. It was nothing I could put my finger on, but I was very uptight, a normal reaction for a POW. I knew firsthand about beatings and suffering and pain and starvation and humiliation and shame. All of these things we POWs had learned to encounter as part and parcel of our daily living. By this time I was even comfortable with thoughts of death. Death was no longer a frightening bugaboo. All of us, those of us who had survived the prison camps thus far, had seen a lot of death. All of us had seen friends and comrades die, some violently, some passing as quietly as the whisper of a soft breath. For myself, I knew that on more than one occasion I had been to the very edge of death, that I had already experienced everything except the final ultimate moment. No, it was none of these things that struck this little bit of fear into my heart. I think, instead, it was simply not knowing. Once I got the hang of this new coal mining thing, once I knew the best and the worst that I could expect, once I had worked in the mine for a few days, then I could settle down, then I could handle it.

Half a mile from the camp to the mine. For most of the way the path ran along the edge of a small river, almost dry now with just a trickle of water in the middle of a wide flat bed. A trickle now but probably a torrent at some other time of the year. Our guards didn't hassle us. The sun was up and I was comfortably warm. The sky was a clear morning blue with a few little white clouds scattered here and there, idyllic, should have been a nice day, but it wasn't. Comparatively speaking, any day that something bad didn't happen to me was a nice day, but this day got off to a bad start because things were different. The basic structure of my life as a POW was changing, and I had no control over the change. I think, intuitively, I realized that my coping devices, my little personal strategies for staying alive in the hospital, for working on the farm, even for surviving on the hell ship, might not work for me here. As we walked along I looked at the man next to me. Our eyes met for an instant, but neither of us spoke. What do you say to another man when you're both jumping off a cliff in the dark? "Just keep smiling fella, everything's going to be all right"? Hardly. From past experience I already knew that whatever we were getting into, whatever the Japanese had planned for us to do, I wasn't going to like it.

The mine, above ground, looked like a small dirty village. There were a couple of two- or three-story buildings, sooty black and covered with corrugated tin, that housed machinery for operating the mine below ground and for processing the coal after it had been brought to the surface. In the distance the mine office and one-story buildings that housed the regular Japanese miners and their families. Our destination, our daily destination, was a long one-story building that reminded me of a small-town railroad depot. The room was bare except for a few benches and a couple of large tables. A set of narrow-gauge rails, inclined rails, ran the length of the room, dropped sharply and disappeared through swinging doors. I looked around, curious, trying to absorb everything. The walls were covered with large colored propaganda posters, posters designed to fill Japanese hearts with hatred for the enemy. I remember best the horrible caricatures of Roosevelt and Churchill, horrible caricatures with bulging eyes and gaping mouths and fangs for teeth that were dripping with blood. Roosevelt had claws for hands, one bloody claw hoisting a broken ship from the ocean, bodies of uniformed Japanese falling from the decks. The other claw held a writhing, screaming mass of civilians, men, women, and children, parts of bodies and blood and gore squeezing through the clenched fist. Boy, oh boy! No wonder the Japanese people hated Americans.

The uniformed soldiers left the room, left us in the care of a few older Japanese miners who were to work with us underground, who were to be our teachers, our supervisors. A wrinkled little old man pushed and shoved and tugged at our clothing until he had nine of us in a corner of the room. Not a word of English from him, not a word of Japanese from us. Through signs and gestures and finger taps on his chest and on ours, he indicated that we were his crew, that we were to follow him. It was OK with us. Next, our new "honcho" led us to a table piled high with batteries and headlamps, and gave us our first lesson in how to be coal miners. Very patiently, all the while chattering to us in a language that none of us understood, he demonstrated how to strap a battery over the right backside, how to let the connecting wire run up the back to the miner's cap with the headlamp on its front.

We were more comfortable now, loosening up. The guards were out of sight and this little old man wasn't threatening. He was trying, so we tried. Might as well make the best of it.

I screwed up momentarily. My battery wasn't on right. Had to get it over my backside so it wouldn't rub my hipbone raw. And I couldn't find the light switch, couldn't turn the damn thing on. The old man demonstrated with his lamp. Once I found the switch the rest was easy.

One light wouldn't turn on. Probably due to a weak battery. We didn't have to tell the old man. He saw the trouble, took the bad light and put it on the floor next to the wall, and helped us rig a new one. Our honcho looked at us, nine POWs properly attired with batteries and headlamps. He seemed satisfied. Sometimes it's amazing how well humans can communicate without the spoken word.

I had no time to speculate. A rattling noise, a whoosh of air and a string of Toonerville trolleys came through the swinging doors. Little trolley cars with no front, no back, no sides. Just ten straight-backed benches and a tin roof. Frankly, they looked like hell. Either they were a hundred years old, or they had seen a lot of action. The tin roofs were twisted and dented and buckled like a kid's toy that had been stepped on. It was obvious that wherever those cars went, a lot of rocks had fallen on the roofs.

Though we bitched among ourselves at the battered appearance of the trolleys, we were still above ground in a well-lighted room. The real mine, the working mine, lay beyond the swinging doors, deep, deep in the bowels of the earth.

Our honcho shooed us into the first car, four men to a seat. He sat beside us. The rest of the prisoners and their foremen loaded up somewhere behind. I sat on the outside. Our honcho sat on the bench next to me. Funny, I worked with him, worked for him for almost a year and he never had a name. We didn't have names either. He would chatter in Japanese, show us what he wanted us to do, and we would try to do it. Once underground, wherever he led, we followed. When he worked, we worked. When he stopped to eat, we stopped to eat. When he was ready to go home, we got ready to go home. All in the dark, without clocks, without words. It was a very strange existence.

With signs our foreman warned us to keep arms and hands inside the trolley. Didn't know why, but one look at the dented roof convinced me that he was right. The trolley cars lurched, and we started down into the mine. Another whoosh of air as the front car forced open the swinging doors. It was pitch dark inside with only a tiny light bulb every hundred feet or so to indicate the way. Gravity pulled us down the steeply sloping tracks, and a steel cable running from the rear car to a winch house somewhere above ground kept our speed under control. Even with my headlamp I could barely make out the sides of the shaft as we rattled along, down, down, down.

What lay ahead at the bottom of this tunnel? I had never been in a mine before; in fact, none of us had. This was an entirely new experience, and we were understandably nervous. Damn the war and damn the Japanese. I didn't like this one little bit.

We talked a little, a good sign. Things were always better when we could chatter, when we could loosen up.

Now and then a falling rock bounced off the roof. From the sound of it, sometimes a little one, sometimes a bigger one. I kept my hands well inside the car. Our Japanese honcho seemed perfectly relaxed, comfortably at home with the situation. I took my cue from him and tried to relax. That first trip was weird. What if the whole thing fell down on us?

I looked behind me. There were three cars in the train. I could see the head-lamps of the other POWs but beyond their headlamps, absolutely nothing, nothing but blackness. Ahead of us the combined light of our lamps pushed the darkness away, kept it always a few feet ahead of the lead car, then nothing. The impenetrable blackness sucked up the light like a sponge sucks up water. In spite of my conscious effort to relax I was damned uncomfortable; every muscle was tense. My heart was pounding, and I caught myself holding my breath from time to time. I tried an old standby rule: in a strange situation watch the old-timers, and do what they do. I watched our honcho out of the corner of my eye. Didn't help a bit. Honcho seemed perfectly at ease, but hell, why not, he'd probably been down in the mine a thousand times. For me, this was my first, and I was scared shitless.

Down, down, down, always further into the blackness. I agonized over every bump in the track, every lurch of the rickety little trolley. Strange thoughts kept running through my mind. Perhaps from a long ago catechism class or a vaguely remembered Sunday sermon, but I clearly recalled hearing the words, "the depths of hell," and I wondered if we stayed on this track long enough, went down deep enough, would we finally get there?

The sight and sound of a thin sheet of water falling from the roof just ahead caught my attention. As our trolley passed I got wet. Water cascaded from the roof and soaked my clothing. It was over in a second. There was nervous laughter because everybody in the outside seat got wet. I thought nothing of it. The mine was warm. What was a little water?

Three months later I found myself pushing and shoving to get an inside seat on the trolley. Going into the mine getting wet didn't matter. The mine was warm and the clothes would dry out. But going out of the mine when it was winter, when there was snow on the ground and the temperature was well below freezing, wet clothes would damn near freeze on my body before we got back to camp. To compound the injury, if my clothes were wet I couldn't sleep in them and I needed to sleep in everything I owned, pants, shirts, even my overcoat, just to fight off the bitter cold of the Japanese winter.

Eventually our trolley train reached the bottom of the inclined shaft. We had reached the working level of the mine. How long from the top? Ten, maybe fifteen minutes. How far down? Don't know, maybe a quarter of a mile, maybe half a mile, straight down.

We piled out and started walking, following our wrinkled little honcho along a level tunnel with a set of narrow-gauge rails down the middle. We walked in silence, the stillness broken only by the rustle of clothing, the sound of breathing, the crunching sound of coal dust under our feet. I can't speak for the other prisoners, but for myself, my mind, all of my faculties were absorbed in looking, feeling, sensing, concentrating mightily on quickly learning all there was to know about the mine. Instinctively I sensed that I had to familiarize myself with every little detail that in order to survive I must learn to live on friendly terms with this new and hostile environment.

A hundred yards into the main tunnel and my group, my nine men and our honcho veered off to the left. The larger group, about eighty prisoners, went on to work somewhere else in the mine. This new tunnel, a lateral shaft leading away from the main tunnel, was much smaller, most places only about five feet in height. We stayed bunched up, single file but close together. Close up, the circle of light from my headlamp only illuminated a small piece of the man ahead of me. If I looked at the back of his head the rest of him was in darkness, out of sight. I stayed close, reached ahead with one hand, touched him on the back. Didn't want to feel alone down here. I had to walk bent way over. My six-foot-two frame didn't fit well in a five-foot-high tunnel. I stumbled along, awkward, clumsy. If I looked upward I couldn't see the cross ties under my feet. If I looked down I banged my head against the timbers that supported the roof. Now and then I heard a grunt, a muffled "goddamn," or "sonofabitch" and knew that someone behind me had banged his head. A couple of twists and turns and I was completely lost. The mine was a maze of unused and abandoned laterals. It was getting hot in the mine. My clothes were damp with sweat. We came to a small room off to one side, not a room really, just a square hole dug into the earth on one side of the shaft. This was the lateral office, an office because it had one small electric light dangling from a wire and a hand-cranked telephone on the wall. Still without words we followed our honcho's lead and stripped, each man putting his clothes and binto box in a neat pile on the dirt floor. So, here I was in my work uniform — rubber-soled, split-toed tennis shoes, black canvas leggings from ankle to knee, the old familiar G-string, a battery and a headlamp. Our honcho, stripped to a G-string like the rest of us, motioned to us to follow him. We were coal miners now, and he was going to put us to work.

We were talking now, chattering back and forth among ourselves. I was beginning to feel confident that I could handle this new situation. There were no guards, no weapons in sight and our one Japanese miner didn't pose much of a threat. Maybe, just maybe, this wasn't going to be so bad after all.

It was hot, at least in our part of the mine. It was very hot. Already I was sticky-sweaty. The temperature must have been well over a hundred degrees.

One of our crew said that this was swimmin' hole weather where he came from. Georgia from his accent. Told us that rivers were low and the water was almost standing still, just warm enough to be comfortable. Said fish almost jumped out of the water to get on the hook, big lazy catfish just beggin' to be caught. Sounded like a place I'd like to visit someday.

I thought of fried catfish, sweet, juicy, delicious. Catfish dipped in egg batter, then rolled in cornmeal and fried to a crisp golden brown. I remembered a couple of summers when I was a kid traveling with a carnival and we played the fair at Beardstown, Illinois, and the carnival set up on the main streets of Beardstown, and the old brick library with books downstairs and a courtroom upstairs where Abe Lincoln once sat as judge and the very same gavel Abe used still lay on the desk, and in the same block there was an ice cream shop where I could get the biggest chocolate malt in the whole damn world for a dime, and the final day of the fair when the city put on a big fish fry and you could get all the fried fish you could eat, come back as often as you like, for "FREE." Damn, some memories are so good they make you want to cry.

Our Japanese honcho, our foreman, looked distressed. He waved his hands and spoke to us in rapid Japanese. It wasn't going over. We didn't understand. Anger and frustration showed in his face. Suddenly his face brightened. Midsentence he clapped his left hand over his mouth, then pointed to his covered mouth with his other hand. One by one he went to each of us, placed a hand over our mouth and shook his head. Wise old man. Language barrier or not, we got the message. No talking in the mine. What the hell! Prisoners weren't allowed to talk on Alcatraz either.

How can I explain the coal mine to someone who has never experienced it? I might as easily explain colors to a blind man or a symphony to a person who cannot hear. To me the mine was a different world, an alien world, a hostile world. With a strange foreboding I sensed that this mine was as much my enemy as the Japanese soldiers with their rifles and bayonets who waited for my return to the surface.

Yonoroshi:
The Hot Hole

Yonoroshi. That's where I work in the mine, that's where my crew works in the mine. We are nine prisoners and one Japanese honcho Yonoroshi. We learned the name from him because he kept repeating it over and over. "Yon," that's the Japanese word for four. "Oroshi," at least that's the way it sounded to me, "oroshi" must mean the lateral or tunnel where we work. Yonoroshi, number four lateral. I got to know it well. The Japanese called it Yonoroshi. We referred to it simply as "the hot hole."

Generally speaking the temperature in the mine was cool, comfortable, but as soon as we left the main tunnel and turned into Yonoroshi we began to feel the heat. By the time we reached the working face my body would be wet with sweat, rivulets of perspiration running down my legs, squishing out the tops of my tennis shoes. And we were just getting there. The real work hadn't started yet.

Hard, brutal, backbreaking labor and stifling heat — that was Yonoroshi. And in Yonoroshi, everything we did, we did in the crudest, most primitive way imaginable. First thing we did every work shift was to push an empty mine car from the main tunnel, up the length of Yonoroshi to the working face, the place where we actually dug the coal out of the wall. These mine cars were large enough to hold five cubic yards of coal and even empty were heavy as hell, and we pushed them by hand, more than a hundred yards, uphill all the way. Uphill because the lateral was dug on a slight slope, inclined because the only way to get the loaded cars out was to let the force of gravity pull them down the lateral to the main track where a battery powered engine would push them to the mine entrance.

A common danger makes strange bedfellows. I have read of a time when a mountain lion, deer, and poisonous snakes peaceably shared the same bit of high ground during a flood. In Yonoroshi we were not much different. Nine prisoners worked side by side with one Japanese miner. In our year together he never struck one of us, and we never considered harming him. Above ground, outside the mine we were enemies. Our countries were at war. Down here, deep in the guts of mother earth, we were quietly allied against the mine, our common enemy.

It didn't take long for us to learn the reason for the "no talking" rule. The mine was old, at least our part of it, very old, and constantly caving in. These cave-ins weren't the massive kind you see in movies. In my year in the mine there was only one occasion when a lateral caved in completely. Instead, we were harried by many small cave-ins, "falls" we called them, small falls that could cause serious injury, could keep your nerves on edge, and could scare hell out of you.

I learned to be always on the alert, alert like a man who walks barefoot in the dark, knowing in advance there are sharp pointed tacks on the floor but not knowing exactly where they are. I developed an almost uncanny sixth sense for these falls. I learned to speak in whispers and to listen, not only with my ears but with my whole body. "Falls" came out of the blackness, quietly, like a thief in the night, and because I couldn't see them I made every effort to hear them. "No talking." Just work and listen.

Falls were usually preceded by the whisper of a handful of rock or fine coal falling out of the blackness, then, a split second later the bulk of the fall. I became an expert at this game of "dodge the rocks." If the first handful of rock hit me it was like walking past a lawn sprinkler with my eyes closed. I instinctively knew which way to jump to get out of the way. If the first rattle or rock missed me but was nearby, my body moved without conscious thought, trying to move away from, not into the fall. Falls usually came through the narrow space between two timbers on one side of the lateral and spread out fanwise against the other. I found the best way to protect myself from injury was to hear the fall coming and to stand against the wall near the point of the fan. If I guessed wrong and stood on the wrong side, the rush of coal and rock could pin me against the opposite wall. Good as I became at guessing and dodging, I've been buried chest deep as many as three times in a single work shift. Though these falls were mostly fine coal, occasional larger rocks could bruise or break bones. For me, the big damage was usually to my nerves. Scary as hell. Once pinned against the wall, I never knew if the rush of coal would stop at my knees or my neck or if it was going to bury me completely, head and all.

In spite of our fear of these cave-ins we often tried to help nature along. Whenever the honcho went down the hill first we would take a few swipes with a miner's pick and loosen the coal around the bottoms of a couple of support timbers. Hopefully the damn roof would fall in before the next work shift and thus slow down production while we cleaned up the rubble and repaired the damage.

Yonoroshi, the hot hole — the name became synonymous with extreme heat, hard work, and exhaustion, really brutal working conditions. The soldiers, our guards, never came into the mine, and our honcho never used force in any way. He didn't have to; the mine whipped our asses. Trouble began on the first work shift. We couldn't stand the heat. I never got a reading on the temperature, but it must have been high. Just walking the length of the lateral to the work face would leave my body glistening with sweat. Pushing a car uphill or swinging a miner's pick drained both fluid and strength from my body.

Heat exhaustion, that was the problem. There were only nine prisoners on the crew, and it was not unusual for one, two, or even three men to drop in a single shift. It wasn't like sunstroke. Nobody died from it. It was a simple combination of the heat, hard labor, and our impossibly poor physical condition. Marathon runners say they sometimes run into a "wall" near the end of a race, a point at which their body no longer responds. Well, we had our "wall" too. In the "hot hole" prisoners would be working, feel faint, collapse to the ground, and be unable to get up. For me it was the same kind of feeling I get now when I stand up too quickly and the blood leaves my head and I black out. I would be working and without warning find myself on the ground with no memory of falling, just a couple of skinned patches here and there and a terrible weakness. Didn't happen every day, at least not to me, but almost every shift we lost someone. For our own preservation and survival we tried to find an answer to our problem. It was plain to us that we couldn't go on this way and live.

First there was the problem of water. I had a canteen and always carried it full into the mine, but I could sweat out that much in a couple of hours. Down the lateral a couple of hundred feet a trickle of water seeped from the wall. Honcho made a face and indicated that it was unfit to drink. We drank it anyway. Filling a canteen from the seepage was hard and time consuming and honcho didn't want us to waste time. He needed us to work. During a lunch period we took a couple of the timbers we used for roof supports and with some clay to plug up the cracks, built an enclosure around the seepage the size of a large bathtub. Next shift we had a pool of water six inches deep. I drank huge amounts of this supposedly undrinkable water. It helped but not enough. We still couldn't stand up to the heat. The pool became a sort of lifeline like the safe base in a kid's game of tag. Honcho let us go there for water whenever we needed a drink, and it gave us a few minutes respite from work. Then we got smart. A prisoner dropped from heat exhaustion and we dragged him to the pool to splash water on him and to get him a drink. The idea was so simple that even in our half-stupefied state we thought of it. We had a pool, why not use it? We stretched the half-conscious prisoner full length in the six inches of water, head resting on a log. The cool water did the trick. Within minutes he revived and came back to work. The pool became a regular therapy. Collapse from the heat, somehow make your way to the pool and either pour cups of water over your head or stretch out in the shallow pool. I don't know how much good the pool did for our bodies, but it was wonderful for morale. I could be weak from the heat, stretch out in the water for a few minutes and return to work feeling refreshed. At least I convinced myself that I felt refreshed. Among ourselves, among the nine of us, we made up two rules about the pool, two unenforceable rules, which we tried fiercely to enforce. First, no cheating. No going to the pool when you don't really need it, and when you do go, no stalling around. Go and get back. Don't stall around and make the other guys do your work. Second, when you're stretched out in the water, damn it, don't urinate in the pool. Bad enough to have to drink the water ten minutes after some guy's been stretched out in it, but damn it, don't urinate in it. Sometimes even POWs get a little squeamish.

Heat prostration continued to slow down the work in the hot hole, and I imagine our honcho put in a good word on our behalf. After three weeks the camp commander began giving each man who worked the hot hole a weekly ration of salt. Just imagine going without salt for two-and-a-half years, no salt in the food, no salt anywhere. Now, just for the nine of us, two ounces of salt every week. A bonus for working in the hot hole. It wasn't the kind of salt we get on tables at home. It was rock salt, chunky, dirty, looking like pieces of small gravel, but it was salt. And with it, in our camp, the nine of us were kings. Nobody else got any and every prisoner in camp wanted it. I was offered rice, clothing, cigarettes, anything just for a pinch of salt. No dice. I wasn't trading. This little bit of salt just might keep me alive. I carried it with me when I went to chow, hid it in my G-string when I slept or went to work. I lived with it or maybe because of it. The rock salt was hard to use. Couldn't sprinkle it over my rice, it was too chunky. I learned to drop a salt rock into a little water, let it dissolve and mix it with my rice. Wonderful, it really worked. Other times I held a piece of rock salt under my tongue. That was good too. I never traded away any of my salt. I felt I needed it to keep me alive. Besides, the only thing anyone had that I wanted was food and to trade my salt for another man's food ratio would have been terribly wrong, perhaps condemning the other man to death. It would have been like the first days of our imprisonment when a few guys had a little medicine and everybody needed it. The guy with the most to trade got the medicine, some of the others died. I did, regularly, give little rocks of salt to a few friends. Didn't give away enough to hurt me, didn't give away enough to do them any good. They treated the little rocks of salt as if they were gold nuggets. Maybe they were.

What a difference a few ounces of salt can make in men's lives. It made the rice taste better. It cut down on the number of heat prostration cases in the hot hole and allowed us to work more efficiently. And now, with our weekly ration of salt the nine of us assumed special status in the camp. We became the elite, the Palace Guard, the Queen's Regiment. Where before the hot hole had been considered the worst place to work in the mine, now other prisoners were envious of the chance to work there. What a difference a little bit of salt makes.

After the war, after I was returned to the United States, I read a story about a Japanese troop train that had been delayed because something was wrong with the engine. The Japanese soldiers got off the train and beat the engine with bamboo poles. A true story? Maybe. Laughable? Of course. But why? Why such irrational behavior as to beat a steam engine with sticks? If this was a true story, I think the soldiers acted out of sheer frustration at something they did not understand. Now we were something they did not understand. They did not understand Americans, and especially they did not understand American prisoners of war. It was a clash of cultures. We came from different worlds. Japanese students sometimes commit suicide because they fail their university entrance exams. An American kid fails an exam, goes home, catches a little hell from his parents, studies harder and passes the next exam. Recently a Japanese figure skater felt shamed, apologized publicly to the entire nation because she had failed to win the gold medal at the Olympics. An American skater? No shame, "Just wait 'til next year." The point I am making is that because of the differences in language, in ways of thinking, and in cultural background, what we prisoners regarded as irrational behavior on the part of our Japanese guards was often dictated by their sheer frustration. This doesn't excuse their often savage behavior, but it may help to explain it. For an example, one night part of the mine caved in. One of our boys lay trapped under a large rock, one leg crushed so badly it later had to be amputated. The Japanese foreman went berserk. Before the rock was removed he beat the injured man, struck him several times with a length of chain for being so stupid as to be caught under a falling rock.

It's winter, bitter cold and snow on the ground. This will be our fourth Christmas since the start of the war, our third as prisoners.

The first Christmas, December 25, 1941, slipped by largely unnoticed. We were young, we were fresh, and the war, our war, was only a couple of weeks old. We were strong, eager to face the enemy and fight, possibly to the death, for our country. In our innocence we did not yet realize that we were already isolated, cut off, eight thousand miles from home and practically on the doorstep of a ruthless aggressor with vastly superior forces at his disposal. We were confident. We thought a relief convoy was being loaded, probably already on its way, and like kids playing cowboys and Indians, our job was to man the barricades and hold off the bad guys until the cavalry came charging to the rescue. And we were naive. Even when Dugout Doug, our commanding general, hightailed it for the safety of Australia, we failed to realize that we were relatively unimportant, a tiny chip to be cashed in, to be sacrificed to buy a little time in this gigantic game of war.

Now, once again, Christmas. I'm not sure how we knew. I suppose our officers told us. Don't know how they knew either, but I suppose, because they were officers they knew things. Smarter than we were? Not really, but infinitely better educated, better organized, more likely to know such things as where we were, how many men had died, and when Christmas came.

For me, I had long ago lost track of time. Days, weeks, months were no longer important. My time was measured by different intervals, by how long it was since I had been struck by a guard, by how long since I was hurt in the mine, by how long since dysentery had tried to rip my guts out. Somehow though, even as a POW Christmas was important. For me, and I believe for all the other prisoners as well, Christmas was the one day that marked the beginning and the end of an interval of time. We didn't remember birthdays or the Fourth of July or Thanksgiving or New Year, but we remembered Christmas. Undoubtedly this was a holdover from childhood. Recollections of childhood, at least the happy ones, always stay with us — the lights, the carols, the music, the decorated trees. Surely these things had made Christmas the most joyful time of the year. There was the wonder of looking at the magical displays in store windows and slowly walking, big-eyed, through the toy departments, and the anticipation, the hope, that when the waiting was over and the big day finally came, that wonderful things would surely happen.

Sadly enough we somehow transposed this feeling of hope into our POW lives.

As each succeeding Christmas passed we knew with unshakable conviction that before the next Christmas we would be out of here, free from the Japanese, free from this God damned slavery. And as each Christmas passed we hung our hopes on next year.

Though we know by now that we won't be out of here, this coming Christmas, 1944, promises both good and bad. The good, there is a rumor, as yet unverified, that we may once again get a food parcel, our third in almost three years. These food parcels, though only the size of a large shoebox, were filled with wonderful things, a can of corned beef, a can of fish, milk chocolate, soluble coffee, two or three packs of American cigarettes, wondrous things we had almost forgotten about. This was the good. The bad, Sergeant Nelson died just a few days before Christmas. Nelson's death threw a shadow over Christmas, not because he died, hell, half our original number had already passed away. Nelson's death saddened us because of the way he died. We knew for weeks, even months ahead, that he was going, slowly, surely, inevitably going to die, and we watched him go and there was absolutely nothing any of us could do about it. First, he began to stumble, to have difficulty in walking. His body movements were clumsy, uncoordinated. Then his speech began to slow down, became blurred, almost unintelligible. Toward the end he remained stretched out on his tatami mat, unable to move, unable to speak, eyes staring but uncomprehending. One night, hopefully without pain, he died quietly in his sleep.

Nelson died from syphilis. He survived in combat, survived through years of beatings and starvation and slave labor, and now some sneaky, bastardly disease that had lain dormant for twenty or thirty years caught up with him and took him away.

His death both saddened and angered us. Our doctor did everything he could, but without medicine, basically nothing. He had all the food he could eat. We kept him warm and comfortable. Someone was always ready to walk him, sometimes to carry him, to the latrine or the bathhouse, and yet he died.

We knew for weeks ahead that Nelson was going to die. No question about that. But unconsciously, without putting it into words, the entire camp had set the goal of keeping him alive until Christmas. And damn it, he died. Had he lived just a few more days he could have died with his belly full of American food, with perhaps a chocolate bar for dessert and an American cigarette on his lips. Nelson would have liked that.

December 25, 1944. Christmas did come, and with it the long-rumored food parcels. Expectations were high. Major Hogan and his two junior officers made a decision not much to our liking. The food parcels were to be kept under lock and key. The American cigarettes were handed out immediately, three packs to each man, and each man's can of corned beef was to go to the kitchen to be mixed into the general rice ration. Thereafter, each man would be given one item a week from his individual parcel. A wise decision, I suppose, because in this way this tiny food supplement could be stretched out over eight or nine weeks.

Suppertime and the entire camp squeezed into the mess hall and sat at the long wooden tables. Mo Ichi Do was there, sitting at a raised table, and several of the Japanese guards stood around the room, but this time without weapons. In front of each prisoner was a bowl of rice, slightly rounded, more full than usual. There was a bowl of soup, hot, bitter, green tea, a tiny biscuit, and finally, a one-ounce paper cup filled with sake, this last, Mo Ichi Do's contribution to the festivities. We stood at attention while Mo Ichi Do offered a toast to our happiness, Christmas, and to our health. Then he told all prisoners to eat. He was beaming, happy with himself and pleased with his recognition of our holiday. I gave my sake to the guy next to me. I wasn't feeling well, ate my soup and the biscuit, drank the tea and ate half my rice. Damn, for once in my life there was enough food and I couldn't handle it. I gave the remaining half of my rice away. The fellow sitting next to me had no trouble in quickly cleaning up both his bowl and mine.

We sang a few songs, mostly Christmas carols that we sometimes only half remembered, but we managed to slip in "America the Beautiful" without objection from the Japanese. A prisoner seated near Mo Ichi Do's table opened a pack of American cigarettes, shook it so that one cigarette protruded above the others, and graciously offered a cigarette to Mo Ichi Do. Mo Ichi Do, not understanding the gesture, smiled broadly, reached over the table and took the entire pack. Dead silence in the room. Jesus Christ, a whole pack of American cigarettes shot to hell. Highly pleased, Mo Ichi Do shook the prisoner's hand and told him, I much thank you. The prisoner managed a very weak "you're welcome" and the spell was broken. We all began to breathe again. The guards were stiff and ill at ease but relaxed somewhat when prisoners offered them an American cigarette, careful this time to extract and offer a single cigarette instead of the whole pack.

Roland Jollie went to the front of the room and sang a couple of songs straight from the hills of Appalachia. Mo Ichi Do, enormously pleased, gave Jollie another cup of sake and encouraged him to sing some more, then with a knowing look he asked Major Hogan if Jollie was a peasant? I saw Jollie smile as the major nodded affirmatively and said that he was.

After about an hour Mo Ichi Do left. The festivities were over. We straggled back to our barracks, each of us convinced in his own mind that before next year, before next Christmas, by God we're gonna be outta here.

January 1945–August 1945:
Slave Labor in the Coal Mine

The mine was like no other experience on earth. The mine was dark, dirty, often wet, and in Yonoroshi, unbearably hot. It was an unfriendly place, unfriendly and almost evil. I always viewed it with deep suspicion, like a snarling dog that will tolerate your presence, allow you to approach it, but is always ready to take a bite out of your hand. To me the mine assumed an identity, a personality, wicked, malevolent, treacherous, a shapeless unseen something lurking just outside the circle of light cast by my headlamp, watching, waiting, ready to pounce the instant I became complacent and let down my guard even for a fraction of a second.

The darkness was something I never got used to. It seems unnatural for a man to spend so much of his life in the dark. No more unnatural though than to be a prisoner of war. On a normal workshift when my battery and headlamp were functional I lived and worked just behind a little circle of light that limited my visual world. The headlamps were not strong. I could usually see clearly whatever lay directly ahead of me, clearly for about six feet, dimly a few feet farther than that. My world was defined by this circle of light. When I looked ahead the blackness receded a little bit; it closed in behind me. I could move this world wherever I looked, up, down, to the side, but outside my circle of light the blackness was so intense that nothing seemed to exist. There were times when for one reason or another I was working alone and my light went out. I do not think I can fully convey to you what it is really like to be alone in silence, in the dark, a half mile beneath the surface of the earth. Both the silence and the darkness changed from concepts to things, things that had weight and substance, things that stifled me, smothered me, pressed in against me. There were times when I wanted to scream just to make a noise, to drive the silence back, to give myself a little breathing room. And the darkness that enveloped me, I could actually feel its presence. I wanted to flail against it with my hands to drive it away. Darkness and silence, silence and darkness. Is this what it's like to be dead?

Had a most unusual happening in Yonoroshi. We were working as usual in the hot hole and literally working our tails off. For about an hour each shift we got air pressure through a small pipeline, enough air pressure to run a small jackhammer. Like everything else in the mine the air pressure was not dependable, so when we got it we worked hard and fast. Took three men to run the drill, two to support the weight and a third on the handle. While we had air pressure we tried to drill several horizontal holes six feet deep into the working face. Holes drilled and air pressure gone, our honcho placed sticks of dynamite with long copper wires attached, one stick in each hole. Then we shoved rolled-up balls of clay in behind the dynamite and tamped it tightly with a broomstick. The wires from the dynamite were attached to a detonator farther back in the tunnel. If we got good air pressure, if we worked hard enough, fast enough, if we drilled enough holes, if all the lousy dynamite went off, lots of ifs, then the explosion would break up a few feet of coal at the face and give us a start on the night's work. It was all very iffy. If the air didn't last long enough or if we didn't get enough holes drilled, we wasted a lot of effort, couldn't blast, and had to dig the coal out by hand. I had a love-hate relationship with the dynamite. Loved it because when it worked it made my job a little easier, hated it because we were never sure that all the sticks had exploded. Our honcho always waited a few minutes after blasting to make sure it was safe to go back, but still, more than once we were surprised by a delayed explosion. Luckily each time only a single stick and luckily before we were close to the working face. Nerve-wracking as hell to start digging away at the wall, never sure whether or not it would blow up in your face.

On this particular night we were working a few feet ahead of our timbers. Usually we put two vertical supports and a crosspiece, small saplings three to six inches in diameter, every three feet to support the roof as we dug farther into the hill. We had just finished blasting and were starting to pick up the loose coal and load the minecar when rocks started falling. The blast must have loosened a lot of stuff in the overhead. Small stuff at first. We heard it coming and ran like hell. Our Japanese honcho tripped and went sprawling. Before he could get up a rock struck him on the head and he was out. It all happened in a fraction of a second. First the warning, small rocks falling and the running. Bigger stuff was falling now and one of our crew, a kid named Bowden, ran back under the falling rocks and dragged our honcho to safety. They were barely clear when the whole damn roof came down, tons of it. Both men were bruised and hurt but okay. It was a brave thing to do, one man reacting instinctively to save the life of another without thought of race or color or enmity. Bowden was closest and without hesitating he ran into the rockfall and dragged the Japanese out. It took a helluva lot of nerve. Had I been in Bowden's place, had I been the closest one, would I have risked my life to save an enemy? I'd surely like to think so, but before God, I don't know.

A few days later our Japanese camp commander presented Bowden with a scroll, beautifully lettered in Japanese characters on heavy paper commending him for his bravery and thanking him for saving a Japanese life. The scroll didn't do Bowden much good, never got him out of the mine, never got him better treatment or better food, but if he got it home I hope it's hanging proudly on the wall.

We never got back to the working face in this particular lateral. Too much hard rock falling, constantly falling. Got so bad I could look up but couldn't see the roof of the chamber. No way to shore it up, no way to reach the high ceiling with timbers, so the Japanese gave up on it. Next shift my crew changed to a different lateral, still in Yonoroshi, still in the hot hole, but in a slightly different location.

Working conditions in the new lateral were primitive beyond belief. We were back in the Stone Age. Like all the side laterals this one ran at an angle to the larger main tunnel, but sloped upward at such a steep angle that we often scuttled along on all fours. Watching the shadowy figures of my crew making their way upward to the working face I was reminded of children on a playground, trying to climb up a slide, from the bottom up. The roof of the tunnel was low, perhaps only four, four-and-a-half feet roof to floor, low even for the smaller Japanese, pure misery for us taller Americans. This lateral, like all the laterals in the hot hole, was very old. The timbers were rotting, walls and overhead crumbling, always crumbling. It was highly dangerous.

At the time I was waging my own little war of survival. Once I got down in the mine, once my group of seven or eight or nine prisoners broke off from the main workforce and turned into the hot hole, my world narrowed to my own immediate circle of light and those few shadowy figures who worked in the hot hole beside me. Once we turned into the hot hole we were cut off even from the rest of the mine. For the year that I worked there I never knew where the larger group of prisoners went in the mine, never saw where they worked, never knew just what they did. I suppose it could be called a prisoner-of-war syndrome, the forced acceptance, the forced adaptation to whatever circumstances our Japanese captors placed us in. As part of a crew of perhaps seventy prisoners, we lined up together before work and marched together to the mine. We rode together in the trolley cars down into the depths of the mine, but once we split off into Yonoroshi we became that strange little bunch that worked in the hot hole. It was like shutting the door to the rest of the world. And neither gave a damn. In the hot hole we had our own particular problems to contend with and the rest of the world had theirs. At the end of the work shift, somewhere in the main tunnel, we would rejoin the main group of prisoners, become part of the larger world again, but conversation between the groups was minimal. If they bothered to ask if we'd had a tough night in the hot hole we'd usually answer that we'd worked our asses off. Same thing every shift. Maybe a couple of guys got hit with falling rock. Nothin' serious but they'd get a couple of days off in camp.

Sometimes I wished it was me. I wouldn't have minded getting hurt, not badly, just enough to get out of the coal mine, to rest up for a few days. It'd damn well be worth it.

We reached the trolley cars at the bottom of the exit tunnel.

"Hey! Move over you bastard, it's my turn to sit in the middle. I got wet goin' out last night."

Looking back it seems obvious that the Japanese economy was struggling mightily to meet the war effort, and my little crew in the hot hole was scratching away to get a few tons of low-grade coal, at any cost, from laterals that had been abandoned as unproductive many years ago.

Our new lateral, the one with the low headroom, had one saving grace, sort of a trade-off, half good, half bad. A small stream of water came out of the wall from somewhere way up the hill, and this lateral had been abandoned for so many years that the stream had cut a sizable ditch along one wall. The ditch was hip deep, v-shaped, and maybe four feet wide at the top. The iron pipe that brought air to the drilling face lay at floor level along one side. The trade-off was that I could either walk on the floor at the side of the ditch, bent way over and scuttling along like a crab, or I could try to walk upright along the bottom of the ditch. I opted for the ditch. It was hell on the ankles because there was no flat spot in the bottom and I walked in mud and water, but I could use the air pipe as a handrail and sort of pull myself along. At first this ditch was just a ditch, a means of getting to the work face, something to take advantage of to make my life a little easier. Later it came to play an important part in my life.

Above the point where the stream came out of the wall the ditch disappeared and the hard rock that formed the roof dropped to within eighteen inches of the floor. We had to wriggle on our bellies to get past this narrow seam in the rock, to get to the point where the roof went up again to give us a little more headroom. It seems unbelievable now, but in those days it was just a part of my daily routine. We dug coal from above this low place in the mine roof. To get the loose coal past this low point, this eighteen-inch gap in the rock, we literally worked on our bellies. We lay, five men head to foot, each man passing coal down to the next man with a wide-blade, short-handled hoe. Though our little Japanese honcho never struck any of my crew while we worked in the mine, this was brutally hard work and we knew we had to do it. There would always be the rifles and bayonets waiting for us when we came out of the mine. I remembered a line that I had read somewhere in the long ago past. "'Twas a dark stormy night, not fit for man or beast." Down here we were the beasts.

We rotated our jobs in the hot hole. Some shifts I dug coal at the cutting face, sometimes passed coal through the low place in the rock, sometimes worked farther down the lateral, but I hated scraping coal through the low spot the most. I think, subconsciously, the idea of working in such close quarters beneath millions of tons of rock terrified me. After all, I spent day after day after day working in this tiny crack where I could touch the rock beneath me with one shoulder, the rock above me with the other. If this mountain shrugged the tiniest bit the crack could close and I would become nothing more than a bloody spot between two layers of rock.

Having dug the coal from the face, having laboriously and painfully dragged it alongside my body, passing it from the man above to the man below, we still had to move the coal a couple of hundred feet down to the main tunnel. How? Damned if I knew. No way in hell could we push a mine car up that steep lateral. I was stymied, baffled, at a loss, but not the Japanese. There was no shortage of unwilling labor. We were prisoners and we were there to work. At our honcho's direction we laid two sets of iron rails from the main tunnel, two hundred feet up the lateral to a spot fifty feel below where the stream came out of the wall. Each set of rails was a foot wide, and there was a space of three feet between the parallel sets. I was mystified. None of my crew had the slightest idea what we were doing this for. But our honcho knew. He had an idea. I think this must have been the way the Egyptians built the pyramids, on the backs of uncomprehending slave labor.

Still uncomprehending we built a barricade of logs across the width of the lateral near the top of the two sets of rails. We blocked the ditch and raised the barricade two feet above the floor of the lateral. Didn't make a bit of sense. The stream ran through the cracks in the dam and kept on running down the hill. But, though we prisoners were stupid, our Japanese honcho had it all figured out. Next shift he appeared with two long wooden boxes, a pulley, and a coil of steel cable. We carried these things with us into the hot hole. By the end of the work day we had our answer. Yes, we were going to mine coal. Incredible as it seems today, our little honcho had figured a way for nine emaciated prisoners to move tons of coal down three hundred feet of almost impassable tunnel to the main line. Impossible, of course, simply couldn't be done, yet I saw it, worked it, lived it, and to this day, find it hard to believe that we did it. In the end the whole operation reminded me of nothing more than one of the Rube Goldberg cartoons that were popular when I was a kid, a complicated arrangement of gears and wheels and bells and whistles that accomplished practically nothing. This crazy scheme might have been a star in our honcho's crown but it was a pain in our collective asses.

On a normal work shift, first thing we did after stripping to G-strings and climbing up the tunnel was to block off the flow of water where it came out of the rock wall. The stream came out of a small opening, and we blocked it with a tapered chunk of timber driven tight with a miner's pick and held firm with a large rock. Next we wriggled on our bellies through the low place in the tunnel, dropping off five men, flat on their bellies, head to toe, along the way. Two prisoners and the honcho dug coal from the working face and piled it within reach of the first of the belly-downers in the crawl space, who dragged it the length of his body with a short-handled hoe and passed the coal to the second of the belly-downers, who passed it to the third and the fourth and the fifth. At the bottom end of the five man line where the tunnel opened up a bit, the last two prisoners made a single pile of the night's work.

This flat-on-my-belly scraping operation was the part of coal mining that I hated most, hated and dreaded. The idea of working for hours in such a confined space struck a constant note of anxiety, of fear, that I could never shake. And I wasn't alone. My entire crew hated this part of the work with a passion. It wasn't just the brutally hard work or the constant anxiety, it was the innate sense that man, human beings, were never intended by God to live and work like this. Other than to grouse among ourselves, to curse the mine and the miners and the Japanese who put us there, we were never able to verbalize these thoughts, but the anxiety, the unfocused hatred, the dread was always there.

We rotated the various positions among the nine of us, two men and the honcho digging coal from the face, the next five scraping it through the crack in the rock, and the last two piling it up as it came out of the crawl space. My turns in the belly-down line were really three-to-four-hour, wide-awake nightmares. Three-to-four-hour, wide-awake nightmares when I was filled with a combination of rage and fear that I couldn't express. When I was top man in the belly-down line my head was out of the hole, I could look around a bit, I could see the honcho and the other prisoners digging at the face. The second, third, fourth and fifth night in the hole were times filled with negative emotions — fear, rage, frustration. The first man, lying partly on his belly, partly on his side, would drag the coal alongside his body down to his knees. That was as far as he could push it. The second man, head touching the first man's feet, would reach up to arm's length with his short-handled hoe and drag coal alongside his body to his knees and so on until the coal was passed through five men and out in to the higher space below the crack. Trouble was, in the second, third, fourth, and fifth place in line I was for all practical purposes blind and in the dark. In such close quarters my headlamp lit up only a small spot directly in front of my nose. No way could I tip my head back far enough to see the man working above me or look downward enough to see the man below. So in the dark each of us had to reach up as far as we could with the hoe and drag a hoeful of coal down to our knees. There was a lot of ill-natured bitching. The usual complaint was that I was hitting the guy above with my hoe or that I was pushing coal down so fast that I was burying the guy below.

For my part, I bitched and I hollered and I cursed at the man who scraped my shin raw with his hoe, and I panicked as the coal from above piled up around my head. I attacked the pile with a vengeance and passed it on without regard for the man below me. And it wasn't just the close quarters. Naked except for my G-string, it didn't take much squirming to make sore spots, even raw spots on shoulders, hips, and legs. I always thought of calluses as belonging on the hands and feet, but in my belly-downer days, bare flesh against hard rock, I developed heavy calluses on shoulders, hips, and legs. Belly-down scraping took up the first three or four hours of a work shift, but even when we had dragged enough coal through the crack to last the rest of the shift, it was still hard work. We had to get out of the crack. Try wriggling backwards on your bare belly over hard rock.

The first phase of this Rube Goldberg mining operation completed, our honcho let us rest briefly, let the tensions die down. Comparatively speaking, lots of room now, four or five feet of headroom. All of the coal that we had so laboriously scraped through the crack was in one big pile across the ditch. This was the easy part of the night's work. We pulled the plug where the stream came out of the wall and the backed-up water gushed forth with enough force to mix with the coal and form a sort of slurry that flowed slowly down the ditch some sixty or seventy feet to pile up against the log barricade we had built across the tunnel. We scurried frantically to help it along with hoes because any coal left after the water ran out still had to be moved down the tunnel by hand, and sixty feet is a helluva long way to scrape a pile of wet coal.

Phase three. This was where I would spend the rest of the shift. Thus far we had managed to dig the coal from the face, scrape it through the crack, and with the help of the stream, move it seventy feet to the log dam. We still had two hundred feet to go to get it to the main line. Ingenious? Damn right, but stupidly so nevertheless. Rube Goldberg would have been proud of this little crew of POW mining engineers.

Problem now was to move the coal on down to the main line and into a mine car without killing ourselves, and quickly enough so we could leave the mine without meeting the next shift on the way in. No easy task. Our shifts often overlapped, meaning my crew had been down in the hole more than twelve hours.

The pile of coal was now piled up against the log barricade and opposite the two sets of rails we had laid. With a pulley fastened to a timber at the top of the rails we rigged a long cable to the two wooden boxes so that when one box was at the top of the rails the other box was at the bottom. Now to make it work. It seemed simple enough. Everybody helped load the top box. I would hold a horseshoe-shaped bamboo basket on the ground between my two feet and scrape it full with the short-handled hoe. Stoop labor. When my basket was full I would pick it up, carry it to the box, and dump it in. The boxes seemed big, eighteen inches wide, fifteen inches deep, and four feet long. They held a lot of coal. Every man had his basket and every man had his hoe. We all chipped in to fill the box. Then there would be a temporary respite while the loaded box slid down the rails and its weight pulled the empty to the top. This was mechanization at its most primitive.

I liked working the boxes. Sure beat hell out of lying on my belly and scraping coal through the crack. Took two men to handle the boxes. When it was my turn, when the top box was full of coal, I would bang on the air pipe with a miner's pick. Two bangs on the pipe was a signal to the man at the bottom that I was starting down the rails with a loaded box and that he had to be ready to run like hell, to hang on for dear life, while the weight of the loaded box going down dragged the empty to the top. Riding the loaded box wasn't easy. It meant stumbling along with both hands on the box, bent double because of the low headroom, pushing a little here, holding back a little there, doing my damndest to keep it from going off the track and dumping the load. For me, it was terribly hard to scuttle behind the box, bent double because of the low overhead, and struggling to keep the box on the track. I continually either bumped my head and scraped my back against the overhead rock, or stumbled and skinned my knees against the floor. Above all, don't let go, don't lose control of the load. When I fell, and I often did, I had to hang on and be dragged until the weight of my body slowed the box and I could again get to my feet. Somewhere halfway down I would pass the man with the empty box on his way up. We were like ships passing in the night. Neither of us dared take a hand off the box to wave, and neither of us had enough breath left to holler. If I got my load to the bottom without dumping it, the track ended on a flat iron plate, just high enough to extend over the edge of a mine car. With strenuous effort and a heck of a lot of luck, my load would slide off the rails and onto the iron plate just short of the mine car. I could dump the box on the plate, scrape the coal into the mine car with a hoe, put my box back on the track, and have a few minutes to recover while the box at the top was being filled. Then, two bangs on the pipe and the wild run behind the empty to the top.

Two, maybe three, months we went through the same daily routine. We mined coal, scraped it through the crack, and nursed it in boxes down the chute. Day by day as I climbed up the shaft to the working face I became more and more aware of a huge round boulder that protruded from one wall. It worried me. Why? I didn't know. Probably been right there for a million years, certainly sticking out of the wall since this shaft was first dug and then abandoned maybe ten or twenty years ago. Not to worry, but I did. I was always wary of the darned thing, kept my eyes on it till I climbed past, gave it a wide berth and walked by on the far side of the lateral. The boulder became a fixture in my mind, a point of reference in the mine as I climbed up or down the steep lateral, always familiar yet threatening.

One night we had finished work and were climbing down the chute on our way out of the mine. Past the big boulder I felt a rock in my shoe. It hurt and I sat down against the side of the ditch to take it out. Single file the rest of my crew went on down to the main line, made the turn and disappeared. I was alone but my headlamp was working. I knew the way, and I would catch up with them before they got to the trolleys. I pulled off my shoe and felt for the stone. I sensed it and heard it at the same time, a soft thud like a ripe melon dropping to the sidewalk. I never saw it but instinctively I knew the boulder had broken loose and that I was in its path. It happened so fast. My back was toward the boulder but I heard the thud, sensed the movement and tried my best to get out of its way. The realization of what was happening hit me like an electric shock, like that terrible feeling that engulfs your whole body when you suddenly find yourself in mortal danger. I had barely started to react, had hardly formed the thought, when four tons of rock crashed into my hip, smashing my body against the sidewall of the ditch. Luckily my body twisted sideways at the first impact and I avoided the full force of the blow.

I was helpless against the tremendous weight of the rock. It pinned my legs, tore my hands loose from the air pipe, rolled up on the small of my back and stopped. I don't think I was unconscious even for a moment, but I was dazed. When my mind cleared I realized that I was pinned down in the bottom of the ditch, head downhill, with a four-ton boulder sitting on the middle of my back. I knew I wasn't dead but I honestly thought I was going to die. I didn't feel any pain, just a general numbness and the awful weight of the boulder on my back. I couldn't breathe, couldn't get enough air into my lungs to shout, and to make things worse, my headlamp went out. I panicked. I was alone in the dark, upside down, acid from my headlamp battery running over my backside, couldn't move a muscle, and this damn big rock was sitting on me. I tried my damndest to holler for help but couldn't. Wondered if I would have to lie here till the next shift came to work. Wondered if I'd still be alive when they did.

Thank God, I can see headlamps at the bottom of the lateral, hear voices too.

Someone in my crew noticed that I didn't catch up, and they're coming back to look for me. Our honcho too, I can hear his voice. He's a Japanese and I am an enemy and sometimes he's a hard-headed arrogant little bastard, but I know he wouldn't leave me in the mine if he thought I was hurt.

The first man's headlamp picked me out in the darkness. He shouted to the others that he could see me, that I was pinned under that big rock. I was conscious but I still couldn't talk. The whole crew was there. Someone was asking me how I felt and telling me to hang on till they figured a way to get the rock off. I nodded my head. Face down I couldn't see anybody, but I could see the lights from their headlamps moving around. There was a conference going on. Our Japanese honcho was rattling off a string of excited, rapid Japanese. Someone climbed down into the ditch, squatted by my head. I think it might have been Bowden.

He paused there for a second to get the right words to say, then told me there was no way in hell they could get that big rock off my back. It was too big, too heavy, and they didn't have any equipment, nothing. The boulder was jammed against the side of the ditch. All that was holding it in place was a tiny finger of rock. He said they could take one of the roof timbers and maybe pry the rock loose, but if they did it would have to roll right over me, probably all the way to the bottom. He told me I had a hell of a choice, but there was nothing else they could do. They couldn't leave me there and they couldn't get me out. Was I ready? I wasn't ready and I was scared shitless. That monstrous big rock was going to roll over the rest of my body, crush me to a pulp.

What a way to die. Again he told me there was nothing else they could do, asked again if I was ready. I nodded my head, dumbly, wondering just how much dying was going to hurt. I tensed everything and waited. I heard the scuffling behind me, heard the grunts as the crew pried with the roof pole, felt the movement and the weight as the boulder rolled the length of my body. The pressure squeezed out what little air was left in my lungs, pushed my face deep into the mud. Dimly I felt the release of the weight, heard the crashing sounds of the boulder as it bounded down the tunnel tearing out timbers here and there as it caromed along. I pulled my face out of the mud. Somehow I realized I wasn't dead. I was bruised, turned almost black from my ankles to my neck, but the v-shape of the ditch held the boulder up enough, kept it from crushing the life out of me.

We waited. Gradually the numbness faded and feeling came back into my legs. I had to be able to walk, knew I had to walk. There was no stretcher and even had there been one there was no headroom in this lateral. Either I walked out on my own or my crew would have to drag my skinny ass down two hundred feet of tunnel. Hurt like hell but with a lot of help I made it to the trolley cars. Damndest thing. I could push backward with my left leg but to bring it forward for the next step I had to swing it like a wooden leg.

On the way out we passed a crew of Japanese miners, regular miners who worked in another, safer part of the mine. Word travels fast. They already knew somebody had been hurt. They were concerned, sympathetic. I heard the words "itai tocsan" over and over again. "Itai tocsan," hurts very much.

I didn't know how badly I was hurt but the pain was intense, a heavy aching pain that stayed with me for weeks, and sharp jabs of pain, the sharp kind you get when a dentist's drill strikes a nerve. The ache was with me all the time but the sharp jabs mostly when I moved. Took about six weeks to heal to the point where I could walk comfortably and work, and during that time I got the usual POW medical treatment, not so much as a simple aspirin. I was young and somehow my body compensated.

My back healed and I thought everything was all right, but it wasn't, never would be. In 1946, the year after the war, my new wife and I went roller-skating. I was uncomfortable, clumsy as hell, unable to do what I used to do easily. Pre-war I had been a pretty good basketball player, played on the regimental team, and we won the championship on Corregidor just six weeks before the war by barely defeating a tough Philippine Scout team that had two former Olympic players. After the war I played on a young men's basketball team at church. We were soundly beaten, forty-four to nothing. Twenty years later I worked as stevedore superintendent for Matson Navigation Company. Two years after I left the job I was walking down a long pier when someone behind me called me by name. I turned around but the man was so far away I couldn't tell who he was. When he drew close I recognized a mechanic who had worked with me at Matson for six years. First thing I asked was how did he know it was me? He said that he didn't need to see my face because he recognized the way I walked. Turned out that I walked with a little rolling gait that my wife and everyone else knew about, every-one except me. Wasn't till 1979, thirty-four years after the war, that a VA surgeon told me that my back hadn't healed properly and that one leg was nearly half an inch shorter than the other.

Anyway, back in prison camp, "Doc," Major Hogan, our camp comman-der — he was "Doc" at sick call and Major Hogan sir at all other times — told me that he thought I had torn some muscles or ligaments in the small of my back. He told me he would do whatever he could for me at sick call in the morning.

Sick call was a farce. Like the old Army medical exam, if you could hear thunder and see lightning you were able-bodied. Major Hogan presided, but under the direction of a Japanese doctor who spoke no English and a medical orderly who spoke damn little. When Major Hogan examined a sick prisoner he very slowly explained his findings to the orderly, who half understandingly explained to the Japanese doctor. If the Japanese doctor agreed with the diagnosis he nod-ded his head and Major Hogan did what he could. Major Hogan had been with Mayo Brothers Clinic and really knew his stuff, but without either medicine or surgical instruments his hands were tied. The Japanese doctor was OK, somewhat distant and noncommittal but OK. The medical orderly was a real son of a bitch. Often when a prisoner would report to sick call with a high fever or severe dysen-tery, the medical orderly would beat the hell out of him and send him on to work. The Japanese miners hated it. They didn't want sickies or cripples hanging around, just made the job tougher for them. The Japanese Army controlled everything. The soldiers brought us to the mine, the miners had to put us to work. Though they obviously didn't like me dragging around, they were nice about it. After we got out of the trolleys at the bottom of the ramp the crew moved out and left me alone to get to Yonoroshi twenty or thirty minutes later. And for a few weeks our honcho would give me a thirty-minute head start at quitting time so I could get to the trolleys and ride out with the rest of the crew.

"Doc" Hogan's talk with the orderly didn't do me a bit of good. I was sent to the mine with my regular shift. As soon as our honcho saw me limping along he started raising hell, screaming at the other honchos. It was plain to see he did not want me around, didn't want to be responsible for me. On the spot I was transferred to another crew and got what I considered a real cushy job.

My new crew worked in a side lateral that was terribly steep, low headroom here too, and so far up the slope that from the bottom I could neither see their headlamps nor hear their voices. They had rigged a series of steel plates to form a sort of chute so that coal dumped on the plates at the top would slide all the way to the bottom. My job was to stay at the bottom and consolidate the coal, with a short-handled scraper, behind a log barricade with a vertical sliding door opening, something like the water gate in a small irrigation ditch. When the electric engine dropped off a mine car at our lateral, I would open the gate and scrape coal into the car. It was a cushy job but highly dangerous. Everything came down the chute, coal, rocks, pieces of timber, and I was alone at the bottom. The coal came down rather gently, gathering around my ankles as I scraped it into a pile against the logs, but the rocks, the big ones, came flying down with the speed of a fast ball crossing home plate. And I was at the bottom with no place to hide.

After getting knocked on my ass a few times I learned to listen, to distinguish between the sound of sliding coal and the sound of a bouncing rock. I even learned to guess, from the sound, which way the rock was coming down and flatten myself against the safer side of the lateral till it went whistling past. Didn't always work but I got damn good at it.

The mine was wearing me down. I was losing weight, my back was hurting, and it was getting harder and harder to face those damn rocks hurtling out of the darkness, never knowing for sure which way they were going to go. I became a little desperate. I wanted to get out of the mine so badly, if only for a few days, a little time out of the mine to rest up, to gain strength, to sort of regroup in my mind so I could more easily face those damn rocks. I thought of everything and came up with nothing. Whatever I did, whatever excuse I found, it had to be good or that Japanese orderly would simply kick the hell out of me and send me back to work. Others may have tried but I knew of only one prisoner who tried to get out of the mine and made it work. Roland Jollie, a soldier from my own outfit on Fort Drum, poured battery acid on his ass and let it burn, burned almost all the way through the skin. Told the orderly his battery leaked and he couldn't stop it. Must have hurt like hell. Jollie had a scab on his backside as big as my two hands. Didn't get him completely out of work but got him a couple of weeks on a topside detail shoveling coal into mine cars from the settling tanks. I would have settled for that but didn't think it could be worked twice. I suppose desperate problems call for desperate solutions. One night a prisoner with a bad case of dysentery came down the chute to relieve himself. We regularly dug pits farther down the line so a man could squat over the hole, relieve himself, and scrape a little coal over the mess to hide the smell. When he came back there were just the two of us, alone, and I had a stupid idea. It was a really stupid idea, but I was just crazy enough to think of it and he was just crazy enough to help me do it. Quickly we held a short consultation. We both agreed it could be done, and we were both a little crazy. I found two short pieces of log and laid them parallel to each other about ten inches apart and laid my left arm across the gap, wrist on one log, elbow on the other. My friend stood by with a club the size of a baseball bat. I turned my head away and told him to break my arm with the club. He raised on his toes and with both hands brought the club down with all the force he could muster. The thump was sickening. Damn, how it hurt. I looked expectantly at my arm. I could still move my fingers. I gritted my teeth.

"Hit it again," I muttered, "harder this time."

Okay, one more time.

This would surely do it. He raised the club over his head and I closed my eyes as tightly as I could. I was too scared, didn't want to see it happen. Whop! The club came down and my world exploded. I opened my eyes and vomited on the ground. My arm was the size of a football but I could still move my goddamn fingers. I looked at him and he looked at me. We knew we were defeated. Two skinny-assed skeletons trying to change what had to be. I didn't have the guts to take another lick; he didn't have the strength to give it. Besides, there was a headlamp coming up the tunnel. If we were caught doing this there'd really be hell to pay. All my trouble, all my pain never got me a day out of the mine. The honcho thought a flying rock had struck me on the arm, and I went to work with my regular shift.

Weeks went by. My back got better, my mind got worse. I began to think the mine was going to get the best of me and I was afraid that if I quit fighting back I would become like the bedpatients at Cabanatuan, too weary to keep on living, just give up, just lie down and die.

I got my out quite by accident, a real accident. I was working in my usual place, scraping coal and dodging rocks when I got hit by a sneaker. A sneaker was a rock that didn't bounce along in the usual way, making a lot of noise. A sneaker was the one that took a long high bounce way up the chute and came the rest of the way down without touching anything. Just a little noise at the top, a long silence, and boom, there it was slamming out of the dark. This one caught me by surprise, came out of nowhere, struck me on the right shin and sent me sprawling. Scared but not hurt. My canvas leggings protected me. The rock didn't even break the skin.

Next morning my shin was sore and by the third day I suspected I was in real trouble. What was happening to me was one of the real dangers of POW life. Incidents, happenings, little hurts that I would have shaken off easily in civilian life, in our half-starved, run-down condition became life threatening.

When I first crawled out from under my pookow in the morning I could barely stand. I felt searing pain in my leg, felt like it was on fire, but after walking on it for a few minutes the pain went away. At lineup our Japanese commander asked for ten volunteers, ten men who knew carpentry, to transfer to another camp. This was my chance to get out of the mine, maybe my only chance, and I jumped at it. It was the middle of winter and there was snow and ice on the ground. I did not think of the bitter cold; my only thought was to get out of the mine.

I wasn't a carpenter, but I could handle a hammer and saw. My only experience had been helping to build that four-room house and a real estate office with a real carpenter. I had carried and fetched, cut boards to length, and nailed studs and boards wherever I was told. He did the thinking and I helped with the work. Not much, but I did work hard and my boss didn't expect much for a dollar a day.

My leg hurt like blazes, and my shin turned bright red. I was afraid to go to sick call because I knew if the medical orderly saw my leg he would scratch me from the list and send me back to the mine. The morning came when the ten of us were to leave for the new camp. I was delighted at getting away from the mine, and I was worried that the medical orderly might somehow find out that I had a very bad leg. I feared his wrath, but most of all I feared being sent back to the mine.

I slept little, woke early. I wanted to be ready. For what? I didn't know, but I didn't want anything to screw it up. I was elated, almost happy. I was getting away from the mine. The POW has to be an eternal optimist. Look ahead. Don't look back because back there is nothing but pain and misery and suffering. Instead, look ahead, to the future. Of course you can't see what lies ahead. That's what so good about it. The past is a dirty mess, but the future is a clean canvas with nothing on it, and your mind can fill in the blank space with anything you wish. Within reason, of course. Not Mom's apple pie and a warm comfortable bed at home, but at least something better than the past. The future is bright but its very brightness makes it hard to see, dims the vision in your mind. The something better is vague, indistinct, but you know it's there. It's like, like ... well, at least not grubbing coal in the mine.

I looked at my leg. It was huge, swollen and red with a dark bruise where the rock had hit that looked like a chicken egg hiding under the skin. Damn, it hurt. I was somewhat used to the pain but this hurt a lot. Most of the barracks was still asleep, so I had the aisle to myself as I limped back and forth, working the soreness out, getting the circulation going, trying to make the pain go away. Hoped none of the guards would look in and see me before I was able to walk without limping.

So far I had told no one about the infection in my leg. The work crew knew I had been hit by a rock because I bitched a little about the big rocks coming down the chute, and the guys that bunked in my room thought it just a bit of soreness. And Doc Hogan, I hadn't dared go to sick call yet because first I had to get past the orderly. Kept my mouth shut and my pant-leg down and hoped I could walk naturally enough to get past the Jap guardhouse. There were no good-byes. Most of the camp wasn't aware we were leaving. Johnson was somewhere in camp, but he was on the other shift and I rarely saw him. I fell in with the regular day shift and got only a perfunctory glance from the guards at the gate. The mine crew turned one way, ten of us and two guards turned the other. Kiss off. Kiss the mine good-bye. We were all in the same boat. The mine had been beating on us, wearing us down, grinding away at our lives. I was quietly excited. Felt like a kid who had been given a day off from school and didn't know what to do with it.

We walked a mile and a half to a railway station, not a station really, just an empty shack beside the tracks with a footpath leading up to it. The guards were in no hurry; it was a day off for them too. I carried nothing. The clothes on my back, the old mess kit bottom, canteen, and cup. Thank God it was an overcoat day. Took that too.

The guard waved. The train rattled to a stop and we climbed aboard. Except for the boxcar ride from Bilibid prison to San Fernando, this was the first train I had seen in three years. We rode in an old passenger car with real seats. Seats cushioned and covered with a dark green fabric like mohair. This was luxury. I hadn't seen or sat on a padded seat since the surrender. Guards sat across the aisle and left us alone. I got a window seat and pressed my nose against the glass. No villages, just Japanese countryside, but there was a wonderful world out there and I hadn't seen anything except the inside of a prison camp for a long time.

One man in our group asked me if I was a real carpenter. Probably looking for reassurance because he was lying about being a carpenter just like I was. I told him the truth, that all I could do was use a hammer and saw. It wasn't much, but I thought we could get away with it. Of course this was just my opinion, not what I knew but what I desperately hoped for. I didn't think they'd expect any fancy stuff from us. They'd have their own people for that. Just nailing boards together. The Japs knew we were soldiers. If we were carpenters we wouldn't be in the Army.

Outta the mine, outta the mine, outta the mine. The click-clack cadence of the rails echoed the thought that kept running through my mind. Whatever happened tomorrow, at least I was out of the mine. I felt relieved, as if I had been given a stay of execution.

The new camp appeared desolate, just some unpainted one-story buildings on a flat barren piece of dirt. It was late in the afternoon and the day was bitter cold. I huddled shivering inside my overcoat. Wondered what kind of carpenter work a man could do in weather like this.

The barracks was a long building, one long narrow room with a row of cots along either side. I was shown to a cot by a dark-skinned prisoner with a strange accent who told me to wait there. He left. Once again I was the new kid on the block. The room was filled with prisoners, but I was a stranger.

The man standing by the next bunk smiled and held out his hand, called me matey, welcomed me aboard, and told me his name was Charley. Charley offered to show me the strings around the place. I shook his hand, grateful for his offer of friendship. I told him my name was Andy, Andy Carson. It was my first day there and I didn't know the ropes yet.

He must have seen the consternation in my face. His smile broadened. He knew I was an American, said he could tell by the way I talked. He continued talking in a clipped British accent. He told me most of them were British around this camp, British and Dutch. The little dark-skinned fellows were Dutch colonials, Dutch troops from the islands, but their officers were Dutch from the mainland, from Holland.

My mind was reeling. I was unable to make any sense out of what he was saying. British and Dutch. What in hell were British and Dutch prisoners doing here? Where had they come from? It was so strange. For almost three years I had been in camps with only American prisoners. We were so cut off, so isolated, that my world had narrowed down to just us, the prisoners from the Philippines and Japan. I hadn't realized that any other country was in our war. Dimly I began to realize that except for my intimate knowledge of life as a prisoner of war, I had no inkling of what was going on in the rest of the world. It wasn't until I had been released and returned to the United States that I began to understand the full scope of the war.

It had been a long day and my leg was giving me hell. I stretched out on my cot. Charley grabbed me quickly, told me there'd be none of that, matey, the Nips don't allow it. I could sit on the cot if I liked, but I couldn't lie down. And don't muss it up or you'll get us all in trouble.

I got up quickly, smoothed my blanket. New camp, new rules. Must be a lot of things I'd have to learn. My leg was throbbing, burning like it was on fire. I grimaced when I stood up and Charley noticed.

He asked if I was hurting, matey, if I had a blister on my foot. I shook my head and silently pulled up my pant-leg. First chance I had to get a good look at my leg since morning. It was swollen, huge. The skin was an angry red, but the chicken egg under the skin had turned black, and there were a couple of red streaks running above my knee. The whole thing was fevered, hot to the touch.

Charley whistled, told me in his stiff British accent that I had real trouble there. Gorblimey, matey, might be blood poison. I asked him about the medicine in the new camp and got the same old familiar story. There was no medicine, but a doctor came around with the guards before work every morning. Maybe he could get me fixed up.

There was a commotion at the far end of the building. Some armed guards and a Japanese noncom shouting orders. Prisoners standing at attention at the foot of their cots.

Head count. I was told to holler my number out loudly when it came my turn, and for Christ sake matey, get it right, get it right.

The head count started at the other end of the room, prisoners counting off in Japanese, guards and the noncom walking slowly along the line. The count stopped; someone had made a mistake. I heard angry shouting in Japanese and the unmistakable sound of a hand slapping a face, hard. The count started over from the beginning. Three more times the count stopped before it got to me, and three more times there was shouting and slapping. Three more times it started from the beginning. Thank God I had learned to count. I remembered my number, and the guards passed me by without incident because I got it right. Good thing too. The way my leg was hurting I don't think I could have stood up to a slapping around. Took an hour, maybe more. Even after we got it right guards made us go through it three more times. Then they left and it was lights out.

I took off my shoes and slipped under my blanket fully dressed, overcoat and all. It felt good to finally get off my feet. The pain in my leg was intense. Every beat of my pulse sent a surge of pain throughout my entire body, and I tensed against it until my stomach muscles wouldn't tense any more. I knew from the beginning that I wasn't going to get any sleep that night. There was no heat in the barracks. Must be as cold in here as it is outside, I thought, except in here we're out of the wind. Pulled the blanket over my head. It was a trick I'd learned. Pull the blanket over your head, tuck it in tight all around, and the heat from your breath helps to warm things up. Took slow deep breaths to get more warm air under the blanket. Seemingly from a distance I heard Charley's voice, muffled, head under his own blanket. Careful not to attract attention, he told me that we were lucky tonight, matey, sometimes they make us stand at attention the whole damn night. If a bloke really screws up they take away the next meal from the whole damn camp. Sometimes we don't know who did it or what for; they just take away a meal for punishment. Sometimes I think they just make it up. His voice drifted off.

After what must have been hours the pain in my leg eased. If I moved the slightest bit it hurt, but if I lay perfectly still the throbbing receded to a constant dull heavy ache and I fell into a merciful sleep. I wondered if I had jumped from the frying pan into the fire. At least in the mine, in the hot hole, it wasn't freezing.

The lights came on. Everybody up. I didn't want to get up. Like trying to hang on to a dream, I didn't want to let go of the sleep that had masked my pain. Reluctantly I sat up and pulled on my shoes. My right foot was swollen. Had some trouble getting it into the shoe. Mustn't take that shoe off again, I thought, or I won't be able to put it on again. Be running around barefoot in the freezing cold with one shoe on.

Breakfast was a rice ball and a cup of weak bitter tea. Must be the British influence. I'd heard that Englishmen loved their tea. Head count went swimmingly. Once around and it was over. I suspected that the guards were easy on us in the morning because it was time to go to work. At night, on our sleep time, they could drag the count out for hours.

Sick call, such as it was, was held in the morning at the foot of each cot. A prisoner doctor, a Japanese doctor, and four armed guards slowly walked the length of the room. They stopped briefly before one or two prisoners, then moved on. My turn. The cortege stopped in front of my cot.

The doctor saw that I was a new man, asked if I had any problems. I pulled up my pant-leg. The shin was flaming red, fevered, hot to the touch, and the black chicken egg under the skin stood out in bold relief. Both doctors showed immediate concern. Together they probed it, squeezed it, ran their hands over the lump. The four guards had a look but did not touch, chattered among themselves.

The prisoner doctor was Dutch, real Dutch from Holland, but I thought he sounded German. Bet he had gone to medical school in Germany. He said that my leg was bad, very bad. He had no medicines to give me but he would operate on the leg in the morning. The Japanese doctor nodded his head in agreement. He pronounced that the leg was "most seriously."

The Dutchman motioned toward the cot and the Japanese doctor nodded his head. Evidently there was some cooperation between them.

I was excused from work. I could stay in the barracks, and I could sit on my cot, but I could not lie down. Rules, rules, rules, different things I had to remember. If I lay down the guards would beat me, and if a guard entered the barracks I had to stand at attention until he left, then I could sit again. Before leaving the doctor cautioned me once again not to lie down.

The barracks went to work and I was left alone. I spent a very long day sitting, standing at attention, and staring at the walls. No wonder the building was cold. I could see daylight through the cracks between the boards that formed the walls. We were truly a mixed lot in this camp. Americans, there were only a few of us, the English with their funny accent, Black Dutch, the colonials from what in those days was still known as the Dutch East Indies, and the Dutch officers from Holland. Four distinct groups, five if you counted the Japanese, but we never counted them.

My mind was playing tricks on me. I was drifting in and out of reality. The pain from my leg racked my entire body. I knew what was going on, but from time to time there would be a roaring in my ears and my vision would narrow down until I could see only what was directly in front of me. Time went by so slowly. Minutes, even seconds, seemed extended. I waited and longed for the evening head count, for lights out, for those precious hours when I could finally relax, stretch out, get off my feet. Dimly I remember wondering what the doctor meant when he said, "I will operate tomorrow." Did operate mean amputate? Was I going to lose my leg? I was scared.

Sometime during the night I felt a gush of hot liquid on my leg, and a most hideous smell came from beneath my blanket. I was startled into wakefulness. My leg had burst and there was pus, rotten stinking pus, cups of it, all over the place. I was wet and sticky from my knee to my ankle. I pulled up my pant-leg and felt a deep hole in my shin, a deep hole in the flesh where the chicken egg had been. I was frightened, but there was nothing I could do, so I lay back on my cot and waited for the morning lights to come on. Strangely, I was more comfortable now. When the abscess burst, the pressure eased, and the throbbing pulsing pain disappeared like water being sucked down a drain. It still hurt, but now only a heavy dull ache. I tried wiping my hands clean on the blanket, but I couldn't wipe off the smell. Rotten meat smells bad, but hot pus, pure corruption, smells even worse. Couldn't keep my fingers away from the mess on my shin. Could tell in the dark that the abscess went all the way to the bone.

Lights turned on in the barracks. It was still dark outside. A guard was banging on a gong with a stick. Time to get up. I stood at attention for the head count. The smell was hideous. A guard held his nose, made a face as he walked past. Probably thought I'd crapped my pants. I was embarrassed by the smell. Seems incongruous when I look back on it. I was a prisoner of war in some God-forgotten prison camp, more dead than alive, only half conscious from the pain, and I was embarrassed.

The Dutch doctor and his Japanese escort came by early. I was sitting with my eyes closed in a half stupor and wasn't aware of their presence until he spoke. He addressed me as soldier and wanted to have a look at my leg. I raised my pant-leg and exposed my right shin for him to see. This was the first time, in daylight, that I had seen it. Yellow pus was caked on my leg, but around the hole it was wet and sticky. The smell was awful, even to me, and by now I was used to it. Doc took a dirty rag from his pocket, wiped the pus from my shin and examined it carefully, then knotted the same rag to cover the open wound. Gently, very gently, Doc pulled my pant-leg down, then told me that I might have to lose the leg. He had no medicine for pain. In fact, he had no medicine at all. It was very bad that he had no bandages either. The dirty rag was the best that he could do for me.

The Dutchman turned to the Japanese doctor. He was angry and obviously trying to control his anger. He told the Japanese that this was beyond his control, that he could not, would not, be responsible for my medical treatment. The Japanese made some notes on a pad. They moved away and there was some conversation that I couldn't hear, some conversation between the doctors, some between the Japanese doctor and the guards. The Dutchman came back and told me I had permission to lie down, that this time the guards had been ordered not to beat me. Doc told me he was very sorry there was nothing more he could do.

I lay back, relieved that I could at least lie down and get off my feet, only dimly aware that I had just received the typical POW medical treatment and totally unaware that I was entering upon one of my most difficult periods.

Less than an hour later Doc came back along with two armed guards. The commander was sending me back because I could not do the work there. Doc gave me two tins of food to put in my overcoat pocket, tins left behind by prisoners who had died before finishing their food packet. Doc shook my hand, wished me good luck, and was gone. The guards escorted me through the door.

It was cold outside, colder than in the barracks. It felt good at first. The cold sort of pushed the fever back, but the wind whipped up under my coat and in around my neck. I was shivering before we got to the railroad. It must have been early spring because some of the snow had melted and there was mud and slush on the ground. Gone was the elation I had felt only a few days before. My body was tired, heavy, and my spirits were low. I should have had better sense, those few days back. But truly, I had been so focused on getting out of the mine that I had given little thought to my leg beyond thinking it would get better by itself. Now, here I was three days out of the mine and I was a reject, a cripple, and I was going back. There was a puddle of water on the ground. I unwrapped my leg, wet the rag in the puddle, and washed my leg, got rid of as much of the dried and caked pus as I could. The guards watched impassively, sympathetic yet aloof. Regardless of what they felt, their culture would not allow them to be overly concerned with a lowly prisoner. After all, we had committed an unpardonable sin; we had surrendered. I think, to the Japanese soldier we were something like the untouchables in India, to be seen, used, tolerated, but nothing more. I rewrapped my leg with the same dirty rag, and we boarded the train.

There were two other prisoners in the car. Rejects like myself or merely being transferred. I didn't know; the guards kept us apart. The trip back seemed longer than the trip out. Perhaps because the elation was gone and I was down in the dumps. I had felt good about getting away from the mine; now I felt like an escaped felon being returned to jail. Transportation in Japan, prisoner-of-war class, did not include meals. In the afternoon I opened my two tins of food. I had a small tin of brown bread, a much smaller tin of a cheesy, butterlike spread. I cut off a piece of bread with the handle of my spoon and started to eat. The two guards sat across the aisle and ignored me. They hadn't eaten either. I cut off two more pieces, spread them with butter, and offered them to the guards. They politely refused. I think they would have liked the food, but I think my offer embarrassed them. My leg was hurting, hurting like hell, but I tried not to show it. Not that I felt it was macho or manly or anything of that sort, it was just that I felt a little smug, a little personal satisfaction whenever I could hide my hurting from the guards. Not that these two particular guards were the bad guys, they weren't. They had been surprisingly pleasant and agreeable for the entire trip. These guys were OK. But for some of them, the real bastards who enjoyed inflicting pain and seeing me suffer, it became a personal challenge to conceal the pain and deny them the satisfaction of seeing me hurting. It was me against them, and when I won, and I'll admit I didn't win every time, but when I did win it became a small personal victory that the guards probably didn't even know about. A small victory to be sure, but a victory nevertheless, even if I was the only one playing the game. And important, because in the POW camps even such small victories were few and far between.

When I got off the train two guards from the mine camp were waiting for me. We walked the mile and a half to the camp, slowly because I was really dragging ass. They didn't seem to be in a hurry, and it was dark when we arrived. As soon as we were inside the gate the guards turned me loose. I went straight to my old room. My space was empty so I curled up on the mat, fully dressed, and shivered through the night.

Sick call was held in an almost bare room. There was a wooden bench, a chair for Major Hogan and one for the Japanese doctor, and a small potbellied stove. It was the only warm room in camp. I waited my turn, then stood in front of Doctor Hogan. First thing he wanted to know was what was wrong with me, what had happened, why had they sent me back?

I bared the leg, showed him the open abscess, and told him the story. I sat on the bench with my leg stretched out so he could have a better look. The Japanese doctor looked interested. I think he might have been a good doctor, sincere in what he tried to do, but as it turned out, he was full of damn fool ideas. Hogan looked at the leg a long time without saying anything. Then he took a pair of surgical tweezers and began to probe. The tweezers looked like scissors, about four inches long, but with a clamp instead of cutting blades. Doc put a piece of cloth in the clamp and probed through the half-dollar-sized hole. I grabbed the bench with both hands, hard, hung on with all my might. I got to know that bench real good in the next couple of months. It helped, having something to hang on to. If it still exists, bet my fingermarks are on it to this very day. Doc probed, and I grunted and strained. He could stick the tweezers out of sight under the flesh in any direction. Then the Japanese doctor took his turn, had to satisfy himself that his eyes were not playing tricks on him. I was sweating like a river but not from the stove. The piece of cloth on the clamp felt like sandpaper inside the abscess. What had been a dull ache when I came in was now a roaring, burning pain.

Doc Hogan was blunt, right to the point, but he was honest with me and I trusted him. He knew I was in bad shape, and he wasn't sure he could save the leg. He had nothing to work with, nothing. He told me that it wouldn't have made much difference if I had stayed in his camp. Maybe he could have lanced it instead of letting it rot until it burst, but it wouldn't have been much different. Through the orderly Major Hogan conferred with the Japanese doctor. He got permission for me to stay in barracks for a few days, to stay off my feet, and to come to sick call every morning. We'd wait and see what happened.

I got my blankets back, got my clothes back, but my ceramic hot water bottle was gone, given to another prisoner when I left. I never got another one. I was sick, weak, hurting, and depressed. Don't think I could have made it through the next weeks on my own, but the guys in my room got me through. Lucky for me, some were on the day shift, some on the night shift. They had been sleeping together, pooling their blankets and huddling beneath the pile, fully dressed, body-to-body, to survive the bitter cold. By squeezing tight we could fit three bodies under one set of blankets. I slept in the middle. When the day shift went to work two bodies from the night shift took their places beside me. When the night shift went to work the day workers replaced them. I crawled out to eat, to go to the toilet, and to go to sick call. Round the clock, day and night, these men kept me from freezing. Somehow I lived through the next three weeks and gained strength.

After a week of probing, my abscess showed no sign of healing. It was red and raw and continually draining. Doc Hogan had almost no bandages. I had one strip of gauze that could wrap three or four times around my leg but nothing to take care of the drainage. Doc got me a stack of toilet paper. Japanese toilet paper, in those days, didn't come in rolls. It came in sheets like typing paper. I would take ten sheets, fold them in quarters to give me forty thicknesses and plaster the lot over the hole. If I put it on before I went to sleep, by morning it would be a fully soaked, soggy, stinking mess. Don't know how the other fellows in my bed put up with it.

Anyway, after a week of probing around with my wound showing no sign of healing, our Japanese doctor got one of his hare-brained ideas. He took an iron poker, heated it white hot in the potbellied stove, and seared the raw flesh around the open edges of the abscess. Said he wanted to create some scar tissue, help with the healing process. Hurt so bad I thought I'd surely die. Hated so much I wanted the Japanese doctor to die with me. I hated it, dreaded it, but I didn't have the option of going to another doctor for a second opinion. I was a prisoner of war and this guy owned my body. He could do with it pretty much as he pleased. Twice a week they burned me with the poker and twice a week the scabs sloughed off and the hole didn't get any smaller. Something was missing in my body and I just wouldn't heal. After the first week Major Hogan took over and under the Japanese doctor's direction used the hot poker. Somehow it made a difference. I knew Major Hogan as caring, knew he would hurt me as little as possible, knew he was shielding me from the Japanese doctor.

The infection was gone, not from my leg, it was still draining gobs, but gone from the rest of my body. I was better, stronger, and the Japs put me back to work. Not in the mine, I wasn't ready for that yet, but they put me to work weaving bamboo baskets in camp. Four of us, one a prisoner who had lost part of his leg in a mine accident, two with broken bones that were healing, and myself, sat on the floor and made horseshoe-shaped baskets for the miners. We took bamboo, soaked it in water until it became extremely pliant, cut it into strips and wove it into baskets. The miners put a basket between their feet, scraped it full of coal, then carried the loaded basket to a mine car and dumped it. Crude, certainly, but I swear, that's the way these people mined coal. We made baskets all day, knocked off work when the day shift came in from the mine. I began to follow the day miners into the bathhouse where they stripped and tried to wash off some of the coal dust in a common tub. I couldn't go into the common tub because the stinking drainage from my leg would contaminate the water for everyone, but in the corner was a little tub just big enough for one person to sit in with legs drawn up under his chin. Tentatively I filled it with the hottest water I could stand and when the guards didn't object sat in it until the miners were out of their tub. No one else used my tub, hell, no one wanted to use it after I had dirtied the water. Day after day I sat for half an hour in my tub. Though my abscess didn't heal, I think this daily hot soaking helped hold down the infection.

I can see that I've been talking as if I were the only person in the world, as if the other hundred and ninety prisoners in my camp didn't exist. They did exist, and while, in my mind, I shut them out, each of them was waging his own particular struggle for survival. It was just that for me, during this most critical period, the rest of the world ceased to exist. I think my body, in an unconscious struggle against death, shut off every function it could do without, including some of the mental ones. I lived in a stupor, in a half-comatose state. For instance, I don't remember the names or the faces of the men who slept beside me in those three terrible weeks. I do remember the press of bodies in my dark little cave under the blankets, of sharing the bodily warmth that kept me alive. I know I must have eaten, and I know I didn't eat in barracks, but I don't remember going to the mess hall. I remember, clearly, my daily sessions in the hot tub, soaking my leg, but I don't remember how I got there. The hot tub was the high point of my day. And I remember the daily sessions on the bench at sick call, the searing flashes of pain as Doc applied the white hot poker to the raw flesh of my abscess. And I remember the pain in Major Hogan's eyes, brown eyes behind rimless glasses, as he applied the iron. I think he was a gentle man, before the war used to clean surgery with white sheets and nurses and anesthetics, and I believe this crude butchery hurt him almost as much as it did me.

So, five weeks now. The abscess shows no visible sign of healing, but I am stronger. The little Japanese medical orderly, the SOB who seems to make these decisions, has decided that I am too strong to sit on my ass weaving baskets and is enraged because the civilian miners refuse to take me into the mine. I am caught in the middle and can see trouble ahead. This guy is a mean one and will get even if he can. The miners compromise by putting me to work in the settling pits above ground. I don't know whether to laugh or cry. I've escaped the wrath of the orderly but even though it's early spring it's still very cold. I'll have to work my tail off to keep from freezing.

The settling pits were concrete-walled enclosures, walls five feet high, with a gate in one wall and some narrow-gauge rails running in. Coal from the mine was dumped into a crusher, which turned it into a powder. The powder was carried along a sluiceway in a slurry and dropped into a pit. Water drained out, the coal remained behind. When the pit was full enough we opened the gate and shoveled wet coal dust into railcars. Another part of the mine pressed the dust into briquets for use in the hot little fires in Japanese kitchens.

Six of us prisoners worked the pits. All of us were beaten or broke up badly enough to be a liability in the mines, yet we considered ourselves to be the lucky ones. Anything was better than the mine itself. We worked, in the pits, for an old patriarch who wore a beard, smoked a pipe, and tried to be kind to us. He had a one-room shack for his office, a one-room shack with the ever-present potbellied stove. He'd take us into his office at lunchtime and let us sit around the stove and eat our rice and get warm. He didn't speak English, so while we scooched close to the stove and ate our rice and talked, he usually sat back in a corner and smoked his pipe and nodded. He even looked the other way if we lingered a minute or two after the go-to-work whistle blew. He was a nice old man.

In camp we had a new Japanese sergeant in charge of the guards. He was an older man, maybe in his mid-forties and he had seen front-line action against American troops. Apparently he had been wounded, survived, and been sent to us while he recovered. He was tough but fair. We liked him. His attitude was entirely different from that of the Japanese soldiers who had never seen combat. None of this making up an offense and beating the hell out of you for something you didn't do, none of that. If you broke a rule he was on your ass, hard. If you didn't he left you alone. Even POW life is easier when you know where you stand.

We had a few American cigarettes still left from the last Christmas food parcel.

One day we traded some of these to a miner for a little raw rice. We cooked the rice in mess kits on top of the old man's potbellied stove, left it there to cook while we worked the pits. Unfortunately, four of the guards dropped in to get warm, found the rice, knew it was contraband, and beat the living hell out of us. When we went into camp at the end of the day we stood a brief inspection in front of the guardhouse before the guards dismissed us to barracks. The six of us were pretty well marked up and the old sergeant noticed. He dismissed the crew but kept the six of us and the four guards standing at attention. I know I didn't understand the words but I damn well got the gist of what went on next.

The sergeant pointed to us six miserable prisoners and wanted to know what had happened to us. Why were we beaten? The guards explained and the sergeant nodded his approval. We had broken the rules. Maybe he would do a little beating himself. The old sergeant actually grabbed hold of the first prisoner, raised his sheathed bayonet for the first blow, then stopped in midair. I could only guess at what came next, but I think my guess was pretty close to the truth.

The sergeant wanted to see the rice. He was shouting now. What had happened to the contraband rice?

The guards had eaten it.

The sergeant exploded into rage. I think he felt the guards had lost face by beating us for an offense and then committing the same offense themselves. He grabbed the first guard by the front of his helmet and shook it fiercely. The man's head rattled around like a loose pea in a pod. Then one by one he beat each guard with the flat of his bayonet. He did a thorough job. When he knocked a man down the soldier would spring to his feet, snap to attention, and bow before waiting for the next lick. Anger appeased, the old sergeant stood feet apart, hands on his hips, and glared fiercely at us for a long moment. Then with a disgusted growl he waved us on to barracks. Tough but fair.

Eight weeks now since I first hurt my leg and the darn thing wasn't getting any better. Both Major Hogan and the Jap doctor checked it out at sick call. I trusted Major Hogan but the Japanese doctor, I'm not so sure. He may not be a real doctor. In the Philippines there were several thousand prisoners at Cabanatuan but no Japanese doctor, not even an orderly. It didn't make much sense to think that they would suddenly give us a full-time doctor for two hundred men. This guy had to be some kind of a quack. At best he probably knew less about medicine than our Army medics.

Doc was probing, showing those scissors clamps out of sight under the flesh, moving them around. It hurt, damn right it hurt. Doc told me that this was necessary because the abscess had to heal from the inside out. Otherwise the darn thing would just fill up with pus and we'd have to start all over again. Doc was probing deep, not looking at me when he told me we might have to take the leg off below the knee.

This was quite a shock, but hell no, I wasn't going to let them take my leg.

Doc told me that we didn't have a hell of a lot of choice. Doc said "we," but I knew he meant me. I had to make the choice. He was looking me straight in the eye, and I knew he wasn't bullshitting when he told me that either the leg started to heal or we amputate or I was going to die. I couldn't face losing my leg, so I asked him to wait a little while longer. It wasn't bravado, nothing like that. I think it was simple denial. In my mind I was still six foot two, two hundred twenty pounds, able to run, jump, play ball, do anything I pleased. In my mind I still had a great body, and there was no room in this vision for a guy with one leg. Besides, I had seen a prison-camp amputation already, and it had scared the hell out of me. I didn't see the actual surgery, just the before part and it had stayed in my mind. I'll never forget that young boy getting ready for surgery. I last saw him the day I left the hospital to go back to work on the farm. He knew the foot had to come off, and he was sick with worry and fear. I don't blame him. Just the thought of what he was going through would have driven me crazy.

You'd think, even in a hellhole like Cabanatuan, the Japanese would have provided some kind of minimum medical facility. They didn't. Our doctors had to perform miracles with nothing, no beds, no sheets, not even hot water unless they carried it from the kitchen in buckets. Our doctors had no sanitary facility, no rubber gloves, no medicine, no anesthetic, nothing, not even whiskey. It was tough on us, but it must also have been heart rending for skilled physicians and surgeons to watch us die and be able to do nothing about it.

Here was an American soldier, like most American soldiers just a kid really, who had already laid his life on the line in combat, and now he had to lay it on the line again. Did he have clean sheets, a soft bed, a good night's sleep? Hell no. Did he have X-rays, blood tests, an EKG? None of that either. He spent his pre-op night on the bamboo slats like the rest of us. Medical advice? Our doctors did the very best they could with the nothing that they had.

Take this piece of rope and tie it around your leg just below the knee. Make a tourniquet, twist it tight with a stick. Loosen it every twenty minutes to let the blood circulate, then tighten it again. Keep this up for twenty-four hours and your leg will be so numb you probably won't feel any pain when we cut through the flesh, but when we hit bone there's nothing more we can do for you.

Go ahead, cry for the kid. I never knew if he made it or not.

Anyway, Major Hogan was on my side. Leave the leg alone. Let's wait and see. He talked the Jap doctor into giving me a couple of days in barracks. Maybe if I stayed flat on my back, maybe if I wasn't standing on the leg all day, working on it, maybe it would get better, maybe. I found an old piece of rope behind the kitchen, tied one end to a rafter, made a loop in the other and lay down with my foot in the loop, my leg in the air.

A couple of days of this and our Japanese doctor got another one of his asshole ideas. He was going to revolutionize the practice of medicine. He had plenty of patients to choose from. Somebody was always getting hurt in the mine, and there were usually fifteen or twenty semicripples, rejects from the mine, lying around camp trying to heal. Our Japanese doctor asked me to cooperate in the usual polite Japanese fashion. He sent two armed guards to escort me to his office. What for? What did he want from me?

I found out sooner than I wanted. There were six of us "volunteers." One prisoner was ahead of me, and I watched him go through the crazy experiment. The prisoner, stripped to a G-string, lay on his side on a bare wooden table, knees drawn up under his chin, arms tight around his knees. His back was toward the Jap doctor. Doc Hogan was there but off to one side. He wasn't in on this. The Jap doc drew a line with something red, from the point of the prisoner's hip straight down to the spine, then went in with a needle and did a spinal tap. God, that needle was huge, three-and-a-half or four inches long and as big around as a thick pencil lead. I watched the prisoner quivering as the needle went in and knew I was in for a hell of a lot of trouble. My turn next. I had no choice. The guards at the door had bayonets fixed to their weapons.

I climbed to the table, hugged my knees with my arms, closed my eyes and waited. The first prisoner had left the table a little wet. Sweat or urine, I didn't know. I might leave a little of both. Doc Hogan stood by my head, put a hand on my shoulder.

The Japanese doctor was going to take out some spinal fluid and replace it with a vitamin B concentrate. I knew I had better not move because I knew all my nerves ran through my spinal column. If I jerked around the sharp end of the needle might cut a nerve and I would be crippled for life.

Just one more thing to worry about. I made up my mind not to move but wondered if I'd have the willpower to stick to it. I'd watched the needle go into the first fellow's back. We were skin and bone but I swear, that needle went in all the way to the hilt.

My turn. I felt the cold wetness as the doc drew the line, then the needle. It wasn't a sharp pain, more a deep dull hurting that seemed to envelope my whole body. I felt as though a tremendous weight was pressing on my back, a weight heavier than I could possibly stand. I wanted to shout, to scream out, to pull away from the needle, but knew if I made the slightest sound or movement I would break and thrash about and screw up the whole thing. Fear, not guts or willpower, just plain fear made me hold still. Doc was clumsy, at least I thought he was clumsy. I felt the tip of the needle strike bone, felt it grate against my spine. No good. The doc pulled it out part way and tried again.

Maybe four times he probed before the needle grated on bone and slipped off between the vertebrae and into the spinal column. Blessed relief while he withdrew spinal fluid and replaced it with his vitamin B. Who knows what the hell he put in there? And then the needle came out. It even hurt coming out. It was over. Well, not yet. I've been told that the proper procedure after a spinal tap is to let the patient lie motionless for an hour or two. Keeps you from getting a bad headache. Doc pulled the needle out, slapped me on the butt, and sent me back to barracks. Before I got there my head exploded, felt as if the top of my head was coming off. The Japanese doctor kept me in barracks for a couple of weeks after that but the trade-off was the needle, every other day. Wish my leg would hurry up and get better. I was better off in the mine.

Life was hard. I wasn't being beaten, I didn't have to go to work, and I was being fed, though never enough. By POW standards I had a pretty good life, but for me, this was a most difficult time. I was tired, just plain worn out both physically and emotionally. My back had not healed properly after the accident in the mine and was giving me a lot of pain. My abscessed leg wasn't getting any better and to make matters worse I was swelling up again. Water retention, wet beri-beri, some damn vitamin deficiency. My legs puffed up and my scrotum hung like a grapefruit. Simply put, my body was wearing out. No, let's face it. My body was worn out. I had tapped the last of my body's resources. My physical bank account was way overdrawn. Emotionally I was in even worse shape. The constant hurting was like carrying a heavy weight that I was unable to put down. I hated the daily sick call with the squeezing and probing and general fooling around with my abscessed leg, and every fruitless visit resurrected the nightmare of possible amputation. And I dreaded those spinal taps. I feared the pain, but most of all I feared having the Japanese doctor poking around in my spine with a dull needle. I was afraid that sooner or later I would jerk around or he would make a mistake somewhere deep in my spine and screw me up for good. I knew I was in danger of lapsing into that don't give a damn state where mind and body say "throw in the towel, we've had enough," and the man simply lies back and dies.

I was hungry, always hungry. No more so, I suppose, than anyone else. I think it was just at this particular time I felt hunger more. Metabolism was the key. For most of us, those who had survived thus far, our bodies and metabolic rates had reached a compromise with the meager rations. For me the break-even point was about one hundred twenty pounds. If I ate everything in sight I could maintain that weight and still do an average day's work. At this time though, with my abscessed leg and the wet beri-beri, with the mental stress of possible amputation and those damn spinal taps, and with the constant hurting, my body was putting out more than it was taking in. I became obsessed with food, or rather, the lack of it. I could get hot water from the kitchen, and I drank it in huge quantities trying to keep a full feeling and assuage the hunger. On rare pleasant afternoons I lay outside the barracks and pretended to gain strength from the warmth of the sun. And I schemed how to get more food. Gradually an idea took shape, a rather disgusting idea but an idea nevertheless. I would build a trap, trap rats, and eat them. The very thought of eating rats was revolting, but no more revolting than the thought of dying.

I scrounged the camp and found a wooden crate behind the kitchen. It was just right for my purpose. I knocked it apart and salvaged four slats of equal size, about five inches wide and fifteen or sixteen inches long. Using nails from the crate I made a box trap, a simple square tunnel the length of the slats. At one end I rigged a sliding wooden door which, when the trap was triggered, dropped into a groove and sealed that end. The other end of the trap posed a problem. Rats are smart. Had to let the rat see through the trap, make it think the box was open at both ends. Solved this problem by asking Roland to bring home a couple of pieces of the thin copper wires that ran from the detonator to the dynamite when they blasted in the mine. I laced this wire crisscrossed, back and forth across the open end of the trap. It looked like it might work. A rat could see through but could not get out when the trapdoor fell down. Crude but workable. A wire ran down through the top of the trap between the rat and the bait. The slightest touch on the wire triggered the trap, and the sliding door dropped down locking the rat inside.

The rat trap was ready for its first trial. Now what to use for bait? Not even a rat would be stupid enough to go into the trap without bait. The only bait I had was my ration of rice. Here I almost gave up my scheme. It really wrenched my soul to put part of my evening meal in the trap for bait. After lights out and everything was quiet I carefully set the trap and baited it. Where? In the latrine, of course, the dirtiest place in camp and the likeliest place for rats. Three, maybe four times during the night, I got up to check the trap. Nothing. Maybe I wasn't so smart after all. Last time I checked the door was down. It was pitch dark but I could hear the scurrying inside. I had a rat. Elated, I picked up the trap, rat and all. It was heavy. Must be a big one. Suddenly I realized that I hadn't thought this thing through. I had a rat, he was in the trap, but how was I going to get him out? Reached my hand in? No way. Couldn't wait because the rat was thrashing about threatening to break out of the flimsy box at any second. It was the middle of the night and there were no guards patrolling through the camp. Trap under my arms I went outside and filled one of the wash tubs with water, then immersed the trap, rat and all. Took only a matter of seconds.

I took the dead rat out of the trap and my stomach lurched. A dead rat is bad enough but a wet dead rat can make even a POW lose his supper. For a moment I was tempted to give it up, to throw the damn thing away, but my mind was made up; I would try it just this once. Skinning the rat, cleaning it was the hardest part. There was no way to kid myself. I knew damn well I was skinning a rat. After I skinned it, got the guts out, cut off the head and the feet and the tail, it looked remarkably like a squirrel. I stuck the long heavy wire through the body and out the neck, opened the fire door to the boiler that heated water for the bathhouse, and hung the rat over the coals. A few turns of the wire and half an hour later it was well done.

I was squeamish at first, but not for long. Hunger is a great motivator. Rat meat is tasty. It is all gray like the dark meat on a chicken, smells good, and is greasy with fat. It wasn't much of a secret. Too many men had seen me building the trap, and too many men had smelled the meat cooking. Another POW offered me half his rice for half my rat, and I instantly made the trade. Suddenly I was in business. There was a waiting list for my rats. Didn't last too long though. Demand was greater than the supply. Other traps were built. A prisoner could get in a fight if he tried to set a trap by someone else's latrine. The rat population was decimated. My trap was stolen. I couldn't find the trap, and I couldn't find material to make another. Didn't matter though, prison camp was like that. Doc, Major Hogan, performed one of his minor miracles and my circumstances got better.

Time for sick call. Time for the usual daily squeezing and probing and burning on my abscessed leg. Time for my almost daily battle of wills. The battle wasn't with Doc. Major Hogan was one swell guy. The battle wasn't even with the Japanese doctor. My personal fight was with the Japanese medical orderly. He was the little SOB who seemed to delight in our hurting. I had the feeling that he was always just watching, waiting and watching like a cat watching a bird on the lawn, waiting for me to cry out, to beg Doc to ease up, to stop whatever he was doing on my leg. And it gave me deep pleasure to deny the little bastard his satisfaction. I stretched my leg out on the bench for the usual ordeal.

Major Hogan spoke as he looked at my leg. He had heard that we were eating better down there. Down there referred to the lower section of the camp. I told him we were doing the best we could with what we had. He said they were dirty and full of germs. Be sure the boys cook them all the way through. So far neither of us had said the word "rats." I let Doc know that they were very well done, cooked almost to a crisp. This satisfied him and he never mentioned it again.

All things considered, eating rat meat wasn't so bad. We were slowly starving and it wasn't too hard for a hungry man to close his eyes and pretend he was eating something else. It was killing the damn thing, skinning it out, removing the guts and cutting off the head and tail and feet. It was doing all of these things and knowing full well that what you were handling was a filthy, dirty rat. This was what made a man sick to his stomach.

With me, Major Hogan was always right out front, no bullshit, no evasions. This time it was at regular morning sick call. Straight out he told me he thought he could do something for me but it was going to hurt a lot.

That was no big news to me. Every time he probed or used the hot poker it hurt like hell anyway. I nodded for him to go ahead with it.

Without another word Doc took a pair of bandage scissors, the kind with the flat round tip on the end of the lower blade to make sure the scissors slip easily under bandages, and began cutting. The scissors went through my flesh easily, almost as though he was cutting a piece of paper. Doc hadn't asked me if I was willing or even if I was ready; he just started cutting. Three or four blade lengths down and a couple up and it was over. It hurt, but completely apart from the pain there was another sensation. I don't know if I heard it, felt it, or merely sensed it, but when the dull scissors cut through flesh I felt as though Doc was ripping a piece of heavy canvas, thread by thread. It hurt, hell yes it hurt, a deep dull hurting like a slow burning fire that kept getting hotter and hotter. I watched Doc cut, stupefied by the pain. Didn't bleed much, but the blood was dark, dirty. Major Hogan opened the abscess wide for six or seven inches, scraped dirty smelly crap from the inside with a knife. I was visibly shaking and grabbing at the bench underneath my ass for all I was worth. The Japanese orderly was watching, but the only satisfaction he got was that I threw up on the floor. I hope he had to clean it. Doc closed the gaping wound in my leg, closed it but didn't sew it up. After it stopped bleeding he wiped it clean and wrapped it with a rag.

Through the orderly, Doc talked with the Japanese doctor and got me a couple of days in the camp hospital. No wheelchairs there. I limped across the yard to the hospital room, found the only empty bed and lay down. I was drained, exhausted, finished for the day. After sick call Major Hogan came to my bed. He was smiling and I could tell he was highly pleased.

Doc told me my friend, the Japanese orderly, was in trouble. Doc knew I hated the orderly's guts. The Japanese orderly had picked up a dose of VD and was afraid to report it to his own people so he came to the major for help. He sneaked the key and let the major into the medical storeroom. There was plenty of medicine in there, mostly American stuff, but the Japs didn't want to give it to us. Doc found the medicine the little guy needed and at the same time filled a pocket with sulfa tablets. Just what he needed to fix me up. He handed me several of the tablets and told me to take them by mouth. Doc always talked while he worked. He crushed some of the tablets into powder, opened my leg, and sprinkled sulfa directly into the wound. Now I just had to wait, wait and see what a good doctor and a little medicine could do.

With the help of Major Hogan's know-how, the Japanese orderly's VD, and a pocketful of sulfa pills, I was up and walking in two weeks, ready for the mine in three.

It was springtime, warmer. No more necessity for sleeping together to keep from freezing. I felt like a new man and knew my days of grace in the hospital were almost over. One pleasant afternoon Mo Ichi Do gathered the sick and crippled, the rejects from the mine, and took them for an outing along the river. A few of them, the strongest, carried empty buckets. These were men who had been banged up in the mine, injured men who were considered, even by the Japanese, too sick to work. With Mo Ichi Do in the lead the little group moved slowly, some of them on crutches. Trying hard to be a nice guy, the lieutenant took them to a wide flat sandbar in the riverbed and turned them loose to catch frogs. Said it would be "good for their healthy." They caught hundreds of frogs. Even the prisoners on crutches caught frogs, tiny little green ones that all stretched out were no more than an inch and a half or two inches long. The lieutenant was right. It was "good for their healthy." These men had seen nothing except the inside of the high wooden fence around the camp and the inside of the mine for most of the year. Getting out of camp, even under guard, gave their morale a boost.

The frogs were donated to the hospital, the eight prisoners too sick or too hurt to get out of bed. I sat on my bed with a pail of water full of floating frogs, all dead, and skinned and cleaned frogs. These tiny fellows peeled like a banana. Hold one by the foot, grab a frog toe between fingernails, and pull down. One pull for each leg and the froggie was skinned. Pull out the guts with thumb and forefinger and the frog was ready for the skillet. The kitchen fried them, and we each got half a cup of assorted frog. We ate them, heads, feet, bones and all. There were toads mixed with the frogs, but once they were skinned out I couldn't tell the difference. Half a cup of frogs once every three years really didn't affect my diet, but I thought it did, and with the thinking, thought I felt better. It was a naive sort of self deception that everyone practiced. Grab onto the tiniest ray of hope, and milk it for everything it was worth. Half a cup of frogs might not do the body any appreciable good, but it made the soul feel better. I once traded some rice for a small tin can full of fish bones. I knew they had already been boiled until the last shred of nourishment was gone, but I traded anyway, boiled them again, and from the weak fish taste and the weak fish smell, convinced myself that I was eating fish soup.

The time was April or May, 1945, the final year of World War II. The handwriting was on the wall. The war was drawing to a close, but none of us could see it. From our perspective inside the prison-camp walls, nothing changed, at least to us nothing changed. There were some subtle indications that the winds of war were blowing in a different direction, but I never recognized them.

Lieutenant Nakamura, Japanese camp commander, was basically a nice guy, but he gave his guards a free hand to run the camp. Never the lieutenant, always the guards. They were the ones that raised hell with us. A basic rule was that a prisoner had to snap to attention and bow whenever a Japanese soldier came into view. One of their favorite diversions was to sneak up on us unseen and slap us around for a while for not showing proper respect. There was a difference. Nakamura was from the Japanese upper class, the guards were peasants. Nakamura kept his distance, even from them. While the guards were going through morning exercises under the direction of the old sergeant, the lieutenant would perform a ritualistic dance with his samurai sword uttering the most fierce shouts with each stroke of the blade.

Occasionally the lieutenant, without his sword, would come down to our barracks, sit very stiffly, and try to hold a polite conversation with a prisoner. He spoke mostly of himself but he was ill at ease. And we listened politely, most politely. It would have been life-threatening to do anything else. After two or three such visits, usually in the evening, the lieutenant began to let the cat out of the bag. One evening after the usual polite inquiries about "How is your healthy?" the lieutenant stated that he felt his family position demanded that he follow the warrior tradition. He was requesting a transfer to the front-line combat unit. Then the bombshell question. Mo Ichi Do wanted to know the best way to surrender to an American soldier.

What a question. Here was a clue, right under our noses, that the war was going our way, that it was possibly drawing to a close. And we missed it. For myself, I suppose I had been cut off from the world for too long a time. I had no concept of the war. For three years my only life had been the inside of a prison camp and a work detail on the farm or in the mine. And always, day and night, under the domination, the threat of rifle and bayonet. My vision had narrowed until I was aware only of American prisoners and Japanese soldiers. It would have taken an incredible leap of the imagination to think of an American army knocking at the gates of the Japanese empire. We didn't take the lieutenant seriously and considered his polite questioning as his way of convincing himself that he was a generous and kindly camp commander. Perhaps he was, I'll never know. Japanese camp commanders had a way of remaining aloof, somewhat distant. They remained polite, courteous, and never dirtied their hands with prisoners. But their soldier guards did the dirty work and the officers either gave the orders or looked the other way.

In some ways the lieutenant was naive and childish. He had never seen an American face-to-face, except as a camp commander to prisoner, and then only after we had survived years of starvation and brutality. He thought we were typical American soldiers, and his idea of combat was like a child playing cowboys and Indians, like St. George slaying the dragon. He was going to the front to cut great swaths among the enemy with his samurai sword. I think I became involved in these infrequent evening talks only because I was there, in barracks, available, at least while my leg was healing. I found these little conversations difficult, emotionally disturbing. How do you speak casually to a man who holds your life in his hands? What do you say? As we talked, these forced, contrived talks, enmity lay heavy between us. To us, though we might not hate him personally, he was the personification of everything we hated. We hated his country, his army, his uniform. We hated everything he represented. And this hatred between men who would have readily killed one another on the battlefield, though sometimes concealed, was always between us, always just beneath the surface.

That particular evening in early summer the lieutenant approached his topic in a roundabout way. He was stiffly polite as he inquired about our healthy.

Of course our healthy was good. Didn't matter what we said, our healthy was going to stay the same, lousy. Then he asked about the food, asked if the food was good.

Silence. He ignored the silence and nodded his head approvingly. He thought the food was very good.

One look at our skinny bodies and any fool would have seen that the food was insufficient both in quantity and quality. We were half starved.

He asked if we were being treated well. Of course the answer was yes. What else could we say without chancing retaliation? We had to say what he wanted to hear. The next question was a stunner. He wanted to know who we thought was going to win the war.

Absolute silence. The conversation was getting dangerous. The lieutenant became angry, raised his voice. He told us we must answer his question. We were prisoners and must answer. He asked again who we thought would win the war.

The Americans, of course. It wasn't what the lieutenant wanted to hear, but I think it was the answer he expected. He was shaken. He remained quiet for a long minute, regained his composure, and without looking directly at us, wanted to know for the second time that evening, how to surrender to an American soldier. The words came almost in a whisper, then more urgently he said that we must answer his question, we must answer. I missed the significance of this completely. I thought the question rhetorical, thought he was testing us, playing with us. We had been prisoners too long. Here in a simple question was the answer to our prayers and we missed it. This Japanese officer could not have conceived such a question had the war not been going badly for Japan.

His voice became threatening and he shouted angrily that we must answer. He was plainly angry, angry at himself for having shown his vulnerability to such lowly creatures as prisoners, and angry at us for having seen his weakness.

Under threat of a beating, or worse, we gave the lieutenant some almost fatherly advice. It was difficult because with his limited English, even though he understood the words mostly, he was not able to fully understand their meaning. Very slowly, very carefully, trying to walk the thin line between being beaten for not answering and being beaten for giving the wrong answer, we tried to explain.

First we told him that we were not typical American soldiers. We were the dregs, the survivors of three years of Japanese imprisonment. A well-fed American farm boy would not in any way resemble the emaciated skeletons in his camp. He appeared confused, didn't understand. We kept insisting that American soldiers were big and strong.

But you are American soldiers. His insistence was almost childish. I don't think he realized the terrible ordeals we had been through or how many of us had died before this scraggly handful of survivors had been put under his command.

Secondly, we tried to tell him that he would probably never get the chance to use his sword against American troops. What I wanted to say but didn't dare, was that American soldiers were not going to hold still while he played samurai games with his sword. They were more likely to take the sword and ram it up his...

Lastly, we told him that American troops, on attack, would not be interested in prisoners. The rule of thumb was, "if it moves, shoot it." His only chance to surrender would be to find a place to hide, wait until the first wave of men and tanks had passed, then try to give himself up to support troops. He left us, still unconvinced.

The lieutenant got his transfer but never made it to the front lines. He was at Nagasaki, waiting to be shipped out when the second atom bomb destroyed the city.

Looking back I realize that the lieutenant had practically told us that the war was drawing to a close, that Japan was defeated. Wish at least one of us had been able to put the pieces together. It would have made those last months so much easier to bear.

And why us, why enlisted men? I think the lieutenant would have lost face had he revealed his innermost feelings to our officers. To enlisted men, the lowest of the low, I think the damage to his ego was less.

While the lieutenant was still our camp commander, a nice thing happened. A very old hand-cranked phonograph and four American records appeared in the mess hall. We were allowed to play them at meal times and in the evening. Four records. I remember them to this day. "Mandy Is Two," Bing Crosby at his best. A nothing song from a cowboy movie, "I've Got Spurs." The third, a little melody about a "castle in the air." And last, "That Old Black Magic Has Me in Its Spell."

Wondered where the lieutenant found them, how he got his hands on them. Were they the spoils of war, loot from Manila or Singapore? And why this magnificent gesture after so much hell and brutality? Why?

For a while we thought the lieutenant was doing us a favor, trying hard to be nice. But no, these records were current. When I got home in November '45, "That Old Black Magic" was still a top tune. More likely, some Japanese big shot sensed his inevitable defeat and let a Red Cross shipment come through, maybe to make amends, maybe to create goodwill.

It was back to the mine for me. My back hurt and I walked with a heavy limp, but the Japanese orderly made the decision. I could walk; therefore I could work. For all my scheming, my rather desperate attempt to be transferred to another camp, I had come full circle. I was going back to the mine. My two months or so out of the mine had not been what I hoped for. Still I was philosophical about it. Things could have been worse. I could have lost my leg or even died. Here again was one of those strange coincidences where a series of totally unpredictable events came together and helped me to survive. Impossible to predict, but each piece of the puzzle had meshed perfectly with each of the others. Time, place, and event had coincided for my benefit. My being sent back from the other camp, the Japanese medical orderly getting a venereal disease, opening the medical storeroom, Major Hogan stealing a pocketful of sulfa pills, me being there and needing them at that precise time. Had any one of these things not fallen into the precise pattern I would surely have lost my leg, possibly my life.

I went back to the mine with a new outlook. In spite of the suffering I had undergone these past couple of months my emotional state had improved. I had passed through that apathetic state where my need to get out of the mine at any cost consumed my every thought. I felt better about myself, more in control, more secure. Work in the mine would still be rough, but I no longer felt the need to run from it. Emotionally I had become the aggressor. I felt I could handle it.

This was my first spring in Japan. I hoped it would be my last. I'm not sure but I think it was April or May. The bitterness of winter was past and the snow was melting rapidly, almost gone. The little rivulet in the river bottom had grown into a sizable stream. Even for a POW spring can be a promise of things to come. There was a new attitude in camp, vague, subtle, intangible as hell, but a change nevertheless. We had survived what to us was a harsh winter, days filled with bitter cold. True, on the walk from the camp to the mine I saw rice farmers, sometimes children, walking barefoot without apparent discomfort while I was in danger of frostbite. Probably because at half my normal weight I had no fat to keep me warm, no calories to burn to generate heat. Regardless, I felt better about myself. At some subconscious level I enjoyed springtime, enjoyed seeing the greenery sprouting in the fields, enjoyed the quiet promise of summer warmth yet to come. Realistically, the last three years had been brutally hard, both physically and emotionally. We had been reduced by our captors to an almost subhuman standard of living, and now, this springtime promise of a warmer, gentler summer was something even the Japanese couldn't take away from us. At some level, which I am sure we did not understand, I think our feelings were akin to the mystic rituals of the ancients, the promise of new life, the rites of spring.

Food wasn't any better. The guards still slapped me around from time to time, and I was forced to work even harder in the mine, but there were changes, little changes in attitude and behavior that I sensed rather than understood, changes that were totally inconsistent with the Japanese idea of how to treat prisoners of war. First there was the victrola and the four records. And we started working longer shifts in the mine. Every few days we would work an extra two or three hours, for the emperor. But instead of just forcing us to work these extended hours, the Japanese gave each of us a tiny biscuit as a reward. Not very Japanese, not at all. As the ultimate final gesture, they scrounged up a very skinny old cow and let one of the prisoners care for it and milk it. Of course, most of the milk went to the Japanese but now and then a little went to our weakest prisoners. These were little things, a small biscuit once a week, the cow that I never saw, even the phonograph and the music. None of these things eased the rigors of my daily life. None of these things eased the hunger in my belly or made work in the mine easier or safer. None of them eased the constant pain in my back and leg. Maybe, just maybe, the sound of American music on that scratchy old phonograph eased the ache in my heart. Maybe, for wiser men, these changes in the Japanese pattern of behavior might have been a good omen, a sign that the war was drawing to a close, an indication that the Japanese sensed their impending defeat and their future accountability for their treatment of prisoners. For us, we were too tired from the long struggle just to stay alive, too occupied with the daily routine of slave labor, hunger, sickness, pain and mistreatment to see beyond the walls of the camp and the depths of the mine.

In midsummer we heard the rumble of thunder in the distance. For the first time the guards rushed us into the air-raid shelter. They came in too, and we sat there for hours. Was this a drill? A test? Had they dreamed of some new way to harass us, to take away our rest between shifts in the mine? And why now? After months and years of don't give a damn, why were they suddenly so solicitous of our welfare? We were in a little valley and the thunder was from the other side of the hills. The third trip to the air-raid shelter happened on a clear day, not a cloud in the sky. A prisoner commented that it couldn't be thunder. There were no clouds. Had to have clouds to have thunder.

He was right. I just hadn't noticed. Took the trips to the shelter as just so much more harassment from the Japanese. Silence in the dugout. This required some thought, and we were not used to thinking, at least not in this direction. Lately my thinking had been limited to the ever more difficult task of keeping Andy Carson alive. My concern was what went on in camp and in the mine. My thoughts rarely jumped over the camp fence. Now, deep in my unconscious there was a tiny spark of hope. I snuffed it out before it became a flame. We had nothing yet. No use building up false hope. We had been through this so many times. Take it slow, take it easy. We had learned to live with the isolation from the rest of the world, to live with hunger and beatings and slave labor, but to allow oneself once again to be tricked into a false sense of hope would be a self-imposed cruelty. To us, after three years, thinking about getting out of the prison camps was like grabbing at a ray of sunlight that shines through a knothole. You can see it, but when you reach for it, it isn't there and the emotional letdown is terrible.

We thought for a while that it might be Jap artillery, practicing, but that didn't make sense. Why would they bring us into the shelter so their own artillery could practice? They surely weren't shooting at us, and why the air-raid shelter? The Japanese had never acted like this before.

I thought it, we all thought it. Not thunder, not artillery, what's left? Could be bombs, bombs sound like that. We'd heard a lot of bombs during our five months of fighting. We knew firsthand what bombs sounded like. Sure enough, could be bombs, and if they were they had to be American. The Japanese weren't bombing their own people. I'm sure we all thought it, longed to believe it, but the very idea was too far-fetched to put into words. American bombs. I tucked the thought away in some deep corner of my mind. Maybe, in the middle of the night I would dare to bring it out and secretly roll it around in my mind like a sweet piece of candy under my tongue.

In the mess hall there was a postcard beside each bowl of rice. Fill out the card. The Japanese said they would select some of them to be read over the radio. We grab at it. We haven't been allowed to write letters, so after three years this is our first chance to communicate with loved ones at home. The postcards are preprinted and there are boxes to be checked.

My health is good, fair, poor.
I am treated well. (Only one box here to be checked.)
The food is good, fair, poor.
I am happy. (Again, only one box to check.)

At the bottom of the card there are two lines for a personal printed message.

I fill out my card. It's easy. I know damn well that if I don't say I am healthy, I am well treated, the food is good, and I am happy, my card will have no chance to be read over the air.

Johnson and I make a pact. In the personal message printed on the bottom, he will mention my name and on my card I will mention his. Major Hogan collects the postcards and turns them over to the Japanese. That's the last we see or hear of them.

When I finally got home in November '45, I was surprised to find that my mother knew Johnson's mother. Johnson's postcard had been read over the air. An American operator had picked up the message and relayed it to the Red Cross, who in turn relayed it to Johnson's mom. Again, through the Red Cross, Johnson's mom got my mother's phone number and called her to let her know I was still alive. It's really a small world.

Meanwhile, I was sent back into the mine. No matter that I was sick, that I was in a lot of pain, that I couldn't walk without a severe limp, our Japanese medical orderly had decided I was workable and I must return to work. One of the guards who regularly escorted us to and from the mine was Big Stoop, so named after a comic book character of our time. He was big, monstrous for a Japanese. He never spoke, even in Japanese, just plodded along dumbly at the rear as we walked from camp to the mine. We considered him ignorant, even stupid, a rice farmer who probably had never worn a pair of shoes before he was forced into the army. He was big, gentle, and as impassive as the cow we regularly robbed of her morning ration of bran. Big Stoop was the butt of many verbal asides as he slouched along behind us. We enjoyed him, enjoyed making smart-alec remarks out loud because we knew he didn't understand. He was one of POW life's little pleasures. We literally thought him too dumb to hit the ground with his hat. We were certain that if his life depended upon it, Big Stoop would be unable to find his ass with both hands.

On our way to the mine we passed near a farmer's cottage, and close to the path we followed, a rickety stable with a single cow. On this particular morning first light was just beginning to show on the horizon but it was still quite dark, dark enough for our little scheme to work. The plan was to wait until the first guards and the first prisoners had passed the stable, then have a man at the end of the line delay Big Stoop long enough for two or three prisoners in the middle to dash unseen to the stable, grab a handful of bran from under the cow's nose and get back into line before Big Stoop got there. We had done this many times, and it always worked to perfection. It was really a terrible risk because theft was punishable by a beating that stopped just short of death. We never got much, no big haul, just two or three handfuls of rough sour bran that tasted like dry weeds, but we ate it dry, gladly, thinking that if it nourished the cow it might do our starving bodies some good. More pity the unknowing cow who shared so many of her breakfasts with us.

At just the right time the prisoner designated to distract Big Stoop pretended to have a pebble in his shoe. I was near the end of the line and I both saw and heard the action. The prisoner sat down and started unlacing his shoe. Big Stoop nudged him with his foot, urging him silently to move on. The prisoner continued unlacing his shoe. Big dumb Big Stoop, he never hurt anybody. Big Stoop pushed the man again, harder, this time with his hand. I distinctly heard one prisoner warning the other, saying that you'd better come on, he's getting hot under the collar. And I heard the reply that it didn't matter none because this dumb son of a bitch don't know his ass from a hole in the ground.

With one tremendous swoop with his open hand Big Stoop sent the prisoner sprawling, then told him to get up and get back into line, in perfect English. So much for Big Stoop. End of story. POW life was full of surprises.

In the mine, because I was still crippled by the earlier back injury, I got the best and the lousiest job of my entire POW career. I sat in a tiny alcove cut in the side of the tunnel, just room enough for me to be out of the way. No bench or chair, I just sat cross-legged on the ground. There was a tiny lightbulb and a hand-lettered sign that read, "No absens." Phonetic spelling but I got the meaning. Prisoners brought me baskets of wet clay, left the clay with me, and disappeared. I was alone for the ten or twelve hours, however long the shift lasted.

My job was to take handfuls of clay and shape it into rolls the size of a broomstick, rolls four or five inches long. We used these to tamp in behind the dynamite before we set off a charge. Easy work because I only had to use my hands. Good thing too, nothing else worked.

Over my head there was a leak in the air line. Air escaped with a high piercing scream that hurt my ears, gave me headaches and nearly drove me out of my mind. The noise never stopped. I wrapped the pipe with a rag, tried to stop the leak with a wad of clay. Nothing worked. I wrapped wads of clay in a cloth and tied the wads over my ears. Didn't do any good. Eventually I became two distinct persons. Sounds crazy, doesn't it, but that's the only way I can describe what happened to me. My body functioned on one level, hands automatically shaping clay rolls and stacking the rolls in baskets. My mind, as a separate entity, concerned itself almost entirely with fighting off the shrill, ear-piercing sound. The noise in my head became physical, assumed substance. The shrieking air not only filled my head and pounded against my brain, it began to be a weight over my whole body. Going to my workplace was like wading into a pool of water that got deeper and deeper as I approached the source of the sound, and when leaving, I actually felt like the pressure on my body decreased as I got away from the noise. This was a difficult period. Easy work physically but psychologically devastating.

On looking back it sometimes seems that the year in Japan was easier than the two-and-a-half years in the Philippines. Not so. More likely it was just that those of us who survived had learned to bend with the wind, to somehow adapt and adjust to each new situation. Take a man who rows a boat for the first time. He will get sore spots, even blisters on his hands. But if he keeps on rowing day after day the blisters will turn into calluses that will protect his hands from further injury. In a similar fashion we POWs, emotionally sore and blistered from the traumatic changes in lifestyle the Japanese forced us to endure, formed emotional and psychological calluses that helped us hang on until late summer 1945.

August 1945–November 1945:
Japan Surrenders and
We Come Home

Though I never knew what day it was, I remember that the month began like any other month in the last three years. August 1945 began like any other month in the last three years. August 1945 began just like August 1944 or '43 or '42. At first glance there were differences. Mining coal was different from building an airstrip or working the farm at Cabanatuan or riding the hell ship. But the realities of life as a prisoner of war were always with us. Our perimeter was marked by barbed wire and patrolled by Japanese soldiers with rifles and bayonets, and the hunger, the brutality, the misery never changed.

The end came quietly, so quietly that none of us even suspected that the day of liberation was near. One morning the day shift lined up for roll call, the usual routine before marching off to the mine. When roll call was over the guards sent us back to barracks. This had never happened before. I supposed the machinery in the mine had broken down. Maybe the hoisting mechanism that took us into and out of the mine needed repair. What the hell, a day off was a blessing.

My mind was busy, full of speculation as I walked back to barracks. I kicked off my split-toed miner's shoes, walked barefoot into the room and stretched out on my tatami mat. If we weren't called out again I could rest, maybe sleep a couple of hours before the noon meal. Suddenly I jumped to my feet, startled. I realized that on my way back from roll call I had walked directly in front of one of the guards without snapping to attention and bowing. Ordinarily this would be considered a deliberate insult and punishment would be immediate. Damn, I fully expected the guard to come raging into the barracks, to slap me around, maybe to keep me standing at attention for the rest of the morning. Nothing happened, nothing at all. Surely the guard must have noticed my flagrant violation, and I knew he would never, never pass up the opportunity to raise a little hell. Still, nothing. It was strange behavior, too strange not to check out. Screwing up my courage I walked to the mess hall and back, each time deliberately passing in front of the guard without bowing. Nothing.

In barracks, in our room, the six of us excitedly held a little conference. No work today and the guards were leaving us alone. What the hell was going on?

Two days of this, no work for the day shift, no work for the night shift. And the guards ignored us, left us alone. Then the word came down. I don't know how we got the news. There was no formation, no announcement, no cheering, no jubilation, just a so-far groundless rumor passed from one man to another. The war is over. Japan has surrendered.

Just like that. The war is over. Don't know who started it or where the news came from. Didn't matter, we weren't going to believe it anyway. Nothing had changed. We were still prisoners and the guards still sat behind the machine guns in the guard towers. The war is over. Oh yeah, and maybe it's gonna rain tomorrow.

A week passed and another rumor. A Red Cross representative had visited the camp, told us to mark the camp with a Red Cross. Nobody saw him come. Nobody saw him go. Did he speak to the Japanese or did he meet with our officers? Nobody knew. If our officers knew anything they damn sure kept it quiet. Maybe they did not believe it either. Maybe they didn't want to get our hopes up. Maybe it was just another bullshit rumor.

No bugle call in the morning. I awakened of my own accord and lay under my pookow for a few minutes, vaguely surprised that there was so much daylight and wondering how I had slept through the bugle. We went to mess hall for breakfast and I noticed that the guards were gone. All the old-timers had disappeared during the night and in their place were a bunch of fifteen- or sixteen-year-old kids, young boys in uniform carrying rifles and bayonets and looking like they did not really know just what they were supposed to do.

Toward the end of the second week we heard the sound of aircraft engines and saw American planes in the distance. We knew there was a large POW camp, camp #17, a few miles away across the valley. We stood on the highest ground in camp and watched in silence, still not daring to believe what we were actually seeing. The planes soared and circled and one by one dropped their loaded parachutes and disappeared into the distance. Finally there was just one plane left, flying in huge lazy circles. Thank God he was a determined pilot. Took him forty-five minutes to find us. Our camp was so small, so hard to find. The plane, a huge four-engined bomber, passed over us, circled again and came in low so we could almost reach up and touch it. The pilot flew that bomber like a stunt plane, waggled his wings as he passed as if to let us know he really knew we were there. As the plane approached for the third time we saw the bomb bay doors open in the distance. Our camp was too small to take a direct drop without the danger of killing some of us, so the parachutes dropped into a rice paddy a quarter of a mile away. One more circle, one more wing waggle and our plane flew off out of sight. It was weird. We stood there in silence, not talking, still not daring to believe, not knowing what to do.

After a minute or two of stunned silence we went to the camp entrance, removed the bar from its rack, and pushed open the high wooden gate. The new guards, the kids with rifles, made no move to stop us. Every prisoner who was able to walk went out the gate. On the way we found an old wooden-spoked farm wagon and pushed it along to the paddy. Barrels, boxes, cans of food were scattered in the mud. We piled everything into the wagon. Japanese civilians, farmers from the nearby village, stood by and watched but made no move either to help or to interfere. I found a small can of fruit cocktail, top popped open cleanly by the impact. Ate it on the spot. Ate the whole damn can sitting right there in the mud.

The sudden end of the war caught our military by surprise and because the Air Force was the only arm of the military that could reach us, the job of getting immediate aid to POWs fell to them. Totally unprepared, the Air Force simply stuffed whatever they had on hand in the way of food and clothing into fifty-gallon drums, hung the drums on parachutes, and dropped them to us. After that first airdrop we found ourselves with a mishmash of wonderful treasure. There were tins of corned beef, Spam, and canned milk, even gallon cans of tomato catsup. There was a whole barrel full of cigarettes and little hard-candy squares called Charms and more chewing gum than I had seen in all my life. And there was a barrel full of olive green mechanic's coveralls. I got a pair that must have been intended for a guy ten feet tall. I cut them in two at the middle, pulled the bottoms up to my chest and let the top hang down like a jacket.

When our bombers made that first parachute drop of relief supplies, there was a bit of comic relief in the rice paddy. Japanese farmers in the paddies stopped their work to stare at the American planes. When the drop was made a chute carrying a drum filled with gallon cans of catsup failed to open. The heavy drum struck the ground with terrific impact, the tins of catsup burst open and catsup sprayed over some of the villagers. Having already heard of the terrible devastation caused by the atom bombs at Hiroshima and Nagasaki, these simple farmers thought they too had been bombed, and covered with catsup, thought they were dying.

The Japanese now gave us an abundance of rice, all we could eat, and our cooks mixed in the corned beef and Spam. For the next three weeks I walked about with a pocket filled with chewing gum, another pocket filled with candy, and a belly full of rice. This was a time of mixed emotions. On the one hand we knew that we were free and that at long last we were going home. On the other hand we were still living in a prison camp with armed guards on the walls. Unable to go to the Americans, we had to wait where we were until the Americans came to us. The waiting was terrible.

No more work in the mines. We had nothing to do except lie around, rest, fill our bellies with rice and candy and chewing gum and wait. The gate remained open. The guards didn't bother us, and little by little, gradually testing, we began to make short forays outside the camp. A half mile out, a half mile back; this was about all our exhausted bodies could handle.

With a couple of comrades I walked to the small cluster of farmhouses we had passed so many times on the way to the mine. We traded, extra clothing, candy, cigarettes, chewing gum, whatever and as much as the farmers wanted, for five very small, very old, very scrawny chickens. That evening we had chicken with our rice, and during the night, each of us with a plate of chicken beside our sleeping spaces, the three of us finished off the five chickens.

Another day, my only other trip outside the camp, we found a small store with bottles of what appeared to be soda pop behind the counter. We negotiated a trade, candy for soda pop. Turned out to be plain unflavored carbonated fizz water. We drank it anyway. Farther down the street we found a barbershop. A single chair with a single barber, an old Japanese woman of sixty or seventy years. Again, candy and chewing gum proved to be the currency of the day. We couldn't communicate verbally, but I held out the candy and chewing gum and she motioned me into the chair. Looking back, I am still somewhat shaken by my stupidity. Just a few days ago all Japanese, this old woman included, had been the hated enemy. And just a few days ago our atom bombs had devastated two of Japan's major cities, yet on that day, with sublime confidence in the immortality of youth, I let this Japanese woman shave my face and neck with a straight razor.

Five weeks had passed since our captors stopped sending us to the mine, five weeks that seemed like five years. The war was over. Japan had surrendered. We were free. My feelings swung back and forth, high one minute, low the next. I wanted to believe with all my heart. Good Lord, how I wanted to believe. But almost three-and-a-half years as a prisoner had taught me to be cautious about exposing my innermost soul to the possibility of crushing disappointment. In effect we were in limbo. We were free, but we were still prisoners. We were free, but we were still in the prison camp. We were free, but armed Japanese still patrolled the camp. To my prison-conditioned way of thinking, the war's end, the Japanese surrender, even the possibility of freedom, none of these things seemed to matter. The important thing was very simple. If I am really free, then why am I still here?

September 17, 1945. I only know the date because I've seen it on my military record. September 17. Completely unannounced, a convoy of Japanese trucks drove up to the camp gate and without any fanfare we climbed aboard and were driven off. The Japanese made sure there was no one left in barracks, no one asleep or unaccounted for, and in ten minutes we were gone. We left everything, simply rode away. I wore the prison uniform I had on at the time. We talked, but during that short ride, maybe a couple of miles, not one man dared put his thoughts into words. Were we really free? Were we really going home? Maybe. And maybe we were just going to another camp. After all, we hadn't seen our first American soldier yet and the damned Japanese still had us by the tail. Maybe, maybe.

Our convoy stopped beside a railroad. No buildings, no railway station, just an engine and a few passenger cars. We loaded aboard two of them. The train ride was slow with lots of stops and starts and long periods of waiting in between. Didn't know it then because I couldn't see much of what was going on, but we must have been picking up prisoners from other camps along the way. The whole trip, short but very slow, took four or five hours.

Late in the afternoon we passed through Nagasaki, right through what must

Two prisoners after release from Santo Tomas prison camp. (Photo courtesy of American Ex-Prisoners of War, Arlington, Texas.)

have been the center of the blast. By this time we were hanging out the windows. The scene was devastation, absolute, utter devastation. As far as they eye could see, almost nothing remained except piles of rubble. Here and there I saw remains of concrete buildings, roofless, windowless, gutted, only parts of concrete walls still standing, and we passed the twisted skeletons of a couple of one-story factories, now just a memory of crumpled steel, nothing inside, nothing outside. The tracks ended and we disembarked. Here, farther from ground zero, a few battered structures were still standing.

Our Japanese escort led us to a long enclosed pier on the Nagasaki waterfront. They stayed outside and we walked through the door into American control. I was a little dazed at the suddenness. On one side of the door I was a prisoner of the Japanese. On the other side I was a free American soldier. It would take a while to sink in. That damned POW mentality was still in control. On the outside I was free. On the inside I was still a POW, afraid to open up, afraid to go ahead and embrace the thing I wanted most, afraid to let anyone else know just how vulnerable I really was.

The American military, our rescuers, handled us with utmost delicacy. There were no orders to do this or to do that, to line up over here or stand there, nothing, not even an announcement over the loudspeaker. They just left us alone to walk about the pier, talk among ourselves, and slowly begin to accept our freedom.

At one end of the pier a Navy band, a bunch of kids in Navy fatigues and little white hats, were playing their hearts out. Old songs, new songs, songs I had never heard, as long as there were POWs on the pier they never stopped playing. Off to the side were a couple of desks, a few Navy corpsmen, clerks, medical doctors, waiting to check us in. They sat patiently, watching us mill about, letting us come to them when we were ready. The big attraction was a makeshift counter in the center of the shed. Behind the counter a Red Cross nurse was busily passing out coffee, milk, and doughnuts. She was short, overly plump, already showing gray in her hair, but she was beautiful. She could have been any guy's mother. Always smiling, sometimes smiling and crying at the same time, she handed out coffee and doughnuts until she must have been exhausted.

Belly full of doughnuts and soul filled with music, I approached one of the desks. No big to-do. I didn't even salute. Just a casual "Welcome home soldier and give me your name, rank, serial number, and the name of your last military unit." "Private First Class Andrew D. Carson, Regular Army 19056693, E Battery, 59th Coast Artillery." That was all there was to it. Simple, quick, and I was in. A couple of questions from the doctor, then, "Better send this one to the *Sanctuary.*" Sanctuary? What an odd name. I immediately envisioned the *Sanctuary* as some kind of stockade where armed American soldiers would protect us from the Japanese. Didn't matter. I'd have walked into hell if they'd said the word. A Navy doctor asked me if I wanted to go on a stretcher or if I could make it on my own. My answer was that a couple of weeks ago I had been a working coal miner. I didn't want a stretcher. Point me in the right direction and show me where to go.

A Navy medic escorted me to another room, a makeshift shower already heavy with steam. He told me to strip down and toss my clothes on a pile to be burned later. He gave me a bar of soap, told me to scrub down, get clean, and pick up a towel as I went out. The room was filled with POWs, some still showering, some toweling off at the other end. I scrubbed and soaked and scrubbed some more until I was clean, then dried with the towel. Clean, damn right I was clean, but not Navy clean, not yet. A medic stood by with a huge Flit gun, told me to close my eyes, and put a big squirt of delousing powder in my hair, another couple of squirts to the groin. I had to turn around, bend over, and spread my cheeks. One more squirt of delousing powder and I was clean — this time, Navy clean.

The medic handed me a pair of white pajamas and some slippers, told me to get dressed, and led me to the door that would take me to the *Sanctuary.*

Through the door and I got my first glimpse of the *Sanctuary,* a large, white, hospital ship moored at the side of the pier. I walked up the gangplank and into a little bit of heaven. In my ward on D deck there were doctors and orderlies in white coats, Navy nurses in crisp white uniforms, and bunks three tiers high, each with a soft mattress covered with a clean white sheet. I had never seen so much white cleanliness in all my life. A nurse tried to give me a top bunk but I couldn't make the climb so we settled for a middle one. I climbed in. The fellow in the bunk next to me, another ex–POW, asked me in a British accent if I fancied a candy and offered me a bag of lemon drops. I thanked him, popped one in my mouth and lay back on the soft mattress with its big pillow, closed my eyes, and relaxed. I think it was at that moment that my release from prisoner-of-war status began to seem real.

A doctor came by my bunk, checked to see that I had no open wounds or open sores and that I was not in need of emergency medical treatment. He cautioned me to take things easy, to eat the food in the mess hall and leave everything else alone for a few days. "Give your stomach a chance to get used to the new diet."

An hour later a line formed at one end of the ward. Probably for some kind of medical treatment. The Brit in the next bunk, already an old-timer because this was his second day on the ward, gave me a nudge with his elbow. "C'mon, matey," he said, "Coca-cola and candy bar time." When I got to the head of the line Doc handed me a Coke and a candy bar without saying a word.

All my life Coke has been an American tradition, an integral part of the American culture, but none ever tasted so good as that first one on the *Sanctuary*.

When I think back, I sometimes wonder at the oddness of our behavior. During the entire release process, from the first rumor of the war's end through the airdrop of food and supplies, the release from camp and the train ride to Nagasaki, the reception on the pier, even the hospital ship, there wasn't a single outburst of cheering, of excitement, or jubilation. We went through the whole process of release without any outward show of emotion.

I spent six days on the *Sanctuary*, six days of eating, resting, wandering around on deck in the warm sunshine and unknowingly soaking up radiation. No medical treatment except the usual series of inoculations that every recruit gets when he first enters military service. The ship kept the kitchen open twenty-four hours a day. At any hour, day or night, an ex–POW could go into the kitchen and get a steak, a sandwich, a bowl of soup, anything he wanted. I ate until my stomach hurt and as soon as it stopped hurting I ate some more. In those six days I gained fourteen pounds. Not solid weight, of course, I probably carried most of it around in my stomach and intestines, but on the scale my actual body weight went up fourteen pounds.

On the seventh day I was transferred to the *Haven*, another hospital ship and after another couple of days, when the ship was fully loaded, we made a leisurely voyage to Okinawa and anchored out in the harbor. Landing craft came alongside to take us in to the shore. Much to my disgust the doctors refused to let me climb down the ladder into the landing craft. Instead, they strapped me into a litter and lowered me by crane. I was embarrassed, felt they were treating me like a baby. There was water sloshing around in the bottom of the boat and my ass was getting wet, so the crew loosened the straps and let me stand up and look over the side. I held my breath as the landing craft held a steady course and drew closer and closer to a rocky beach, and was much surprised when the landing craft turned out to have large rubber-tired wheels that carried us out of the water, across the rocky beach, and along a black-top road.

Next stop was a field hospital on Okinawa. I was given a cot in a tent. Weather was nice, the food was good, and twice a day a Red Cross worker came through the tent with candy, sodas, cigarettes, writing paper, toothbrush and shaving gear, lots of little things that made living easier. Because my records were still somewhere behind me, I got another series of shots. It did no good to protest; the doctors were firm. No records, take the shots. Two weeks on Okinawa and I was put on a hospital plane for a long flight to Manila. The day-long flight was a miserable experience. We were happy because we were on one more leg of the trip home but terribly embarrassed by events on the flight. The hospital bunks, tiered along both sides of the fuselage, were filled to capacity with ex-prisoners, most of whom had never before been on a plane. The two nurses were young, kind, attentive, and did everything possible to make us relaxed and comfortable. Actually they were part of our trouble. On one side of the plane there was a hose with a funnel attached to the end. The idea was to urinate into the funnel, and the urine would pass through the hose and out the bottom of the plane. Practical, efficient, a damn good idea. But use it? In front of the nurses? No way. Not a man moved. And our bellies were full of rich American food. The plane was not pressurized and when we reached altitude our bellies became bloated and we started passing gas. The nurses pretended not to notice, but I'm sure they did, and it was a relief to everyone when we got our feet back on solid ground.

Manila, to us, was just another tent city; only this time it was a replacement depot instead of a field hospital. We were somewhere near the city but far enough away that even the tallest buildings were out of sight. The heat was stifling, and I had nothing to do except sit on my cot and sweat. Those prisoners who were seriously ill had been left on the hospital ship and the rest of us, although somewhat weak and still suffering from malnutrition, were thought to have no immediate health problems. My only medical attention was another series of shots. My records never caught up with me, and I was inoculated five different times before I got home and was discharged from the service. I began to feel like a human pincushion.

At the replacement depot we POWs were treated differently from the regular soldiers. We had no records, no money, no clothes, so everything we needed was given to us free. In lieu of money, each prisoner was given a slip of paper with a list of items that were available at the canteen on a daily basis. Three cans of beer a day, a couple of candy bars, a pack of cigarettes, toothpaste, shaving cream, little personal items that a soldier usually needs. We went to the canteen tent, selected the things we needed, and the clerk checked them off our list with a pencil. Nobody seemed to mind if we erased the pencil mark and went back for another candy bar.

I was only at the replacement depot for ten or twelve days, but each day seemed endless. Freedom was wonderful and the Army gave us the VIP treatment, but freedom wasn't enough. I was impatient. I wanted to go home. Every day that my name wasn't on the departure list was a disappointment. I didn't understand at the time, but now I realize that the military deliberately stalled us a little, hoping to fatten us up before letting the folks at home get a look at us.

Met my old friend Floyd Buckner at the replacement depot. Like me, he was anxiously waiting to be shipped home. He was terribly underweight but otherwise seemed OK. He was a little embarrassed because Army dentists had already extracted all of his teeth and he couldn't get dentures until he got back to the States. I met three or four men from my old outfit. Checking back and forth about who died here and who disappeared there, it seemed that there weren't too many of us left.

Bored as hell with the waiting I often strolled about the camp to see what was going on. Near the edge of the camp a group of fifty Japanese prisoners were clearing debris from a road. This time the tables were reversed. These Japanese were our prisoners. Curious, I stopped to talk with the lone American soldier who was guarding them. He was frustrated, said they didn't understand English and he wasn't getting much work out of them. I knew the Japanese were being treated well. They ate the same food that we did, and their Army fatigues were clean and new. I borrowed the soldier's rifle and picked a Japanese prisoner who seemed to be the group leader. I didn't touch him, didn't threaten him, didn't even raise my voice, but with lots of sign language and my stupid pig–Latin Japanese I convinced him that I had been their prisoner for three-and-a-half years and that it was time to go to work. My soldier friend was pleasantly surprised at how much the Japanese accomplished the rest of the afternoon.

The day finally came when my name was on the list along with Johnson and Buckner. Next morning we were trucked to the docks and loaded aboard a regular troop ship, by coincidence the same dock where I had landed in the Philippines nearly four-and-a-half years ago. This sea voyage would be the last leg of our journey. Home alive in forty-five! We were finally going home.

It was an idyllic seventeen-day trip. Seas were calm all the way. Nothing to do except eat, sleep, and lounge around on deck in the warm sunshine and dream of home. The regular soldiers did all the work. I overheard a sergeant complaining to an officer that they helped in the kitchen, cleaned up the living areas, and swabbed the decks while we weren't doing any work. The officer said that because we had been prisoners, orders were to leave us alone. He thought we were all crazy anyway.

My newly issued combat jacket was stolen. I left it on my bunk when I went to chow, and when I came back it was gone. Too bad. I liked it and I missed it. I think the taker must have been one of the regulars because all POWs already had one of their own. No matter though. How could I be concerned about an article of clothing when I was on my way home?

Our ship, the *Marine Shark*, was on its maiden voyage and darned if it didn't have engine trouble. We were dead in the water for a long, long twenty-four hours. Everyone breathed a sigh of relief when the rhythmic throb of the engines started again.

The ship's crew rigged a canvas screen aft of the deckhouse, and we saw a different movie every night. We sat on the open deck, on the hatch covers, or climbed in the rigging and watched. I remember best a couple of Humphrey

Bogart–Lauren Bacall films. Great pictures, great actors. I liked them. These movies offered both entertainment and a break from the everyday dullness of the ship's routine. More important, they gave us a glimpse of America, of buildings and automobiles and people on the streets, a gradual reintroduction to things we had almost forgotten. We were fascinated as we experienced old memories anew.

Midmorning and the loudspeaker ordered all POWs to the stern of the ship for what the troops laughingly called a short-arm inspection, an inspection where you drop your pants in front of the doctor and he checks you for venereal disease. The doctors waited but no POWs showed up. There must have been a psychologist on the ship because in the afternoon the announcement was repeated, only this time they offered every POW a quart of frozen milk after the inspection. The line was long and it formed quickly. What can you do with a quart of frozen milk? I sat in the warm sunshine, tore a couple of inches off the top of the milk carton and ate mine like an ice-cream cone.

The big day was at hand. The ship's captain announced our impending arrival at the port of San Francisco. We would dock at ten o'clock the next morning. Nobody slept. I lay on my bunk fully awake and fully dressed. Never took my shoes off. Hours before the first streaks of light appeared in the sky, the bunks were empty and the decks were full. Johnson and I found our favorite spot on the deck and we waited. Believe me, the waiting was hard. The seconds dragged by, and the ship seemed to be moving ever so slowly. We got our first glimpse of the Golden Gate Bridge about eight o'clock. The Golden Gate, truly magical words to returning servicemen and women. Voices were low and eyes were wet. We steamed under the bridge, crossed the finish line an hour later. Veterans will tell you, the underside of the Golden Gate Bridge is beautiful too. And as we steamed past Angel Island, my embarkation point nearly five years earlier, we saw a message painted on the hillside, painted in huge white letters for all returning servicemen to see. The message? WELCOME HOME, WELL DONE.

Appendix A

Vol. 132　　　WASHINGTON, WEDNESDAY, APRIL 9, 1986　　　No. 42

Congressional Record

American Salute to Cabanatuan Prisoner of War Memorial Day

• Mr. Wilson, Mr. President, through a joint resolution of the Congress and a Presidential proclamation, April 12, 1982, was designated "American Salute to Cabanatuan Prisoner of War Memorial Day." The Cabanatuan Memorial is located in the central valley of Luzon, Philippine Islands, at the site of the infamous Cabanatuan Prisoner of War Camp. Here, nearly 3,000 American servicemen—veterans of Bataan, Corregidor, and other fiercely contested areas throughout the Philippine archipelago—died of disease, starvation, execution, and other brutality and neglect at the hands of their captors.

10,300 battle weary, starved, disheartened survivors of the rigors of combat in Bataan's jungles, all "Battling Bastards of Bataan," died on the 85-mile march enroute to their first POW camp, Camp O'Donnell. In June 1942, following the surrender of the Corregidor garrison, most of the American servicemen who had survived the hell of the Bataan Death March and the horror of the O'Donnell POW Camp were joined with those captured on Corregidor and elsewhere throughout the Philippines at the Cabanatuan POW Camp. This camp was the principal camp in which the Americans were held during the war.

In the fall of 1944, the Japanese transferred more than 1,600 Cabanatuan prisoners to "hell ships" destined for Japan, where they were to be used as slave laborers working in the mines, dock areas, and factories. Because these ships were unmarked, they were attacked by U.S. aircraft.

The casualties resulting from those attacks which destroyed two of the three ships on which the POW's were being transported, together with the deaths which resulted from starvation, disease, and exposure during the 49-day trip between Manila and Japan, accounted for 90 percent of those prisoners having perished during that indescribably gruesome voyage.

The 500 American prisoners who had not been moved from the camp because of illnesses were liberated in January 1945 by a team of American Rangers, Alamo Scouts, and Filipino guerrillas. These units overcame a Japanese force of 1,000 to lead the American prisoners on foot and on water buffalo drawn carts to freedom.

Of the 25,000 American servicemen who were in the Philippines at the outbreak of World War II, only some 5,000 are living today. Battle deaths and the depredations and cruelty they suffered while prisoners account for the major loss among those most unfortunate men.

I ask that we remember today the bravery of these men who fought and suffered for the freedom we enjoy. It is especially important that we regard the Cabanatuan Memorial as a combined Filipino and American effort which pays tribute to the dedication of both our people to the cause of freedom. It is an important and enduring testimonial to the historic friendship and cooperation of the two nations and to the gallantry and sacrifice of the individuals who participated in a joint quest for honor, freedom, and peace.

Appendix B:
Hell Ships —
Just What the Name Implies

Let me state here that the ship which transported my group of prisoners to Japan, the *Nisso Maru*, came through unscathed. Although our convoy was attacked by submarines and other ships were sunk, the *Nisso Maru* was not hit. Deaths on the *Nisso* were due to the conditions of confinement during the voyage. We were the lucky ones. Prisoners on the ships listed below were not so lucky.

Shinyo Maru
Of 750 prisoners, 82 survived the sinking.

Arisan Maru
Torpedoed and sunk. Of 1,759 prisoners,
there were 6 or 7 survivors.

Oryoku Maru
Bombed by American planes and sunk.
About 1,500 prisoners were aboard.
About 550 survived the sinking.

Brazil Maru
Transported most of the survivors from
the *Oryoku Maru*. Of approximately 550
prisoners, about 250 survived.

Enoura Maru
Carried the rest of the survivors from the
Oryoku Maru. About 30 prisoners died
en route.

The above-listed ships carried American POWs. Other ships carrying mostly British, Dutch, and Australian prisoners were sunk with terrible losses.

Junyo Maru: About 5,000 aboard. About 1,000 survived.

Rakyuo Maru: About 1,600 aboard. About 600 survived.

Kachidoki Maru: About 2,400 aboard. About 600 survived.

Military History
of Andrew D. Carson

Andrew D. Carson enlisted in the United States Army on March 20, 1941, at Fort MacArthur, San Pedro, California. He was shipped to the overseas embarcation station on Angel Island in San Francisco Bay and then to Corregidor. He was assigned to I Battery, 59th Coast Artillery Regiment, Philippine Department, where he trained on 12-inch mortars and 12-inch disappearing rifles.

In September 1941 Private Carson was promoted to Private First Class and transferred to E Battery, 59th C.A.C., stationed on Fort Drum, where he served until his unit surrendered to the Japanese on May 6, 1942.

Upon surrender, Private Carson's unit was separated from the main body of prisoners for two weeks for "special severe punishment," then transported through Bilibid prison and on to Cabanatuan Prisoner of War Camp #3 near San Fernando, Philippines.

After seven months, Camp #3 was disbanded and all prisoners there were taken to Cabanatuan Prisoner of War Camp #1, where Private Carson remained for almost two years.

In July 1944 Private Carson was taken to the port of Moji, on Kyushu, the southern island of Japan, then to Fukuoka, Camp #23, where he remained until the end of the war.

In September 1945, prisoners at Camp #23 were taken by rail to Nagasaki, where they were turned over to American troops at the docks. From Nagasaki Private Carson arrived at San Francisco on November 1, 1945. He was discharged from the Army on February 4, 1946. All prisoners having been given an automatic one-rank promotion upon return to United States custody, Carson was discharged as a corporal.

Carson's military awards include three Presidential Unit Citations from the United States and one Presidential Unit Citation from the Philippine Government, the Purple Heart, the Bronze Star, the Prisoner of War Medal, and medals for Philippine Defense, Pacific Theatre, American Defense, and Good Conduct, as well as the Victory Medal. Carson was also awarded two honorary medals by the Philippine Government: Philippine Liberation and Philippine Independence.

Index